Unveiling Empire

The Bible & Liberation

An Orbis Series in Biblical Studies

Norman K. Gottwald and Richard A. Horsley,
General Editors

The Bible & Liberation Series focuses on the emerging range of political, social, and contextual hermeneutics that are changing the face of biblical interpretation today. It brings to light the social struggles behind the biblical texts. At the same time it explores the ways that a "liberated Bible" may offer resources in the contemporary struggle for a more human world.

Already published:

The Bible and Liberation: Political and Social Hermeneutics (revised edition), Norman K. Gottwald and Richard A. Horsley, Editors

Josiah's Passover: Sociology and the Liberating Bible, Shigeyuki Nakanose

The Psalms: Songs of Tragedy, Hope, and Justice, J. David Pleins

Women and Jesus in Mark: A Japanese Feminist Perspective, Hisako Kinukawa

Liberating Paul: The Justice of God and the Politics of the Apostle, Neil Elliott

Becoming Children of God: John's Gospel and Radical Discipleship, Wes Howard-Brook

Discovering the Bible in the Non-Biblical World, Kwok Pui-lan

Biblical Hermeneutics of Liberation: Modes of Reading the Bible in the South African Context, Gerald West

Apocalypse: A People's Commentary on The Book of Revelation, Pablo Richard

Go Preach! Mark's Kingdom Message and the Black Church Today, Brian K. Blount

Shall We Look for Another? A Feminist Rereading of the Matthean Jesus, Elaine M. Wainwright

Asian Biblical Hermeneutics and Postcolonialism: Contesting the Interpretations, R. S. Sugirtharajah

The Bible & Liberation Series

Unveiling Empire

Reading Revelation Then and Now

Wes Howard-Brook
and
Anthony Gwyther

ORBIS BOOKS

Maryknoll, New York 10545

Fourth printing, February 2002

The Catholic Foreign Mission Society of America (Maryknoll) recruits and trains people for overseas missionary service. Through Orbis Books, Maryknoll aims to foster the international dialogue that is essential to mission. The books published, however, reflect the opinions of their authors and are not meant to represent the official position of the society. To obtain more information about Maryknoll and Orbis Books, please visit our website at www.maryknoll.org.

Published by Orbis Books, Maryknoll, NY 10545-0308

The figure of Cybele astride a lion has been taken from Maarten J. Vermaseren, *Cybele and Attis: The Myth and the Cult* (London: Thames and Hudson, 1977).

Manufactured in the United States of America

Library of Congress Cataloging-in-Publication Data

Howard-Brook, Wes.
    Unveiling empire : reading Revelation then and now / Wes Howard-
Brook and Anthony Gwyther.
       p.   cm. — (Bible & liberation series)
    Includes bibliographical references and index.
    ISBN 1-57075-287-7 (paper)
    1. Bible. N.T. Revelation—Socio-rhetorical criticism.
    2. Imperialism—Religious aspects—Christianity—Biblical teaching.
    I. Gwyther, Anthony. II. Title. III. Series.
    BS2825.2.H68   1999
    228'.06—dc21   99-35040
                                               CIP

Contents

List of Tables, Diagrams, and Figures

Acknowledgments

The notion of two people who have never met collaborating on a book from homes on opposite sides of the ocean seems unlikely at best, and possible only in our high-tech world. When Ched Myers first suggested it to Wes and Anthony separately, the first reaction was to scoff. But, as an e-mail conversation ensued, the possibility became a probability and the probability a gift to us both. We thank Ched Myers—writer, teacher, storyteller, campfire liturgist, and friend— for planting the idea that became this book.

As readers will soon discover, this book attempts to combine scholarly investigation of the book of Revelation with inquiry into the practical consequences of Revelation for people attempting to follow Jesus on the way of discipleship. We are very grateful for all those communities of faithful discipleship who have kept us honest in avoiding the temptation to interpret biblical texts without regard for the real world. Specifically, the global network of Catholic Worker communities has been a constant inspiration, as have other communities such as Jonah House in Baltimore, and the Open Door in Atlanta.

Numerous biblical scholars and teachers have been supportive of this project. Among them have been Sharon Callahan, James Eblen, Kathryn Rickert, Barbara Rossing, and Jeff Staley in the United States; and Ray Barraclough in Brisbane. The incisive work of Jacques Ellul, William Stringfellow, and Daniel Berrigan in bringing Revelation alive for discipleship has been a great inspiration to us.

More personally, Wes is thankful for those who have listened appreciatively to each unfolding insight, especially the members of the Sunday Night group: Aarne, Andrea, Brian, Don, Eddie, and Randall. Most of all, though, Wes is immeasurably grateful to Maggie and Peter, who, as is the case with writers' families, have put up with a lot of crazy ideas on the way to the final text. Their love and support are evident throughout.

Anthony would like to thank those with whom he has shared community over the years, the St. Francis community, the West End Catholic Worker, and Mamre. It is in the crucible of community that the power of the imperial hold on us all can be seen most clearly, and the way out of empire emerges in a myriad of ways. To the Tuesday Night Revelation group: Rachael Harrison, Damian le Goullon, Kay McPadden, and Wendy Webster, thanks for the many evenings we struggled to tease some meaning from this forbidding text. Thanks also to Joanne Merrigan and Fr. Peter Maher, whose valuable feedback at various stages of the manuscript shaped what you read today.

Finally, we are grateful to Liz McAllister for her gracious and powerful Foreword. Her years of personal witness against empire have given her authority beyond that of any officeholder in church or government. And, of course, this book would literally not be possible without the trust placed in us by Robert Ellsberg, whose many years of elegant editorial leadership at Orbis have allowed for the birth and growth of what has now become a tremendous body of incisive theological reflection from the four corners of God's empire.

Foreword

In the course of its more than twenty-five years in existence, the Jonah House Community has twice taken up study of the book of Revelation (a weekly study lasting well over eighteen months each time), gathering to ponder the text and its implications for our lives and our world. The sources upon which we relied for clarification were Dan Berrigan's *The Nightmare of God,* Jacques Ellul's *Apocalypse,* and Paul S. Minear's *I Saw a New Earth.*

Unveiling Empire: Reading Revelation Then and Now is a significant contribution to the study of Revelation. It could not come at a better time. Using this work as the basis for study, a community can arrive at a radical outside look, a judgment, a fresh start.

A fresh start—how we long for it amid the terrifying realities that encircle would-be Christians. As a new millennium dawns and we contemplate the wars and genocides of this day, of this decade, of this century, as well as the ongoing devastation of our planet, we are provoked to take up the book once again in order to learn about our time and its relation to God's time.

Does every age, every empire share in such blindness as ours? For two centuries (or more) of American life, the myth of a special covenant between our nation and God has assured us a protected, quasi-permanent status in the world; the myth has made us, sustained us, put us on top, but, above all, mystified us. A more modest place in the universe is beyond imagining. And what we can't imagine, we can scarcely bring to pass.

And because we believe we have arrived, there is nowhere to go. People carry the look of those without hope. The covenant may be breaking up or it may be hardening its terms, condemning us to death. No one seems to know which is happening or even to care; either outcome or interpretation seems equally unbearable. In such malaise, Revelation offers a place to stand: outside, apart from the consensus. It is not a text capable of being understood directly; thus the need and the value of the research and study that Wes Howard-Brook and Anthony Gwyther have completed.

The authors remind us that in each section of Revelation it is not the spectacular that is important; the spectacle is the environment, or illustration, or parable, or allegory about who Christ is and what he does. When we develop an unhealthy curiosity about the spectacular in the Apocalypse we become interested in what is only an envelope.

Thus, when we read in 1:1, "To show to his servants what must soon take place . . . ," it is a misunderstanding to think that what follows is a description of historical realities to come. Instead, what is announced is the theme of imminence. It is not the "what must come" that is essential, but the "soon." The Apocalypse is a book of imminence, of urgency, but not an imminence that is counted in days. It is the imminence of God in time; it is the clash between two irreconcilable and unimaginable dimensions: eternity and time, the wholly other and the similar, the not yet and the already, the absolute and the contingent.

Prophecy may be familiar to us. We understand in it three movements: a reminder of the past (what God has done for us), a solid political analysis of the present (in which we come to grasp the relationships among the forces that are at play in our own present), and, derived from that, a conclusion, implying an exhortation: if you do not do x, y, z, behold what is to happen. . . . Apocalypse is not prophecy. All this is foreign to apocalyptic, which doesn't speak of concrete political events that take place in unfolding history. It speaks of a brutal invasion of catastrophes of which nothing is said except that they will take place, are perhaps already taking place. In apocalyptic we are spectators to events, while in prophecy we are called to change what we foresee. At most in apocalyptic we are advised to flee or hide. The apocalyptist is first of all a seer; the prophet is a hearer.

But prophecy and apocalypse meet at the point of hope. And the one who understands is encouraged not only to persevere but to become a witness, an actual sign of the emergence and the power of God in history. The Apocalypse reveals that history is fundamentally, essentially, a crisis. At the same time, it discloses the reality of history. As Dan Berrigan has written:

> The history of empires is a vast dreary network, chiastic, cyclic, wearying, of moral clichés. Empires are like aging spiders limping on, weaving the same old ragged webs. They know only one thing to do. They secrete one pattern in their guts. They act not so much out of enterprise as out of dying instinct. Killers even in their last days; what else is there to do?

And how do we relate to that history? Participating in history, assuming any "progress" in history—in a real sense these end as we enter the world of Revelation.

And what replaces it?

- Faith in the living presence of God and in God's desire and ability to reveal himself to us.
- Familiarity with the story and witness of Jesus and the conviction that that story and witness are alive and decisive.
- Reliance on the power of God to determine future developments. Jesus' disclosure of God's purpose embraces not only the present situation (our own world today) and the events shaping it but also the whole chain of future consequences. The present, the past, the future are dependent on the revelation God entrusted to Jesus.

- Becoming servants of Jesus Christ and pledging ourselves to serve and obey Jesus whatever the cost.
- Being constantly engaged in a dialogue with Christ and the Parent and welcoming the role of a prophet like the author of Revelation who relays a message from God to us in the dialogue. Faith that a message such as John's, when authentic, will exert power to bless or to curse.

If we don't enter into these essentials, we will misconstrue the message. And it is well to keep in mind the warning of William Stringfellow:

An obstinate misconception associated with the gospel of Jesus Christ is that the gospel is welcome in this world. . . . That it can be heard in its own integrity . . . found attractive by people, become popular, and, even, be a success of some sort. This idea . . . is bluntly contracted in Scripture and in the experience of the continuing biblical witness in history from the event of Pentecost to the present. . . . Categories of popularity or progress or effectiveness or success are impertinent to the gospel.

With significance, *Unveiling Empire* notes that the site from which Revelation is written is a penal colony in which John is imprisoned because of his vocation and his loyalty to the message of God. He is not alone in his predicament. He and we, his readers, are partners with one another and with Jesus in agony, royal power, and loyal endurance.

Agony is ordeal, distress, tribulation, suffering. What more can we expect amid the distress of our world?

Royal power is partnership with Christ in his kin-dom. We share his royal power and are in agony as a result of exercise of that power because our victory remains as hidden as the victory of Good Friday. No wonder! The powers of the earth jealously guard their hegemony over all who dwell on the earth—what else could Iraq or Yugoslavia mean today?

Loyal endurance is patience, steadfastness—the spiritual alchemy that transmutes suffering into dignity. It involves stubborn refusal to give in under fire, alert watchfulness against deception, eagerness to make our testimony credible to the enemies of God, discernment of the inner roots of fear and anxiety, readiness to forgive, and the joy discovered within the pain. Loyal endurance is *the major ethical thrust* in John's book. It is a gift of the text to those who take it seriously. Let's! And, in so doing, let us fulfill the dream of Wes and Anthony that *this book light an apocalyptic fire in us that will allow the Empire of God to be revealed more fully in the world through us and those with whom we walk on the Way of the Slaughtered Lamb.*

Elizabeth McAlister

Introduction

Reading Revelation

This book is written by two authors who *care* about the meaning of Revelation. It is an attempt to take seriously the challenge of apocalyptic literature, from its origins in antiquity to its use and misuse in our own day. Apocalyptic literature has always been an effort to respond to very basic human questions that transcend time and place: How do we live in a world rife with evil? Does God care about our predicament? Will justice finally be found on earth? What happens when we die? These and other questions live in the heart of humanity. The book of Revelation offers powerful, poetic answers to them.

The authors care not only because the questions are important but because we are trying in our own ways from different outposts of empire to live lives faithful to the Crucified and Risen One. This is not now, and has never been, an easy thing to do. We believe that Revelation offers great insight as to how this is both necessary and possible. We also recognize that many sincere Christians have refused to read Revelation or have put it aside for various reasons. This book is an attempt to recover the power of Revelation for our time.

THE PURPOSE OF THIS BOOK

Our book is not a verse-by-verse commentary. Rather, it provides resources that we hope will be helpful for a reading of Revelation faithful both to its original context ("then") and meaningful today ("now"). One of the limitations of many popular works on Revelation is that they do not sufficiently situate the text within the social and historical context out of which John of Patmos's visions took place and were written down. Therefore, we have explored both the roots and branches of apocalyptic literature generally, as well as the specific setting of Revelation within the Roman Empire of the first century C.E. With this background in mind, we proceed to address Revelation thematically, attempting to respond to what seem to be the central concerns both of the text itself and of intelligent, faithful readers in our time. This book, therefore, is not the definitive work on Revelation, but, we hope, a step toward recovering its power for today's Christian readers. We engage the scholarly literature, but are writing not simply for scholars but for others, like ourselves, who are intrigued by the power of Revelation and are sincerely discerning what its call might be for our lives. As two authors who had not known each other personally before we collaborated on this book, we each came to Revelation with different issues in our hearts and minds. These differences, though, were within the framework of a broader commonality of purpose and vision. From opposite sides of the Pacific we have asked similar questions and been challenged and inspired by similar people, communities, and movements.

I, Anthony (to borrow a phrase from Revelation), am from Australia, having spent most of my life in Sydney and Brisbane, two cities on the Pacific seaboard. For me, the situation in Australia has been somewhat analogous to the situation of the Roman province of Asia for which Revelation was written. While the citizens of Asia looked to the great Roman Empire for security, prosperity, and as a source of culture, in my lifetime Australians have looked toward the United States for these same things. Here our security has been purchased by a military alliance with Washington that has led us to war in Vietnam and Iraq. Economists from Chicago and Harvard tell us that the free market is the panacea for all our ills, and so our economy has been privatized and globalized, with benefits for some and costs to others. But it is probably the importation of cultural commodities from across the Pacific that epitomizes our relationship with the "great city." From our earliest days young Australians are inculturated with icons of American culture. We begin by learning our alphabet from *Sesame Street*. We then graduate to Hollywood, McDonald's, Nike, and Calvin Klein. Nothing of this is imposed upon us. Rather we seek it out; we desire to become part of the "great city." We believe we will find happiness and satisfaction there. I have long had inklings that Revelation might speak to this situation. My theological education had made it clear that beneath the weird imagery Revelation took a critical stance toward the Roman Empire. My experiences among the homeless and traumatized of our cities shed some light on the harsh realities imposed by empire on so many people. My desire to recover the authentic message of the scriptures for our time compelled me to investigate Revelation and see whether it could live up to its promise.

I, Wes, living in Seattle, Washington, U.S.A., recognize that even the opportunity to study and write this book is a sign of the privileged imperial situation in which I live day to day. I come to Revelation, though, because of a rather indirect acknowledgment of its power among adult participants in Bible study programs I have been presenting in recent years. At the end of each series, I invite people as part of the evaluation process to rate on a scale of 5 (= most) to 1 (= least) which parts of the Bible they might be interested in studying in future programs. Most portions garner scores between 3 and 5, but Revelation is different. There are a few 5s, but also a lot of 1s. But they are 1s with *feeling*: exclamation points, underlines, a large "NO!" written in the margin. This expression of resistance was saying something strong about the power, for better or worse, that Revelation held in peoples' hearts. Another factor for me is the frequent questioning that comes my way along this line: "My neighbor (friend, coworker, child) says that the book of Revelation says that the end of the world is coming, and that you can tell because . . . . What do you think?" My inability to answer these heartfelt questions led me first to study Revelation for myself, then to discover the absence of a resource aimed at helping with this pastoral need among mainstream Christians in our culture. For the past few years, I have been living and breathing in two worlds: that of a middle-class, educated male of privilege in the security of the United States, and that of a follower of Jesus trying to become intimate with some of the wisdom of my ancestors in faith.

We live on opposite shores of the Pacific Ocean, yet long before we knew each other we had already become "blood brothers." On September 17, 1988, Anthony and five friends from the Catholic Worker movement in Australia boarded the USS *New Jersey,* a battleship in the United States Navy, while it was docked on the Brisbane River. Their intention was to unmask the *New Jersey*'s long history of bloodshed in Korea, Vietnam, and Lebanon. To this end they poured their blood on the sixteen-inch guns and on the front deck of the battleship and recited prayers to cast out the spirit of evil embodied in the warship. Less than a year later, Wes, as part of a community he was then a member of, called Galilee Circle, boarded this same ship on Hiroshima Day 1989 as it sat in Seattle's Elliott Bay on tour as part of the annual Seafair summer celebration. Wes, along with another, unfurled a banner with a quotation from then Seattle Archbishop Raymond Hunthausen: "Our Nuclear War Preparations Are the Global Crucifixion of Jesus," while others poured blood and ashes on the same sixteen-inch guns and a display of Marine paraphernalia. Both Anthony's and Wes's actions were part of our ongoing commitment to the biblical call to witness both *against* the forces of death that beckon and seduce us and *for* the life-giving way of Jesus that conquers death by accepting violence rather than inflicting it. Our reading of Revelation flows out of and deepens this commitment to nonviolent public witness as part of the task of faithful discipleship.

We believe that our reading of Revelation has something new to offer people concerned with the meaning of the Bible in their lives and in their world. We have not only engaged the scholarly, "objective" work on Revelation but have also been inspired by the writings of people such as William Stringfellow and Daniel Berrigan, whose revelations about Revelation have engaged their lives and ours. These aspects of who we are and what resources we have used have led us to depart in important ways from prevailing interpretations of Revelation.

WHAT'S DIFFERENT ABOUT OUR APPROACH?

For most of its history of interpretation, Revelation was thought to have been written in a time when the churches were suffering a great persecution. Revelation, it was believed, was written to help the followers of Jesus maintain their faith amid distress, with the promise that the imminence of the End would bring to a close their great tribulation. This traditional view does not fit with the emerging consensus among historians that finds no evidence for a widespread or systematic persecution of Christians in first-century provincial Asia. Rather, the evidence of both historical documents and the text of Revelation itself suggests that it was seduction by the Roman Empire from within a context of relative comfort, rather than a terrifying persecution, that more accurately describes the situation of the original audience of the book of Revelation.

The book of Revelation was addressed to a circle of seven discipleship communities—which we will refer to throughout this book by the Greek term, *ekklēsiai*[1]—in the Roman province of Asia. The usual word offered by translators, "churches," suggests much more structure and organization than was present in the first-century discipleship groups. The alternative, "community," has been so abused in our time by its reference to such markedly noncommunal groupings as "the international community," the "business community," and so forth, that we find its use problematic.

Richard Horsley explains:

> While *ekklēsia* came . . . from the Septuagint (the Jewish Bible in Greek) with strong connotations of the "assembly" of (all) Israel, its primary meaning in the Greek-speaking eastern Roman Empire was the citizen "assembly" of the Greek *polis*. *Ekklēsia* is thus a political term with certain religious overtones.[2]

The Hellenistic cities of the eastern empire all had *ekklēsiai,* or citizens' assemblies. The assemblies engaged in civic planning, cultic ritual, and the discussion of issues of concern to the urban citizenry. In our culture the *ekklēsiai* might be labeled a "Town Hall" meeting. The followers of Jesus originally set themselves up as an alternative citizens' assembly. Yet the apparent attractiveness of empire began to entice some members of the *ekklēsiai* back into Rome's orbit.

That the members of the *ekklēsiai* were increasingly attracted to the ways of empire constituted for the author of Revelation (who names himself as John) a grave crisis. What could be more natural than this: that a tiny group of people—say between fifty and one hundred among a population of two hundred thousand in the huge cosmopolitan city of Ephesus—would experience the pressure of going along with the ways of empire just to get by in daily life? For those who were sorely tempted to make their peace with Rome, Revelation unveiled the truth about empire. It revealed empire as both a seductive whore who offered the good life in exchange for obedience and a ravenous beast that devoured any who would dare oppose it. The situation where seduction, rather than the fear of per-

---

1. Throughout this book we use the Greek singular *ekklēsia* to refer to individual assemblies in particular cities and the plural *ekklēsiai* to refer to the collection of assemblies addressed in Revelation.

2. Horsley (1997), p. 208.

secution, consumed the followers of Jesus also accurately describes the situation of First World followers of Jesus today.

Rather than reading Revelation as written about the End—an issue that the passing of time would render more and more irrelevant to the people of the first-century Roman Empire—we read Revelation as written to address what John believed to be the pastoral situation of the seven *ekklēsiai* in their own time and place. As the individual character of the messages to each *ekklēsia* (Rev. 2-3) makes abundantly clear, the followers of Jesus in each city had different challenges to meet in their relationship with the "great city." The majority of the *ekklēsiai* were guilty of collusion with Rome. Only two, the *ekklēsiai* of Smyrna and Philadelphia, did not need to "repent." Their task was to persevere in their resistance to empire and to embrace God's alternative way, to which they were obviously already committed. As for the other five *ekklēsiai*, their task was to renew their commitments to Jesus and each other so as to "come out" of empire. Such a "coming out" can never be a completed task. Rather, the members of the *ekklēsiai* were called to embrace daily the way of God—all the while surrounded by the attractions and threats of empire.

Revelation is a call to have faith in God rather than empire. This call takes place in a narrative through which John tells of his visionary experiences. While many interpreters read each set of visions as recapitulating a single theme, we read these series of visions as containing a "plot." This plot is the story of YHWH's[3] plan for the people of YHWH[4] who live in a world dominated by concentrations of human power. The biblical Story tells of a people called to be "set apart" from the power arrangements that characterized Egypt, Canaan, Assyria, Babylon, Persia, Greece, and Rome. This Story is retold in the visions of Revelation. Revelation shows how in earlier days YHWH had issued stern warnings of disaster to those who lived in opposition to YHWH's covenant with humanity, so that they might repent and embrace the way of YHWH alone. In his visionary experience, however, John saw that YHWH, through Jesus, had activated a new plan. Threats usually did not succeed in bringing people to repentance. Therefore, rather than continue to make prophetic threats to call people to faithfulness, Jesus offered his life in nonviolent witness to the way of God as a new means of leading people to repentance. The raising of Jesus from death was God's vindication of this new plan. The followers of Jesus in the cities of Roman Asia were themselves called to continue the nonviolent witness practiced by Jesus. This is how the disciples of Jesus were to live in the midst of empire.

We interpret this "plot" as a deliberate rewriting of the biblical Story. As such, Revelation brings forward and completes the entire biblical tradition. This is not

---

3. Throughout the book, we use the transliteration of the original Hebrew name for God (YHWH) rather than the vocalized "Yahweh" or the generic "Lord" in order to preserve the sense of power and mystery attached to the divine name, a theme central to Revelation.

4. We find ourselves compelled to use sometimes awkward circumlocutions such as the one contained in this sentence in order to avoid gender-specific language for God.

to say that John deliberately wrote Revelation as the last book of the Bible—the biblical canon as we have it did not exist in John's day. Nor is it meant as a counterpoint to Genesis: the beginning of creation and the destruction of creation. Rather, in weaving the language and imagery of the Hebrew scriptures into his book, John consciously appropriated the biblical style and saw himself as writing with biblical authority. John had a profound knowledge and grasp of the Hebrew scriptures. It is as if John had eaten the scroll of the scriptures himself (cf. Rev. 10:9-11) and had creatively re-presented them on the pages of his book.

The strategy we have adopted in reading Revelation is simple. We have attempted to take seriously the fact that Revelation is a carefully crafted literary composition within the genre of apocalyptic literature. We believe that the text was not written with esoteric intent but was intended to engender real changes in the daily lives of the members of the Asian *ekklēsiai* in their relationship with the Roman Empire. We have endeavored to discover the implications of how Revelation both reflects and critiques the social world in and for which it was produced. In this we have tried to avoid the two "either/or" interpretive pitfalls that have often characterized recent biblical interpretation. One is the belief that written texts are valuable only for the light they shed on the historical world that produced them. The opposing belief is that written texts are wholly independent of the social world of their origins. These have been labeled the "historical-critical" and "literary-critical" methods of interpretation, respectively. We instead use both the available social/historical information about the Roman Empire of early Christianity and the narrative signals provided within the text of Revelation itself to come to grips with what the text is trying to convey. Although the linguistic style of Revelation may seem strange to modern readers familiar perhaps only with the Gospels and epistles among biblical texts, we will show how much of its imagery and form arises from the treasure trove of the more than five-hundred-year-old apocalyptic tradition received and creatively engaged by John. Thus, we seek to be attentive both to the *context* in which John wrote and to the *way* in which he wrote.

Despite the spiritualized and politically disengaged interpretations of scripture that have become the norm in our churches, seminaries, and Bible study groups, it is clear to us that Revelation, like all the other biblical texts, was involved in a pitched battle over issues of spirit such as economics and politics. What was and remains at stake in the biblical texts was and is what it means to live life in accord with the way of YHWH alone. The divine pretensions of pharaohs, kings, and emperors were and are nothing more than a parody of the true sovereignty of YHWH. Because Revelation took seriously the world of the Roman Empire—and declared it a blasphemous caricature of God's sovereignty over the world—we can take our own world no less seriously. Revelation spared nothing in its critique of empire. In being faithful to John and his vision, we must submit our own world to the same no-holds-barred critique. Revelation does not lend itself to neutrality. The passion with which Revelation was so obviously written typically repulses or engages readers. We have both found ourselves challenged by this obscure book and felt the call to sharpen and deepen our practice of discipleship. Our reading of Revelation has left us with an awareness of how deeply we are mired in Babylon, but it has also left us more keenly seeking New Jerusalem.

In many ways Revelation is a bizarre book. Its lurid and violent imagery renders the book almost opaque to us who are steeped in Western modes of discourse. For a variety of reasons most of us have neglected or refused to pick up the book, let alone familiarize ourselves with its contents. Because of this unfamiliarity with the text, we urge you to read carefully the text of Revelation itself before, during, and after your study of our book. We attempt to provide *an* interpretation of Revelation, but in no way can it substitute for your own reading of the primary document. Perhaps the best encouragement to pick up the text directly is contained in the opening words of Revelation: "Blessed the one reading these words of prophecy" (1:3).

AN OUTLINE OF THE BOOK OF REVELATION

As an aid to your reading of the book of Revelation, we present here an outline of the text. This is not *the* outline but simply one of many possible road maps to help lead you through the intertwined series of visions and metaphorical images that make up the text. We assure you that Revelation is not the work of a deranged mind, but is a carefully crafted work of literary art, whose depth and subtlety we are just beginning fully to appreciate.

- 1:1-8   Prologue/Greeting

- 1:9-3:22   Messages to the Seven *Ekklēsiai* in Asia
  - 1:9-20   Introduction to the Messages
  - 2:1-3:22   Prophetic Messages to the *Ekklēsiai* in Asia (each with same structure):
    - Command to write:
    - Address to angel of the *ekklēsia* by name
    - Title(s) for Jesus
    - What Jesus "knows"
    - Name of opponent
    - Threat against opponent
    - "Hear what the spirit says"
    - Reward for those conquering

- 4:1-5:14   Vision of the Heavenly Court, the Sealed Scroll, and the Lamb
    The heavenly liturgies, 4:8-11; 5:8-14
    The opening of the scroll leads to the next vision . . .

- 6:1-8:1   Vision of Empire and the Cry for Justice—The Seven Seals Are Opened

Four contain the horses/riders of empire
Fifth contains the cry of those executed by empire
Sixth unveils the heavens
> *The heavenly liturgy, 7:9-17*
The seventh seal leads to the next vision . . .

• 8:2-11:19   Vision of YHWH's Plan for Repentance—Seven Trumpets
and a Second Scroll
The "old plan": heralded by trumpets that sound warnings to repent
or else
The "new plan": announced in the second scroll as nonviolent witness and resurrection
> *The heavenly liturgy, 11:15-18*
The seventh trumpet leads to the next vision . . .

• 12:1-14:20   Vision of the Woman, the Dragon, the Two Beasts, and the
Seven Messages
The woman gives birth; war begins in heaven
The war continues on earth led by the two beasts of empire
The earthly liturgy of empire, ch. 13.
> *The heavenly liturgy, 14:1-5*
14:1-20 The Seven Angels with Seven Messages

• 15:1-16:21   Vision of Judgment—The Seven Angels with the Seven
Bowls
> *The heavenly liturgy, 15:2-4*
The apocalyptic judgment of evil

• 17:1-22:9   The Vision of the Two Cities
17:1-19:10 The Vision of Babylon as Fallen
> *The heavenly liturgy, 19:1-8*
19:11-20:15 The Vision of Judgment and Victory
21:1-22:9 The Vision of New Jerusalem

• 22:9-21   Epilogue

REVELATION'S AUTHOR

Unlike other apocalyptic texts, Revelation does not claim to have been written by a revered figure from the past, such as Adam, Enoch, Abraham, Daniel, or
Ezra. Rather, Revelation presents itself as written by a contemporary of the Asian
ekklēsiai, a fellow traveler, someone who shared the distress, the empire, and the
endurance of the followers of Jesus in the cities of Asia (1:9). Revelation is
John's attempt to convey in words the visions that had seized his entire being on
the island of Patmos, fifty miles across the Aegean Sea from the city of Ephesus.

There is general, but not universal, scholarly agreement that John's presence on the island was the result of social sanctions imposed on him by imperial authorities. This is the meaning of John's statement that he was on Patmos "on account of the word of God and my witness to Jesus" (1:9).[5] Yet if John experienced imperial sanctions for his public witnessing to Jesus, why was he still alive to tell the tale?

In Roman law, the *status* of a condemned person was more critical than the crime committed for determining the penalty. People with high social standing were likely to be banished for crimes for which people with lesser social standing would be punished by execution. There were a variety of forms of exile that could explain how John might have found himself on Patmos. First, John could have voluntarily chosen exile after a sentence of death had been passed on him. Second, he may have been permanently or temporarily banished to the island, possibly experiencing the loss of property and citizenship rights. Finally, he may have been permanently or temporarily banished from his home territory, and chosen to live on Patmos.[6] The actual mechanism of John's exile is a matter of speculation, but it is intriguing that John seems to have possessed sufficient social status to avoid the more severe penalty of execution.

Various philosophers, orators, writers, and other elite social critics had been exiled by Rome for daring to challenge the imperial *mythos*, and John seems to have been among their number. Yet John, through his visionary experience on Patmos, presented a message more radical than that of any of his contemporaries. John did not criticize this or that ruler, this or that imperial dynasty, or even this or that empire. John did not advocate a change of leadership or call for political or economic reform. Rather, John saw from the heavenly perspective granted to him that *empire in itself* stood in contradiction to the ways of God, and that communities that embraced YHWH's covenant were the faithful ones. We cannot know the exact circumstances that led John to this island. Yet Revelation tells us that it was the power and truth of the visions he had while there that led this person of high social status to reject completely empire as a way of life. John's willingness to trade his privileged social location in Roman society for life among the struggling *ekklēsiai* represents John's "coming out" of the "great city Babylon." In this John is like those of us whose birthright, skin color, education, or connections have bought us some measure of imperial privilege today.

Another vexing question is the relationship between John and the other New Testament authors. The apostle Paul spent much time in Ephesus (Acts 19:10; 20:17-38). Laodicea is mentioned in the letter to the Colossians (2:1; 4:13, 15, 16). Recent interpretations of Paul's writings suggest that Paul had both a more apocalyptic worldview[7] and was more critical of the Roman Empire[8] than was

---

5. The Greek text leaves room for ambiguity. John may also have gone to Patmos on a missionary journey or to take a retreat after a previous journey.

6. Aune (1997), p. 79.

7. Elliott (1995), pp. 140-80.

8. Ibid., pp. 181-230; Horsley (1997).

usually thought. The Gospels of Mark, Matthew, and Luke also contain significant sections of apocalyptic discourse (Mark 13; Matt. 24:1-44; Luke 21:5-36). While nowhere in Revelation does John cite his fellow Christian writers, his worldview is consistent with theirs. The major difference is that Revelation is a wholly apocalyptic discourse, whereas Paul and the Synoptic writers only briefly use the apocalyptic genre.

People frequently wonder about the connections between the "Johns" of the New Testament. Did the apostle John—one of the "sons of thunder," the brother of James (Mark 3:17)—write the Gospel of John, the Revelation to John, and/or the three letters that bear the name John? Numerous hypotheses have been developed to prove any number of variations on the authorship of these five texts. Perhaps David Aune's summary of the matter is the most that can be said about the issue:

> While the final editor-author of Revelation was named "John," it is not possible to identify him with any other early Christian figures of the same name, including John the son of Zebedee or the shadowy figure of John the Elder. The otherwise unknown author of Revelation in its final form was probably a Palestinian Jew who had emigrated to the Roman province of Asia, perhaps in connection with the first Jewish revolt in 66-70 CE.[9]

Just as we can only speculate about John's life story, neither can we know the source of John's authority among the *ekklēsiai*. John clearly names himself as a prophet to the Christians in Asia (22:6, 9), and labels his book as a prophecy (1:3; 22:7, 10, 18, 19). Yet nowhere does John claim the authority of the office of bishop, presbyter, or deacon that Ignatius of Antioch commended as the structure of the Asian churches only a matter of years after Revelation was written. Although he did not claim hierarchical office, John expected his book to be read aloud in gatherings of the *ekklēsiai*, and his words to be taken seriously. Perhaps most crucially, though, John expected those who receive his book to be prepared to lay down their lives on the basis of the truth of his visionary experiences. Whether John was a traveling prophet or a member-in-exile of one *ekklēsia* in Asia, it was his absolute conviction that the Word of God had revealed to him the true character of empire and that this should be sufficient authority for his fellow Christians.

HOW TO USE THIS BOOK

As noted at the outset, this book is not a commentary but a collection of what we hope will prove to be helpful resources for your own engagement with Revelation. As a way to help you decide which of these resources might respond most immediately to your concerns and needs, we provide now a brief overview of each chapter.

---

9. Aune (1997), p. lvi.

Chapter 1 begins by taking seriously the modern anxieties that lead many people to seek "wisdom from on high" as a way of finding the "truth" about our lives. We start with an investigation of the modern phenomena of premillennialism and its doctrine of the Rapture, the belief that Jesus will come suddenly at a specific historical moment to carry off true believers to a heaven above. This particularly American tradition and its "prophecy readings" of apocalyptic texts have become, for believers and skeptics alike, the prevailing interpretation of Revelation today. The chapter also surveys modern apocalyptic phenomena that serve for many as substitutes for Revelation in seeking "heavenly" insight: near-death experiences, UFO and alien abduction experiences, New Age phenomena, and Marian apparitions.

Revelation, contrary to the first impression of many mainstream Christians, did not arise from a vacuum. To help readers situate Revelation within its own tradition, chapter 2 explores the roots and branches of apocalyptic literature. It includes a survey of apocalyptic writing in the Hebrew scriptures, New Testament writings, and noncanonical Jewish apocalypses. It begins with an examination of Jewish resistance to the Seleucid Empire two hundred years before Jesus, contrasting the Maccabean ideology of armed insurrection with the praxis of nonviolent resistance to empire proclaimed in the visionary apocalyptic of Daniel. This is followed by a look deeper into the roots of apocalyptic which preceded Daniel in the period after the Babylonian exile during which the Persian Empire controlled Jerusalem. We show here how a split within God's people over how to respond to the "charms" of empire developed into the apocalyptic tradition upon which Daniel, John, and others built. The chapter concludes with a brief description of apocalyptic literature in the period just before and contemporaneous with the book of Revelation.

Chapter 3 contains a portrait of urban life in the province of Asia in the first-century Roman Empire. This includes an overview of the political, economic, cultural, and mythic dimensions of Roman provincial society. This was the context in which the members of the *ekklēsiai* were called to practice radical discipleship; hence, it is the necessary background to a reading of the book of Revelation.

Chapter 4 explains how differing concepts of time and space between cultures like the United States and Australia, on the one hand, and the cultures of the ancient Mediterranean, on the other hand, have left us with a view of apocalyptic in general and Revelation in particular that is preoccupied both with the future and with a heaven that is ultimately unconcerned with our earthly existence. These cultural differences have been a major contributor to the modern misreading of Revelation. We offer in place of these anachronistic misunderstandings a way of looking at Revelation's spatial and temporal language that respects the mind-set of both John and the *ekklēsiai* to whom he wrote.

Chapter 5 explores the "plot" of Revelation as a way to come to grips with the text's language of violence and vengeance that repels so many readers today. This plot is encapsulated in the story of the two scrolls and their message of violence, justice, repentance, and nonviolence. This chapter examines Revelation's review of history, which begins with YHWH's hope for repentance by way of prophetic warnings, and the "new plan" practiced by Jesus, the Lamb who was slain, who nonviolently witnessed to the truth of God, who was executed for this witness and vindicated by being raised by God.

Chapter 6 portrays the apocalyptic cities of Babylon and New Jerusalem. The two cities are, respectively, how empire and authentic human community look when viewed from the perspective of "heaven." The master metaphor of the two cities includes the command to defect from Babylon to become instead a citizen of New Jerusalem. We explore how this is to be achieved by the difficult, yet glorious, daily practice of life-embracing ways of being in the midst of empire. We show how the path of discipleship is intended to be one of celebration and joy, not the "perpetual Lent" through which it is sometimes caricatured by those who would trivialize the gospel and implicitly approve of empire.

Chapter 7 offers a look at the scenes of worship and liturgy in Revelation. These scenes were written to call the members of the *ekklēsiai* to renew their faith in God and in Jesus and to remind them of the ongoing support they experience from the "heavenly" choir of angels and witnesses. This heavenly worship is expressed in overtly political language: worship of God precludes worship of empire. John's apocalyptic liturgical vision provides a sharp contrast between the seductive yet satanic worship of empire and the joyful celebration of the one, true God.

Chapter 8 is a sort of "post-game wrap-up" which reviews the action in the "battle of myths" between empire and God. We look at how the Roman myths of Empire, Peace, Victory, Faith, and Eternity are appropriated by Revelation and applied not to Rome but to the faithful followers of Jesus. Revelation claims that by embracing the way of God and rejecting empire, the followers of Jesus *already* have true empire, victory, and eternity.

We conclude by asking ourselves the hard question of how Revelation speaks to us today. Chapter 9 presents a case for the argument that nation-states are no longer the bearers and promoters of empire. Instead, the phenomenon of global capital has become the "empire" that dominates our world today. We take a hard but clear-eyed look at how we are seduced by this empire into acceptance of its own mythic claims to divine legitimacy, and how Revelation calls followers of Jesus to resist it and to be faithful to the ways of YHWH in the midst of this empire.

Our engagement with apocalyptic literature generally and with Revelation specifically has challenged, excited, and sometimes overwhelmed us with the power and with the implications of these writings for our way of life. We hope that this book will light an apocalyptic fire in you that will allow the Empire of God to be revealed more fully in the world through you and those with whom you walk on the Way of the Slaughtered Lamb. We are grateful for your willingness to engage along with us the beautiful, disturbing, faith-filled visions that comprise the final book of the Bible.

1

"Behold, A Door Was Opened in Heaven"

Seeking Wisdom from On High

Blessed is the one who reads aloud the words of the prophecy, and blessed are those who hear and who keep what is written in it; for the time is near.
—Rev. 1:3

For thousands of years, humans have struggled to create a meaningful pattern out of the apparent chaos of events that surrounds their lives. The Bible begins with a dream-memory of a time in which our ancestors lived, for a brief moment, in harmony with each other, the earth and its creatures, and their Creator. But once Adam and Eve are expelled from the garden and the fiery cherubim sword blocks their return, history threatens to become little more than a sequence of rebellions, wars, wrong turns, and dead ends. Is there a way out of this seemingly endless stumbling in the dark? Is there "more" to life than meets the ordinary eye?

At the other end of the biblical collection is the book of Revelation. Ever since its appearance late in the first century of the common era, people have searched its sometimes bizarre imagery for hints of a grand answer to the mystery of life. In our time, it has become largely the domain of "students of prophecy," the preachers and teachers who claim to find in its narrative a chronology of the End. Much of the incredibly popular literature of this movement places pieces of Revelation's story within a Story of its own, which culminates in a grand scenario of vindication and destruction, highlighted by the "Rapture," in which the faithful remnant of "true Christians" are taken up bodily into the sky with the returning Jesus to escape the force of God's wrath poured out on the unbelievers down on earth. Most mainstream Christians, having heard only rumors of Rapture and some of the other aspects of the prophecy students' Story, have tended to write

1

off the entire book of Revelation as either utter nonsense or as hopelessly impossible to understand in a "rational" way.

The price of this ignorance is high. Whether mainstream Christians like it or not, Revelation is one of the most powerful texts in the Western world. It has been used and abused to support a wide variety of social movements, from the modern-day Branch Davidians incinerated at Waco and the Heaven's Gate community, who committed mass suicide to seek solace in spaceships, to the second-century Montanists and the thirteenth-century Apostolic Brethren.[1] Commentaries on Revelation have been written by such diverse thinkers as Isaac Newton and D. H. Lawrence. It has inspired an enormous array of writers, from Emily Dickinson[2] to journalist Hunter S. Thompson.[3] Its underlying schema of history has inspired, consciously or unconsciously, Hitler's notion of the Third Reich and Karl Marx's dream of the revolution of the proletariat.[4] To allow the interpretation of Revelation to be controlled by a particular group of Christians is to throw away one of the church's most powerful tools for inculcating and sustaining countercultural discipleship.

Part of the appeal of Revelation to those who have enthusiastically embraced it is its apparent engagement with some of the most difficult issues of life. What is the origin of evil? How do we live in the presence of monstrous evil? What is the role of the church in responding to this evil? What happens when we die? Where is God amid our struggles? These and other urgent and eternal questions constantly bubble to the surface of consciousness in people who are attempting to live thoughtful lives. A plethora of alternative sources of "wisdom" have emerged in our culture to help people find answers to their questions. One central feature binds together such diverse, mass-culture phenomena as near-death experiences, UFO sightings and abductions, New Age "channeling," and Marian apparitions: each offers wisdom from "on high," from outside the "ordinary" ways of knowing available to humanity in daily life. One of the main reasons for the popularity of these phenomena, we suggest, is the failure of mainstream Christianity to engage its own sources of wisdom in ways that are equally satisfying for people's search for answers. The book of Revelation is itself, as we will show in chapter 2, the culmination of over five hundred years of "apocalyptic" insight, the fruit of a tree with deep roots going back to ancient Persia. To allow its power to be lost to mainstream Western culture is to push people to grasp at whatever straws they can find. We propose in this book a modest effort to restore Revelation to its rightful place within the canon of texts beloved and studied by the church.

---

1. "[T]here is surely a thread leading from Monte Rebello [where the Apostolic Brethren were killed] in 1307 to Waco in 1993" (Thompson [1996], pp. 67-68). See Keller for a survey of groups following the "apocalypse script" through the centuries; Robbins and Palmer for a survey of recent apocalyptic groups.

2. Norris (1997), pp. 210-19.

3. "I still read the Book of Revelation when I need to get cranked up about language" (Hunter S. Thompson in *Atlantic Unbound* interview, August 26, 1997 [http://www.theatlantic.com/unbound/graffiti/hunter.htm]).

4. Grosso, pp. 174-75, 181-202; Engels.

To enable this restoration, several tasks are in order. First, it is important to take a direct look at the prophecy readings of Revelation. The hostility, confusion, embarrassment, and even fear that many mainstream Christians may feel when they hear apocalyptic, end-of-the-world scenarios preached at them by fundamentalist family members, neighbors, or work colleagues can be dissipated by having an empathetic understanding of what these interpretations are about. We might be surprised to find that the long tradition of "premillennialism" offers, beneath the surface absurdity of some of its conclusions, much from which other Christians can learn.

Second, it may be valuable to examine the apocalyptic, mass-culture alternatives to the Bible noted above to understand the ways in which they sincerely respond to the same real human needs and concerns to which premillennialists' writings appeal. It is all too easy to laugh at supposed alien abduction experiences and similar reports of "heavenly" intervention, but we should not throw out the baby with the bathwater. These books and their authors and interviewees have attracted huge audiences seeking some source of wisdom from "beyond." The questions for which they provide answers are questions that our reading of Revelation will also seek to address.

Finally, we will look at a sampling of "alternative readings" of Revelation from contemporary scholars. For those who reject the premillennialist interpretations of apocalyptic literature, the answer is not some other "correct" reading that claims dogmatic authority. The imagery and symbolism of Revelation are far too open to succumb to any final "answer." What we offer as our reading is simply one that we believe makes sense of the text in light of our own experience and the situation of our world today. A brief, preliminary glimpse at some other interpreters' attempts will help open up readers' imaginations to the power of Revelation and liberate us from captivity to any all-or-nothing approaches.

A BRIEF HISTORY OF THE RAPTURE
IN THE UNITED STATES

Part of the difficulty for mainstream Christians in coming to grips with the doomsday scenarios proffered by premillennialists is confusion over the variety of terms used by and about interpreters of Revelation. "Fundamentalists," "students of prophecy," and "premillennialists" are overlapping but nonidentical groups of people. Various "insider" jargon terms are often thrown around as if listeners already knew the difference between the "Tribulation" and the "Rapture." The glossary on pp. 4-5 provides an overview of the most important of these terms.

The most influential group of interpreters of Revelation has been the premillennialists. The most popular premillennial writer of our time has been Hal Lindsey, whose *The Late, Great Planet Earth* has reportedly sold over forty million copies since its publication in 1970. The success of this book led Lindsey and others to spawn numerous sequels, each providing a new link between the

Table 1

GLOSSARY OF TERMS RELATED
TO APOCALYPTIC WRITINGS

Antichrist. In millennial belief, the evil human who will rule during the Tribulation, only to be defeated by the returned Christ in anticipation of the millennium. Biblically, the term is used only in 1-2 John. However, it has come to refer to "the beasts" in Rev. 13. It is often expected that this individual will come from Europe as head of a restored Roman Empire. He will be the leader of a movement toward a world government that ostensibly eases human suffering and creates peace, but which will turn out to be hell on earth.

Apocalypse. A text written from an apocalyptic perspective, generally categorized as either "historical" (in which the narrator is shown a review and interpretation of some or all of human history by an angelic interpreter) or "other" (in which only personal experience is reported). Apocalypses can have a wide range of characteristics, but commonly include (1) a dream or vision that requires interpretation by a "heavenly" agent; (2) complex symbolic characters and events that relate to the seer's world, past, present, and/or future; (3) an assurance that evil will be punished by God and good rewarded at the end of time, which is coming "soon."

Apocalyptic. A worldview characterized by one or more of the following elements: (1) an expectation that the present world situation will come to an abrupt end and be replaced by a new, better world; (2) a belief that things are likely to get worse in the current age before the "new age" comes; (3) the worldview that life takes place on two levels simultaneously: an "earthly" level in which evil or Satan temporarily reigns over sinful humanity, and a "heavenly" level in which God reigns; the "heavenly" level is already victorious over the "earthly" level. In this book, the term is used to refer to a worldview consisting of the third element without the first and second.

Armageddon. In millennial belief, the final battle between good and evil, based on Rev. 16:16, which is to take place after the Tribulation and before the millennium. Literally, the word refers to Mt. Megiddo, a mythical mountain in Palestine derived from texts such as Zech. 12:11 ("plain of Megiddo") and others.

Beast(s), The. Two symbolic creatures named in Rev. 13 as the powers that control Babylon, under the central authority of "the Dragon" described in Rev. 12. The Beast(s) are often used interchangeably with "Antichrist" as a label to demonize individual or institutional opponents or to refer to the demonic figures that fit the prophecy "puzzle" within the understanding of premillennialist writers.

Dispensationalism. The belief that history is divided into fixed units, called "dispensations," in which God has particular plans for humanity. The idea was developed and popularized by John Darby in the 1840s. The current dispensation is "the Church Age," which is sometimes known as "the Great Parenthesis," because believers see it as an interim between the first and second comings of Jesus.

Eschatology. In traditional theology, the study of "last things," that is, heaven, hell, purgatory, and judgment. In millennial belief, the concern with the specific events supposed to happen at the literal "end of time."

Millennium. Based on Rev. 20:4-6, the belief that Christ will return to earth for a literal one-thousand-year peaceful reign, accompanied by "the saints," that is, the "true believers."

Postmillennialism. A branch of millennial Christianity in which believers expect the Rapture to take place *after* the one-thousand-year reign of Christ, which will require preparation on the part of Christians to make the world worthy of Christ's return. Thus, postmillennialists see social action as an important element of their faith practice.

Premillennialism. A branch of millennial Christianity in which believers expect that they will be "raptured" by Jesus *prior* to a one-thousand-year reign by Christ ("the millennium") in which peace will reign. Most premillennialists believe that the Rapture will occur prior to "the Tribulation." Others believe that the Rapture will take place after the Tribulation but before the millennium. Both groups of premillennialists see social action, as well as all human endeavor, as doomed to failure and thus the work of Antichrist when seen as the means to solve social problems and to hasten the Second Coming.

Rapture. A doctrine based on a literal interpretation of 1 Thess. 4:17: "Then we who are alive, who are left, will be caught up in the clouds together with them to meet the Lord in the air; and so we will be with the Lord forever." All millennialists believe that "true believers" will be lifted up from earth to escape the difficulties of this world, while all others will be left behind.

Scofield Reference Bible. A text developed by Cyrus Scofield in 1909, in which the author's premillennialist cross-references and interpretations are included alongside the biblical texts, often confusing readers as to which is which. It has sold over ten million copies since its publication and is the root source for millennial interpreters.

Tribulation. In millennial belief, the anticipated seven-year reign of Antichrist, based on Dan. 11:35; 12:1 and Rev. 7:14; 13:5, which will begin with a period of apparent peace and then turn hellish. Believers in the Tribulation divide themselves into three groups:

> *Pretribulationists.* These believe that the Rapture of the "saints" will come before the Tribulation begins.

> *Midtribulationists.* These believe that the Rapture will come at the middle of the Tribulation, that is, after the period of apparent peace and before the hellish conclusion.

> *Posttribulationists.* These believe that Christians will have to survive the entire Tribulation before they will be raptured. This leads to survivalist movements, which prepare themselves for the Tribulation by gathering caches of food and weapons in underground or remote locations.

apocalyptic texts of the Bible—which the genre's writers refer to as "prophecies"—and the current day's political and cultural headlines. Lindsey's *The 1980s: Countdown to Armageddon* contains, after its speculative take on current events, what became the veritable blueprint for Reaganism. It is crucial to understand, however, that the right-wing politics of patriotism frequently associated with conservative Christianity have nothing whatsoever to do with the tradition of premillennialism in which Lindsey and his ilk purport to be based. As explained by conservative Christian writer Timothy Weber,

> In the political analysis that follows [his interpretation of scripture], Lindsey leaves his premillennialism behind; that is, he never demonstrates how his diagnosis of and prescription for American political and social life has anything to do with biblical prophecy. His observations and remedies come out of right-wing political ideology and have nothing to do with premillennialism per se. . . .
>
> An analysis of his footnotes reveals that his understanding of America's current political, social, and military condition comes almost exclusively from Barry Goldwater's *With No Apologies* (1979) and the conservative Coalition for Peace Through Strength. . . .
>
> Jerry Falwell . . . has done much the same thing.[5]

The mainstream media, however, have utterly failed to make this distinction, leaving the indelible impression upon liberal and progressive Christians who have not taken their own look at these writings that the book of Revelation is inextricably (and necessarily) bound up with the Christian right. The frequent use of apocalyptic rhetoric by Reagan himself seemingly provided further evidence of this link. For example, Reagan's branding of the Soviet Union as the "Evil Empire" amid the threat of nuclear war seemed to many to flow directly out of Revelation and to call for an endless U.S. weapons buildup.

The fact is that Lindsey and his fellow ideologues, by attempting to blur the lines between premillennialism and peace-through-strength patriotism, have betrayed the tradition of which they purport to be "students." To understand the depth of this betrayal, we need to investigate the history of this tradition, especially as it has expressed itself in the United States since the Civil War.

For biblical interpreters, the role of the United States has always been highly ambiguous. The association between the so-called New World and Revelation began with Columbus, who thought that he had discovered the biblical New Jerusalem:

> Of the New Heaven and Earth which our Lord made, as St. John writes in the Apocalypse . . . He made me the messenger thereof and showed me where to go.[6]

---

5. Weber, pp. 219-21.
6. Quoted in Keller, p. 159.

In the minds of the first religious interpreters of the New World, America was often interpreted in imagery that combined the Garden of Eden, the Promised Land, and the Endtime City-on-a-Hill. Seventeenth-century New England preachers such as Cotton Mather and eighteenth-century successors such as Jonathan Edwards frequently gave eschatological meaning to the colonial adventure.[7] There was a shadow side, of course, to this projection of joy and light: the legitimation of the genocide of the indigenous people as "savages" who stood in the path of the fulfillment of scripture. The nineteenth-century outcome of this view of America-as-Promised-Land or as New Jerusalem was the doctrine of Manifest Destiny, which entitled the European Christians to claim the continent from the Atlantic to the Pacific as somehow a gift of God.[8] This tradition continues to find its echoes in our time in the implicit belief of most U.S. citizens that their own way of life—that is, "democracy" and capitalism—is "superior" to other ways and is somehow "destined" to envelope all societies.

Alongside this positive interpretation of the United States, though, another has developed. As the settlers were transformed from residents of small, isolated, colonial towns and villages to urban dwellers caught up in national and international affairs and cultural developments, a more pessimistic strain of interpretation developed. As historian Sydney Ahlstrom expresses it, "Immigration, exploitation, dislocation, loneliness—and, very significantly, the financial panic of 1837—darkened the dream."[9]

Precisely at this time a figure emerged whose work would become the foundation of the tradition known as "dispensationalism": John Nelson Darby. At first he found his vocation as a priest in the Anglican Church of Ireland in 1825, but soon became deeply distressed at the "ruin of the church" at the hands of politicians. In 1828 he joined and became a promoter of a fledgling group of dissidents, the Plymouth Brethren. Out of this association, he developed an overarching interpretation of the Bible which saw history as divided into seven periods, or "dispensations." History, in Darby's scheme, would culminate in the reign of Christ for a thousand years (the "millennium"). For now—meaning the time between Jesus and the millennium—the church existed in the "great parenthesis."[10] Darby based his scenario primarily on readings of apocalyptic passages in Ezekiel and Daniel in the Hebrew scriptures, and the book of Revelation and First Thessalonians in the New Testament. It displaced the sense of America-as-New-Israel with a future role for a restored, actual nation of Israel in Palestine. With the association between America's self-image and the fulfillment of God's covenants with biblical Israel severed, the way was opened for powerful critiques by premillennialists of important aspects of American culture in coming years.

Darby's scheme lay in wait for two further events which would cause it to burst forth on the American scene: the Civil War and the Reference Bible of

---

7. Boyer, pp. 68-73.
8. Strozier, p. 171.
9. Ahlstrom, p. 475.
10. Ibid., pp. 808-11; Weber, pp. 16-24; Boyer, pp. 88-90.

Cyrus Scofield. During the years of the war itself, most evangelical preachers and writers continued to interpret America as God's instrument for achieving the divine will. As Charles Strozier writes,

> [T]he Civil War was the first time (and I would add the last) in our history that there was a virtually unanimous feeling among northern ministers that the war was hastening the day of the Lord and was a climactic test of the redeemer nation and its millennial role.[11]

A classic example comes from Lincoln's Second Inaugural Address amid the terror of seemingly endless bloodshed:

> Fondly do we hope, fervently do we pray, that this mighty scourge of war may speedily pass away. Yet, if God wills that it continue until all the wealth piled by the bondsman's two hundred and fifty years of unrequited toil shall be sunk, and until every drop of blood drawn with the lash shall be paid by another drawn with the sword, as was said three thousand years ago, so still it must be said "the judgments of the Lord are true and righteous altogether."

Or in the words of a prominent evangelical preacher on the occasion of Lincoln's funeral on Easter 1865:

> The great battle of Gog and Magog is being fought on the gory field of Armageddon, which is the American Republic—a contest between freedom and oppression, liberty and slavery, light and darkness—and O how that conflict has raged during the past four years![12]

In the aftermath of this wrenching national experience and the struggles that came with postwar industrialization, many Americans began to yearn for a time when such events would not need to be replayed again and again across the span of history. Darby's dispensationalism, as popularized by Cyrus Scofield, provided just the answers many were seeking.

Scofield himself served in the Confederate Army, then had a religious conversion in 1879, becoming a pupil of leading premillennialist James H. Brookes.[13] During the later years of the nineteenth century, Scofield worked Darby's system of dispensations into what would become and continues to be the key resource for premillennialists: The Scofield Reference Bible. Published in 1909, Scofield's text physically places his interpretations and cross-references so close to the biblical texts themselves that many readers do not distinguish text

---

11. Strozier, p. 175.
12. Rev. Rolla Chubb, quoted in Strozier, p. 177.
13. Ahlstrom, pp. 809-10.

from interpretation. This, of course, is a key to the authority of Scofield's work: the unalerted reader can easily take Scofield's own comments as the "word of God."

Scofield's text quickly became the primary source for premillennialist speculation, selling over ten million copies by the 1990s.[14] As America reached the end of the century, further difficulties led to an increased desire for an "end" to the struggle. Massive waves of immigration, the crush and disease of rapidly expanding cities, the displacement of many from rural farmlands to urban factories all contributed to a sense that something was deeply wrong in the United States.

Christian response to these events soon took three turns down very different paths. Traditional evangelicals decided that what the times called for was a heavy dose of revivalism. It had worked in 1740s New England,[15] and had worked again during the "Second Great Awakening" in the early nineteenth century.[16] Under the leadership of people such as Dwight L. Moody and Billy Sunday, revivals swept across the scene like wildfire. The excesses of the movement were pilloried in such works as Sinclair Lewis's book *Elmer Gantry* (1927), but the revivals were effective among many in responding to the vices of drinking, gambling, and the like.

A second response was the advent of the "social gospel." This movement, given classic expression in Walter Rauschenbusch's 1907 book *Christianity and the Social Crisis*, saw the gospel as the key to repairing the rent in the social fabric. It expressed enormous confidence in the progression of humanity from a "primitive" past to a golden future, in which social ills such as poverty and war would be eliminated. Rauschenbusch and his companions saw the primary role of the churches as awakening its members both to the horror of current conditions and to the moral necessity of getting one's hands dirty in the process of seeking improvement. Out of this movement came the theological discipline of social ethics, and the new profession of social work.

For the most part, premillennialists saw the social gospel as the work of the devil. While the social gospelers expressed hope and trust in the ability of humans to become the "hands" and "feet" of God, premillennialists saw this hope as a misguided and misdirected waste of time running contrary to God's purpose. As Timothy Weber writes, premillennialists believed that,

> God had absolutely no intention of saving the world before the second coming of Christ. His chief purpose in this dispensation was to "visit the Gentiles, to take out of them a people for his name" (Acts 15:14), not to convert the world. . . .
>
> Christians, therefore, must be content with their minority status and with the apparent failure of their cause.[17]

---

14. Boyer, pp. 98-99.
15. Bushman.
16. Ahlstrom, pp. 415-29.
17. Weber, p. 70.

Rejection of the social gospel was part and parcel of the rejection of the entire edifice of modernity, from liberal theology and the tools of historical-critical Bible exegesis to unionism and popular democracy. On the one hand, premillennialists saw these cultural developments as attempts to put trust in human effort rather than solely in God. On the other, they began to see the decline of the United States as a sign of the approaching Endtimes, in which the ancient biblical prophecies would be fulfilled. As this way of thinking developed in opposition to the growing success of the social gospel and liberal theology in the mainstream churches and seminaries, premillennialists became more and more willing to offer harsh criticism of the entire American project.

With the approach of World War I, this opposition took what appears in retrospect as an ironic turn. Premillennialists issued strong criticism of the war buildup and its accompanying patriotic fervor, while "liberal" theologians charged premillennialists with presenting, in the words of University of Chicago professor Shirley Jackson Case, "a serious menace to our democracy."[18] The following quotation from premillennialist Reuben Torrey in 1914 might sound surprising to the modern ear:

> To love a country simply because it is one's own country and to stand by it no matter of what injustice it is guilty towards other and weaker nations is radically and thoroughly un-Christian. The sentiment, "My country, may she always be right, but my country whether right or wrong," has been quoted and requoted until some almost seem to think it a portion of the Word of God. It is a thoroughly vicious statement. It justifies the most unjustifiable wars and the most devilish conduct in war. We should love our country . . . but we should not love our country at the expense of other countries. We should not justify our country when she is in the wrong. We should not join hands with the multitude of our countrymen to do evil to other nations. We should seek the peace and prosperity and welfare of other lands as well as our own. We should not seek to always put the best construction on our own acts and the worst construction on the acts of other nations. The law of love should be the law of nations as well as the law of the individual. The fair-sounding word "Patriotism" is often used as a cloak for the basest and meanest conduct. In Christ Jesus there is neither Jew nor Greek, Barbarian, Scythian, German, Englishman, Russian, or American, we are all one in Him.[19]

Similarly strong premillennialist critiques of other cultural phenomena usually thought to be criticized by those on the far left, such as the excesses of corporate wealth, exploitation of the poor, and the control of the media by moneyed interests, can be found at this time.[20] In light of the interpretation of Revelation

---

18. Ibid., p. 120.
19. Ibid., p. 123.
20. E.g., Boyer, p. 94.

to come, it is worth remembering this critique of "the world" by early-twentieth-century premillennialists.

From a more apocalyptic perspective, premillennialists found World War I to provide ample grist for the fulfillment-of-prophecy mill. The movement was greatly strengthened by its "success" in predicting much of the national postwar realignment in Europe, all on the basis of the interpretation of biblical prophecy.[21] Soon after, though, another cultural development arose which premillennialists could not refute so easily: the theory of evolution.

It is at this point in history that premillennialism and fundamentalism can become fused in one's mind unless one pays careful attention. The latter phenomenon developed with the help of, but at least partly independent of, premillennial dispensationalism. Fundamentalism proper was a reaction to the growth of liberal theology in the wake of the Civil War. After World War I, the nascent movement grew rapidly as a response to modernism in all its forms, especially those that directly challenged the authority of the Bible, such as evolution. From 1910 to 1915, with the financial support of the Stewart brothers, who had made a fortune in the oil business,[22] three million copies of a series of twelve pamphlets called "The Fundamentals" were distributed free of charge to United States Protestant leaders throughout the country. This in turn led to the World's Conference on Christian Fundamentals in Philadelphia in 1919 and the founding of the World's Christian Fundamentals Association.[23] The power of fundamentalists led to two highly charged denominational controversies within the Northern Baptist Convention and the Northern Presbyterian Church. The result was that many fundamentalists abandoned the mainstream denominations to form their own churches and related institutions.

The most famous confrontation between fundamentalists and liberals during this period was the Scopes "monkey" trial of 1925. Former presidential candidate William Jennings Bryan, representing the prosecutor, the state of Tennessee, was ruthlessly mocked by journalist H. L. Mencken, while school teacher Scopes was defended on the charge of teaching evolution by the nationally known attorney, Clarence Darrow. The case was immortalized in the film *Inherit the Wind*. Mencken's journalistic exposure of some of the absurdities of the biblical literalism poorly defended by the outmatched Bryan led many to believe that fundamentalism would be relegated to the dustbin of history.

While the Scopes trial "convicted" a naïve biblical literalism of foolishness, premillennialism was working hard to develop a measure of intellectual respectability. The founding of Dallas Theological Seminary in 1924—the future training ground of people such as Hal Lindsey—and Westminster Seminary in 1929 provided a base from which prophecy readings of scripture could develop away from the harsh eye of the secular media. Throughout the 1930s, these and other institutions, including the numerous "Bible institutes" founded to train lay

---

21. Weber, p. 112.
22. Lyman and Milton Stewart were the founders of the Union Oil Company (Boyer, p. 100).
23. Weber, p. 161.

workers and missionaries,[24] developed a solid foundation of scholars and other ministers to promote the premillennialist viewpoint.

Premillennialist Endtime speculation was nurtured during the 1930s by the use of two new forms of presentation: the "prophecy novel" and radio evangelism. But nothing set premillennialist fervor in motion like two events that followed upon each other in the 1940s like bolts from the sky. The first of these was the development and use of the atomic bomb. While most mainstream secular thinkers responded to the bombing of Hiroshima and Nagasaki with relief that the war was over and awe at the power of the bomb, premillennialists saw the bomb as a certain sign that the End was near. For the first time, the meaning of a powerful, apocalyptic passage from scripture seemed clear:

> But the day of the Lord will come like a thief, and then the heavens will pass away with a loud noise, and the elements will be dissolved with fire, and the earth and everything that is done on it will be disclosed. Since all these things are to be dissolved in this way, what sort of persons ought you to be in leading lives of holiness and godliness, waiting for and hastening the coming of the day of God, because of which the heavens will be set ablaze and dissolved, and the elements will melt with fire? But, in accordance with his promise, we wait for new heavens and a new earth, where righteousness is at home. (2 Pet. 3:10-13)

Premillennialist writing in the late 1940s and 1950s interpreted the bomb as solid evidence that the time of prophetic fulfillment was near. Premillennialists looked from this point forward upon attempts to limit weapons development as a futile effort to resist the divine imperative. While many Americans spent the 1950s learning to locate their nearest fallout shelter, premillennialists began to look more and more for the Second Coming of Jesus and the Rapture that would protect them from the "inevitable" nuclear war.[25]

The second, and even more portentous event for premillennialists, was the reestablishment of the nation of Israel for the first time in two thousand years. The relationship between premillennialists and Jews/Israel is very complex and defies easy explanation. On the one hand, as conservative evangelicals, most premillennialists had a certain, sometimes unconscious contempt for Jews for failing to acknowledge Jesus as Messiah, and, in the eyes of some, being responsible for his death. On the other hand, the dispensational system established by Darby and elucidated by Scofield and his successors recognized an ongoing and essential role for the Jews and Israel in God's Endtime plans. Throughout the century, premillennialist writings vacillate between abhorrence and condemnation of anti-Semitism and a condescending attitude just short of racial hatred. An example

---

24. For example, under the leadership of president James Gray, the Moody Bible Institute expanded from a staff of 42 and a student body of 1,100 in 1904 to a staff of 280 and a student body of over 17,000 in 1931 (Weber, p. 45).

25. Boyer, pp. 117-20, 135-36.

from leading turn-of-the-century preacher and writer Arno Gaebelein illustrates the tone that continued through mid-century: "the Jew has no need whatever of the organization or institutions of historical Christianity. All he needs is personal, saving faith in his own Jewish Messiah, the Christ of God, nothing more."[26] He went on to add that orthodox Jews are the prophesied remnant, in contrast to the "international Jews, the political-financial schemers . . . [who] will worship the Beast."[27]

Despite this ambivalence toward Jewish people, premillennialists had always been active and vociferous supporters of Zionism, because their apocalyptic scenario depended entirely upon the existence of a restored nation of Israel. Now, in the wake of World War II, the most important sign of the End had happened in their midst! A breathless, even frantic, search began for ways to show that other prophetic signs were being fulfilled and that the End was near. The ensuing Cold War provided all the signs that most premillennialists needed to imagine that Jesus' return was indeed imminent.

One of the longest-running—and, from the perspective of historical criticism, most bizarre—interpretations of scripture within the dispensational system was the association of geographic places in Ezekiel 38-39 with counterparts in modern-day Russia. The key verses are Ezek. 38:2-4:

> Mortal, set your face toward Gog, of the land of Magog, the chief [Hebrew *rosh*] prince of Meshech and Tubal. Prophesy against him and say: Thus says the Lord GOD: I am against you, O Gog, chief prince of Meshech and Tubal; I will turn you around and put hooks into your jaws, and I will lead you out with all your army, horses and horsemen, all of them clothed in full armor, a great company, all of them with shield and buckler, wielding swords. (NRSV)

The Hebrew word *rosh*, which the New Revised Standard Version translates (properly) as "chief" (or "head"), was translated by the Prussian scholar Wilhelm Gesenius in the 1830s as a proper name, hence, "Magog, prince of Rosh."[28] While controversial at the time of Gesenius, this translation was seized upon by Darby and Scofield and became an essential element in the Endtime schema. In Gesenius's version, "Rosh" was an early form of "Russia," "Meshech" was "Moscow," and "Tubal" was "Tobolsk." While historical-critical scholars insisted that these ancient place-names bore no relationship to the modern world—and that *"rosh"* was not a place-name at all—premillennialists constructed elaborate scenarios out of a combination of these passages from Ezekiel and others from Daniel and, of course, Revelation. It was this tradition that was tapped by Hal Lindsey in the 1970s and made the popular basis of virtually all premillennialist speculation until the collapse of the Soviet Union in 1991. It is important to

26. Quoted in Weber, p. 153.
27. Ibid., p. 187.
28. Boyer, p. 154.

remember, though, that this tradition did not imply that a better-armed United States would triumph over Russia as part of God's plan. Rather, the United States was mostly irrelevant to the images of Armageddon that focused on a final invasion of Israel by the Russian army.

Of course, the invasion has not happened and appears less likely with the passing years. Mainstream Christians who now may feel inclined to laugh at the foolishness of the premillennialist apocalyptic scenarios should pause, however, before doing so. An aspect of the tradition that has allowed premillennialism to flourish over such a long time span is its flexibility in the face of changing events. In contrast to some early apocalypticists who attempted to predict the exact date of the End, most premillennialist writers have avoided such obvious traps, using rhetoric about the "nearness" of the End rather than its precise arrival. Furthermore, as Lindsey's work demonstrates, these writers present themselves as "students of prophecy" rather than as authoritative interpreters, or even as interpreters at all. Their task is to "decode" texts rather than to "interpret" them. Like good detectives, they appear always willing to adjust or abandon a hypothesis in the face of new evidence.[29] Their followers seem equally willing to forgive mistakes and eagerly await the next attempt to put the pieces of the puzzle together.

While these Cold War scenarios were being spun out in the 1950s-1970s, premillennialists were also taking frequent aim at what they saw as other U.S. cultural signs of the approaching End. Among their targets were television (described by one writer as "that speaking idol . . . the mouth of hell"),[30] consumerism, advancing technology, changes in gender roles in the family and workplace, the advent of the New Age movement, rock and roll, and homosexuality. One thing was certainly true about premillennialists: they were willing to look American culture in the eye and not flinch. Of course, they had no desire to repair the damage or heal the wounds; such malignant forces were simply further evidence that the Second Coming was getting closer and closer, and hence, the Rapture of the true believers.[31]

Recent expressions of this search among premillennialists for signs of the End sound utterly absurd to most mainstream Christians, but are taken with great seriousness by their proponents. The attempts to decipher Revelation's mysterious "666" are legion, as have been the efforts to match "the Beast" and the "Antichrist" (not, by the way, found in Revelation) with specific persons. One of the most repeatedly named prophetic events that premillennialists watch for is the reestablishment of the Roman Empire as a ten-nation confederacy, in fulfillment of the image of the "ten-horned beast" of Daniel 7. The growth of the European Common Market into a ten-nation unit by 1981 was witnessed with great excitement, which, however, began to fade as its membership expanded to twelve

---

29. O'Leary, p. 78.

30. David Wilkerson, quoted in Boyer, p. 237.

31. One of the best presentations of this attitude is found in Mojtabai (1986), a set of interviews and analysis of workers at the Pantex nuclear weapons plant in Amarillo, Texas.

by the late 1980s.[32] Not surprisingly, other writers "discovered" new evidence for the larger membership figure itself being a fulfillment of scripture.[33]

What lessons might we learn from this brief survey of history? First, it is unfair and inappropriate to write off all who speak of the Rapture and other apocalyptic endings as being "wackos" or ignorant. Within their own systems and methods of interpretation (despite the disclaimers that interpretation is taking place at all), premillennialists are consistent and rational readers of what they see as "evidence."

Second, they are willing to engage in clear-eyed and well-informed social analysis of both the United States and the world political and economic situation, a practice that many mainstream churches have abandoned as too depressing or too complicated. Their cultural critique defies easy categorization as left-wing or right-wing, given the scope of ills, both personal and collective, that they are willing to name.

Third, they take the Bible seriously as a source of wisdom, even if much criticism can be leveled at their selectivity of texts and their sometimes outlandish associations between biblical and current events. In a time when many mainstream Christians seem more embarrassed than enlightened by the biblical stories, premillennialists continue to look primarily to the ancient texts and the lives of the first Christians as models for their own behavior and tools for understanding the world in which they live.

Fourth, premillennialists believe deeply that God is active in history and is concerned with the fate of humanity. It often seems that many mainstream Christians imagine God much as the deist founders of America did: as the "clockmaker" who created the universe and set it in motion, then stood back and left its fate wholly in human hands. God can be appealed to in prayer, but do we really expect a concrete answer? For premillennialists, the answer is a resounding, Yes! While the Rapture may not be the means by which many people can imagine God acting, at least the premillennialists believe that God continues to be God, powerful and involved in the fate of humanity and the earth.

Finally, premillennialists have looked deeply into the human condition and know, consciously or unconsciously, the needs and concerns that preoccupy people, the shadowy fears and anxieties that come out in dreams and therapy sessions but are often untouched by mainstream Christianity. This raises the question of how and why premillennialism works, a topic to which we now turn.

WHY IS PREMILLENNIALISM ATTRACTIVE?

For decades, most liberal or progressive church leaders saw fundamentalism and premillennialism as sideshows outside the big tent of the church that would

32. Boyer, pp. 277-78.
33. Ibid.

attract a few ignorant and gullible people from among the masses but would never attract intelligent, sophisticated Christians. Similarly, these church leaders often acted as if they expected premillennialism to disappear like a tired fad, the curiosity factor having been spent.

Needless to say, these predictions were utterly wrong. Polls and studies show that millennial belief has always been popular across a wide swath of Western society, including both lower and upper classes, the little and much educated, and people from a diversity of ethnicities. As noted, some of this century's most powerful premillennialists were also successful businesspeople or intellectuals. Charles Strozier's excellent study *Apocalypse: On the Psychology of Fundamentalism in America* shows how such belief can be found in the New York City of the 1980s from Harlem to Wall Street. A 1980 Gallup Poll showed that 62 percent of Americans had "no doubts" that Jesus would come again.[34] Despite the collapse of the Soviet Union, prophecy books continue to be written and sold in droves. Make no mistake: premillennialism seems here to stay.

What is its appeal? Why do intelligent people believe in the Rapture? Early attempts to explain the attraction of premillennialism relied on what sociologists call "deprivation" or "relative deprivation." This theory suggests that people who have no power in a society and are unlikely to get any through the normal channels are attracted to ideas that suggest that the worldly powerful will be destroyed by divine intervention.[35] However, as the data above suggest, premillennial belief extends far beyond those who could fairly be characterized as "deprived."

Conservative evangelical writer Timothy Weber suggests that the appeal is largely "religious": "most premillennialists accept the doctrine [of the Rapture] because they believe that the Bible teaches it."[36] This, however, begs the question of premillennialism's appeal in the first place. Weber responds to this query by claiming that premillennialism "has maintained its appeal among conservative Protestants also because it seems to be empirically verified by current events."[37] But this only pushes us to a slightly different question: What is the appeal of what Weber calls broadly, "conservative Protestantism"?

Communication theory scholar Stephen O'Leary comes at the issue from another angle. O'Leary's premise is that apocalyptic thinking in general appeals to two basic "problems" inherent in the human situation: time and evil. Within the first problem are questions such as: Is there an end to time? What happens when I die? What is the purpose of history? Within the second problem are concerns such as: Where did evil come from? Will evil ever be defeated? (Note that this question also invokes the problem of "time.") What is "our" relationship with the "other" deemed responsible for the presence of evil in our world? O'Leary argues that the popularity of systems such as premillennial dispensationalism rises or falls to the extent that "answers" to these questions provided by the dom-

---

34. Ibid., p. 13.
35. Weber, p. 228; O'Leary, p. 9.
36. Weber, p. 230.
37. Ibid., p. 231.

inant cultural voices fail to satisfy people.[38] In presenting a thorough analysis of the rhetorical methods of writers such as Hal Lindsey, O'Leary concludes that premillennialism's success depends on its ability to persuade its audience that its own "explanation" of the problems of time and evil fit the historical situation of its audience better than other explanations.[39] That is, if America's own myths are unable to account for the situation in which people live, people will look elsewhere for answers. Premillennialism is simply one of several available systems of belief offering such answers. In other words, as long as politicians and advertisers continue to appeal to people's pursuit of the "American dream" of self-made, family-based, happy-faced prosperity, premillennialism and other forms of apocalyptic thinking will prosper.

Psychologist Charles Strozier reaches this same conclusion from the perspective of his own discipline. He notes that

Fundamentalists' broken narratives profoundly distort time, a break that is rooted in experience. The past is separated off, to be remembered only as an object lesson. . . . The present, in turn, is profoundly degraded and full of evil. God is furious, and about to end it all. The handful of the faithful must keep struggling, but they are persecuted and doomed to failure. Things can be delayed but not solved. . . . The only hope lies in the mythical transformation of the future.[40]

Strozier sees the fundamentalists he studied personally for five years as rational people seeking meaning in a chaotic world where the traditional sources of meaning have become bankrupt. He castigates the mainstream churches for failing to understand how the popularity of premillennialism should be read as a harsh critique of the mainstream churches' own failure to respond to real human needs:

[To] dismiss fundamentalist theology as the kind of fanciful imaginative scheme fit only for comic books is an elitist judgment that reflects more than anything the anger of mainline Christians who have seen their churches emptied by the message and enthusiasms of fundamentalists.[41]

Another effort to understand the appeal of apocalyptic comes from outside the United States scene, from the German theologian Ulrich Körtner. In his magisterial work of theological reflection, *The End of the World: A Theological Interpretation,* Körtner argues from the perspective of existential philosophy that apocalyptic responds to what he calls "apocalyptic world anxiety." This term refers not to a particular social situation and fears of an imminent End, but to the universal recognition that life is finite, and that we all stand powerless to change

---

38. O'Leary, p. 197.
39. Ibid., p. 13.
40. Strozier, pp. 44-45.
41. Ibid., p. 88.

that essential aspect of our human condition.[42] He argues that "Apocalyptic can be understood as a form of pastoral care for those in anxiety."[43] Körtner warns, however, that there is a latent flip side to this pastoral function, in which apocalyptic adherents divide the world into the "saved" and the "condemned" and actively yearn for the destruction of those perceived as "outside" the holy circle.[44]

Theologian Catherine Keller sees a risk in what Körtner notes as the dark side of apocalyptic's function as pastoral care. She calls this risk "the apocalypse habit."[45] This is, briefly put, the tendency to act out one's life as a series of "apocalypse scripts," patterns in which life is seen as an either/or moral duality requiring unity in the face of "the enemy" and the expectation of an eventual cataclysmic showdown. She warns that such "scripts," taking their cue from Revelation, frequently label *passive* forces as impersonally feminine, for example, virgin-bride or lecherous whore, and *active* agents as impersonally masculine, for example, Messiah or Satan. This is, indeed, the shadow side of premillennialism, expressed in numerous cultural forms in the United States, such as the *Rambo* or *Terminator* films.

What all these observers make clear is that premillennialism is responding to real and deep needs of the human person which transcend a specific cultural moment but are more acutely felt in times of social confusion and stress. And there can be no doubt that the world generally, and the United States in particular, is in a situation incredibly attractive to apocalyptic "answers." As Strozier notes,

> In [fundamentalists'] groping attempt to relate their beliefs to ultimate dangers [such as nuclear and environmental threats], they are at least dealing with authentic issues—unlike most of our culture, which foolishly acts as though the end of the cold war has wiped out the nuclear threat.[46]

In addition to the "apocalyptic" threats of weapons and environmental collapse, the United States faces—despite the official rhetoric of economic prosperity and social stability—declining literacy, increased poverty and disparity between the wealthy few and struggling many, the highest rates of incarceration and government-sponsored executions of any country in the Western world, ongoing and seemingly intractable racism and fear of immigrants, and declining participation in democratic processes. Some of these conditions will be examined in more detail in the final chapter of this book with an eye toward how new readings of Revelation might provide some fresh hope for Christians living amid this injustice and evil. For now, the point is simply that there are strong grounds for concluding that the turn to premillennialism for answers comes out of both a

---

42. Körtner, pp. 56-57, 94-96.
43. Ibid., p. xi.
44. Ibid., pp. 221-22.
45. Keller, p. 11.
46. Strozier, p. 66.

deep sense that something is wrong and the failure of mainstream Christianity or other mainstream Western cultural institutions to provide meaningful responses to this anxiety and stress.

NEAR-DEATH EXPERIENCES, UFOS, MARIAN APPARITIONS, AND THE NEW AGE

For many people, of course, premillennialism is seen as carrying too much right-wing baggage to be appealing. Harsh or hypocritical Christian childhoods have turned many away from the possibility that churches have anything meaningful to say to their struggles. The sheer improbability of the Rapture leads others to seek alternative sources of hope.

The past decades in particular have seen an explosion of apocalyptic wisdom sources offering a response to anxiety. This section will look briefly at a few of these phenomena with focus on the question, How does each of these phenomena serve as a substitute for the book of Revelation, however unconscious such a process of substitution may be to their proponents or their adherents? Perhaps by studying how Americans and others have found hope in stories of, for example, near-death and UFO encounters, we might gain insight into how an alternative reading of Revelation might provide a more solid, and more truly Christian, source of wisdom.

Near-Death Experiences

The term "near-death experience" burst into Western consciousness in 1975 with the publication of the best-selling book by Dr. Raymond Moody, *Life After Life*. In approaching the topic as a matter for scientific investigation, Dr. Moody's book invited readers scornful or suspicious of traditional religion to find hope and comfort without dogma or other institutional restrictions. The "discovery" that some people who have come close to death have experienced something like a visionary transport into a "heavenly" realm of light, love, and acceptance swept across America with evangelical fervor. Dr. Moody and his numerous successors became staples of television and radio talk shows, popular magazines, and other mass media. Moody's success became, as Carol Zaleski has noted, "a template against which to measure future near death reports."[47] This template required, according to Zaleski, that narratives discussing near-death experience (NDE) contain the following characteristics:

1. An author "seen as a moderate and reasonable professional, rather than as an impassioned metaphysician. . . . He begins by disarming skeptics with the confession that he, too, was a skeptic at first, and even now remains baffled by what he has to report."

---

47. Zaleski (1987), p. 103.

2. The narration contains "an introduction designed to win trust and a conclusion defending the validity of the visions."
3. A sense of humor
4. Research procedures are placed before the reader
5. A confession of bias
6. Purported unanimity among reports as a key to validity
7. An argument against the idea that outcomes match social expectations
8. Convergence of evidence beyond subjective factors
9. Quantitative analysis[48]

All of these factors fit what the writers understand to be the way their readers
learn and accept new ideas: a "revelation" or vision presents valid "information"
only if it can be shown by scientific, objective criteria to be a "normal" experience, albeit one previously "undiscovered." Within this paradigm, skepticism is
valued to the extent that it calls for "proof." However, those who remain uncon-
vinced by the evidence presented by the narrative are implicitly or explicitly considered "closed-minded," something like those scientists who rejected the
insights of Galileo or Einstein before their discoveries became commonplace.[49]
As we will see, this paradigm is equally applicable to other "otherworldly"
sources of wisdom, such as encounters with extraterrestrials.

Dr. Melvin Morse's *Parting Visions: Uses and Meanings of Pre-Death, Psychic, and Spiritual Experiences* (1995) provides a typical example of the almost
desperate need of scientifically oriented near-death researchers to distance themselves from anything sounding "religious" or, worse, "New Age." Morse, who
has published several best-sellers on near-death experiences, especially in children, repeatedly informs his readers that his insights are "hard-core science, not
philosophy or religion or speculation."[50] He insists that he does "not have a religious faith" and has "a violent allergy to anything remotely 'New Age.'"[51] He
writes that much of what he has found "would be easy to write off . . . as being
new-age fluff if science itself hadn't already ridden to the rescue."[52] Although he
frequently chastises the medical establishment for being unfairly cynical about
near-death experiences, his own conclusions are aimed directly at them. At least
six times, he refers to "the circuit boards of mysticism" in the right temporal lobe
of the brain, using this techno-metaphor to appeal to his scientifically oriented
audience.[53] Throughout his book, Morse attempts to walk the fine line between
"hard-core science" and "spirituality" for people for whom the latter term is
freighted with emotionally repelling baggage. Only the slightest hint is provided
that the work which has engaged him for more than fifteen years is rooted in
ancient stories of contact with the Other.

48. Ibid., pp. 153-60.
49. E.g., Morse, p. 140.
50. Ibid., p. 136.
51. Ibid., p. 152.
52. Ibid., p. 121.
53. E.g., ibid., pp. 43, 44.

How does the NDE narrative pattern compare with the visionary experience of John of Patmos reported in the book of Revelation? Consider the parallels in the following table:

Table 2 PARALLELS BETWEEN NEAR-DEATH EXPERIENCE NARRATIVES AND THE BOOK OF REVELATION	
Near-Death Experience	*Revelation*
Sense of being lifted out of "ordinary life" to a vantage point "above" one's body or the room one is in	"After this I looked, and there in heaven a door stood open! And the first voice . . . said, 'Come up here . . .'" (4:1).
Encounter with a "being of light" or a person dressed in white	"His head and his hair were white as white wool, white as snow; his eyes were like a flame of fire" (1:14).
	Numerous references to heavenly angels, e.g., "And I saw another mighty angel coming down from heaven, wrapped in a cloud, with a rainbow over his head; his face was like the sun, and his legs like pillars of fire" (10:1).
An experience of one's life history passing before one's eyes	"I know your works, your toil and your patient endurance" (2:2).
Receipt of a "message" to be transmitted to others upon one's return	"Now write what you have seen, what is, and what is to take place after this" (1:19).
Content of message: warning to others to transform their lives in accordance with a higher wisdom	The thrust of the whole book—e.g., "Remember then from what you have fallen; repent . . ." (2:5).
A vision of a "heavenly city," e.g., "In its total energy configuration, the galaxy looked like a fantastic city of lights."[54]	New Jerusalem, e.g., "And in the spirit he carried me away to a great, high mountain and showed me the holy city Jerusalem coming down out of heaven from God. It has the glory of God and a radiance like a very rare jewel, like jasper, clear as crystal" (21:10).

---

54. Benedict in Bailey and Yates, p. 43.

The NDE narrative, while eschewing the "religiosity" of Revelation according to the "template" developed by Moody, contains numerous parallels to the language and imagery of the biblical text. Researchers insist that the pattern of near-death narratives is independent of the previous religious experience or socialization of the experiencer.[55] This is an important part of the message conveyed by the popularizers of NDE narratives. For example, Moody himself claims—perhaps ironically, given the parallels in the table above:

> In fact, in all the reports I have gathered, not one person has painted the mythological picture of what lies hereafter. No one has described the cartoonist's heaven of pearly gates, golden streets, and winged, harp-playing angels, nor a hell of flames and demons with pitchforks.[56]

What Moody pejoratively labels "the cartoonist's heaven" and hell is, of course, the heaven and hell of Revelation, minus the demonic pitchforks. As we shall see, modern "scientific" interpreters of Revelation seem also to be embarrassed by Revelation's heaven and hell, attributing John's description to a "literary device" rather than something stemming from an actual visionary experience. Thus, with differing agendas, those favoring scientific method react to Revelation in opposite ways: the NDE writers believe in the veracity of the vision while rejecting religion, while the biblical commentators accept the religion while rejecting the vision.

Almost never mentioned by the modern NDE popularizers, however, is that near-death and "post-death" narratives are hardly a "discovery" of Western scientific inquiry, but rather can be found throughout Western history, firmly ensconced in the context of Jewish and Christian traditions. Carol Zaleski's excellent work *Otherworld Journeys: Accounts of Near-Death Experience in Medieval and Modern Times* traces such reports back through Greco-Roman traditions to ancient Egyptian and Middle Eastern narratives, as perhaps found even in Upper Paleolithic culture.[57] The slightly broader but related tradition of "otherworld journeys" independent of near-death experience became the basis for much apocalyptic and other extrabiblical Jewish and Christian literature of the ancient world, some of which will be considered in chapter 2.[58]

This ancient literature served several functions that parallel the cultural role of NDE narratives in our own time. A primary purpose of both is what theologians call *theodicy*, or the defense of God's justice in the face of the existence of evil. In apocalyptic and other "journey" literature, this is accomplished by showing the visionary that, despite possible appearances to the contrary, God is firmly in charge of the world, and that those practicing evil will be punished after death, even if their evil seems to succeed in this world.[59] This serves the additional func-

---

55. Ring in Bailey and Yates, p. 185.
56. Moody, p. 97.
57. Zaleski (1987), pp. 13-19.
58. Collins and Fishbane; Cohn.
59. E.g., Zaleski (1987), p. 20.

tion of warning those still living to conform their lives to the divine order or risk postmortem judgment. This belief has survived in the "fire-and-brimstone" preaching tradition once common throughout America but now virtually absent from mainstream Christianity.

In modern NDE narration, this function takes a different form. Gone are the threats of fiery purification and judgment. In their place is a liberal, pluralistic notion of "everything's okay." As Zaleski states,

> In today's upbeat near death literature, however, which invariably depicts the universe as friendly to human interests, the questioning [found in medieval accounts] has been transformed from an ordeal into an affirmation. The being of light communicates, but never excommunicates.[60]

The medieval theme of the "two deaths"—the victorious death of the hero and the unsavory death of the sinner—has been replaced by a post-death vision where all is light. Zaleski says,

> those who flock to buy books on near death experience want to hear that they will not be robbed of the satisfaction of continued personal existence; they do not want to hear that they will be held accountable for sins.[61]

Thus, theodicy has become universal salvation. Even a self-described lifelong, violent bully and callous, wartime mass murderer can be welcomed by the Light without the slightest hint of punishment for one's crimes.[62]

Near-death accounts in which the visionary experiences hellish visions or auditions are very rare in the published literature.[63] Attempts to interpret these few frightening and dark visions in the face of the apparently overwhelming number of joyous reports often suggest that it is the experiencer's own fear of "letting go" rather than something inherent in the post-death world that produces such imagery.[64] However, it may well be that the paucity of such reports has as much to do with the interviewer's questions seeking to elicit the kind of report that will be popular with the book-buying public.[65]

Another important function shared by both ancient and modern near- and pre-death narratives is the restoration of access to a higher realm, imagined as having once been available to human experience but having since been closed off because of the distractions of life in this world.[66] Pediatrician Melvin Morse sees

---

60. Ibid., p. 128.

61. Ibid., pp. 36-37.

62. Brinkley. The author very openly describes his long-term tendency toward selfishness, violence, and coldheartedness as if to suggest that if someone as terrible as I am can be welcomed with open arms by the Being of Light, so will you!

63. Ring in Bailey and Yates, p. 184.

64. E.g., Greyson and Bush in Bailey and Yates, p. 214.

65. Zaleski (1987), p. 149.

66. Ibid., pp. 3-4.

this as a primary value of his research. The visionary experience provides comfort and security in the face of death for people to whom religious faith no longer serves this function.[67] Morse states, "The importance of near-death studies is not what they teach us about life after death, but rather the spotlight they shine on the spiritual impoverishment of our own lives."[68] In this modern form, however, access to "heaven" is a purely individualistic matter, occurring solely after death to each person one at a time. At the same time, near-death narratives provide an implicit social critique of the dominant culture as materialistic, selfish, and ignorant. However, the encouraged response to this social decay is almost identical to that of premillennial fundamentalism: trust in the Light (Jesus), and you will be saved from the destruction to come. Personal transformation is essential, but social transformation is rarely considered.[69]

In sum, the modern genre of near-death literature serves as a substitute in many ways for apocalyptic literature such as Revelation. It invites its audience, whom it presumes to be open to scientific inquiry over and against religious "revelation," to trust in the truth of its visionary reports. Such trust is intended to provide security and comfort in a world gone astray by adherence to false messages of materialism and selfishness. It offers wisdom from "above" that removes the "veil" of ordinary experience. By watering down or removing altogether a sense of sinfulness or need for repentance, it appeals to a mind-set that balks at "superstitious" or "primitive" notions of "hell." What it fails to offer, though, is any sense of call to community or mission, other than to promote the "gospel" of the near-death experience itself. As Zaleski concludes, "The one article of faith . . . is that there is life after death. On that single platform, enthusiasts of near death experience can raise an entire edifice of nonsectarian, healthy-minded religion."[70]

Unlike Revelation, near-death literature does not call its followers to live in accordance with a different vision from that of the dominant culture. Rather, it unapologetically invites adherents to fit their newly discovered "wisdom" directly into the dominant culture's way of life. For example, a near-death experiencer lamented that upon his return from death's door, he could no longer watch television because of the "false" and "violent" images it portrayed. However, through the "help" of friendly "Father Bob," the misfit regained his place in his world: "Perhaps the most important thing he did for me was to help me to . . . accept life. . . . And it did help, you know. I'm back to watching television. I even like the boxing matches! I've come a long way!"[71]

Conservative Christian evangelicals have often seen this secularized spirituality as a tool of the devil, as they do any ideology that does not explicitly rely on

---

67. Morse, e.g., pp. 129-31, 140.
68. Ibid., p. 151.
69. Cf. Ring in Bailey and Yates, pp. 187-90, where a series of transformative effects are noted, all of which apply exclusively to the individual's personal self-consiousness.
70. Zaleski (1987), p. 145.
71. Quoted in Zaleski (1987), p. 140.

Jesus for salvation.[72] Mainstream Christians need not feel compelled to demonize near-death experiencers. However, when one takes account of the call of Revelation, near-death narratives appear as hollow and trivialized alternatives. While not inherently diabolic, their tendency toward individualism and salvation-without-repentance runs contrary to the thrust not only of Revelation but also of the entire sweep of biblical narrative.

UFOs and Alien Abduction Experiences

Paralleling the popularity of near-death narratives over the past two decades has been the amazingly fertile field of books about sightings of UFOs and contacts and abductions by extraterrestrials. The UFO "craze" has its modern roots in the sightings by pilot Kenneth Arnold in 1947 of a group of nine mysterious objects flying in apparent formation near Mt. Rainier in Washington. What Arnold described as objects "moving like a saucer skipping across water," reporters misunderstood and reported as objects *shaped* like saucers.[73] Thus, the term "flying saucer" came into common parlance. A Gallup Poll showed that within two months of Arnold's report, over 90 percent of Americans had heard of "flying saucers."[74] Significantly, most reports after this time described UFOs as relatively flat, round objects, in contrast to late-nineteenth-century reports that described cigarlike ships.[75] At once, a key question became, Are observers reporting "real" experiences, or are their reports conscious or unconscious projections from images previously planted in their minds?

The UFO literature presents a dizzying array of tales, including such tantalizing topics as purported government conspiracies to cover up the evidence of alien landings, detailed reports of abductions and other invasive experiences, speculations about "ancient astronauts" and their influence on biblical and other ancient civilizations,[76] and a furious debate over the "reality" of interstellar travel. For our purposes, we will focus on the more narrow question, Are UFO reports serving as a technologically "acceptable" substitute for apocalyptic literature such as Revelation?

UFO experiences can be divided roughly into three basic categories: (1) visual sightings of an inexplicable occurrence in the sky; (2) alleged "contacts" by extraterrestrials, either via a spaceship or a telepathic communication; and (3) alleged "abduction" experiences, in which a human is physically taken aboard an extraterrestrial ship and subjected to various tests. Each of these categories provides a different mode in which modern, rationalistically oriented persons can find hope from "the heavens."

---

72. Ibid., p. 103.
73. Thompson (1991), p. 13.
74. Ibid., p. 4.
75. Ibid., pp. 3, 13.
76. Von Daniken (1970) has reportedly sold over fifty million copies throughout the world (Thompson [1991], p. 112).

The first wave of UFO reports in the 1950s after Arnold's "creation myth"[77] largely involved the first category, aerial sightings. Initially, these reports were considered by many sectors of American society[78] to be possible evidence of extraterrestrial contact by intelligent life. Scientists, journalists, and government officials scrambled to either prove or disprove the claims. However, as more bizarre and doubtful reports of actual contact[79] began to merge in the public's mind with "objective" stories, many scientists began to distance themselves from the entire phenomenon, as did skeptical journalists. Meanwhile, government officials worked hard to contain the stories, providing much fuel for conspiracy theorists' fire.[80] The result was a split between the new field of researchers known as "ufologists" and the scientific, journalistic, and government establishments. This battle for credibility and "proof" determined the following three decades of debate.

Starting in the 1950s, various individuals began to report not only sightings but also actual contact with extraterrestrials. While some of these reports were more or less obvious hoaxes, others could not be so easily explained away. Many included supposed messages from the visitors regarding the need for humanity to end its evil ways before it was too late. Significantly, a common message in this early Cold War period was the need to end nuclear weapons testing.[81] Contactee tales continued throughout the 1960s and 1970s, leading to the frequently frightening reports of actual abductions by "aliens."[82]

While the proponents and debunkers of the "scientific" truth of these reports continued to battle, a new perspective relevant to our study was introduced by Dr. Carl Jung. His 1959 book *Flying Saucers: A Modern Myth of Things Seen in the Sky* explored the possibilities that these reports were what he called "visionary rumors" generated from within a social setting of instability and repressed spirituality.[83] Jung, abstaining from siding one way or the other in the scientific debate, interpreted the phenomenon in terms of the need for modern people to find "salvation" from sources other than the religious and mythological:

> The present world situation is calculated as never before to arouse expectations of a redeeming, supernatural event. . . . Consciously, however,

---

77. Thompson (1991), pp. 11-13, argues that Arnold's story became a "creation myth" with which subsequent accounts interacted.

78. Interestingly, most, but not all, of the early reports came from U.S. observers.

79. The key account at this time was the 1952 experience of George Adamski, a renowned occult devotee from Southern California, who claimed to have been contacted by "Venusians" whose spaceship landed in the Nevada desert. His book based on this "experience" was a best-seller and spawned several other similar books in the 1950s.

80. Thompson (1991), pp. 6, 25-28.

81. Ibid., p. 29; Whitmore, pp. 73-74.

82. The socially and politically loaded use of the term "alien" to refer to extraterrestrials has been explored by, among others, Jodi Dean in "The Familiarity of Strangeness: Aliens, Citizens, and Abduction" (http://www.press.jhu.edu.journals/theory_&_event/v0001/1.2dean.html).

83. Jung, pp. 9-14.

rationalistic enlightenment predominates, and this abhors all leanings to the "occult." Desperate efforts are made for a "repristination" of our Christian faith, but we cannot get back to that limited world view which in former times left room for metaphysical intervention. Nor can we resuscitate a genuine Christian belief in an after-life or the equally Christian hope for an imminent end of the world. . . . This attitude on the part of the overwhelming majority provides the most favourable basis for a projection, that is, for a manifestation of the unconscious background. . . . It is characteristic of our time that the archetype, in contrast to its previous manifestations, should now take the form of an object, a technological construction, in order to avoid the odiousness of mythological personification. . . .

[UFOs may be] a spontaneous answer of the unconscious to the present conscious situation, i.e., to fears created by an apparently insoluble political solution which might at any moment lead to a universal catastrophe. At such times men's eyes turn to heaven for help, and marvelous signs appear from on high, of a threatening or reassuring nature.[84]

At the same time, Jung noted that, despite the rejection of the mythological and naïvely religious within the intellectually sophisticated segment of the population, which he presumed to include his readers,

The Middle Ages, antiquity, and prehistory have not died out, as the "enlightened" suppose, but live on merrily in large sections of the population. Mythology and magic flourish as ever in our midst and are unknown only to those whose rationalistic education has alienated them from their roots.[85]

Jung's book opened up the interpretation of the entire UFO phenomenon beyond the either/or debate between proponents and debunkers and allowed a wide range of disciples to take a shot at explaining these reported experiences. As Keith Thompson notes, "the old school was interested only in aliens; the new school saw parallels between angels and aliens."[86]

This opening up of conversation has led to many insights of relevance to our topic. For example, some have observed the parallels between contactee reports and stories about religious prophets. John A. Saliba writes,

[The] contactee experiences a religious growth and acquires a status or prestige that surpasses that of other humans. . . . The contactee becomes a person set apart. . . . Moreover, contactees can acquire a sense of duty, destiny, and mission, which further sets them apart and, in typical prophetic expression, usually evokes ridicule and/or persecution.[87]

---

84. Ibid., pp. 22, 131.
85. Ibid., pp. 63-64.
86. Thompson (1991), p. 47.
87. Saliba, p. 51. See also Thompson (1991), p. 144: "The contactee is cast as a modern prophet,

Others have noted the similarities between UFO narratives and folkloric and mythic themes recurrent in the world's oral and written literature, especially within the social sector outside "official" loci of knowledge and truth.[88] The leading proponent of these links has been French astrophysicist and computer scientist Jacques Vallee. Throughout three decades of study, Vallee—who became the model for the character played by François Trauffaut in Steven Spielberg's film *Close Encounters of the Third Kind*—has attempted to show how such disparate phenomena as modern UFOs, Celtic "fairy faith," medieval sightings of "cloud ships," and biblical reports of "heavenly" visitors are part of "a deep stream in human culture known in older times under various other names."[89] However, Vallee also expresses frustration at what he perceives as the narrowness of scientists in seeking wisdom connections beyond what they can "prove." He says about his fellow researchers, "Ufology . . . has become such a narrow field of specialization that the experts . . . are so busy rationalizing the dreams of other people that they themselves do not dream anymore."[90]

Not surprisingly, UFO reports have challenged the materialist paradigm of modern scientific inquiry. While some scientists have adamantly refused to consider UFO phenomena as a sufficiently "serious" subject of study, others have tentatively allowed their premises to be reviewed. A leading voice within this group has been Harvard psychiatrist emeritus John Mack. This eminent professor has—similar to the work of Dr. Melvin Morse cited above with regard to near-death experience—challenged his own and his peers' assumptions about the nature of "reality": "Our materialist concept requires that we choose: are they in the spirit world, or are they in the real world? . . . What it means is that we must rethink our whole place in the cosmos!"[91]

Dr. Mack continues,

[W]e've so cut ourselves off from any sense of a divine design that we wouldn't know it if it were there! People talk about God in church, but they don't really believe there's any divine design. It's like with Joan of Arc: it's okay to have rules about God, as long as you don't experience conversations directly with God. They've burned people for that! . . . to actually experience a robust intelligence operating with some stake in the fate of the earth. . . .

I was raised as the strictest of materialists . . . So this phenomenon has got me very agitated, sort of puzzled.[92]

---

an intermediary between recalcitrant mortals and extraterrestrial helpers intervening to save humankind from its reckless ways."

88. Thompson (1991), p. 151.
89. Vallee (1969), p. 56.
90. Ibid., p. 25.
91. Quoted in Bryan, p. 132.
92. Quoted in Bryan, pp. 273-74.

Mack's exploration of this realm beyond the purely material leads him to provide a metaphor with clear apocalyptic implications:

When [the UFOs] arrive you are looking at ordinary reality as a movie screen. When they come it is like someone shines a bright light behind the movie screen and obliterates the screen. What we perceive as the movie screen, what we call ordinary reality, they burn through, proving it's only a construct, a version of reality.[93]

Mack's anguished encounter with the UFO phenomenon reveals the existence of a strong current within American culture with regard to otherworldly contact. While implicitly committed to the "religious" worldview of scientific materialism, many people unconsciously yearn for evidence of something "more," which can provide a way out of the mess into which we have put ourselves as a species. One of the pointers toward that "something more" is the persistence of UFO reports that cannot be explained away through traditional science. For some, they suggest that "reality" and "imagination" are not mutually exclusive categories. Rather, according to folklorist Peter Rojcewicz,

there exists a continuum of experiences where reality and imagination imperceptibly flow into each other, [as through a] crack between worlds . . . where one realm passes through and blurs the boundary between two realities—for example, the mundane and the sacred, the material and the imaginative—that are simultaneously perceived by the same witness.[94]

This, of course, is precisely what lies behind all apocalyptic literature from the ancient world, as we shall see in chapter 2. Apocalyptic "obliterates the screen" of ordinary reality to reveal the "more real" world made available through visions and other "paranormal" experiences. In the absence of an active engagement with texts such as Revelation, UFO encounters provide one lens through which modern people can recover this sense of bifurcated reality. Religious studies scholar Carl Raschke notes that UFOs serve as "agents of cultural deconstruction [via a] process whereby long-standing and pivotal 'structures' of thought and action are dismantled so that new, more fluid, and semantically fruitful modes of reflection can take place."[95] Their popularity should not be ignored by those seeking to understand the role of apocalyptic literature in our time. As Thompson notes,

For now, the main significance of UFOs for society may well rest not so much in their extraterrestrial origins, or lack thereof, as in the fact that a

---

93. Quoted in Bryan, p. 276.
94. Quoted in Thompson (1991), p. 191.
95. Quoted in Thompson (1991), p. 186.

sizable segment of society believes and behaves as if they are real, regardless of the available evidence.[96]

Much of the research noted thus far has dealt with interpretation of individual reports of UFO contact. But what of those who have formed new religions and cults around reports of extraterrestrial encounters? What might sensational stories such as the 1997 "Heaven's Gate" mass suicide in a wealthy suburb of San Diego teach us about our modern loss of interest in Revelation?

Of the numerous religious groups that have developed in response to an interpretation of the book of Revelation, the Heaven's Gate group was the only one to our knowledge to have been developed out of an alleged UFO contact experience. Known early in its history as "human individual metamorphosis," or HIM, the group was founded in the 1970s by Marshall ("Do" or "Bo") Herff Applewhite and Bonnie Lu ("Ti" or "Peep") Nettles. The pair responded to a visionary experience by Applewhite while the two were camped along Oregon's Rogue River. Suddenly, Applewhite "realized" that the two were "in fact" the two witnesses "predicted" in Rev. 11. Through his vision, they "discovered" that they were incarnate beings from "the next kingdom," what the New Testament quoted Jesus as calling "the kingdom of Heaven." The "cloud" in which Jesus ascended after his resurrection was "what humans refer to as UFO's [sic]," in Applewhite's words.[97]

With this recognition, Applewhite and Nettles bounced around the country over the next decade, attracting sporadic followers. Sociologists Robert Balch and David Taylor infiltrated the group in 1975 and provided important information on the group's early development and ideology.[98] Then suddenly Bo and Peep took their followers underground, no longer seeking further initiates. Just as suddenly, Bo and his followers reappeared in 1993 (Peep had died of cancer in 1985), believing now that their lift-off into the "Next Level" would take place within a year or two. The weaving together of themes from the now several-decades-long "tradition" of UFO encounters and from Revelation led to the mass suicide of forty people, who believed that their death would take them, via the comet Hale-Bopp, to the "heavenly realm," which they interpreted as literally in the sky.[99] Through it all, Heaven's Gate writings insist that their project is not about "religion" but rather about the development of human potential. Biblical texts are cited as "evidence" that the wisdom taught by Bo is ancient, rather than as calls for commitment to a covenant with a divine Creator. Thus, Applewhite's ideology was a bizarre hybrid of premillennialist biblical literalism and many UFO proponents' yearning for a message from above. It was sufficiently com-

---

96. Thompson (1991), p. 244.

97. First Statement of Ti and Do, March 1975. All Heaven's Gate documentary references come from the Heaven's Gate Internet Website, replicated at http://www.netcentral.co.uk/steveb/gate/index.html.

98. Balch, pp. 137ff.

99. Statement of February 15, 1997.

pelling to lead the group's members calmly to end their earthly lives in reliance upon its truth.

Numerous other groups have been spawned as responses to alleged communication from extraterrestrials. For example, the Unarius group was created in 1954 after Ernest Norman claimed to have received clairvoyant communications from Mars and Venus. Norman and his wife, Ruth—who became known to members as "Uriel"—claimed to have lived past lives as Jesus and Mary Magdalene.[100] They preached that the "Space Brothers" would land in the year 2001 and would usher in a golden age of logic and reason via their "vehicles of light."[101] In a now familiar refrain, Uriel insisted that their teaching was a "science" and not a "religion."[102] Their message, promulgated via "transcripts" of channeled speeches from extraterrestrial beings, included the urgent need for humanity to develop a "higher consciousness" before it's too late. Unarius reached a peak of popularity in the 1980s and continues to this day.

Groups such as Unarius have their roots in the nineteenth-century "spiritualism" of Madame Blavatsky and her Theosophical Society, which also claimed telepathic contact with Venusians.[103] For many, though, it was the prevalence of UFO sightings and contact stories in the 1950s-1980s that made such accounts seem credible, while simultaneously pushing the alleged extraterrestrials' origins to more and more distant interstellar outposts, away from the prying eyes of modern telescopes.[104]

Heaven's Gate, Unarius, and their ilk represent a phenomenon that, we claim, would be unlikely to find popular support among persons familiar with the kind of non-premillennialist readings of Revelation presented in this book. Once one understands the nature and purpose of ancient apocalyptic literature, techno-substitutes such as UFO encounters will lose their apocalyptic appeal.

The New Age

> One reason for the increased interest in shamanism is that many educated, thinking people have left the Age of Faith behind them. They no longer trust ecclesiastical dogma and authority to provide them with adequate evidence of the realms of the spirit or, indeed, with evidence that there is a spirit.[105]

The numerical icon "the Sixties" carries an abundance of meaning for those who lived through that mythical decade as well as those who went before and came after who were buffeted by its sometimes gentle, sometimes stormy winds. The transition in American—and by the power of cultural imperialism, much of

---

100. Tumminia and Kirkpatrick, pp. 86-87.
101. Ibid., p. 90.
102. Ibid., p. 99.
103. Melton, p. 6.
104. Ibid., p. 9.
105. Harner, p. xi (preface to third edition, 1990).

the Western world's—culture from the sleepy and apparently conformist 1950s to the rebellious and antiauthoritarian 1960s was one filled with extremes of emotion and reaction. For the purposes of this book, we would like to focus on one aspect of that tumultuous period in asking the question, How did innocuous slogans such as "Flower Power" become transformed into the frequently apocalyptic visions of what is loosely called "the New Age"?

Contrary to many evaluations of the student political movements that generated anger, violence, and substantial social change, we believe the basic vision that motivated young people to protest the excesses of their government and corporate leaders was a deeply conservative one. That is, spokespeople such as Free Speech Movement leader Mario Savio at Berkeley in 1964-65 aroused in their listeners a commitment to the possibility that American constitutional government, if practiced according to its stated principles, would produce a society that truly provided "liberty and justice for all." Such thinking expressed deep hope and trust in the basic structure of U.S. society. The initial diagnosis of the 1960s' first leaders was that the patient was simply "sick," and needed a cleansing of the "cancer" that had produced the Vietnam War, southern racism, corporate greed, environmental degradation, and political corruption.

A mere two or three years later, however, another vision was taking shape among America's youth. The "system" was not merely sick but rotten to its core. Images of rebirth began to arise from other speakers and writers. An entire litany of slogans appeared that, when juxtaposed to the status quo, expressed a deep desire for a complete replacement of the existing system with another that was waiting to be born. Consider the comparison in the table on the following page of the 1960s' status quo with the alternative society that was being envisioned.

The question is not how many children of privilege whose parents' hard work in corporate America created the luxury for them to dream of "free love" actually "tuned in, turned on and dropped out," in the pithy slogan of Harvard professor cum LSD guru Timothy Leary. Rather, the point is that a large percentage of the demographic segment that became known as the "Baby Boomers" became infused with a dream of a society radically different from the one they had inherited from the Silent Generation, the Baby Boomers' parents.

At first, this set of images had no "transcendent" authority, however. It was as much a product of the Age of Reason as any scientific hypothesis. It was no coincidence that the birthplace of much of this alternative vision was the college campus, where young people were exercising their minds independently of their parents and learning tools of social analysis and, sometimes, Marxist theory. For some, this was sufficient warrant for work that sought to transform America. For others, though, there was a deep need for a "higher" source of wisdom to legitimate the vision. Young people looked at the Christian churches and often saw nothing but hidebound rules and restrictions, governed by the gilded institutions of official religion. On the one hand, the "Jesus freaks" and "born again" movements gained some success in providing a brand of Christianity that appealed to 1960s youth. On the other, though, most youth interpreted these phenomena as con games, attempting to "sucker" them into signing up for an outdated and

Table 3
CULTURAL IMAGES OF THE NEW AGE
COMPARED TO THE 1960S STATUS QUO

Status Quo Images	Alternative Images
Vietnam War	Make love, not war
"Without chemicals, life itself would be impossible" (Dow Chemical slogan)	"Organic" as literal and metaphorical value
Marlboro Man	Hippie communes
Alcohol and tobacco	Marijuana and LSD
Suburbs and shopping centers	"Back to nature" and handmade crafts
Gemini and the NASA space program	The Age of Aquarius and astrology

superstition-ridden religion. Many began a search for wisdom from on high in any place except the Bible.

Two events symbolize this transition. When the Beatles—quintessential "successes" of corporate mass culture whose initially innocuous songs challenged nothing—went to India to meditate with the Maharishi Mahesh Yogi, Eastern religion was suddenly discovered by Western youth. At the same time, a UCLA film student named Jim Morrison called his fledgling rock group "The Doors" after the British novelist Aldous Huxley's underground classic *The Doors of Perception*. Huxley's 1950s experiments with psychedelic drugs (legal at the time) led him to postulate a theory of perception that suggested that socialization by mainstream culture was closing off all but a trickle of what the senses perceived and the mind interpreted, and that drugs such as mescaline and LSD could reopen these constricted faucets. Morrison's act of naming brought Huxley's thought into the minds of many young people, who now could associate taking drugs not with escape but with discovery and knowledge.

The link between psychedelic drugs and "revelations" of otherwise hidden wisdom was strengthened by the series of books by Carlos Casteneda which introduced southwest Native American shamanism to American youth. His classic *The Teachings of Don Juan: A Yaqui Way of Knowledge* (1968) provided Huxley's theory with an authentic and ancient source of tradition. Before long, any of the world's traditions, from Buddhism and Hinduism to wide varieties of North and South American indigenous wisdom, became sources of insight for many. The cardinal rule seemed to be: as long as it's not the religion of our parents, it must be true.

This, of course, was partly an expression of the eternal struggle of one generation to find its own way in the shadow of the parents. The famed "Generation Gap" was nothing unique to this time period. However, there was something real going on that continues to bear fruit to this day. With the success of the Broadway musical *Hair* and its catchy soundtrack, many truly believed that they were witnessing the "dawning of the Age of Aquarius."

Beyond the alliterative attraction of the phrase lay a popular perception that human fate—and indeed, the fate of the planet—was about to be transformed because of the movement of the sun from one zodiacal constellation to another. As Damian Thompson puts it,

> For most New Agers . . . the shift from Pisces to Aquarius is a once-and-for-all apocalyptic event, one which would have been inconceivable until the development of an apocalyptic world-view in the West. For the Age of Aquarius is essentially the longed-for, perfect age, albeit one whose dawn may be attended by terrible cataclysms.[106]

Thompson's analysis reveals how a movement that had begun with "Flower Power" had become rooted in traditions that not only proposed an "unveiling" of a deeper reality but anticipated an actual, historical coming of that New Age amid wrenching violence and judgment.

As the 1960s moved into the 1970s and beyond, many hippies demurred to the inevitable and took their places amid the machinery of empire. As a recent radio station advertisement put it, "Woodstock" had become "stock portfolios." But for many others, the abandonment of drugs and rock 'n' roll did not mean abandonment of spiritual pursuit. An ongoing fascination with indigenous wisdom traditions began to develop its own, unstructured tradition and even minor institutions, such as New Age bookstores and magazines, and "power" products such as pyramids and crystals.

An example of this development can be seen in the popular book from which this section's opening quotation was taken, *The Way of the Shaman* (1980) by self-described "atheistic anthropologist" Michael Harner. The author, who reports on his decades of work living with various indigenous tribes of South America and his study of shamanism among other tribal peoples of the globe, offers a series of exercises and techniques for bringing ancient shamanic wisdom to the people of the West. Building on the work of Casteneda, Harner invites his readers to become shamans as he has done, which he claims is not a religion but simply a practice of healing wisdom. To inspire his readers to undertake this journey of discovery, he recites a story of his own, firsthand experience of shamanic insight among the Conibo people deep in the Amazon forest. He begins by not-

---

106. Thompson (1996), p. 198.

ing his hope that perhaps his stories "will convey something of the incredible hidden world open to the shamanic explorer."[107] He continues by describing in powerful detail how the village elder brewed a potion from native vines, which Harner was instructed to drink. The experience led Harner through a series of powerful visions during which he thought he would die. His visions included the following imagery:

> Within this celestial cavern [to which he felt that he had been transported], I heard the sound of water grow louder . . . the moving scene resolved itself into something resembling a huge fun house, a supernatural carnival of demons. In the center . . . was a gigantic, grinning crocodilian head, from whose cavernous jaws gushed a torrential flood of water. . . . [Later], I became conscious, too, of the most beautiful singing I have ever heard in my life, high-pitched and ethereal, emanating from myriad voices. . . . [Still later], I needed a guardian who could defeat dragons, and I frantically tried to conjure up a powerful being to protect me against the alien reptilian creatures. One appeared before me. . . .[108]

Upon completing his experience, Harner was anxious to share his "secret" with others to protect himself from the fear that what he had learned "was only intended for the dying."[109] The only outsiders to whom he could turn were, ironically, a pair of Christian evangelists from the local mission station. When Harner told his story to them, he says that

> they exchanged glances, reached for their Bible, and read to me the following line from Chapter 12 in the Book of Revelation: "And the serpent cast out of his mouth water as a flood. . . ." [They] seemed to be awed by the fact that an atheistic anthropologist, by taking the drink of the "witch doctors," could apparently have revealed to him some of the same holy material in the Book of Revelation.[110]

One might also add, of course, the similarities between the celestial choir Harner heard and those in Revelation. However, rather than pursue these parallels with the evangelists, Harner rushed off to seek "a professional opinion" from "a blind shaman who had made many excursions into the spirit world."[111] Finding what he sought, Harner then devoted his life to the pursuit of knowledge of this ancient tradition. What is interesting for our purposes is how quickly Harner bypassed the possibility that the book of Revelation itself might have been written by someone who had tapped into precisely the same wisdom source as had

107. Harner, p. 1.
108. Ibid., pp. 3-5.
109. Ibid., p. 6.
110. Ibid., p. 7.
111. Ibid.

his blind shaman. Christianity, beclouded by "ecclesiastical dogma and authority," was simply not a place to go for those who had "left the Age of Faith behind them."

The popularity of Harner's and many other books that offer Western audiences a "rediscovery" of ancient, indigenous wisdom underscores just how much the institutions of Christianity have failed in their sacred mission of transmitting their own "ancient indigenous wisdom." Indeed, Harner's only other reference to the church is in blaming it for wiping out Europe's own shamanic tradition by labeling its practitioners as "witches" subject to burning, not respect.[112] For millions of people whose perception of Christianity is either the caricature of biblical faith presented by television evangelists and the more hysterical "prophecy students" or the sometimes authoritarian, pompous patriarchy of popes and bishops, the faith of Jesus has been severed from the roots it shares with the tradition of Harner's blind shaman. For these people, mainstream religious leaders are simply "old men," while Eastern and American indigenous religious teachers are "elders." By recovering the original power of the book of Revelation (and the rest of the New Testament), Christianity still has a chance of speaking to this eternal apocalyptic need for wisdom that transcends the senses and the powers of reason.

Marian Apparitions

The final "alternative" source of apocalyptic insight cannot really be called alternative, given its uniquely Christian, and indeed, Catholic, source. The phenomenon of Marian apparitions has been reported since at least the fifth century, according to its devotees.[113] Without delving into the vexing question of the "reality" of such reports, our question remains, How does the popularity of this phenomenon express an ongoing desire for apocalyptic insight first promised to Christians two thousand years ago?

Whereas near-death experiences, UFOs, and New Age wisdom often share a sense of resistance to being characterized as "religious" phenomena, Marian apparitions are explicitly and demandingly such. While some may question whether any particular category of human experience can be called "religious,"[114] people who report a vision of the Blessed Mother are clearly claiming to be "revealing" something about the reality of Christianity's primary beliefs. Some apparitions have resulted in cross-cultural understandings that seemed to be blocked by "normal" means, such as the Aztec Juan Diego's vision of Our Lady of Guadalupe in Mexico in 1531, an appearance clearly linked in tradition with the "woman clothed with the sun" in Revelation 12.[115] In the past two centuries, however, and especially in the recent series of visions reported at Medjugorje,

---

112. Ibid., p. 41.
113. Connell, p. 40.
114. Zimdars-Swartz, p. 156.
115. For a modern treatment of this apparition as expressing great liberating power, see Rodriguez (1996).

Bosnia, what many of these visions purport to reveal is a message as apocalyptically charged as anything found in the book of Revelation or the related literature of the first century.

A few examples will show just how "apocalyptic" (in the ordinary sense of the
word) some of these recent vision reports are. Devotee Janice Connell, author of
numerous books on the topic of Marian apparitions, summarizes a few of the
twentieth-century narratives by noting that the "Blessed Mother is filled with
love. . . . But she is also firm. She is decisive and unrelenting. . . . " Connell then
goes on to say that "[o]minous portents of global destruction induced by humans
lend an urgency to the current Marian apparitions reported all over the world."[116]
She begins her summary by citing the 1980s appearances to seven children in
Rwanda in which Mary was reported to predict that "rivers of human blood"
would flow there. Later, she quotes a visionary message heard in a remote
Ukrainian village in the 1950s as predicting that a "catastrophe is imminent just
as in the time of Noah. Many will die, not from flood but by fire. . . . Never in its
history has humanity fallen so low. This is the age of the kingdom of Satan."[117]
Repeatedly, like the premillennialist prophecy students, Connell links signs of
social disaster with Marian messages of imminent judgment if people do not
repent.

In contrast to the premillennialists, however, the visions cited by Connell and
others do not envision an inevitable End. Rather, they threaten destruction only
if people fail to repent. What is required as evidence of repentance? Practicing
solid, pre–Vatican II Catholicism seems to be the command of Mary's Son,
whose will the visions usually purport to be expressing. Regular reciting of the
rosary, belief in the real presence of Jesus in the Eucharist, and obedience to the
pope are the prescriptions offered. Across decades and oceans, this is the oft-
repeated set of practices that will save humanity from the fruits of its own disobedience.

Interestingly, this call for Catholic devotional piety has met with caution, and
even resistance, from the highest levels of the church's hierarchy. This has been
most clear when visionary narratives purport to offer heavenly insight that runs
contrary to official church teaching. For example, the appearances at San Dami-
ano, Italy, which began in the midst of the Second Vatican Council, offered a
Marian message that claimed that receiving communion in the hand would be a
sacrilege. Given that the council had just authorized this practice, an Italian official refuted the authenticity of the vision on the grounds that the Blessed Virgin
could not condemn an act that had been approved by the pope.[118] Similarly, the
1962 vision at San Sebastian de Garabandal in Spain involved the visionary's
claim to have received communion from an angel. Numerous church officials
objected that an angel, because it was not an ordained priest, was not empowered
to consecrate a host.[119]

---

116. Connell, p. 9.
117. Ibid., p. 269.
118. Zimdars-Swartz, p. 116.
119. Ibid., p. 141.

This conflict between purported visionary experience and official religious teachings is, of course, nothing new: Christianity itself is founded on precisely such claims by Jesus and the apostles Paul and Peter. It reveals the ongoing struggle between what the Catholic Church officially calls "private revelation" and ecclesiastical dogma. As an American Jesuit theology professor noted in 1959 in response to the claims made by the Fatima visionary Lucia, "What happens to belief in the infallible *magisterium* of the Catholic Church if the claims of an individual, even of a woman as sincere as Sister Lucy, are treated as the word of God?"[120] This question is one anyone who attempts to understand the book of Revelation must take seriously: When do we put our trust in the visionary experiences of individuals that conflict with our inherited religious traditions?

The topic of the apocalyptic implications of Marian apparitions would not be complete without consideration of the greatest apocalyptic appearance of them all: the visions at Fatima, Portugal, in 1917 to three shepherd children. The Fatima narratives—and there are many, by devotees, skeptics, and the generally curious—have engaged the imagination of Catholics and others for eight decades. Much of the appeal lies in the tantalizingly secret messages allegedly given by the Blessed Mother to the visionaries, especially to Lucia, the only one to survive past early adulthood. From the first hint soon after the initial appearances that Mary had given apocalyptic messages to the children, to the release of Lucia's version of the first two of three "secrets" in her 1941 *Third Memoir*, the Fatima apparitions have had the faithful guessing about God's message about the fate of humanity. The *Third Memoir* reported that the then twenty-four-year-old secrets included a vision of hell and the call for the consecration of Russia to the "Immaculate Heart" of Mary. Of course, the initial vision coincided nearly exactly with the Russian Revolution, and the revelation of the secrets coincided with the era of Stalin's terrible repression. When Catholics in Europe and America heard that there was a "third secret," which Lucia would not reveal to the public but, in accordance with another visionary experience, would send to the pope for safekeeping, many were beside themselves with curiosity. As World War II ended and the Cold War began, the apparent fulfillment of the prediction that the world's fate might turn on the sanctity of Russia, as revealed in the second secret, made the mystery of the third secret something that occupied officials at the highest levels of the Vatican. In 1951, thirty-four years after the original vision, U.S. bishop Fulton J. Sheen proclaimed that in another thirty-four years, it would be Communist Russia itself that would "disappear," and "what will survive will be a Lady reviewing her children in the White Square."[121] In 1957, a text purporting to be Lucia's own narrative of the third secret was sent to Pope Pius XII and has been passed on to all subsequent popes. While none has ever revealed the secret, in a 1980 response to an inquiry about it, Pope John Paul II reportedly

---

120. Quoted in Zimdars-Swartz, p. 212 (italics in original)
121. Quoted in Zimdars-Swartz, p. 207.

seized his rosary and exclaimed, "There is the remedy against evil. Pray! Pray! And ask nothing else. Entrust all the rest to God."[122]

Scholar Sandra L. Zimdars-Swartz, in her excellent volume *Encountering Mary* (1991) explains how "something like a single, transcultural, apocalyptic ideology based on apparition messages has grown up in recent years around the edges of mainline Roman Catholic institutions." She adds:

> Fundamental to this worldview are the images of intercession and inter-vention. It is assumed here that a divinely appointed figure may, on the heavenly plane, intercede with God or Christ, and on the earthly plane, intervene in history to change an otherwise predetermined course of events. Most modern apparition devotees assume that the Virgin Mary has been appointed by God as the chief executor of both of these tasks. . . .
>
> In this worldview and in the apparition messages on which it is based, God is portrayed as most offended by sins of a particular kind . . . working on Sunday, swearing in her son's name, neglecting to attend Mass, mock-ing religion, and eating meat during Lent—all transgressions against a rit-ually defined sacred order.[123]

As we will show, the book of Revelation portrays a God "offended" by sin of a different sort. For now, it is important to understand how powerfully Marian apparitions serve for some as an assurance that, despite the "chaos" of the mod-ern world, it is possible for God's order to be restored. Like biblical Israel's priestly establishment in the postexilic period, apparition devotees have placed their trust in the establishment and faithful practice of religious rituals as a pro-tection against God's wrath. But even in that long-past biblical era, there were others who claimed, based on their own visionary encounters with the Holy One, that God wanted more than ritual obedience. We will look closely at this inner-biblical tension in chapter 2.

SOME RECENT ALTERNATIVE READINGS
OF REVELATION

Alongside the premillennialist prophecy readings of Revelation that have developed over the past century, mainstream biblical scholarship has also explored the text. The starting point for the research of most modern scholars is the pioneering work of R. H. Charles, whose two-volume commentary on Reve-lation was published in 1920. Charles adopted the methods and interpretive stance of his day, namely, historical criticism applied from an "objective" per-spective. Although many commentaries to this day follow in the footsteps of

---

122. Quoted in Zimdars-Swartz, p. 218.
123. Zimdars-Swartz, pp. 247-48.

Charles's method and stance, others have taken different approaches. More and more biblical scholars are coming to grips with philosophical and ideological criticism of the supposed "objectivity" of biblical interpretation. An enormous body of literature has developed in recent years attempting to grapple with ideas such as the "role of the reader" in creating meaning, the relationship between the "social location" of readers and their readings, and issues of how the ideological commitments of readers affect how they read biblical (and other) texts.[124] These studies have opened up interpretation to a wide range of new methods and starting points for biblical studies generally. With a text as metaphorical as Revelation, this new interpretive space has brought forth some creative and insightful studies.

The summaries below are meant simply to allow the reader a glimpse into some of the possible angles of approach taken by recent readers of Revelation. It is by no means a comprehensive review of the literature. The works chosen for summary were selected to illustrate the breadth of possibility that awaits the interpreter who remains unsatisfied with prophecy readings of Revelation.

Two Contrasting Approaches to the Astrological Symbolism in Revelation

Revelation purports to tell of things seen "above" the plane of ordinary existence in a realm referred to as "heaven" (Greek *ouranos*). As will be shown in chapter 4, reading Revelation within its ancient cultural context shows that this cannot fairly be reduced to a simplistic structure of heaven = up and hell = down. At the same time, the Greek term *ouranos* is in fact the word for "sky." This has led two scholars to address in very different ways what each sees as the "astrological" symbolism in Revelation.

Bruce Malina is a scholar known largely for his work in social-scientific studies of the ancient Mediterranean world and in biblical interpretation in light of his and others' social-scientific insights. Malina opens Revelation and sees in it a report of things seen in *ouranos*, that is, in the "sky." His starting premise, therefore, is "that the author of the book of Revelation, the prophet John, has his initial, ecstatic vision while considering the vault of the sky."[125] To understand these visions, according to Malina, one must first ask, "What was a first-century Mediterranean taught to see in the sky?"[126] This calls for investigation not simply of the biblical traditions of Israel but also of the Hellenistic and Babylonian traditions of *astrology*. Ancient astrology, Malina explains, bears virtually no resemblance to grocery store horoscopes, which are a trivialization of the impor-

---

124. For recent summaries of some of these discussions, see Staley (1995, role of the reader and "autobiographical criticism"); Moore (1989, language and meaning); Segovia and Tolbert (1995, social location); Eagleton; Jameson; Gottwald and Horsley (1993); Jobling et al.; Schüssler Fiorenza (1988, ideology and commitment).

125. Malina (1995), p. 1.

126. Ibid., p. xv.

tance astrology had in the ancient world. John of Patmos's contemporaries understood the sky—like the other realms of created reality—as populated by a wide
diversity of creatures. Our modern scientific sense of the stars as distant balls of
gas and of constellations as mere connect-the-dot patterns made among inherently unrelated objects must be put aside if one is to grasp the sense of power and
life that the ancients believed to be found in the heavens.[127] The ancients saw the
"stars" (including what we would now call meteors, comets, and planets) move
and deduced from those movements that they were alive.

Malina takes this initial premise and notions about the ancient sense of the sky
and reads Revelation as a book of "astral prophecy," a well-known genre in the
ancient world.[128] This lens allows him to find correlations between virtually
every image in Revelation and ancient astrological lore. His conclusion is that
Revelation portrays Jesus as "one wielding control of the cosmos" from his position "in the sky" and hence he is the Messiah of God worthy of honor and loyalty in place of earthly emperors and the Roman gods and goddesses.

A very different astrological reading comes from the Jungian scholar F. Aster
Barnwell. He notes that his own interest was piqued by the following quote from
Jung's own autobiography, *Memories, Dreams, Reflections*: "I will not discuss
the transparent prophecies of the Book of Revelation because no one believes in
them and the whole subject is felt to be an embarrassing one."[129]

The master psychologist's "brash statement" triggered a cascade of questions
in Barnwell's mind, which led him to take a look at the book that the master had
refused to discuss. Barnwell immediately saw that Revelation "was heavily over-
laden with astrological symbolism," and set himself to work unpacking the
meaning of those symbols.[130] Thus, Barnwell reads the text not as a biblical
scholar but as a student of psychology and the human "transformational process."
His own premise is that "Revelation was produced and written with the purpose
of leaving a record of spiritual initiation of a Christian genre." He derives this
premise from his belief that Revelation reflects the practice of a branch of astrology that understands the discipline as "a technique for the discovery of one's own
individual structures of being."[131] Thus, Barnwell's reading of Revelation sees it
as a "map," written in the symbolism of astrology, to help the reader reach
psycho-spiritual integration from a Christian perspective. In Barnwell's reading,
any reference to the external worlds of Rome and Jerusalem is merely incidental
to the more central message directed to the reflective individual seeking self-
knowledge.

---

127. D. H. Lawrence notes, "It seems as if the experience of the living heavens, with a living yet
not human sun, and brilliant living stars in *live* space must have been the most magnificent of all
experiences. . . . But our experience of the sun is dead, we are cut off. All we have now is the thought-
form of the sun" (Lawrence, p. 51; italics in original).

128. Malina (1995), p. 19.

129. Barnwell, p. 1, quoting Jung, p. 333.

130. Barnwell, p. 2.

131. Ibid., p. 9.

Reading Revelation from within a Context of Political Oppression

As we will see, Revelation is highly critical of "empire," a category larger than but including specific empires such as Rome. Two recent writers have used this prophetic critique as a basis for criticizing empire in each author's own situation as well as for providing hope for their readers who are presently oppressed by empire. Allan Boesak, the once esteemed antiapartheid leader, wrote *Comfort and Protest: The Apocalypse from South African Perspective* (1987) in the midst of black South Africa's struggle to free itself from the remnants of the former Dutch Empire, which colonized South Africa in the seventeenth century.[132] Pablo Richard, a Chilean priest, wrote *Apocalypse: A People's Commentary on the Book of Revelation* (1995) after years of work with base communities throughout Latin America suffering under U.S.-backed local oppression. We will look briefly at Richard's book as representative of the approach taken by both Boesak and Richard.

As Richard notes at the outset, "I first want this book to be read by pastoral agents working with the churches and the basic Christian communities."[133] It serves, therefore, as a form of "pastoral care for those in anxiety" as described by Ulrich Körtner above. However, the "anxiety" in question is not the existential struggle of the privileged but the daily struggle to survive with dignity faced by the poor within an oppressive imperial regime. Richard believes (contrary to the view taken in our book) that Revelation was written "in a time of persecution," that is, a time like that in which he writes. Its purpose is to transmit "a spirituality of resistance" that "offers guidance for organizing an alternative world."[134] In the end, Richard's reading of Revelation largely presents summaries of prevailing historical-critical interpretations. What is different about his and Boesak's approach is that the interpretation places its readers into what the authors see as a world very similar to that of the readers themselves. The readings therefore are new not because they read particular passages in new ways, but because they read them so that the poor and oppressed can find hope amid their struggles for freedom and justice.

Feminist Readings of Revelation

The next pair of readings we examine come from two women scholars who apply their feminist lens to Revelation with differing results. Elisabeth Schüssler Fiorenza is a leading feminist biblical scholar whose work has questioned patriarchal readings of much of the New Testament and offered in place of such readings more egalitarian, inclusive reconstructions of the first Christian communities and the texts that describe them. Over the course of two decades,

---

132. Unfortunately, Boesak's book is out of print; the authors were unable to obtain a copy.
133. Richard, p. 2.
134. Ibid., p. 3.

she has also written numerous books and articles on Revelation. Her recent introductory commentary, *Revelation: Vision of a Just World* (1991), notes that feminist criticism has generally taken two approaches to Revelation. The first
approach is to point out the "androcentric" (i.e., male-centered) language and
imagery of the text, with the goal of criticizing such language and the social
worlds that such language creates. This approach basically gives up at the outset
on the task of recovering meaning in Revelation for women of today, settling for
critiquing sexism.[135] The second approach "understands language as a convention or tool that enables readers to negotiate and create meanings in specific contexts and situations."[136]

Schüssler Fiorenza chooses this second strategy. She notes that this involves
three steps. First, grammatically masculine language is translated into "conventional generic language," the task of much inclusive-language rewriting of biblical and hymnic texts generally. Second, sexual imagery is seen as part of ancient
"convention" which can be "translated" into nonsexist imagery. Third, she reads
Revelation using tools of *rhetorical criticism*, which seeks to understand how
language reveals and conceals power relations within a given culture. Using these
tools and acknowledging her own ideological commitment to the liberation of
peoples, Schüssler Fiorenza finds in Revelation a future-oriented expression of
hope for Christians caught up within the power of empire.[137]

A feminist writer who explicitly follows Schüssler Fiorenza's first feminist
strategy is Tina Pippin.[138] In her book *Death and Desire: The Rhetoric of Gender
in the Apocalypse of John* (1992), she focuses on the imagery that seeks the
"death of the female."[139] She is explicitly unconcerned with the historical context
of Revelation, focusing instead on the "polyvalence of the symbols," especially
those that appear to promote violence against women as part of a vision of
"God's new world." Her reading reflects postmodern sensibilities that recognize
that texts are not generally susceptible to an interpretive "answer," but rather
evoke "readings" from specific readers with their own unique interests and commitments. Pippin's own primary interest is stated clearly: to resist misogyny.
From this perspective, she rejects Schüssler Fiorenza's attempt to "translate"
Revelation's imagery, seeing it as too violent and stereotyped to be worthy of or
susceptible to Schüssler Fiorenza's strategy.

First World Political Readings of Revelation: William Stringfellow and Daniel Berrigan

The interpretive tradition with which we most share an affinity is the strand of
biblical studies exemplified by the writings of William Stringfellow and Daniel
Berrigan. While not biblical "scholars" in the academic sense of the word, their

---

135. Schüssler Fiorenza (1991), pp. 12-13.
136. Ibid., p. 13.
137. Ibid., pp. 26, 36.
138. Pippin (1992), p. 52.
139. Ibid., p. 16.

writings, we believe, reflect a deep resonance with the spirit of John of Patmos. Stringfellow, in *An Ethic for Christians and Other Aliens in a Strange Land* (1973) and *Conscience and Obedience* (1977), sought to "understand America biblically."[140] Both books were written in a time of political, and therefore theological, crisis. As Stringfellow explained: "This book is necessarily at once theological and political for the good reason that the theology of the bible concerns politics."[141] The particular crisis was occasioned by the war in Southeast Asia, the illegal activities and systematic lies perpetrated in the highest office in the land, and the surveillance and harassment of American citizens by various government agencies. Bill Wylie Kellermann explains Stringfellow's approach:

> [He looks] the American beast in the face, without either flinching or failing. He reads America biblically. He unmasks the rule of death we suffer. He names it Babylon.[142]

In naming America Babylon, Stringfellow attempted to apply the message of the book of Revelation to the world of his day. In using Revelation to expose contemporary U.S. reality, Stringfellow "sought to be exegetically responsible," but wrote not in the form of a technical treatise, but as "polemic."[143] As we shall see, it was in just such a spirit that John wrote the book of Revelation itself. Stringfellow's work was not commentary on Revelation but the reverse: Revelation commenting on "us."

The writings of Daniel Berrigan on Revelation, like those of Stringfellow (who had sheltered Berrigan while he was eluding the FBI in the early 1970s), are not technical treatises but poetic biblical reflections on the reality of imperial America. Berrigan's understanding of Revelation was learned under the aegis of the U.S. war in Southeast Asia and the nuclear arms race, both of which he confronted through resistance actions that resulted in long periods in prison. In fact, both *Beside the Sea of Glass: The Song of the Lamb* (1978) and *The Nightmare of God* (1983) were written while Berrigan was spending time in American jails. In these books Berrigan sketched parallels between John's depiction of "Babylon" as embodied in the Roman Empire of his day, and the expression of "empire" in contemporary America. He asks the question: "Bellicose, selfish, self-deluded, icy, absurdly resolute—behold the Rome of the book of Revelation. Behold also America?"[144] In appropriating Revelation for his time and place, Berrigan performed the central apocalyptic function: the unveiling of empire and the concomitant call to a more human way of life. But as with Stringfellow's work, Berrigan's eloquent and powerful reflections did not attempt to provide uninitiated readers with background about the Roman Empire or the biblical history of apocalyptic thinking.

---

140. Stringfellow (1973), p. 13.
141. Ibid., p. 14.
142. Kellermann (1994), p. 3; Stringfellow (1973), p. 34.
143. Stringfellow (1973), p. 16.
144. Berrigan (1983), p. 24.

Each of these recent readings sheds its own light on Revelation; none captures the full meaning of the text. To begin the process of offering our own reading, it is now time to dig into the roots of the apocalyptic tree to discover the sources and struggles underlying the apocalyptic tradition, which was already ancient by the time John of Patmos experienced and wrote down his visions.

REFLECTION QUESTIONS

1. Consider your starting ideas and feelings about the book of Revelation. Consider images from the book that may have become a part of your life, for example, heavenly choirs of angels, hell as issuing smoke and fire, the number 666, and so forth. What *feelings* do you have about these images? What impressions have shaped your preunderstanding of what Revelation might be trying to say?

2. Consider your own attitudes toward premillennialist ideas like "the Rapture," "the Tribulation," and so forth. If you have ever had someone espouse such views to you, have you tried to engage the issues in conversation? If so, what happened? Reflect on why dialogue might have been enabled or blocked in such a situation.

3. Take a look at a book or article about some modern apocalyptic phenomena like those described in this chapter. Pay attention to the author's explicit or implicit assumptions about the relationship between "ordinary" forms of knowing and wisdom taught from "outside" ordinary experience. What do these assumptions say about the intended audience's mind-set? Try this exercise with a group, with each person choosing a different text for reflection.

2

The Roots and Branches
of Apocalyptic Writings

As we have seen, apocalyptic writings—whether based on interpretations of Revelation and other biblical literature or on contemporary substitutes—respond to basic human needs that transcend specific times and places. If prophecy students "search the scriptures" and the signs of the times in an attempt to discern God's will for themselves and their readers, so did John of Patmos in interpreting the meaning of his vision for the people in the Christian communities in Roman Asia.

One of the initial difficulties in trying to understand the meaning of Revelation for our own time is our unfamiliarity with the tradition out of which Revelation was born. To many current-day Christian readers, Revelation sounds "strange," especially in comparison with the Gospels and Paul's letters. Given the final shape of the New Testament canon, Revelation seems to stand out as a one-of-a-kind text. But was it? Is this final book of the Bible a unique creation, or is it the culmination of a long tradition of apocalyptic visionary experiences and their literary records? If the latter is the case, from where did John get his imagery? Would his original audience have been as baffled as we are, or would they have understood exactly what he was talking about?

To begin to explore these questions, we need to go back in time to before Christianity and before the Roman Empire. Our journey will stop at two critical junctions in biblical history. First, we will look at Israel's struggle under the oppressive rule of a tyrant named Antiochus IV Epiphanes, almost three hundred years before Revelation. Next, we will go back over three hundred years further to the period of the reestablishment of Israel in Palestine after the Babylonian exile. Finally, we will explore how these deep roots of tradition manifested themselves in the time of John of Patmos in texts expressing an apocalyptic vision different from that of Revelation.

RESISTING THE SELEUCID EMPIRE

The "Holy War" Ideology of Maccabees

The First Book of Maccabees tells a hero's tale of the sons of Mattathias, especially the favored son, Judas Maccabeus. While formally a part of the deuterocanonical or "apocryphal" books of the Bible, 1 Maccabees has become known for its story of the origin of the Jewish feast of Chanukah (Dedication; cf. John 10:22), during which the restoration of the Jerusalem temple altar is celebrated after its desecration by Antiochus IV Epiphanes, ruler of the Seleucid Empire. The story is one brimming with pathos and power, with those who burn with "righteous zeal" for the covenant of the ancestors. One element, though, is surprisingly absent for a narrative about faith, justice, and courage: the presence of God. When we look at how, in writing the book of Daniel, another segment of Israel's faithful urged its audience to respond to the same social pressures, we will see the power of God present on every page. It is the choice between the ideology of 1 Maccabees and the apocalyptic vision of Daniel that we must first explore to get to the roots of Revelation.

The story of Mattathias and his sons begins with the author's brief summary of the period from the conquest of the Persian Empire by the king of the Macedonians, Alexander the Great, in 335 B.C.E. to the time of Antiochus IV Epiphanes 137 years later. During this period, Alexander's kingdom became divided among his descendants into two subkingdoms, the Ptolemies and the Seleucids—Antiochus was the successor of the latter. The author has little concern with this first interval and covers it in a mere ten verses. The immediate issue instead is the "culture war" between Jews who counsel accommodation to the Hellenistic way of life and those who see this as a sellout of the covenant's command to be a people who follow the unique and exclusive ways of *torah,* the traditional code of instruction that defined Israel's unique heritage and way of life. As John J. Collins notes, the Hellenizers "undoubtedly saw their actions as a liberalization and updating of Judaism. Throughout the Hellenistic world the Jews were regarded as strange and inhospitable because of the exclusivity of their religion."[1]

The position of 1 Maccabees is clear: those who seek to fit in with the dominant Hellenistic culture are called "lawless ones" who "sold themselves to do evil" (1 Macc. 1:11, 16). From the time when the people left Egypt and settled in the land of Canaan until the time of the monarchy, the Israelites had struggled over this holy vocation to be a people set apart. A thousand years earlier, the focal point had been the desire for the prophet Samuel to "appoint for us, then, a king to govern us, like other nations" (1 Sam. 8:5). This, of course, was seen by the author of 1 Samuel as a rejection of God's claim to exclusive reign over the

---

1. Collins (1981), pp. 156-57.

hearts and minds of the Israelites. The consequence of this preference for a human over a divine king led, in the interpretation of the biblical authors, to the punishment of Israel first by the internal oppression imposed by their own kings (predicted in 1 Sam. 8:11-18; fulfilled in, e.g., 1 Kings 12) and finally, to the humiliation of defeat and exile at the hands of Babylon. At the time of 1 Maccabees, the immediate symbol of sellout was the desire to build a gymnasium, which envisioned naked athletic competition and the commensurate urge to cover over the now-visible sign of difference, the circumcised penis. This was accomplished via a painful procedure called epispasm, which involved stretching the existing penile sheath so that it resembled a foreskin. Symbolically, 1 Maccabees suggests that the desire to accommodate to the dominant culture was so strong that the physical pain of epispasm was preferred to the psychological pain of being different.[2]

First Maccabees continues by narrating the military successes of Antiochus. Upon returning from a campaign in Egypt, he found himself short of funds and raided the gold and other valuables within the Jerusalem temple. The narrator tells the story in great detail with the purpose of arousing the audience's emotions against Antiochus. The next step in the building up of readerly hostility against the Seleucid tyrant is to tell of the deceitful attempt to feign peacemaking two years later, only to swoop down upon Israel with plunder, fire, kidnapping, and destruction. Jerusalem is described as a desolate woman, whose "dishonor now grew as great as her glory" (1 Macc. 1:40).

In case readers' righteous fury against Antiochus has not at this point been whipped up into a sufficient frenzy, the narrator pours further fuel upon the fire. Not satisfied with pillage and destruction, Antiochus issues a "universal" edict that "all should be one people" requiring a total abandonment of native customs. It is the ultimate call for a "melting pot" culture: native traditions are to be swallowed up and consumed in the stew of Antiochus's Hellenism. But Antiochus's edict has behind it more force than simply the pressure to conform. He commands that "whoever does not obey the command of the king shall die" (1 Macc. 1:50). Every conceivable ritual and practice central to torah obedience is explicitly prohibited, including the mere possession of the sacred text. The "lawless ones" join in the enforcement by burning torahs and building up altars for idols. In an important point of contact between 1 Maccabees and Daniel (and the Synoptic Gospels), the narrator tells of how the lawless ones went so far as to erect a "desolating sacrilege upon the altar of burnt offering" (1 Macc. 1:54; Dan. 9:27; 11:31; 12:11; Mark 13:14).

But not all in Israel apostatize under this terrible pressure. As 1 Maccabees tells it, "many in Israel stood firm and were resolved in their hearts not to eat unclean food. They chose to die rather than to be defiled by food or to profane the holy covenant; and they did die" (1:62-63). It is in the midst of the crisis that the narrator introduces Mattathias and his sons. After an expression of great

---

2. Cf. 1 Cor. 7:18-23 and Winter, pp. 147-50.

anguish and lament which makes Mattathias in the audience's hearts a faithful Israelite like those of old, Mattathias is confronted by one of the king's officers and encouraged to be the first in the city of Modein to offer sacrifice because, in the words of the officer, "You are a leader, honored and great in this city, and supported by sons and brothers" (1 Macc. 2:17). The promised reward for obedience is to be "numbered among the King's Friends" and to be "honored with silver and gold and many gifts" (1 Macc. 2:18). Will Mattathias and his sons accept the invitation to be honored as friends of empire? We are not kept in suspense for long. In words that powerfully echo his faithful predecessors, Mattathias proclaims "in a loud voice" before all the assembled Israelites:

> Even if all the nations that live under the rule of the king obey him, and have chosen to do his commandments, departing each one from the religion of his fathers, yet I and my sons and my brothers will live by the covenant of our fathers. Far be it from us to desert the law and the ordinances. We will not obey the king's words by turning aside from our religion to the right hand or to the left. (1 Macc. 2:19-22)

The reference to refusing to turn aside to the "right hand or to the left" recalls Deut. 5:32-33 and its numerous, subsequent repetitions:

> You must therefore be careful to do as YHWH your God has commanded you; you shall not turn to the right or to the left. You must follow exactly the path that YHWH your God has commanded you, so that you may live.

Readers may fairly be expected to burst into cheering at Mattathias's powerful words of witness, which, of course, put his entire family's life on the line. But at this moment of great emotion, a lone Jew comes forward to offer sacrifice. In the ideologically charged words of 1 Maccabees,

> When Mattathias saw it, he burned with zeal and his heart was stirred. He gave vent to righteous anger; he ran and killed him upon the altar. At the same time he killed the king's officer who was forcing them to sacrifice, and he tore down the altar. Thus he burned with zeal for the law, as Phinehas did against Zimri the son of Salu. (2:24-26)

The closing reference is to Num. 25:7-15, when Phinehas stopped the "plague" of Ba'al worship by running his spear through the bellies of two idolizing Israelites. Mattathias's bold act of violence is thus given implicit divine sanction by this act of scriptural recall. But, one might ask, was this truly the will of God, or is it the author's "spin" on an act of "zealous" violence?

The story does not pause to address this question, however. Instead, it narrates Mattathias's call for a guerrilla army to join him in the caves. A group of these, who are described as those "seeking righteousness and justice" (1 Macc. 2:29), are confronted on the sabbath by the king's troops. But the cave-dwellers choose death over the apostasy of fighting on the sabbath, and a thousand persons are murdered by Antiochus's army.

One might imagine the story continuing in this mode, celebrating martyrdom for God's *torah*. But instead, we find Mattathias and his friends discerning that this path will lead only to the utter destruction of Israel. The ironic consequence is clear: they must break the sabbath in order to save it. They organize an army, which sweeps through the land, striking down the "lawless ones" and "forcibly circumcis[ing] all the uncircumcised boys that they found within the borders of Israel" (1 Macc. 2:44-46).

After much success in opposing Antiochus, Mattathias makes a curiously two-voiced deathbed speech to his children that begins with the command: "Now, my children, show zeal for the law, and give your lives for the covenant of our fathers" (1 Macc. 2:50). Giving their lives, of course, is precisely what Mattathias and his friends did *not* do! Having practiced vengeful violence, Mattathias begins by preaching martyrdom. He then calls upon his sons to "remember the deeds of the fathers" by reciting a very selective litany of Israel's heroes, including warrior-leaders such as Joshua, Caleb, and David, and excluding all the prophets except Elijah. He closes with a warrior's pep talk to "avenge the wrong done to your people. Pay back the nations in full, and heed what the law commands . . ." (1 Macc. 2:67-68). This is indeed what his sons do, with Judas Maccabeus at the command. Portrayed as a new Joshua, Judas and his troops march through the land, reconquering territory that Antiochus had commandeered and more.

First Maccabees revels in each stage of Judas's victorious travels through Palestine. The battles are described with relish, Judas is constantly courageous, and Israel is restored to its greatest international prestige since before the exile. Yet even this piece of ideological hagiography cannot deceive its readers as to one essential: there is not a word "from above" to legitimize Mattathias's chosen path of "just war." It is the *culture of Judaism* that has been defended, not obedience to the living God (cf. Josh. 3:10; 1 Sam. 17:26; Dan. 6:20, 26). Indeed, nowhere in 1 Maccabees is God or YHWH even mentioned! What has been narrated is the struggle of human beings to maintain the traditions of their ancestors in the face of enormous pressure from the dominant culture. The "winning" prescription is "righteous" violence. But not all in Israel thought that the way of Mattathias was truly the path of the faithful ones. Beyond the spectacular scenario of Mattathias's and his sons' swordsmanship lay an even greater battle, one not under the power of human hands.

Daniel's Apocalyptic Call for Nonviolent Resistance

The book of Daniel is, in many ways, unlike any other in the Hebrew scriptures. The first six chapters are a collection of stories presenting Daniel as a new Joseph: one of God's people who finds himself favored in the court of an imperial monarch because of his ability to interpret the monarch's dreams (Gen. 40-

42).[3] With Dan. 7, however, the book takes an apocalyptic turn. Suddenly, it is Daniel who has dreams and "visions of his head as he lay in bed" (Dan. 7:1). The visions are of great, hybrid beasts who "came up out of the sea" and who are given great power. The fourth beast has ten horns, and a "little" horn which is seen to be "coming up among them." Then, all at once, the scene shifts to reveal a great throne and "an Ancient One" with clothing as "white as snow" sitting upon the throne. Fire streams out from the Ancient One's presence, and a "thousand thousand served him and ten thousand times ten thousand stood attending him." It is a judgment scene in which the fourth beast is put to death and the dominion of the other beasts is taken away. Then, "one like a human being coming with the clouds of heaven" appears and is presented before the Ancient One (7:13). This one is given "dominion and glory and kingship, that all peoples, nations, and languages should serve him" for an "everlasting dominion." Ironically, Daniel the dream interpreter is terrified by his own dream, and turns to one of the throne attendants for help. The interpretation that follows reveals the dream to be a political allegory in which each of the beasts is a king. The "little horn" "shall speak words against the Most High, shall wear out the holy ones of the Most High and shall attempt to change the sacred seasons and the law" (7:25). But the little horn's power will be taken away and "given to the people of the holy ones of the Most High" (7:27).

What does this bizarre dreamscape have to do with the Maccabees and the fight against Antiochus IV Epiphanes? While the story world of Daniel is placed in the court of the Babylonian king Nebuchadnezzar during Israel's exile in the sixth century B.C.E., scholars generally agree that the author's world was that of Israel during the reign of Antiochus, who is the "little horn." Thus, Daniel's dream and its interpretation generate an alternative plan of response to the oppression to which the Maccabees respond with armed violence. It is the first fully apocalyptic vision in the Bible; we will soon look at its visionary predecessors within other prophetic books of the Hebrew canon. To understand the significance of Daniel's alternative, we must briefly examine some other elements of his visions that follow this initial dream-vision in Dan. 7.

In chapter 8, Daniel has another vision, which presents the same "earthly" scenario under a different set of apocalyptic symbols. But again, Antiochus is a "little horn," which this time "grew as high as the host of heaven" (8:10). The historical link with the Maccabean struggle becomes clear in 8:13 when the vision speaks of "the transgression that makes desolate," that is, "the desolating sacrilege" of 1 Macc. 1:54 noted above (see also, Dan. 9:27; 11:31). Daniel's second vision is interpreted by Gabriel (who is not called an "angel"), who explains that the little horn "shall be broken, and not by human hands" (8:25). This is the first

---

3. Although not written in the apocalyptic genre, these initial stories illustrate and support Dan. 7-12's apocalyptic advice: faithful martyrdom, not guerrilla warfare or cultural accommodation, is God's will for those fated to live within empire. See, e.g., Dan. 3, the story of Shadrach, Meshach, and Abednego, who, willing to be martyred, are miraculously saved from death in the fiery furnace. The apocalyptic sections of Daniel, however, offer no such miracle, counseling actual martyrdom instead.

key point of difference between the Maccabean and Danielic programs: whereas Mattathias and his sons take upon themselves the prerogative of destroying Israel's enemy, the apocalyptic vision insists that Israel's salvation lies in the power of God.

Daniel's succeeding visions continue to spiral apocalyptically around the question of how to respond to the Antiochan oppression. Much of the imagery will be recycled into John of Patmos's own vision nearly three hundred years later. For our present purposes, though, the focus remains on the social and covenantal implications of the visions for the Israelites at the time of Antiochus. In Dan. 11, "one in human form" gives Daniel a visionary summary of the same history of Hellenistic control of Palestine and the wide region as that presented by the narrator of 1 Macc. 1. When the history comes to the period of Antiochus IV Epiphanes, the narrative notes:

> He [Antiochus] shall seduce with intrigue those who violate the covenant; but the people who are loyal to their God shall stand firm and take action. The wise [Hebrew *maskilim*] among the people shall give understanding to many; for some days, however, they shall fall by sword and flame, and suffer captivity and plunder. When they fall victim, they shall receive a little help, and many shall join them insincerely. (Dan. 11:32-34)

Daniel's vision shares with the ideology of Mattathias the need for the "loyal" to resist Antiochus's program of cultural indoctrination. However, whereas the Maccabean vision called for loyalty to *torah*, Daniel calls for loyalty to *God*. This is certainly not the radical distinction it became in the worldview of Paul, the apostle of Jesus. It does, however, introduce an element that was wholly absent from Maccabees: what is at stake is not simply ethnic preservation but conformance to the divine will. John J. Collins says of the *maskilim* who are promised the gift of understanding that "[t]here can be little doubt that the author of Daniel belonged to this circle and that the instruction they impart corresponds to the apocalyptic wisdom of the book."[4] Thus, from within this circle of literate apocalypticists comes a revelation that calls for the loyal to be willing to "fall by sword and flame and suffer captivity and plunder" rather than inflict violence upon the enemy. The entire Maccabean war is put aside as nothing more than "a little help," which is basically irrelevant from the perspective of the deeper reality seen within the vision.

Why should anyone accept suffering rather than inflicting it in defense of one's land and one's people? In other words, what alternative source of hope does the apocalyptic vision propose to the Maccabean offer of an ethnically cleansed homeland? The answer is found in Daniel's most startling innovation,[5] presented in the final chapter of the book:

---

4. Collins (1992), p. 385.

5. The difficult-to-date "Isaian apocalypse" (Isa. 24-27) contains what may be a source for Daniel's vision: "Your dead shall live, their corpses shall rise. O dwellers in the dust, awake and sing for joy!" (Isa. 26:19). See Albertz, pp. 570-75; Brueggemann (1998b), pp. 188-216.

At that time Michael, the great prince, the protector of your people, shall arise. There shall be a time of anguish, such as has never occurred since nations first came into existence. But at that time your people shall be delivered, everyone who is found written in the book. Many of those who sleep in the dust of the earth shall awake, some to everlasting life, and some to shame and everlasting contempt. Those who are wise shall shine like the brightness of the sky, and those who lead many to righteousness, like the stars forever and ever. (Dan. 12:1-3)

It is Michael, "the great prince," not Mattathias, who is the "protector" of the Israelites. And at the time of the deliverance he brings, a new thing is said to be expected: *resurrection* of those "who sleep in the dust of the earth." This predicted resurrection is different from that of later Christian thought: those who are raised live their restored existence on the earth, not in an unearthly "heaven." It is this promise of resurrection which gives Daniel's apocalyptic alternative its "hook." The divine blessing is on those who are willing to accept the suffering inflicted by empire rather than return it in kind, a task made possible by the knowledge given to "the wise" that God's appointed agent is already at work defeating the enemy on the other side of the apocalyptic divide. This is *not* a call for *passive* endurance; the *maskilim* must remain ever vigilant in resisting the temptation to fit in with the dominant culture around them. Daniel's dreams provide a way to live through the suffering inflicted upon Israel without, in Walter Wink's phrase, "becoming what they hate."[6] To accept Daniel's program over that of the Maccabees as the divinely blessed response to empire is to engage in active, nonviolent resistance to evil, "armed" with the assurance that God has already provided the "victory."

THE ROOTS OF DANIEL'S APOCALYPTIC VISION

In many ways, Daniel, like Revelation in the New Testament, stands apart from the other books of the Hebrew scriptures. It is certainly the only text that presents a wholly apocalyptic perspective on oppression at the hands of Israel's external enemies. However, important traces of its visionary imagery and prophetic worldview can be found in even earlier biblical works. An understanding of when and why these earlier narratives arose will help us to gain perspective on the task of reading Revelation while resisting the Rapture.

"The Heavens Were Opened and I Saw Visions of God": Visionary Imagery in Israel's Exilic Prophets (Jeremiah, Ezekiel, and Second Isaiah)

Throughout most of Israel's early history, covenant faith held that God was actively involved in history, saving the people of God as a whole from their exter-

---

6. Wink (1992), p. 13.

nal enemies. Long before the modern myth of "progress," Israel's prophets and historians envisioned a course of history that was leading toward a definitive goal: the joyous coming of the nations to Zion to become incorporated into the Holy People. Nowhere is that hope expressed with more clarity and beauty than in the book of the prophet Isaiah:

> In days to come the mountain of YHWH's house shall be established as the highest of the mountains, and shall be raised above the hills; all the nations shall stream to it. Many peoples shall come and say, "Come, let us go up to the mountain of YHWH, to the house of the God of Jacob; that he may teach us his ways and that we may walk in his paths." For out of Zion shall go forth instruction, and the word of YHWH from Jerusalem. He shall judge between the nations, and shall arbitrate for many peoples; they shall beat their swords into plowshares, and their spears into pruning hooks; nation shall not lift up sword against nation, neither shall they learn war any more. (Isa. 2:2-4)

Along the path of history, however, a terrible stumbling block was placed in Israel's way: the conquest of Judea and the destruction of Jerusalem by Babylon and the deportation into exile of Israel's intellectual elite. The exile was a redefining event for Israel and its scriptural tradition. In the wake of this terrible experience of dislocation, the priestly and scribal elite went to work attempting to forge a future from the ruins of Jerusalem.

For the Deuteronomistic Historian—the final editor of the traditions compiled in the books from Joshua through 2 Kings—the meaning of exile was that Israel was being punished for the "original sin" of desiring to be "like the nations" in demanding a human king to rule over the people (1 Sam. 8). In this vision, Israel would be allowed to continue its journey with its God only if the institution of the monarchy was abandoned as dream and as reality.[7]

This tradition has substantial points of overlap with the work of the prophet whose ministry bridged the gap between monarchy and exile, Jeremiah. In fact, some have ventured to speculate that Jeremiah or one of his circle was responsible for the point of view expressed in the Deuteronomistic History.[8] Jeremiah's vision was of a monarchy-free and temple-free Israel governed by the direct relationship between YHWH and YHWH's people:

> The days are surely coming, says YHWH, when I will make a new covenant with the house of Israel and the house of Judah. It will not be like the covenant that I made with their ancestors when I took them by the hand

---

7. Polzin (1989), p. 79, argues on compositional and rhetorical grounds that the entire Deuteronomistic History is anti-monarchical. In this, Polzin breaks from previous scholarship, which saw both a pro-monarchy and an anti-monarchy strand in the final edition of the history.

8. Friedman, pp. 146-48, 208-10; cf. Albertz, pp. 382-99, distinguishing the theological goals and texts of the "Jeremiah Deuteronomists" from those of the circle that authored the Deuteronomistic History.

to bring them out of the land of Egypt—a covenant that they broke, though I was their husband, says YHWH. But this is the covenant that I will make with the house of Israel after those days, says YHWH: I will put my law within them, and I will write it on their hearts; and I will be their God, and they shall be my people. No longer shall they teach one another, or say to each other, "Know YHWH," for they shall all know me, from the least of them to the greatest, says YHWH; for I will forgive their iniquity, and remember their sin no more. (Jer. 31:31-34)

However, Jeremiah offered no specific program for how this covenant-in-the-heart would shape a restored community. It took the visionary power of another priest-prophet, Ezekiel, to provide a specific conception for the eventual restoration. Standing on the shores of the Babylonian irrigation channel Chebar, Ezekiel found himself overwhelmed by a series of experiences of divine power and glory unmatched in the annals of previous prophets. The reports of his experiences, especially Ezek. 1-3, 8-10, and 38-48 must have seemed bizarre to those who first heard them. Their imagery combines elements from a tremendous variety of sources: ancient Canaanite storm-god manifestations, memories of the Exodus, stories of the prophet Elijah's heavenly travels, and Babylonian epics apparently absorbed during the prophet's time in exile. Many of these images return in Revelation: the four living creatures "full of eyes," the heavenly throne, the heavenly scroll that tastes like honey, the voice sounding like "many waters," the darkening of the sun and moon as signs of judgment, the battle of Gog and Magog, the tree(s) of life growing at the center of the restored world.[9]

At the heart of Ezekiel's vision is the detailed description of a temple in Jerusalem (Ezek. 40-48). It follows upon his vision of the valley of dry bones that return to life, an allegory for the recovery of Judea by those "dead" in Babylon (Ezek. 37). Together these visions provided a tremendous source of hope for the exiles, offering as they do assurance that YHWH would continue to bless them, their land, and—in the vision of the priest-prophet—their cultic traditions. Ezekiel's mystical accounts are not "apocalyptic" in the precise way we are using the term in this book (see p. 4). That is, they are not inviting their hearers to live differently *now* because of the deeper reality that has been revealed to them by the seer. Rather, Ezekiel's writings were intended to allow the exiled elite to maintain hope that someday soon the physical land of Judea would again become their home and that in the meantime YHWH remained their God.

Ezekiel, like his prophetic predecessor Jeremiah, upon whose work Ezekiel draws frequently,[10] expresses great ambivalence about Babylon. On the one hand, Babylon is a polluted land filled with idolatry, described in nearly pornographic terms in relation to the "whorings" of daughter Jerusalem (Ezek. 16 and 23, especially 23:14-17). On the other hand, though, Babylon is YHWH's instrument of

---

9. Our count shows more than 130 specific passages from Ezekiel echoed directly or indirectly in Revelation.

10. Blenkinsopp, p. 7.

divine punishment for Jerusalem's sins (17:16-20) as well as those of the neighboring lands of Tyre (26:7ff.) and Egypt (30:22-26). The resolution of this tension must await a later period in history, when the immediate question before Ezekiel and his audience—Is YHWH still our God?—has been definitively answered.

Ezekiel was not alone among the exiles envisioning a restored Jerusalem. The prophet known as Second Isaiah—the author of Isaiah 40-55—also attempted to provide hope during the sojourn in Babylon. This writer fills his pages with recollections of YHWH the divine warrior, a theme borrowed originally by Israel's writers from the Canaanite traditions of Ba'al the storm-god.[11] As Claus Westermann writes,

> What Deutero-Isaiah is seeking to do by this means is, in the time of his people's deep affliction, to make them recapture the vision of God as great and majestic; for only such a God can be imagined powerful enough to bring about the new miraculous deliverance.[12]

Another tactic in the strategy of Second Isaiah is the use of behind-the-scenes peeks into the workings of the Divine Council, where YHWH consults with his advisors over the fate of exiled Israel. Included within this tactic is the ancient form known as the "covenant lawsuit." The thrust of this tactic was to show that, despite the exile, YHWH remained enthroned as the heavenly king, more powerful than the other gods.[13] Through the combination of the imagery of the divine warrior and that of the heavenly king, Second Isaiah succeeded in reminding the exiles that YHWH was Creator, controller of world history, and the maker of deliverance, all the attributes necessary to be the One upon whom Israel could continue to rest its hopes. Here, in a few verses, is the sum of Second Isaiah's message:

> Sing, O heavens, for YHWH has done it; shout, O depths of the earth; break forth into singing, O mountains, O forest, and every tree in it! For YHWH has *redeemed* Jacob, and will be glorified in Israel. Thus says YHWH, your *Redeemer,* who formed you in the womb: I am YHWH, *who made all things, who alone stretched out the heavens, who by myself spread out the earth;* who frustrates the omens of liars, and makes fools of diviners; who turns back the wise, and makes their knowledge foolish; who confirms the word of his servant, and fulfills the prediction of his messengers; who says of Jerusalem, "It shall be inhabited," and of the cities of Judah,

---

11. See generally Cross.

12. Westermann, p. 14; also Cross, pp. 107-11.

13. Westermann, pp. 15-17; Cross, pp. 186-90. Westermann notes: "Deutero-Isaiah took the other gods seriously, more so, indeed, than any other previous prophet. . . . Had Deutero-Isaiah's intention been to prove that these had no real existence, such a procedure [as the heavenly lawsuit] would have been pointless. What he here demonstrates is that their pretensions to divinity were baseless—a very different thing" (p. 17).

"They shall be rebuilt, and I will raise up their ruins." (Isa. 44:23-26, emphasis added)

A mere two verses after this passage, Second Isaiah, whose period of public ministry lasted beyond that of Ezekiel, offered his audience a shocking prophecy of the all-powerful YHWH's ways:

> who says of Cyrus, "He is my shepherd, and he shall carry out all my purpose"; and who says of Jerusalem, "It shall be rebuilt," and of the temple, "Your foundation shall be laid." Thus says YHWH to his anointed [Hebrew *mashiah*], to Cyrus, whose right hand I have grasped to subdue nations before him and strip kings of their robes, to open doors before him—and the gates shall not be closed: I will go before you and level the mountains, I will break in pieces the doors of bronze and cut through the bars of iron, I will give you the treasures of darkness and riches hidden in secret places, so that you may know that it is I, YHWH, the God of Israel, who call you by your name. For the sake of my servant Jacob, and Israel my chosen, I call you by your name, I surname you, though you do not know me. I am YHWH, and there is no other; besides me there is no god. I arm you, though you do not know me, so that they may know, from the rising of the sun and from the west, that there is no one besides me; I am YHWH, and there is no other. (Isa 44:28-45:6)

Who is this Cyrus, who is both YHWH's "shepherd" and "messiah," one chosen by, but unaware of, YHWH? He is none other than the king of Persia, the increasingly powerful nation that would soon replace Babylon as the premier empire of the Mediterranean. How impossible it must have seemed to traditional piety that YHWH would anoint a ruler from among the nations to liberate the chosen people! Yet this newness is at the heart of Second Isaiah's vision of YHWH as the Lord of all history.

> Do not remember the former things, or consider the things of old. I am about to do a new thing; now it springs forth, do you not perceive it? I will make a way in the wilderness and rivers in the desert. The wild animals will honor me, the jackals and the ostriches; for I give water in the wilderness, rivers in the desert, to give drink to my chosen people, the people whom I formed for myself so that they might declare my praise. (Isa. 43:18-21)

The references here seem to point directly to the announcement of the messianic role of Cyrus and the reversal of the shame of exile expressed by First Isaiah in terms of jackals and ostriches (Isa. 34:12-14). The "way in the wilderness" is the path from exile (Exodus) to restoration, made possible by the "new thing" of a leader from among the nations. The honor YHWH will receive from the "wild animals" certainly suggests the expansion of YHWH's sovereignty to include foreigners such as Cyrus. It is this tradition celebrating YHWH's free-dom to do a new thing that will inspire his successors as they grope for ways to express their visions of how the present should be shaped as something new, but always in light of the past ("the people whom I formed for myself").

The message of Second Isaiah, while powerful and unprecedented in its con-tent, was fully consistent in style with that of Israel's great prophets of the time of the monarchy. It remained for the situation after the exile to call forth a new kind of message, one that would provide the root for Daniel's message and, ulti-mately, for that of Revelation, too. The work of Second Isaiah remained to be completed through the writings of another prophet, one deeply influenced by his predecessor, so much so that his writing became part of the canonical book of Isaiah.

"For I Am about to Create New Heavens and a New Earth": The Battle for Justice and Fidelity under Persian Imperial Rule of "Yehud"

Second Isaiah's prophecy about Cyrus turned out, of course, to be true. Cyrus's conquest of Babylon in 538 B.C.E. produced the most powerful empire that the ancient world had known up to this time.[14] With this strength in place, Cyrus embarked on an imperial policy nearly the opposite of that of King Neb-uchadnezzar of Babylon and his successors. Whereas Babylon centralized power within its own realm through forced exile of the elite leaders in its conquered lands, Cyrus developed strong local control over Persia's colonies, which helped to protect Persia from its greatest threats, first Egypt and later Greece.[15] Thus, it was in Cyrus's own political interests to send back to their homeland the mem-bers of the exiled elite who had proven to be most skilled in governmental admin-istration and most supportive of a foreign regime.

Cyrus's plan required the return to their land of members of two important groups: the priests who had led the Israelites-in-exile in worship in Babylon itself and the scribes and other royal elite who had served in the Babylonian govern-ment during exile (cf. Ezra 2).[16] Upon their return, of course, they found a land already populated by the descendants of the people who had been left behind when the elite had been carried off to Babylon some fifty or sixty years earlier.[17] The elite, with the contempt for the rural working class that has been all too com-mon throughout history,[18] set about trying to control and eventually to exploit those whom they referred to pejoratively as "the people of the land."[19]

---

14. Berquist, p. 23.

15. Ibid., pp. 25-26.

16. Hanson (1979), p. 226.

17. In fact, the first deportation took place as early as 597 B.C.E., as reported in 2 Kings 24:12-16, with the final deportation, accompanied by the destruction of the temple, in 586 (2 Kings 25).

18. Cf. John 7:49 and the regular pattern of contempt for the indigenous spirituality of earth-based peoples that has been expressed by urban-based religious authorities throughout Christian his-tory.

19. Cf. Berquist, p. 37, who notes that Second Isaiah "does not consider the plight of the inhab-

Scholarly Reconstructions of Postexilic Yehud. We know little about the process by which this returned elite came to dominate a land occupied by their former compatriots, a land now called by the Persian colonial name Yehud, meaning "peace." In fact, during the reign of Cyrus, the biblical record tells us virtually nothing apart from the fact of the return itself. It is not until the powerful and long-reigning Darius (reigned 522-486 B.C.E.) that we begin to see how the "blessing" of Persian "liberation" began to be put into question by a group of dissidents whose specific identity remains one of the great mysteries of biblical history.

A wide collection of biblical texts appears to express one viewpoint or another on the questions of Israel's reconstruction under Persian imperial rule (see table 4, p. 63 below). The books of Ezra and Nehemiah purport to be historical reports, although, as we shall see, they appear rather to be pro-Persian propaganda promulgated by Persian representatives in the Yehud government. The books of the prophets Haggai and Zechariah (or at least Zech. 1-8) seem to come out of this period as voices in support not only of the Persian regime, but also specifically of the temple rebuilding project that was at the top of the agenda of the returnees. Finally, the closing chapters of Isaiah, 56-66—often known as Third Isaiah— along with Zech. 9-14, seem to speak in opposition to an element of Yehud's leadership, whose identity we consider below. Furthermore, the priestly "winners" consolidated their victory by offering a revisionist history of monarchy in the two books of Chronicles. Because we are proposing here a fresh perspective on this conflict, it might be valuable to pause for a moment to review the state of the question among biblical scholars and historians.

Two primary questions focus the discussion. First, who were the various groups whose voices are heard in these biblical texts, and what was each group's relationship with the Persian Empire? Second, what role did a rebuilt temple play in each group's vision of the future? Nineteenth-century opinion was led by the scholarly giant Julius Wellhausen, whose monumental work left the stamp of his opinions across the entire scope of modern understanding of Israel's history. Wellhausen's view, in a nutshell, was that postexilic Israel, haunted by the bitter memory of the monarchy's failure, recreated its religious tradition apart from its political structures, a notion Wellhausen believed to be supported by Persia's interest in maintaining colonial calm. This led to the exaltation of institutionalized law over what Wellhausen considered to be the superior personal faith of Israel's ancestors.[20] Thus, in Wellhausen's view, the postexilic restoration meant a withdrawal from the world into the internally structured certainty of the realm of legal code.

Later interpreters found much to criticize in Wellhausen's synthesis, not the least of which was his all-too-apparent distaste for Judaism.[21] Martin Noth

---

itants of the land, even though they would far outnumber the emigrants. The Babylonian Jews' claim to the land of Yehud would be the only claim worthy of consideration."

20. Summarized in Berquist, pp. 3-6.
21. Silberman.

reversed Wellhausen's causation. He saw the key to Yehud's reconstruction in Persia's "wise" policy of encouraging local religious expression as a means of keeping imperial peace. However, Noth saw this Persian "tolerance" as a means by which Yehud could develop internally with little interference from the imperial regime. This idea of Persian tolerance was criticized by Peter Ackroyd, who noted that Persia used either conciliation or force when necessary to quash rebellion.[22]

The greatest effort at putting together the seemingly disparate views expressed within the biblical texts of this period, though, was that of Paul D. Hanson in *The Dawn of Apocalyptic* (rev. ed. 1979). Because we take issue specifically with Hanson's reconstruction, it is important to understand the main lines of his theory. One should note at this point that all of these attempts at reconstructing Yehud's postexilic situation are necessarily speculative. Beyond the biblical texts themselves, there is precious little independent evidence upon which to test one's theory.

Hanson saw postexilic Yehud as dominated by what he called the "hierophants," that is, the priestly elite claiming ancestry from Zadok, one of King David's priests, whose descendants became the key leadership in Solomon's temple under subsequent kings and in Ezekiel's vision of the restored temple.[23] These Zadokites were the ones whom Cyrus sent back to Palestine to restore order in accordance with the vision of Ezekiel, their great exilic proponent.

The hierophants, in Hanson's view, were initially opposed by a rival group of priests who sought to reconstruct Israel along the lines of the vision of Second Isaiah. Where the Zadokites focused on temple reconstruction, the "visionaries," as Hanson refers to them, ignored the issue of temple in favor of a renewed sense of YHWH's presence in the cosmos itself. To support his view, Hanson utterly ignores the canonical structure of Third Isaiah, and rearranges it according to his norms of poetic style and meter, seeing the "better" poetry as evidence of earlier texts and the "chaotic" poetry as evidence of later texts.[24] Having thus reshaped the order of texts to fit his theory, he "proves" his theory with a chronological reconstruction of a situation in which the "losers," that is, the Third Isaiah visionaries, "give up" on politics in favor of an apocalyptic inbreaking of YHWH's power at some point in the unknown future. Obviously seeing apocalyptic as a dead end, Hanson's own ideological perspective is made clear in the following commentary:

> [Third Isaiah presents] a familiar pattern by which oppressed groups in widely divergent historical periods have sought to resolve the tension between brilliant hopes for the future and harsh present realities which threaten to crush those hopes, that pattern being an ardent longing for a return to a past golden era. . . .

---

22. Summarized in Berquist, pp. 6-7.
23. 2 Sam. 8:17; 1 Kings 1:34ff.; cf. Ezek. 40:46; 43:19, etc.; Hanson (1979), pp. 228–40.
24. E.g., Hanson (1979), p. 168.

[It is] a harking back even beyond the historical events of the dim past to the timeless, primordial events of myth which offer total escape.[25]

Sociologically, Hanson's view is based on the theory of "deprivation" espoused by Karl Mannheim and Ernst Troeltsch, grounded in the work of Max Weber. This theory suggests that millennialism generally arises from conditions in which segments of a society find themselves "deprived" of power, and seek "justice" in a powerful event which will turn the tables.[26] The key for our purposes is in Hanson's statement that

Modern sociologists like Mannheim and Weber have demonstrated convincingly that powerful officials ruling over the religious or political structures of a society do not dream apocalyptic visions of the revolutionary overthrow of the existing order of things. Temple priests are not likely candidates for apocalyptic seers, not, that is, so long as they are in control of their temples.[27]

The deprivation theory has been demolished by both subsequent sociologists as well as by scholars of millennial movements.[28] Recently, Stephen L. Cook has presented a thorough critique of Hanson's reconstruction which took direct aim at the statement quoted above, showing convincingly that texts such as Ezek. 38-39 (Gog and Magog), Zech. 1-8, and the book of Joel are both apocalyptic *and* priestly in origin.[29] In addition to not considering all the available apocalyptic biblical evidence, Hanson's viewpoint suffers from failing thoroughly to consider the biblical evidence that reveals important clues to alternative motivations behind Third Isaiah, namely, the books of Ezra and Nehemiah. Finally, Hanson's derogation of apocalyptic as an otherworldly escape from "reality" reveals more about his own ideology of social change than it does about the struggle in postexilic Yehud. For example, he fails to see how apocalyptic language and imagery functions as a "political cartoon" and offers "a deeply penetrating critique of political systems."[30]

In place of Hanson's reconstruction, we offer the following model through which to read Third Isaiah (and Second Zechariah), on the one hand, and Haggai/First Zechariah and Ezra/Nehemiah, on the other. As we will show, although we cannot know precisely the contours of Third Isaiah's audience, it is clear that the text comes from a group of literate, engaged, and profoundly committed followers of YHWH who see the dominant culture's acceptance of accommodation to the Persian Empire as a terrible sellout of Israel's tradition of "YHWH alone."

---

25. Ibid., p. 90.
26. Note that this same theory was used to explain the popularity of millennialism today also; see p. 16 above.
27. Hanson (1979), pp. 233-34.
28. See, e.g., Yarbro Collins (1984), p. 106; Festinger; Strozier.
29. Cook (1995).
30. Myers (1981), pp. 8-9.

Rather than relying on empire, Third Isaiah, in imagery coming from traditional prophecy, divine warrior motifs, and perhaps even using Persia's venerable Zoroastrian tradition against itself, urges Yehud to return to its reliance on YHWH for its stability and strength.

Because the various texts, their authors, and their social situations can become confusing for readers not familiar with them, we offer table 4 on the following page as an overview of the "players" and their situations.

As one can see from the table, the situation is complex. For our purposes here, all we propose to do is to show how the prophecies of Third Isaiah confront those who would accommodate to the Persian Empire in much the same way as Daniel does for his own time vis-à-vis the Seleucid Empire, and as John of Patmos does vis-à-vis the Roman Empire.

The Pro-Imperial Biblical Perspective. The story begins with the Persian cheerleader Haggai. As commentators have noted, his enthusiasm for temple-building seems totally out of place among the prophets. As Elizabeth Achtemeier expresses it:

> He crops up in the midst of the goodly fellowship of the prophets like a misguided stranger from the wrong part of town. No cry for social justice escapes his lips, no assurance that God dwells with the humble and contrite. Instead, he reeks of something that smells very much like the external and superficial religion of which we would all like to be rid.[31]

Haggai's mission is to convince the returned exiles that YHWH's favor is tied to the rebuilding of the temple. The subtext, of course, is that YHWH is on the side of Persia, whose idea it was to build the temple in the first place (Ezra 4:3; 5:13; 6:3). Haggai's goal is to cover over the accommodation to empire involved in temple building with appeals to biblical tradition. He links Yehud's economic woes to the ancient Deuteronomic curses (Hag. 1:6-11; cf. Deut. 28:22-24, 38-40), assuring his audience that the curse will be removed if the temple is rebuilt. As concrete symbols of the continuity between preexilic and postexilic temples, Haggai speaks not only to the returned elite but also directly to Joshua and Zerubbabel (Hag. 2:1ff.). The former was a Zadokite priest in direct descent from the last Zadokite before the exile (1 Chron. 6:12-15; 2 Kings 25:18-21), while the latter descended from King David (1 Chron. 3:17) and had been appointed by King Darius of Persia as governor of the colony of Yehud. Both Joshua and Zerubbabel figure greatly in all the pro-Persian texts at issue; however, their role is purely symbolic. Neither speaks nor acts on his own, but rather is spoken of and acted upon (e.g., Zech. 3). Haggai's message is simple and to the point, and, according to his own text, effective at once in arousing Joshua and Zerubbabel into leadership of the building project.

---

31. E. Achtemeier (1986), p. 95.

Table 4

TEXTS INVOLVED IN STRUGGLE OVER POSTEXILIC RESTORATION

Text	Time of Events (B.C.E.)	Traditions Called on for Support	Central Message
Supporters of the Persian Empire and the Zadokite Priestly Temple Builders			
Haggai	520	Deut. (against its own anti-monarchic tradition)	YHWH calls on you to rebuild the temple with Joshua and Zerubbabel as symbolic leaders
1 Zech. (chs. 1-8)	520-518	Deut.; Jer.; Ezek.	YHWH calls you to rebuild the temple while maintaining covenantal justice; Jerusalem is to be center of multicultural worship
Ezra	Chs. 1-2 538-537 Chs. 3-6 520-518 Chs. 7-10 458-455(?)	Ezek.	YHWH and the kings of Persia call for the rebuilding of the temple and the establishment of a priestly hierarchy to officiate there; foreigners are to be excluded from the temple and from families of the elite
Neh.	445-432(?)	Deut.; Ezek.	Build the temple walls; exclude foreigners; reduce social and economic exploitation enough to maintain a work force in support of the wall-building project; live under the combination of God's law and Persian royal law so that there will be peace.
Supporters of the People of the Land and the Covenant with YHWH			
3 Isa.	During Nehemiah's rule	2 Isa.; divine warrior	YHWH alone is Yehud's security, not the Persian Empire; God's people include all those who trust in YHWH from any nation; no temple
2 Zech.	Between 518 and 432(?)	Isa.; Jer.; Deut.; Zech.; divine warrior	YHWH will send a messiah, who will be rejected by the elite; YHWH alone will defeat evil for the sake of a remnant.

Behind the screen of temple piety, however, Haggai's message can be read as one of pure political accommodation to empire. At the time of his proclamation, Persia's greatest threat under King Darius was the rebellion of Egypt from the empire. Yehud lay almost directly between the two powerful nations. It was the policy of Darius to support the rebuilding of local temples as part of the wider strategy of maintaining imperial control through the establishment of strong colonial governments under the watchful eye of the king.[32] In the specific situation of Yehud, a temple in Jerusalem would establish a well-located base from which food and weapons could be distributed to the tremendous army marching south to Egypt in 519-517. The arrangement was simple and effective: the Zadokite elite would make sure that the "people of the land" produced enough food for the troops, in exchange for which Persia would pay the Zadokites and their partners for the temple construction and support Zadokite authority within the rebuilt temple system.[33] The result: a widening gap between the wealthy Zadokites and their supporters, on the one hand, and the desperately poor indigenous farmers, on the other.

First Zechariah is also a spokesman for the Persians, but his message runs deeper than that of Haggai. His rhetoric is couched in reports of visionary experience, which, for the first time in biblical history, requires an angelic interpreter (cf. Dan. 7:15ff.; 8:16ff.; etc.). His first vision is of a heavenly horse patrol, who report that "the whole earth remains at peace" (Zech. 1:11). Jon Berquist interprets this report as assurance to the Yehud elite that imperial Persia has indeed achieved political control of the whole world.[34] Zechariah attempts to defuse concern that the temple project is simply a political accommodation by proclaiming, "Not by might, nor by power, but by my spirit, says YHWH of hosts" (Zech. 4:6).

First Zechariah's message is about more than temple building, though. He appears to want to offer a compromise between parties at two ends of the spectrum regarding Yehud's reconstruction. On the one hand are the Zadokite priests, who would establish a strict purity code, beginning with the establishment of ethnic purity both within the priesthood itself and more broadly among the elite, stemming from a narrow interpretation of Ezekiel's exilic vision. This group apparently sees *chaos* as the primary threat to Yehud's future. This chaos is best avoided through the twin pillars of *temple* (i.e., Persian protection) and *torah* (i.e., Zadokite authority over holiness). On the other hand are those who would open up access to YHWH's people to all who come to worship in Jerusalem, regardless of the temple. This group sees *covenant infidelity* as the key threat to peace. They see a secure future as dependent on a different pair: *exclusive obedience to the rule of YHWH* (i.e., rejection of Persia's "peace") and *ethical behavior*. First Zechariah offers something for each group. For the former, he supports the rebuilding project and the authority of Joshua and Zerubbabel. For the latter, he insists on repentance by the elite (Zech. 3:2-8) and justice (Zech. 7:9-10; 8:16-17).

---

32. Berquist, p. 53.
33. Ibid., pp. 61-62.
34. Ibid., p. 71.

We have no idea how First Zechariah's message was received at the time of its pronouncement. But we do know that within a few decades, chaos *and* injustice of the grossest sort were rampant in Yehud. The Zadokite priest-scribe Ezra arrives on the scene from Babylon sometime in the mid-fifth century. Armed with a decree from the Persian king Artaxerxes to all the colonial treasurers in the "Province Beyond the River" (which included Yehud) providing him carte blanche (Ezra 7:21-22), Ezra takes charge of the situation. Artaxerxes allows Ezra to consolidate Zadokite power by exempting the entire temple administration from imperial taxes (Ezra 7:24)—then the clincher:

> All who will not obey *the law of your God and the law of the king,* let judgment be strictly executed on them, whether for death or for banishment or for confiscation of their goods or for imprisonment. (Ezra 7:26, emphasis added)

What Haggai kept hidden and First Zechariah allowed only slightly into the open, Ezra reveals for all to see. *Torah* is now in service to foreign empire, an accommodation previously unimaginable in Israel's memory. There remains only one impediment to the Zadokite program. In Ezra 9:1-2, a report is presented to Ezra from the "officials" that

> The people of Israel, the priests, and the Levites have not separated themselves from the peoples of the lands with their abominations, from the Canaanites, the Hittites, the Perizzites, the Jebusites, the Ammonites, the Moabites, the Egyptians, and the Amorites. For they have taken some of their daughters as wives for themselves and for their sons. Thus the holy seed has mixed itself with the peoples of the lands, and in this faithlessness the officials and leaders have led the way.

Ezra responds with a dramatic gesture of ritual repentance, a fast, and a prayer for guidance. The bottom line: "make confession to YHWH the God of your ancestors, and do his will; separate yourselves from the peoples of the land and from the foreign wives" (Ezra 10:11). All existing family bonds are broken and wives and children sent away. The Zadokite program of purification—all in service of Persia—is complete.

But from the imperial perspective, one task remains. This story is told in the book of Nehemiah, which is focused exclusively on the accomplishment of this task: the rebuilding of the walls of Jerusalem. Nehemiah's journey from royal cup-bearer in Persia to construction superintendent in Jerusalem is described, of course, from the Zadokite perspective. We must read between the lines a bit to see beneath the veneer of piety into the underlying politics of the situation. For instance, Nehemiah's travels purport to be grounded in his grief over the sorry state of Jerusalem, a situation brought suddenly to his attention by a delegation from Judah. In reality, however, Persia kept close tabs on the colonial conditions through its network of governors and its temple-based administrations. Some seventy years or more had passed from the first release of exiles until the time of Nehemiah. It strains credulity to imagine Nehemiah, a privileged member of the Persian royal household, as utterly unaware of the situation in Judah until this report arrives. The more likely scenario, consistent with the message of Ezra and external historical documents, is that Nehemiah was sent by King Artaxerxes to Yehud to bring order to the chaotic situation.

While Nehemiah's attention is focused exclusively on the wall construction project, the narrator allows one incident to intrude that reveals a tremendous amount about what was really going on in Yehud.

> Now there was a great outcry of the people and of their wives against their Jewish kin. For there were those who said, "With our sons and our daughters, we are many; we must get grain, so that we may eat and stay alive." There were also those who said, "We are having to pledge our fields, our vineyards, and our houses in order to get grain during the famine." And there were those who said, "We are having to borrow money on our fields and vineyards to pay the king's tax. Now our flesh is the same as that of our kindred; our children are the same as their children; and yet we are forcing our sons and daughters to be slaves, and some of our daughters have been ravished; we are powerless, and our fields and vineyards now belong to others." (Neh. 5:1-5)

In other words, the imperial program, administered by and profited under by the Zadokites and their elite compatriots, has resulted in the systematic impoverishment and oppression of the "people of the land." Rebellion is in the air; Nehemiah, the imperial delegate, must do something so that the twin work forces of farmers and construction laborers will not go on strike or worse. Nehemiah acts swiftly and definitively.

> I was very angry when I heard their outcry and these complaints. After thinking it over, I brought charges against the nobles and the officials; I said to them, "You are all taking interest from your own people." And I called a great assembly to deal with them, and said to them, "As far as we were able, we have bought back our Jewish kindred who had been sold to other nations; but now you are selling your own kin, who must then be bought back by us!" They were silent, and could not find a word to say. So I said, "The thing that you are doing is not good. Should you not walk in the fear of our God, to prevent the taunts of the nations our enemies? Moreover I and my brothers and my servants are lending them money and grain. Let us stop this taking of interest. Restore to them, this very day, their fields, their vineyards, their olive orchards, and their houses, and the interest on money, grain, wine, and oil that you have been exacting from them." (Neh. 5:6-11)

The nobles' silence is telling. Of course they have been oppressing the people! This is hardly a surprise. In fact, Nehemiah admits that he is among those who are exacting interest and appropriating the peasants' property. It is as if the U.S.-backed puppet leader of a Latin American country had gathered the leaders of the oligarchy together and announced, like Louis in the film *Casablanca*, that he was "shocked, shocked," to find that exploitation was taking place. All that is shocking is that Nehemiah is bothering to name the obvious and require that it cease at once!

What is more shocking, though, is the response of the nobles and officials.

> Then they said, "We will restore everything and demand nothing more from them. We will do as you say." And I called the priests, and made them take an oath to do as they had promised. (Neh. 5:12)

Suddenly, they agree totally to change their ways! There is no note of repentance or admission of wrongdoing. Instead, what we are witnessing is a power play: Nehemiah is issuing an imperial edict, not appealing for conversion of heart. They *will* stop because the stability of Yehud requires it. But, of course, the wall building goes on. So we should not imagine some sort of jubilee in which the captive workers are set totally free (cf. Lev. 25:10ff.), but rather, a reform equivalent to raising the minimum wage, providing better working conditions, and so forth.

The Anti-Imperial Biblical Perspective. It is precisely at this point that the long-simmering opposition to the entire imperial program bursts into the open in the text known as Third Isaiah. Juxtaposing a few key texts (see table 5 on the following page) will show how this unknown prophet's words struck directly at the heart of the Zadokite accommodation.

As is apparent from these texts, Third Isaiah stood in direct opposition to the entire Zadokite program, seeing it as simply a reiteration of the sins of Judah's own imperial past. Solomon and his successors had made themselves rich by exploiting the people through the building and maintenance of the first temple, exchanging the covenant for a military security state (see, e.g., 1 Kings 4:21-27; 5:13ff.; 9:15ff.). As noted above, the Deuteronomistic Historian deduced that monarchy was the "original sin" of Israel, because it replaced their unique covenantal birthright and its call for exclusive trust in YHWH with an exploitative hierarchy that depended on international deal making, just "like the other nations" (1 Sam. 8). However, that writer had the luxury of hindsight, weaving his critique back into a story already completed with the fact of the exile. Third Isaiah, on the other hand, spoke directly to a situation in which his people's perspective had been systemically repressed in favor of Ezra's public "interpretation" of the law for the people at Nehemiah's behest (Neh. 8:8). Thus, Third Isaiah needed a new-yet-old language with which to make his claim that his way was the "true" path of YHWH. His rhetoric needed to appeal to ancient memories of YHWH's power and authority, while also speaking clearly to the exigencies of the present moment. To do this, he developed a unique blend of history and myth, of traditional prophetic ethical exhortation, and what scholars call "proto-apocalyptic" use of the imagery of YHWH the divine warrior.

Table 5
CONTRAST OF KEY TEXTS IN NEHEMIAH AND THIRD ISAIAH

Nehemiah	*Third Isaiah*
Then those of Israelite descent separated themselves from all **foreigners** (9:2; also 13:3) Thus I cleansed them from everything foreign (13:30)	Do not let the **foreigner** joined to YHWH say, "YHWH will surely separate me from his people." . . . And the foreigners who join themselves to YHWH, to minister to him, to love the name of YHWH, and to be his servants, all who keep the sabbath, and do not profane it, and hold fast my covenant—these I will bring to my holy mountain, and make them joyful in my house of prayer; their burnt offerings and their sacrifices will be accepted on my altar; for my house shall be called a house of prayer for all peoples. (56:3, 6-7)
The God of heaven is the one who will give us success, and we his servants are going to start building; but you [the Samaritans, i.e., the "people of the land"] have no share or claim or historic right [Hebrew *zikkaron,* rare in Hebrew scripture] in Jerusalem. (2:20)	Upon a high and lofty mountain you have set your bed, and there you went up to offer sacrifice. Behind the door and the doorpost you have set up your symbol [Hebrew *zikkaron*]; for, in deserting me, you have uncovered your bed, you have gone up to it, you have made it wide; and you have made a bargain for yourself with them, you have loved their bed, you have gazed on their nakedness. (57:7-8)
[See passage quoted above, 5:1-5.]	Look, you serve your own interest on your fast day, and oppress all your workers. (58:3)
You see the trouble we are in, how Jerusalem lies in ruins with its gates burned. Come, let us **rebuild the wall** of Jerusalem, so that we may no longer suffer disgrace. (2:17)	Your ancient ruins shall be rebuilt; you shall raise up the foundations of many generations; you shall be called the **repairer of the breach** [Hebrew *peresh,* broken wall], the restorer of streets to live in. *If* you refrain from trampling the sabbath, from pursuing your own interests on my holy day; if you call the sabbath a delight and the holy day of YHWH honorable; if you honor it, not going your own ways, serving your own interests, or pursuing your own affairs. (58:12-13)
The **gates of Jerusalem are not to be opened** until the sun is hot; while the gatekeepers are still standing guard, let them shut and bar the doors. (7:3; also 13:19)	**Your gates shall always be open**; day and night they shall not be shut, so that nations shall bring you their wealth, with their kings led in procession. (60:11)
(use of wood and stones to build gates and walls under oversight of Nehemiah on behalf of Artaxerxes)	Instead of bronze I will bring gold, instead of iron I will bring silver; instead of wood, bronze, instead of stones, iron. I will appoint Peace as your overseer and Righteousness as your taskmaster. (60:17)

Nehemiah	*Third Isaiah*
(Nehemiah orders economic reform, 5:6-11.)	The spirit of YHWH God is upon me, because YHWH has anointed me; he has sent me to bring **good news to the oppressed, to bind up the brokenhearted, to proclaim liberty to the captives, and release to the prisoners;** to proclaim the year of YHWH's favor, and the day of vengeance of our God; to comfort all who mourn. (61:1-2) YHWH has sworn by his right hand and by his mighty arm: I will not again give your grain to be food for your enemies, and foreigners shall not drink the wine for which you have labored; but those who garner it shall eat it and praise YHWH, and those who gather it shall drink it in my holy courts. (62:8-9)

Thus, in contrast to Hanson, there is no reason to attempt to rearrange the canonical text of Third Isaiah into a supposed "better" order that sees the more apocalyptic language as a "giving up" of politics in favor of pie-in-the-sky dreams. Rather, the order of Third Isaiah's text, as Norman Gottwald has shown, is structured concentrically into what is known as a "chiasm," a pattern in which the key message is at the textual center, surrounded by "rings" of parallel passages that reinforce or deepen the primary message.[35]

A: 56:1-8: salvation to foreigners
  B: 56:9-57:13: indictment of wicked leaders
    C: 57:14-21: salvation for the people
      D: 58:1-14: indictment of corrupt worship
        E: 59:1-15a: lament/confession over sins of the people
          F: 59:15b-20: theophany of judgment/redemption
            G: 60-62: proclamation of redemption
          F': 63:1-6: theophany of judgment/redemption
        E': 63:7-64:12: lament/confession over sins of the people
      D': 65:1-16: indictment of corrupt worship
    C': 65:17-25: salvation for the people + new heavens/earth
  B': 66:1-6: indictment of wicked leaders + exclusion of faithful from cult
A': 66:7-24: salvation to foreigners + mission of foreigners to foreigners

At the heart, therefore, of Third Isaiah's writing is the proclamation of salvation and jubilee for the poor and oppressed—that is, the workers conscripted by the Zadokites on behalf of the Persian Empire—found in Isaiah 60-62.

---

35. Gottwald, p. 508.

But surrounding this soaring song of salvation are harsh critiques of the Yehud establishment, accompanied by promises that the divine warrior will not for long sit back quietly and watch his people be exploited. YHWH proclaims:

> I am about to create new heavens and a new earth; the former things shall not be remembered or come to mind. But be glad and rejoice forever in what I am creating; for I am about to create Jerusalem as a joy, and its people as a delight. I will rejoice in Jerusalem, and delight in my people; no more shall the sound of weeping be heard in it, or the cry of distress. No more shall there be in it an infant that lives but a few days, or an old person who does not live out a lifetime; for one who dies at a hundred years will be considered a youth, and one who falls short of a hundred will be considered accursed. They shall build houses and inhabit them; they shall plant vineyards and eat their fruit. They shall not build and another inhabit; they shall not plant and another eat; for like the days of a tree shall the days of my people be, and my chosen shall long enjoy the work of their hands. They shall not labor in vain, or bear children for calamity; for they shall be offspring blessed by YHWH—and their descendants as well. Before they call I will answer, while they are yet speaking I will hear. The wolf and the lamb shall feed together, the lion shall eat straw like the ox; but the serpent—its food shall be dust! They shall not hurt or destroy on all my holy mountain, says YHWH. (Isa. 65:17-25)

It is YHWH, not Artaxerxes, Nehemiah, and their ilk, who will reconstruct Jerusalem! And with that reconstruction will be abundant life with justice for all the people. One can easily read the concluding parable of the wolf and lamb, lion and ox and serpent as a political allegory, in which the wolf/lion are the Zadokite partnership and the lamb/ox are the exploited workers.[36] In this reading, the serpent—a common Persian religious symbol—represents the Persian Empire itself, which will be brought down by the divine warrior, just as was the original serpent in Gen. 3:14 (cf. Rev. 12:9; 20:2). Thus, Third Isaiah, while not a visionary like Ezekiel or First Zechariah, "sees" beyond the surface of the official story into the deeper reality of YHWH's eternal rule. It is this pattern—the refusal to be taken in by imperial propaganda which masks itself as divine truth while insisting on the exclusive authority of YHWH—that anticipates the more fully apocalyptic writing of Daniel and, ultimately, of John of Patmos.

Who was Third Isaiah and what social group did he represent? We should remember that any attempt to answer these questions is necessarily speculative. There is simply not enough evidence on which to build a clear-cut case. Nonetheless, there are some hints in the text and its context that enable us to make an educated guess different from the prevailing scholarly speculations.

---

36. The allegorical use of these animals is common throughout the Bible (e.g., Gen. 49:27 [Benjamin as ravenous wolf]; Ezek. 22:27 [Babylonian officials as wolves]; Isa. 40:11 [God's people as lambs]; Gen. 49:9 [Judah as a lion]; Ps. 57:4 [exploiters as lions]).

First, we recall that Hanson's view, as noted above, claims to see behind Third Isaiah's words a group of "visionary" priests who were excluded from power by the Zadokites and are now seeking vengeance from the hand of YHWH. His perspective depends on the sociological theory of "relative deprivation," in which social groups excluded from power become "millennial" as an outlet for their "real world" frustrations. A related perspective comes from Jon Berquist, who positions early apocalyptic in Yehud within "middle-class, middle management discontents [who] argue for the destruction of their own society . . . as a response to their own frustrations with a status quo in which they participated and from which they benefited but which they felt they could not control and use to their own advantage and for the right purposes within society."[37] Berquist's view is based on the theory of "*perceived* relative deprivation" in which "persons with relatively high standards of living, but who are poorer than their colleagues, often feel a sense of inadequacy and dissatisfaction."[38] The problem with both Hanson's and Berquist's starting points is that they assume, like modern free-market economists, that people act virtually exclusively out of self-interest, and financial self-interest at that.

Our starting assumption, therefore, is different from that of both Hanson and Berquist. What if, rather than self-interested politicians or bureaucratic career climbers, the Third Isaiah group were educated, non-Zadokite priests who dared to continue to believe that the ancient covenant between YHWH and the people remained the best and truest way to live? What if they were people willing to renounce some of their own privilege and status on behalf of the voiceless construction workers and farmers who were being systematically exploited by the nobility? Such a social location would place the Third Isaiah group not as "visionaries" disconnected from "real politics" nor as disaffected careerists, but rather as active dissenters who were willing to risk hostility and rejection in order to stay true to the covenant tradition of their ancestors. As we will see, such a place in society is precisely from where, we suggest, John of Patmos wrote down his own manifesto of faithful resistance to empire.[39]

Third Isaiah was apparently not alone in rejecting the imperial accommodation with Persia. Just as this anonymous prophet built on the work of his prophetic predecessor, Second Isaiah, so too did such a prophet follow upon the heels of First Zechariah. While the writings of Second Zechariah found in Zech. 9-14 cannot be tracked as tightly as can those of Third Isaiah in opposing the

---

37. Berquist, p. 185.

38. Ibid., p. 184.

39. Cf. Albertz, pp. 503–7, who argues for the origin of Third Isaiah from among the impoverished lower classes themselves as a means to persuade elite sympathizers to give up some of their comfort and privilege on behalf of the oppressed. The flaw in Albertz's theory, however, is the unlikelihood that illiterate farmers and construction workers could compose a work as intertextually rich and as compositionally crafted as Isa. 56-66. Thus, it seems more likely that the text arises directly from a portion of the elite sufficiently sympathetic to the plight of the poor to risk their own social dislocation in order to express their solidarity with those whose cries reach the ear of YHWH.

specifics of the Zadokite scheme, it is clear that the rhetoric of these chapters is also harshly critical of what it perceives to be an oppressive status quo in favor of the rule of the divine warrior.

> Ask rain from YHWH in the season of the spring rain, from YHWH who makes the storm clouds, who gives showers of rain to you, the vegetation in the field to everyone. For the teraphim utter nonsense, and the diviners see lies; the dreamers tell false dreams, and give empty consolation. There-fore the people wander like sheep; they suffer for lack of a shepherd. My anger is hot against the shepherds, and I will punish the leaders; for YHWH of hosts cares for his flock, the house of Judah, and will make them like his proud war horse. (Zech. 10:1-3)

Second Zechariah's use of the divine warrior motif reaches its bitter climax in Zech. 13-14, where the split between the evil shepherds and the faithful remnant becomes a matter of final divine judgment:

> In the whole land, says YHWH, two-thirds shall be cut off and perish, and one-third shall be left alive. And I will put this third into the fire, refine them as one refines silver, and test them as gold is tested. They will call on my name, and I will answer them. I will say, "They are my people"; and they will say, "YHWH is our God." (Zech. 13:8-9)

After this great separation, we are told that "a day is coming for YHWH," in which "YHWH will go forth and fight" (14:3). Cosmic signs accompany this bat-tle, including the absence of cold or frost, the establishment of continuous day, and the flowing of living waters out from Jerusalem. On this day, "YHWH will become king over all the earth; on that day YHWH will be one and his name will be one" (14:9). Those who refuse to recognize YHWH's divinity will suffer the greatest punishment possible for a desert people: "there will be no rain upon them" (14:17). As Hanson comments, "With Zechariah 14 one enters the period of full-blown apocalyptic literature."[40] There is little doubt that Daniel's visions of cosmic forces overcoming Israel's earthly oppressors stand in a continuous line of tradition with this passage from Second Zechariah, composed around three hundred years earlier. The common theme is clear: for those who have been unjustly exploited by those in political power, God provides a vision revealing how the faithful ones *will* be vindicated.

From Third Isaiah to Daniel: Judea Steeped in the Apocalyptic Brew of Zoroastrianism

Despite the powerful protests of Third Isaiah and Second Zechariah, the Zadokite-Persian deal had been sealed. It was another hundred years until Persia

---

40. Hanson (1979), p. 369.

finally collapsed before the superior might of Alexander the Great in 335 B.C.E. During this period, Yehud's elite were certainly exposed to the dominant religion of Persia, the ancient tradition of Zoroastrianism. It was during this period of Persia's imperial triumph that the perhaps thousand-year-or-more-old stories of Zoroaster were compiled into the scriptural collection known as the Avesta.[41]

Contained within this collection was a powerful myth of the battle between good and evil, embodied in the cosmic war between the creator god Ahura Mazda and his evil enemy Angra Mainyu. Zoroaster, living long before the establishment of the Persian nation, probably developed this myth out of his people's experience of invasion by hostile bands of marauders. It expressed the hope that good and truth would triumph over evil and falsehood, so long as devout Zoroastrians helped Ahura Mazda by living in accordance with truth. The Zoroastrian creed was spiritually egalitarian; all persons, regardless of social status or class, were called upon to participate in the salvation of the world from the forces of falsehood.[42]

Norman Cohn, a leading scholar of Zoroastrianism, claims that Zoroaster himself expected the imminent victory of Ahura Mazda and his followers. When it did not happen, the myth was expanded to include the prophecy of the coming of a savior known as the Saoshyant. This figure would appear just when it looked as if falsehood would finally defeat truth. His appearance would come about through the bathing of a virgin in a sacred lake in which the seed of Zoroaster himself will have been held, guarded by 99,999 souls of the righteous dead. The virgin, whose name meant "She Who Conquers," would become pregnant with this seed and give birth to the Saoshyant. Her offspring would then spend fifty-seven years resurrecting the righteous dead and assembling them for a final battle against Angra Mainyu. The latter would be defeated, and the Saoshyant, by gazing lovingly on the world, would usher in the final and eternal era of true peace known as the "making wonderful." While not thought to be imminent, the coming of the Saoshyant was an event watched for by devout Zoroastrians.

As Cohn points out, Zoroastrianism was clearly the religion of Darius and Artaxerxes, as can be seen by inscriptions on their tombs.[43] However, a stable empire needs a spirituality that does not lead people to expect mammoth change to come over the world at any time in the near future. Instead, imperial Persia sought divine legitimation and a sense of longevity by making major modifications in the tradition handed down from the time of Zoroaster himself. This major innovation, developed not later than the first half of the fourth century B.C.E. by Zoroastrianism's scholar-priests (i.e., the counterparts of Yehud's Zadokites), replaced the expectation of the Saoshyant with the doctrine of successive world ages. While traditions vary, each extant version of the Zoroastrian myth from this period presents the story of multi-thousand-year periods comprising "limited time" before the arrival of the "making wonderful" at the End. Of course, this

---

41. Cohn, pp. 79-80.
42. Ibid., p. 89.
43. Ibid., p. 102.

meant that the entire sequence of ages would need to be completed before the final triumph of truth. In this revised scheme, a saoshyant was to be expected for each age, whose victory would simply lead to the beginning of the next age rather than to the "making wonderful" itself.

It was this form of Zoroastrianism that was promulgated and practiced during Palestine's period of colonial subjugation. There can be little doubt that the eventual imagery of historical ages found in Daniel was influenced by Yehud's exposure to Persia's dominant religion for nearly two hundred years. Another critical belief within Zoroastrianism that was taken up by Daniel with powerful rhetorical effect was the idea of bodily resurrection. Such a concept was just as controversial during the time in which the Avesta was composed as it would be to Greeks during the apostle Paul's missionary travels (e.g., 1 Cor. 15). In anticipation of disbelief in such a counterintuitive doctrine, the Avesta contains both a question from a doubter and Ahura Mazda's response, which concludes with the question, "If I made that which is not, why cannot I make again that which was?"[44] The doctrine of bodily resurrection became, of course, a key element in the apocalyptic program of encouraging *hypomonē*, that is, long-standing, faithful resistance[45] to empire that might lead even to death at the hands of the powers of evil (Rev. 1:9; 2:2; 2:3; 2:19; etc.).

Furthermore, other elements of Zoroastrianism also made their way into what became the traditions of Jewish apocalyptic. For example, Zoroastrianism preached the presence and power of demonic spirits who assisted Angra Mainyu in his efforts to deceive people into following the false path.[46] Their counterparts were called *fravashis*, winged warriors not unlike the cherubim seen by Ezekiel, Daniel, and John of Patmos, whose function it was to guard the living, especially in times of war. Zoroastrians also believed in a netherworld in which the souls of the damned would be punished, a doctrine otherwise wholly unknown to Judaism but clearly taken up in apocalyptic writings. All of these doctrines filtered into the imagination of Yehud's literate classes, only to be remolded and brought out centuries later in service of YHWH.

Perhaps ironically, still another feature arising from Jewish subjugation under Persia was the development of the character of Satan. While modern-day Christians often imagine Satan as the leader of an "evil empire," his origins were much more humble. He began as a cosmic counterpart to the Persian spies known to Yehud's elite as roving intelligence officers probing the colonies for disloyalty.[47] They were called "the king's eye" or "the king's ear," a function that the cosmic

---

44. Quoted in Cohn, p. 97.

45. Usually translated as the more passive "patient endurance," F. Hauck notes "*hupomenê* becomes a prominent virtue in the sense of courageous endurance. As distinct from patience, it has the active significance of energetic if not necessarily successful resistance . . ." (*TDNT,* vol. 4, p. 580). It is the noun form of the verb used by Third Isaiah in the Septuagint translation of Isa. 64:3, *hupomenousin,* "waiting" for YHWH. Cf. 4 Macc. 1:11; 7:9; etc. (twelve times in 4 Maccabees) for similar use of the noun in connection with martyrdom.

46. Cohn, pp. 91-92.

47. Pagels, p. 41.

Satan takes on most famously in the book of Job. In apocalyptic form, Satan—also known in some texts by other names such as Azazel, Belial, or Beliar—combines this accusatory function with the more explicitly evil role of Angra Mainyu as purveyor of falsehood, violence, and destruction. It has been one of the great powers of the apocalyptic imagination over the centuries to take familiar political, historical, and mythical images and creatively to rework them to provide a message of hope for a new situation. The development of the character of Satan, so central to the book of Revelation, is simply one example of this ability.

JEWISH APOCALYPTIC BRANCHES AFTER DANIEL

The Composite Book of First Enoch

As we have seen, much of the social struggle over how to resist empire and the powerful imagery of the divine warrior generated by the postexilic crisis made their way into the book of Daniel during the Seleucid Empire in the second century B.C.E. Daniel, though, was not the only apocalyptic book purporting to show the way out of this struggle. The book of *1 Enoch* as we now have it, is a composite of individual apocalypses, accounts of visionary journeys, ethical exhortations, and astronomical speculations. As yet scholars have not been able to link many of its parts to specific, external social circumstances, nor is the specific location of its composition and exposure known.[48] What is clear, though, is that its general purpose is to address problems related to Jewish life within the Hellenistic cultural setting.

Table 6
APOCALYPTIC COMPONENTS OF THE BOOK OF ENOCH

Section	*Date*	*Theme*	*Important Elements*
Book of Watchers (chs. 1-36)	Composite: pre-167 B.C.E.	God's wisdom and power will triumph	Throne vision; heavenly journey
Animal Apocalypse (chs. 85-91)	Approx. 167 B.C.E.	Victory is in God's hands; the righteous participate in God's victory through holy war	Animals as symbols for human leaders/enemies
Apocalypse of Weeks (ch. 93)	Approx. 160 B.C.E. (?)	The "elect" will be saved from among the wicked; new heaven and new earth	Division of history into ten periods; use of "7" and multiples

---

48. Collins (1984), pp. 36, 38-39.

The first section (see table 6) is known as The Book of the Watchers. Its ostensible setting is during the prehistoric period of Enoch, son of Cain, who was reported to have lived the "perfect" length of 365 years (Gen. 4:17; 5:23). In the Book of the Watchers, Enoch is called by the "Watchers," the heavenly beings known to the biblical tradition as the "sons of God" (Gen. 6:2), to pronounce judgment upon the Watchers themselves for the sin of having mated with human women. In Genesis, it is this sin that leads God to call upon Noah to prepare for the great Flood. In the book of *Enoch,* however, a much more elaborate scenario is presented. Judgment is declared directly upon the Watchers themselves, after which Enoch is taken up into heaven for a tour of the heavenly realms. On the tour, he sees a dazzling array of heavenly features that were known to Ezekiel centuries earlier and are again revealed to John of Patmos: God on a jeweled throne surrounded by cherubim, fire flowing like water, the home of the four winds. Throughout the journey, angels are seen to assist God in overseeing the creation. Enoch is himself guided by the angel Uriel (Hebrew for "fire of God"), who shows him a place in which a great and lush mountain is surrounded by harsh, arid desert. Uriel explains that these are the places in which the "Eternal King" will place the blessed and the accursed, although no specific basis for the judgment is given. These locales are holding areas until the final judgment, when God will make his dwelling for eternity on a transformed earth.[49] The entire journey seems to be presented so that readers will be inspired by the awesome power of the divine Creator and Judge of all to live holy lives. As John J. Collins notes, "Enoch's journey has no close parallel in the Hebrew scriptures, and it does not appear to be closely modeled on a nonbiblical source either."[50] Although the overall genre and structure of the Book of the Watchers appears to be unique, individual images have their origin in Babylonian, Persian, and biblical sources.

The second apocalyptic section of the book of *Enoch* is called the Animal Apocalypse. This text bears strong resemblance to Daniel in its allegorical presentation of historical, political figures as various sorts of animals. It is a report of a dream narrated by Enoch to his son Methuselah. The allegory begins with Adam and continues throughout the primal history through the Exodus and the monarchy. It culminates in the time of Antiochus IV Epiphanes, portraying Judas Maccabeus as a heroic "horn." The allegory presents Judas as the hero of the conquest that leads to God's establishment of an earthly judgment throne within a restored and glorious Israel. Thus, the Animal Apocalypse, in direct contrast to Daniel, purports to reveal God endorsing the use of the sword against the Seleucids.[51]

The final apocalyptic section is the *Apocalypse of Weeks.* This brief text contains no visionary dreams nor heavenly journeys. Instead, it presents a schematized historical overview, almost certainly based in the Zoroastrian idea of the Ages.[52] The historical review leads to a moment of eschatological judgment in which the author, borrowing directly from Third Isaiah, proclaims, "And the first

---

49. Collins (1995), p. 48.
50. Collins (1984), p. 44.
51. Albertz, pp. 588-90.
52. Collins (1984), p. 50.

heaven shall depart and pass away, and a new heaven shall appear" *(1 Enoch* 93:16). The text provides assurance amid chaotic social circumstances that God the Creator remains, as always, fully in control of events.

This brief overview shows that the tradition of imagery and ideas that developed first in the postexilic period and continued into the Hellenistic period provided fertile ground for the apocalyptic imagination.

Jewish Apocalyptic during the Roman Empire

As we have seen, writers like Third Isaiah and Second Zechariah provided a foundation upon which later writers could build. Later writers continued this now-several-hundred-year-old tradition when confronted with the new power of Rome.

The amount of apocalyptic literature arising from this period is vast, taking up one thick volume in the most widespread collection.[53] For our purposes, we would like to highlight briefly a few of the most important texts from around the same time period as Revelation. Our goal is to show how much of the imagery flowing from these apocalyptic roots made its way into texts beyond Revelation itself, sometimes with very different ideological results. One theme found throughout many of these texts is that the Roman Empire is Babylon and its lures must be resisted by those faithful to the ways of YHWH.

Table 7
SELECTED JEWISH APOCALYPTIC TEXTS
FROM THE ROMAN IMPERIAL PERIOD

Text	Date	Theme	Important Elements
Dead Sea Scrolls	Approx. 100 B.C.E.-50 C.E.	Jerusalem will be purified by triple messiahs (priest/warrior/prophetic); the holy remnant will be restored to earthly authority via holy war	Light/dark imagery; cosmic war; elect/condemned segments of community
4 Ezra	70-100 C.E. (post temple)	Justice of God after destruction of temple	Cosmic interpretation of history; dream-visions; resurrection of judgment; angelic interpreter; many images parallel to Rev., including Rome as Babylon
2 Baruch	70-100 C.E. (post temple)	Salvation from this world comes to those Jews who obey the *torah*	Symbolic visions
Fifth Sibylline Oracle	70-100 C.E. (post-temple)	Rome will be punished for destroying the temple	Rome as Babylon; Nero *redivivus;* final battle between "the stars"

---

53. J. H. Charlesworth.

Qumran. The vast collection of Dead Sea Scrolls found in the desert at Qumran testifies to an apocalyptic community that survived the Roman occupation of Judea for perhaps as long as two hundred years. Scholars differ over whether the community actually lived in the desert or whether the location where the documents were found served some lesser purpose while the members of the community lived secretly amid other Jews in Jerusalem.[54] In either case, the Qumran texts reveal a community of Jews fiercely resistant to accommodation to imperial Rome or its Hellenistic predecessor.

Unlike self-contained, individual texts such as 4 Ezra and *2 Baruch,* the Qumran documents apparently served a variety of roles for their community. What is clear is that the community members waited in anticipation of a triple-messianic event that would restore justice and righteousness to Jerusalem. An actual holy war led by the three messiahs, in contrast to the "heavenly" scenarios of Third Isaiah, Daniel, or perhaps 4 Ezra, is envisioned. The members of the community would serve as messianic troops, following the leaders back into a purified Jerusalem. In this respect, the Qumran community fell between the viewpoint of the Maccabees and that of Daniel. Like the Maccabees, they saw actual violence as a necessary weapon in the fight against evil. Like Daniel, however, they did not see the initiation of violence as their own prerogative, choosing instead to await God's powerful act of liberation and justice. The destruction of the Jerusalem temple, however, also destroyed the hope of this community, leaving some perhaps to turn to post-temple texts such as 4 Ezra and *2 Baruch* to explain the disaster.

There is much imagery in common between the Qumran texts and Revelation, including the characterization of the enemy as beastlike and as serving Satan, and the call for holy war, which would be accompanied by signs in the earth and sky.

Fourth Ezra. The text known as Fourth Ezra or Second Esdras responds to Jewish despair after the destruction of the Jerusalem temple in 70 C.E. Like most apocalypses, however, it is set in an earlier time period through which it interprets the present of the author. Like Daniel, it presents its story from the imagined setting of Babylonian exile. Its fictive narrator is, of course, the priest-scribe Ezra, whose historical role we examined earlier.

Fourth Ezra consists of two major parts. In the first, Ezra is taken up into heaven for a series of dialogues with the angel Uriel. The form is similar to the dialogues between Job and God. Here, though, the issue begins as a collective rather than an individual question: Why are the Babylonians (Romans) thriving while we, your chosen people, continue to suffer endlessly? Uriel's first response is to remind Ezra that God's ways cannot be discerned fully through human ways of knowledge; revelation from heaven is necessary (4 Ezra 4:10). The second response is that God has created not one world but two, and the first is about to "pass away" (6:20; 7:50). This passing will happen in stages, leading to the final destruction of evil and the resurrection of the just.

---

54. Golb.

This provokes Ezra's ultimate question of justice: Why are so many born only to be destroyed, and so few born for eternal joy? Uriel's response gives a natural world analogy: the rarity of precious gold and jewels amid the clay and dust. Ezra, however, remains stubbornly unsatisfied. The text teaches that human frustration and despair are primarily the results of failing to trust deeply enough in the ways of God.

The second part of the book is visionary. In this section, the text reinterprets Daniel's vision of the beasts/kingdoms (Dan. 7). Ezra's vision reveals a coming Messiah who will destroy Babylon/Rome and restore earthly Israel to glory. In this scenario, Ezra is cast as a new Moses, who gives not *torah* but direct revelation from God.[55]

Fourth Ezra finds hope in the salvation of a tiny remnant of the just after a final confrontation between good and evil. It despairs of the idea of understanding God's ways, counseling instead for the practice of righteousness by those who have been called to do so. It is a thoroughly Jewish document and yet it shares much of Revelation's call for the ongoing practice of covenant justice in the midst of empire. Table 8 shows some of the traditional imagery and language shared with Revelation.

Second Baruch. Contemporaneous with 4 Ezra is the text called *Second Baruch.* In fact, many scholars believe that *2 Baruch* was composed in direct response to 4 Ezra.[56] Unlike 4 Ezra, *2 Baruch*'s story world is set *before* the fall of Jerusalem to Babylon. The unmitigated grief expressed by Ezra is forestalled in *2 Baruch* by a direct assurance from God that the temple which will be destroyed is not the "real" one. Rather, there is an eternal, heavenly temple, which God has always and always will preserve. From this perspective, Baruch is assured that nothing of ultimate importance is happening when the earthly edifice is demolished.

Whereas 4 Ezra is largely pessimistic about human ability to understand God's ways and, therefore, to live a just life, *2 Baruch* is more optimistic. While presenting a scenario of cosmic war in which the Messiah saves the day similar to that in 4 Ezra, this text does not belabor the question of the number of the saved. Rather, it insists that *torah can* be practiced, and that those who do live according to its ways will be saved. In this regard, it takes up the universality of Third Isaiah (Isa. 56:6-7).

The text ends with a vision interpreted by the angel Ramiel, in which history is shown to pass in periods, as in Zoroastrianism. But unlike Persian apocalyptic thought, *2 Baruch* fits squarely within the emerging rabbinic Judaism of the post–70 C.E. era.[57]

---

55. Collins (1984), pp. 167-68.
56. Ibid., pp. 179-80.
57. Ibid., p. 178.

Table 8
SELECTED IMAGES AND PHRASES
FOUND IN BOTH 4 EZRA AND REVELATION

Image	Revelation	4 Ezra
Command to write down the vision	1:11	14:6
Sound of many waters	1:15	6:17
Falling down before an angel and being touched by the angel	1:17	5:14-15; 10:30
Tree of life	2:7	2:12
Crowning of the faithful	2:10; 3:11	2:42-48
White clothes as sign of worthiness	3:4	2:40
Inhabitants of the earth (negative image)	10 times	19 times
Lion as messianic symbol	5:5	12:31-33
Call for completing the number of martyrs	6:9-11	4:35-37
Cry of "How long?"	6:10	4:33-36
Earthquake as sign of old being replaced by new	6:12	6:11-16
The number of those sealed by God	7:4	2:38
Tribes of YHWH as symbol of God's saved people	7:4ff.	ch. 13
Who are these?	7:13	2:44-45
Beast from the sea	13:1	6:49-52
Countless multitude on Mt. Zion	14:1	2:42
Messiah coming on the clouds of heaven in judgment	14:14	13:3
Blood as high as a horse	14:20	15:35-36
Burning the enemy's body	17:16	12:3
Babylon as image of Rome's seductive power	chs. 17-18	15:46ff.
Messianic mouth as bearing a weapon	19:15	13:9-10
Lake of fire	19:20	7:36
War between messianic army and Beast's army	20:8-9	13:5
Earth/sea giving up dead for resurrection	20:13	7:32
Jerusalem as a glorious woman	21:2ff.	10:25-27
Kings will bring their honor/wealth to God	21:24	15:20-21

Fifth Sibylline Oracle. This apocalyptic book was also written in the aftermath of the Roman destruction of Jerusalem, probably in Egypt. It is characterized by its animosity toward the political powers that surrounded its community of Egyptian Jews, with a special vehemence reserved for Rome. This oracle contains much symbolism that is found in the book of Revelation, particularly that of "Babylon." The writer of the oracle blamed Rome/Babylon for the murder of Jewish people during the Roman/Jewish war:

A great star will come from heaven to the wondrous sea and will burn the deep sea and Babylon itself and the land of Italy, because of which many holy faithful Hebrews and a true people perished. (5:158-61)

Interestingly, the oracle also speaks of woes for the cities to which Revelation is addressed. Thus Sardis, Laodicea, Ephesus, and Smyrna are marked out for torment and destruction because of their wealth and arrogance (5:286-327).

Like Revelation, the oracle condemns "Babylon" for its affluence, its universal political power, and its arrogance and announces the destruction of the city (5:434-46). The book also speaks of a city made by God, "more brilliant than the stars and sun and moon" (5:420-21). But unlike the heavenly city depicted in Revelation, this city did contain a temple that was "exceedingly beautiful" (5:423-24). Like Revelation, the *Fifth Sibylline Oracle* harbors a repugnance of the cults that operated among the people.[58] Thus, Isis is named a "thrice-wretched goddess" (5:484), and her divine partner Sarapis is parodied as "reposing on unwrought stones" (5:487), a calculated insult in a world where fancy stonework was viewed as the only fitting earthly resting place for the gods.

These diverse Jewish texts from the period in which Revelation was written illustrate the variety of apocalyptic perspectives available to help discern where and how YHWH was active in the midst of Roman control. The apocalyptic tradition, with its roots in the postexilic struggle and branches in the Seleucid era, had brought forth much fruit during this period. For some Jews, however, none of these texts seemed to provide sufficient guidance or insight. Some of these people turned to the fledgling communities that were being formed out of the strange idea that the Messiah had already come and had been crucified by empire, but, through God's power, had risen from the dead to reign with God.

CHRISTIAN APOCALYPTIC BRANCHES
IN THE NEW TESTAMENT IN ADDITION TO REVELATION

Although Revelation is the only New Testament text that fits the prevailing scholarly definition of an "apocalypse,"[59] it is far from the only Christian canonical text with apocalyptic passages. We review these briefly here to remind the reader that John of Patmos was not the only pastoral leader among the early *ekklēsiai* who turned to the apocalyptic tradition as a source of language and inspiration.

The Synoptic Apocalypses

In Mark's Gospel, Jesus responds to the disciples' question about the time and the signs surrounding the destruction of the Jerusalem temple with an apocalyp-

---

58. Ibid., p. 190.
59. Collins (1979b), p. 9; Hellholm; Aune (1986). These sources discuss the complex and much debated issue of the genre of "apocalypse," a question not of direct relevance to our topic in this book.

tic sermon (Mark 13:5-37). The passage calls upon many of the images familiar from the tradition, including Daniel's reference to the "desolating sacrilege" (e.g., Dan. 11:31; Mark 13:14). In Daniel's case, the hated object was likely a statue of Zeus placed in the temple by Antiochus IV Epiphanes. In Mark's situation, the object is almost certainly a Roman eagle placed there by the Roman procurator. Ched Myers explains how this passage functions in Mark's Gospel to put Christians to the urgent test of how to respond to the approaching Roman troops on their way to destroy Jerusalem and to put a stop to the rebellion that has wrested control of Jerusalem from Roman hands.[60] Jesus uses this apocalyptic language and imagery to warn the members of the Markan community not to defend Jerusalem but rather to "flee to the mountains." Christians are neither to accommodate to Rome (as did the Jewish historian Josephus) nor to take up weapons against empire (as did the Zealot coalition that temporarily expelled the Romans). Rather, they are to "resist [Greek *hupomeinas*] to the end." Thus, Mark's use of the tradition is for the same basic purpose as his Jewish predecessors: to answer the question of how to live with empire outside your door and all around your town.

Matthew and Luke, writing after the destruction of Jerusalem, reproduce the apocalyptic sermon in modified form. Matthew's immediate pastoral concern is not with war in Jerusalem but with "the increase of lawlessness [Greek *anomia*]," which causes "the love of many [to] grow cold" (Matt. 24:12). The situation in his community is similar to that of the *ekklēsia* in Ephesus addressed by John: "I have this against you, that you have abandoned the love you had at first" (Rev. 2:4). Perhaps some had expected the immediate return of Jesus and were discouraged by the apparent "delay" (Matt. 24:44-51). In other words, the joy of living the gospel has turned into a tiresome task of endless resistance to empire, one that can cause the most faithful disciple, like a salmon constantly swimming upstream, to grow weary. Matthew's use of Mark's apocalyptic sermon, then, serves to bolster endurance in discipleship by restoring not only a sense of joy but also by providing stern warnings about the consequences of letting down one's guard.

Luke's use of the apocalyptic sermon is similar to Matthew's. He "gives away" the secret meaning of the "desolating sacrilege" that Mark and Matthew both kept hidden: "When you see Jerusalem surrounded by armies, then know that its desolation has come near" (Luke 21:20). His focus is on the threat that the disciples will be "weighed down with dissipation and drunkenness and the worries of this life" (21:34), and be unprepared for the advent of the "Empire [Greek *basileia*] of God." Luke thus appeals to his largely Hellenistic community in terms recognizable by anyone familiar with Stoic philosophy. The purpose, however, remains the same: to keep the disciples awake in the midst of the temptations of empire.

---

60. Myers (1988), pp. 331-33.

Paul's Use of Apocalyptic

Paul's usual genre is that of Greco-Roman argument. However, he frequently peppers his letters with apocalyptic imagery which serves as an exclamation point to his reasoned discourse. For example, in 1 Corinthians, we find language such as this:

> My speech and my proclamation were not with plausible words of wisdom, but with a demonstration of the Spirit and of power, so that your faith might rest not on human wisdom but on the power of God. Yet among the mature we do speak wisdom, though it is not a wisdom of this age or of the rulers of this age, who are doomed to perish. But we speak God's wisdom, secret and hidden, which God decreed before the ages for our glory. None of the rulers of this age understood this; for if they had, they would not have crucified the Lord of glory. But, as it is written, "What no eye has seen, nor ear heard, nor the human heart conceived, what God has prepared for those who love him"—these things God has revealed [Greek *apekalupsen*] to us through the Spirit; for the Spirit searches everything, even the depths of God. (2:4-10)

The very basis of Paul's claim to preach is that God's Spirit and Power have revealed to him wisdom that runs directly counter to the "wisdom of this age" and "the rulers of this age." Paul's entire ministry is grounded in his apocalyptic experience of the risen Jesus, which turned the event of the cross from the "appropriate" execution of a blaspheming troublemaker into the transforming victory of God.[61] His message of inclusion of Jews and Greeks, his willingness to abandon the dietary and circumcision rules, and his acceptance of repeated physical abuse and rejection all stem from the "revealing [Greek *apokalupsin*] of our Lord Jesus Christ" (1 Cor. 1:7).

Throughout 1 Corinthians, we see the consequences of this apocalyptic contrast between the "wisdom of this age" and the wisdom of God. Paul counsels the *ekklēsia* not to expect or to seek justice in the imperial courtroom (1 Cor. 6:1-11). He warns them against appearing to accommodate to the imperial and local cult practices (see chapter 3 below) lest it cause scandal within the community (1 Cor. 8-10). He subverts the Stoic metaphor of the body—which was used to legitimate the social pyramid and keep the lower classes peacefully in their places—by emphasizing the equal importance within the *ekklēsia* of all members (1 Cor. 12:12-31).[62] All of these reversals of the prevailing social norms and the counsel to resist the "normal" practices of empire are grounded for Paul in an apocalyptic event.

Another place where Paul's foundation expresses itself in openly apocalyptic

---

61. A. Brown, p. 24; N. Elliott (1995), pp. 142-43.
62. Moxnes, p. 224.

language is in the Thessalonian correspondence. Premillennialists have grounded their doctrine of the Rapture in one of these passages:

> For the Lord himself, with a cry of command, with the archangel's call and with the sound of God's trumpet, will descend from heaven, and the dead in Christ will rise first. Then we who are alive, who are left, will be caught up in the clouds together with them to meet the Lord in the air; and so we will be with the Lord forever. (1 Thess. 4:16-17)

However, far from expressing a literal expectation of a Rapture, in its context, the passage speaks to the royal authority of Jesus in the face of imperial propaganda. A few verses later, for example, Paul quotes the propagandists directly: "When they say, 'There is peace and security,' then sudden destruction will come upon them, as labor pains come upon a pregnant woman, and there will be no escape!" (1 Thess. 5:3). The quoted slogan, "peace and security" (Latin *pax et securitas*), was a favorite of Rome in applauding the results of its conquest of the previously feuding Mediterranean city-states. As Helmut Koester notes, "Paul points to the coming of the day of the Lord as an event that will shatter the false peace and security of the Roman establishment."[63]

If the apocalyptic rhetoric and purpose of 1 Thessalonians is partially hidden to readers in our time, that of 2 Thessalonians could hardly be more plain. After the formulaic opening greeting, the author launches directly into a full-blown apocalyptic discourse. A few verses will suffice to convey the similarity between this text and Revelation:

> For it is indeed just of God to repay with affliction those who afflict you, and to give relief to the afflicted as well as to us, when the Lord Jesus is revealed from heaven with his mighty angels in flaming fire, inflicting vengeance on those who do not know God and on those who do not obey the gospel of our Lord Jesus. These will suffer the punishment of eternal destruction, separated from the presence of the Lord and from the glory of his might, when he comes to be glorified by his saints and to be marveled at on that day among all who have believed. . . .
>
> For the mystery of lawlessness is already at work, but only until the one who now restrains it is removed. And then the lawless one will be revealed, whom the Lord Jesus will destroy with the breath of his mouth, annihilating him by the manifestation of his coming. The coming of the lawless one is apparent in the working of Satan, who uses all power, signs, lying wonders, and every kind of wicked deception for those who are perishing, because they refused to love the truth and so be saved. For this reason God sends them a powerful delusion, leading them to believe what is false, so that all who have not believed the truth but took pleasure in unrighteousness will be condemned. But we must always give thanks to God for you,

---

63. Koester (1997), pp. 161-62.

brothers and sisters beloved by the Lord, because God chose you as the first fruits for salvation through sanctification by the Spirit and through belief in the truth. (2 Thess. 1:6-10; 2:7-13)

Once again, the message, for those familiar with the apocalyptic tradition, is clear: empire appears to be in charge, but only because God allows it to be that way. However, the faithful ones—those who resist the "powerful delusion" of empire's ultimacy—are saved already as "first fruits" (cf. Rev. 14:4).

The Other New Testament Letters

Paul was not the only pastoral letter writer within the first decades of Christianity to counsel resistance to empire in apocalyptic terms. In 1 Peter, for example, we hear this admonition:

Discipline yourselves, keep alert. Like a roaring lion your adversary the devil prowls around, looking for someone to devour. Resist him, steadfast in your faith, for you know that your brothers and sisters in all the world are undergoing the same kinds of suffering. And after you have suffered for a little while, the God of all grace, who has called you to his eternal glory in Christ, will himself restore, support, strengthen, and establish you. To him be the power forever and ever. Amen. (5:8-11)

And in 2 Peter—which expressly refers to itself as a reminder of what was counseled in 1 Peter (2 Pet. 3:1-2)—we hear this:

But by the same word the present heavens and earth have been reserved for fire, being kept until the day of judgment and destruction of the godless. But do not ignore this one fact, beloved, that with the Lord one day is like a thousand years, and a thousand years are like one day. The Lord is not slow about his promise, as some think of slowness, but is patient with you, not wanting any to perish, but all to come to repentance. But the day of the Lord will come like a thief, and then the heavens will pass away with a loud noise, and the elements will be dissolved with fire, and the earth and everything that is done on it will be disclosed. (2 Pet. 3:7-10)

As with the prophecy writers' focus on 1 Thess. 4:17 as a basis for the Rapture, this passage, as noted earlier, is one interpreted by those writers as a prediction of nuclear holocaust. However, we can see that the language is that of the apocalyptic tradition, used once more to warn its hearers not to doubt God's power and thereby to give up resistance to empire.

In sum, Revelation, far from being an isolated example of apocalypticism within the supposedly more ordinary world of the Gospels and Paul, is simply the most exuberant expression of a tradition drawn on throughout the New Testament. The roots of apocalyptic had been growing in the soil of God's people for hundreds of years, bearing fruit from season to season whenever empire appeared as a threat to the ability of the people to remain faithful.

REFLECTION QUESTIONS

1. How do you conceive of God speaking to you in your life? Do you trust your prayer experiences, dreams, the visionary experiences of others, official church statements, or other types of inspiration to guide your own life choices? Why or why not?

2. Which appeals more to you: the Maccabees' approach to empire or Daniel's? Which do you consider is more realistic? Why?

3. What role does "the past" play in guiding you in the present or toward the future? Consider the experience(s) of your personal/family past, ethnic/national ancestors, religious ancestors, or other world historical events. Think of the three or four most important experiences from the past that affect who you are or what you do. Why does or doesn't the past affect your choices and beliefs?

3

Reading Revelation in Context

Imperial Rome and Christianity in the First Century

To understand the need to become familiar with the Roman Empire and its social world in the time of Revelation, consider an example from our own culture. In our newspapers and on our radios and televisions we are daily bombarded with opinions. The social commentators, reporters, shock-jocks, and many and varied experts ply us with their version of the-way-things-are or the-way-things-should-be. Most of us are content to accept the majority opinion. After all, they must know what they are talking about or they wouldn't be in such positions, right? The possibility of critically discerning the truth proffered by these various pundits relies on our ability to go beyond their simple recitation of oft-repeated "truths." A critical analysis of these sources of "information" must involve an understanding of who these people are and for whom they work. We must come to grips with the motives of the media companies and their relationships with the global corporations that control the media, as well as their relations with government.[1] These factors operate in the background, yet they are crucial to an understanding of how the media propagate a particular worldview, as we will see in more detail in chapter 9.

If it is difficult to penetrate the cultural, economic, and political forces that shape our media and go on under our very noses, how much more difficult is it to discover the social forces that shaped the media of ancient societies? This has been a major problem in the historical investigation of ancient cultures, particularly that of ancient Rome. There has been a tendency for ancient Roman histo-

---

1. Noam Chomsky and Edward Herman have analyzed the American media with these factors in mind. They "trace the routes by which money and power are able to filter out the news fit to print, marginalize dissent, and allow government and dominant private interests to get their messages across to the public" (Chomsky and Herman [1994], p. 2).

rians to accept at face value the claims made in the various imperial media. This has resulted in the writing of "history" that has stressed the benefits of Roman rule. These historians have typically praised Roman law, its prosperity, its establishment of peace across a large sector of the known world, and its roads and communications. Not surprisingly, it is these aspects of Rome that were lauded by those who were the friends of the emperors. In describing Rome as beneficent, the historians have merely recycled the words of those who acted as public relations personnel for the empire! Take, for example, the English historian Edward Gibbon, whose six-volume work *The History of the Decline and Fall of the Roman Empire* (1776-88) was one of the most influential historical works of modern times. Gibbon wrote at a critical time in the history of the British Empire. In fact his first volume coincided with the American War of Independence from Britain, and his last with the British occupation of Australia! Gibbon was fulsome in his praise of the Roman Empire. Discussing the period just after the book of Revelation was written, Gibbon wrote:

> In the second century of the Christian era, the empire of Rome comprehended the fairest part of the earth, and the most civilized portion of mankind. The frontiers of that extensive monarchy were guarded by ancient renown and disciplined valor. The gentle, but powerful, influence of laws and manners had gradually cemented the union of the provinces. Their peaceful inhabitants enjoyed or abused the advantages of wealth and luxury. The image of a free constitution was preserved with decent reverence. The Roman senate appeared to possess the sovereign authority, and devolved on the emperors all the executive powers of government.[2]

Was Gibbon's perception of his native British Empire shaped by his view of ancient Rome, or did his wonder at Rome's glory mirror his love for his own empire? Whatever the case, Gibbon and his colleagues are largely responsible for the popular view of Rome as a benevolent empire, a view that is conducive to the interests of the empires of which they are beneficiaries.

While television, radio, the Internet, and the press are the primary media today, ancient Rome possessed less technical but no less sophisticated means of propagating its worldview. The Roman media included temples, monuments, inscriptions, festivals, orations, coinage, games, and so forth. Taken together, these media communicated powerfully the message that Rome was a beneficent and well-ordered society, and that its emperor was the guarantor of peace and harmony.

Two ancient figures characterize this propensity to weave grand images around the Roman Empire. Virgil and Aristides are representative of those who saw the Roman Empire as the embodiment of virtue and justice. They stand at the beginning and the end of the period that began with the establishment of the *imperium* by Augustus (31 B.C.E.) and continued to the reign of Antoninus Pius (138-161 C.E.). This period witnessed the development of the Christian movement from its beginning to its spread across the Roman Empire and saw the writ-

---

2. Gibbon (1869), p.1.

ing of the Christian scriptures. Virgil saw the ascendancy of the emperor Augustus and wrote of his glory. Referring to Augustus, Virgil proclaimed:

> This, this is he whom so often you hear promised to you, Augustus Caesar, son of a god, who shall again set up the golden age in Latium [Italy] amid the fields where Saturn once reigned, and shall spread his empire past Garamant and India, to a land that lies beyond the stars. (*Aeneid* 6.791-95)

Aelius Aristides was an orator from Asia Minor who traveled to the court of the emperor Antoninus Pius in the year 143 C.E. There he delivered his famous eulogy to Rome. In glowing approval of the empire, Aristides described Rome as he saw it:

> No words are good enough for this city, indeed it is impossible to see it as one should. . . . It cannot be otherwise than that there always be here an abundance of all that grows and is manufactured among each people. So many merchant ships arrive here, conveying every kind of goods from every people every hour and every day, so that the city is like a factory common to the whole earth. . . . Cities now gleam in splendor and beauty, and the whole earth is arrayed like a paradise . . . order has returned everywhere, and in everyday life and in the state there is clear light of day. Laws have come into being, and faith has been found at the altar of the gods. (*Eulogy to Rome* 6, 10, 99, 103)

Despite the powerful rhetoric of these friends and propagandists of Rome, most Christian texts offered a view that stood in defiant contradiction to the dominant imperial view of reality. In the period in which Revelation was written, "imperial Rome offered Asians a coherent, ordered structure of reality which unified religious, social, economic, political and aesthetic aspects of the world."[3] An investigation of how Rome constructed this coherent and ordered view and the reality it sought to mask will be the task of this chapter. This will ground our reading of Revelation's resistance to empire.

The *ekklēsiai* to whom Revelation was addressed were located in some of the most important cities of the province: Ephesus, Smyrna, Pergamum, Thyatira, Sardis, Philadelphia, and Laodicea (Rev. 2-3) (see table 10, p. 94). The fact that the communities were located in the *cities* of *Asia* is of critical importance to our interpretation of Revelation. The historical context of the communities requires an examination of how life was lived in the cities of this Roman province. This will involve an exploration of the politics, economics, culture, and mythology of the Roman Empire, particularly as these were found in the Roman province of Asia. As in any society, these elements of the Roman world were not separate realities. Rather, together they constituted a social totality that was interwoven in a web of imperial power. These were the avenues by which Rome held the great and the small, the rich and poor, the slave and free in its orbit.

---

3. L. Thompson (1986), p. 159.

Table 9
TIMELINE: ROME AND EARLY CHRISTIANITY

Imperial Events	*Events in the Early Christian Movement*
JULIUS CAESAR assassinated (44 B.C.E.) Civil conflict in the Roman Republic (40-31 B.C.E.)	
[produces fears of the end of civilization] Octavian's victory over Antony at Actium (31 B.C.E.) ends civil war	
AUGUSTUS (31 B.C.E.-14 C.E.) Octavian named Augustus (27 B.C.E.)	Birth of Jesus (c. 6-4 B.C.E.)
[Roman belief that Augustus had inaugurated a new age]	
TIBERIUS (14-37 C.E.)	Execution of Jesus by Pontius Pilate in Jerusalem (c. 30 C.E.)
	Execution of Stephen in Jerusalem (c. 35)
	Conversion of Saul to Paul (c. 35)
CALIGULA (37-41)	
CLAUDIUS (41-54)	James ("brother of John") executed by Herod Agrippa in Jerusalem (44)
	Council of Jerusalem (48)
	First Thessalonians (c. 50)
NERO (54-68)	Paul in Ephesus (53-55)
	Philippians (c. 55) *1* and *2 Corinthians* (c. 55-58) *Galatians* (c. 56-58)
	James ("brother of the Lord") becomes head of Christian community in Jerusalem (58)
	James ("brother of the Lord") stoned to death in Jerusalem (62)
	Beginning of Christian persecution in Rome under Nero (64)
Beginning of Roman–Jewish war (66) migration of Jews and Christians across the empire	*Gospel of Mark* (c. 68)

Imperial Events	*Events in the Early Christian Movement*
Year of the three emperors (68-69) and civil war in Rome [causes pessimism at fate of civilization]	
VESPASIAN (69-79) ends civil war [bringing belief that the world had again been renewed]	*Colossians* (c. 70s)
Roman capture of Jerusalem and destruction of temple by the general Titus (70). Later to become emperor.	
TITUS (79-81)	
DOMITIAN (81-96)	*First Peter, Ephesians* (c. 80s)
	Gospels of Matthew and *Luke, Acts of the Apostles* (c. 80s)
	Revelation, according to Irenaeus, was "seen" at the "end of the rule of Domitian"
	Gospel of John (c. 95)
NERVA (96-98)	
TRAJAN (98-117)	*1-2 Timothy* (c. 100s)
Correspondence concerning trials of Christians between Pliny and the emperor Trajan (c. 110)	*Letters of Ignatius* and the execution of Ignatius in Rome (110)
HADRIAN (117-138)	
Second Jewish-Roman war (132-135)	
ANTONINUS PIUS (138-161)	
Aelius Aristides delivers *Eulogy to Rome* (c. 143)	

IMPERIAL POLITICS

The people of the Roman province of Asia did not consider themselves to be subjugated or occupied by Rome. Unlike people in Judea, Gaul, or Britain, the people in Asia welcomed rather than resisted Roman rule. In the first century, no Roman legionary forces were stationed there. Rather, the majority of the residents of Asia consented to Roman control of their territory. This, briefly, is how this situation came about.

The province of Asia was incorporated under Roman control in 133 B.C.E. within the larger geographic region of Asia Minor (see map on p. 93). Significantly, this was achieved not by force, but by the granting of territory by King Attalus of Pergamum to Rome.[4] Farther inland, the region of Phrygia was added in 116 B.C.E. The only real resistance to Roman rule came with the temporary expulsion between 88 and 86 B.C.E. of Roman authority from Asia by a local king supported by both the elite and poorer classes. Augustus's victory put an end to war between the Roman elite in 31 B.C.E. This caused the Greek-speaking world to acquiesce to the inevitability and desirability of Roman rule. The speed with which imperial temples were built in Roman Asia after the victory of Augustus demonstrates that the elite, at least, readily embraced it.

With his victory, Augustus brought an end to civil war within the empire. Recognizing the benefits of keeping Asia a harmonious and stable imperial asset, Augustus granted the province a cancellation of the debt it owed to Rome. As Anthony Macro explains: "this engaged the goodwill of all Asia and gave the Hellenists in the cities a basis from which to rebuild not only their homes but their culture."[5] It was this policy of mutual self-interest that encouraged the residents of Asia to accept Roman rule. The imperial policy toward Asia also involved a confirmation of the authority of the existing provincial elite. In first-century Asia this elite included Roman officials, local officeholders, honorable local families—many of whom owned large agricultural estates—and a growing number of wealthy traders. The continuation of their predominance in local government assured their loyalty to Rome. With Roman encouragement, the traditional Hellenistic Council was modified from a democratic, open organization to one based on family standing (that is, social "honor"). In Hellenistic politics, the council (Greek *boulē*) stood at the level above the *ekklēsia* in the hierarchy of local government. By the first century the Hellenistic Council was preserved in form, but property qualifications for membership had been introduced, and life tenure had become the norm.[6]

At the same time, the empire pursued a policy of urbanization, through which it moved more of the population into the cities of the empire. Increased urbanization strengthened the power of the provincial elite by developing a stronger urban base over which they had authority. The elite held a wide range of official and semiofficial duties within the city. These included the construction and maintenance of public buildings (including imperial and other temples); the maintenance of adequate food supplies for the city; the holding of regular public celebrations, games, and festivals; and the maintenance of public order. All these activities were financed by the private wealth of the officeholder. They served to provide social identity and cohesion for urban, multicultural populations.

---

4. Koester (1992), p. 10. A revolt was led by Aristonicus, a member of the royal household, who attempted to seize control of the kingdom after Attalus's death. This was suppressed by a coalition of Roman forces and militias from the Greek city-states of the region. This revolt should be seen as a royal grab for power, rather than resistance to Rome.

5. Macro, p. 660.

6. Ibid., p. 662.

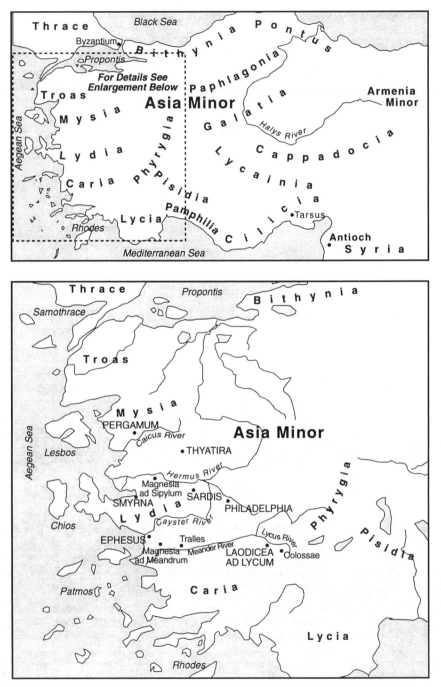

Roman Province of Asia and Environs, first century C.E.
The seven cities of Revelation in capital letters.

Table 10
THE CITIES OF ROMAN ASIA
TO WHICH JOHN IS DIRECTED TO WRITE
IN REVELATION 2-3

Ephesus: The greatest city of the Roman province Asia; the seat of the proconsul and competed with Pergamum for the recognition of its primacy.

Smyrna: A prosperous port city, rivaling Ephesus, and maintains a special loyalty to Rome. Temple to Roma built in 195 B.C.E., and to Tiberius in 26 C.E.

Pergamum: Capital of Asia, the center of imperial worship for the whole region; standing over the city is a great acropolis and an altar to Zeus; also, a temple to Augustus and to Roma, built in 29 B.C.E.

Thyatira: City of traders and artisans without Roman significance.

Sardis: Regional capital of Sydia in Asia Minor. Founded by Seleucids. Lydian wealth was legendary. Sardis was center of Sydian imperial cult in Roman times.

Philadelphia: Like Sardis, a city of Lydia, founded by Attalus II, king of Pergamum in the second century B.C.E. A communication link between Sardis/Pergamum to the west and Laodicea and Hierapolis to the east.

Laodicea: Richest city in Phrygia, known for its banks, its linen and cotton industry, and its medical school and pharmacies.

It was also at this time that the practice of dual citizenship was established. Initially, the elite of the provincial cities were considered citizens of the "city" (Greek *polis*) in which they were born. However, the empire granted Roman citizenship to the wealthier and more influential provincials. This implied the termination of their local financial obligations, an event that would have been disastrous to the local economy. Accordingly, Augustus declared that if provincial people were "honored with the citizenship, I declare that these must nonetheless undertake liturgies in their turn within the community of the Greeks."[7] With this:

> The principle of a dual citizenship (or Cicero's notion that each man has two *patriae* [Latin, "fatherlands"], his hometown and Rome) was thus conclusively established, and was to form the social basis of the running of the Empire for three centuries. The spread of citizenship was to provide a rich harvest of rules and exceptions, petitions and responses. . . . But it does not seem ever to have been claimed subsequently that Roman citizenship affected a man's obligations to his native city.[8]

---

7. The third edict of Augustus to Cyrene.
8. Millar, p. 85.

With this the elite of the cities of Asia were bound by increasingly compli-cated notions of rights and obligations vis-à-vis Rome and their local city. This served to link their fortunes more tightly to those of both Rome and their own city.

Asian cities of the first century competed with one another for imperial honor and privilege. The quaint Australian practice of the "tidy town competition," in which rural villages and towns compete by maintaining gardens and public spaces in good order, pales in comparison with the civic "war" between the cities of Asia. The ancient practice was more like the recent trend to offer huge finan-cial subsidies to corporations, sports franchises, and cultural events such as the Olympics to encourage them to locate in a given city. This, like its ancient coun-terpart, is a form of *patronage*. The Asian civic competition involved the con-struction of imperial temples, and other public buildings and monuments, the use of ever more grandiloquent titles for their city,[9] and the making of embassies by the local elite to the emperor. The tradition of warfare between the Hellenistic city-states, which seemed to have existed since time immemorial, was subli-mated into competitive civic pride.

Roman society was built on a pyramid of *patron–client relationships*. A per-son of higher standing (patron) could offer financial assistance or legal protec-tion (patronage) to a person of lower standing (client). By accepting assistance the client was obligated to offer respect and loyalty to the patron. These rela-tionships existed at the level of the individual, the household, the city, and the province. The emperor was the patron par excellence, and the peoples of the empire his clients. This was an important aspect of the competition that existed among the cities of Asia.[10] The point of this civic competition was to impress the Roman officials that *this* city was the most loyal to Rome in order to encourage a strengthening of Rome's patronage of the city. Peter Garnsey and Richard Saller explain the relationship between the emperor and his subjects:

> the ideology of the good emperor was not so much of an efficient admin-istrator as of a paternal protector and benefactor. Since subjects could not repay imperial benefactions in kind, the reciprocity ethic dictated that they make a return in the form of deference, respect and loyalty.[11]

In competing for the right to host the imperial cult and its festivals, the resi-dents of the Asian cities forged an identity based on allegiance to Rome.

The construction of theaters, gymnasiums, baths, and schools was also an important aspect of Rome's policy of urbanization. This project aimed to co-opt resistance by promoting "civilization." The Roman writer Tacitus described how urbanization pacified the rebellious population of Britain. So successful was this

---

9. An example of claims to greatness in the titles of the major cities is Pergamum's claim to the title "Metropolis of Asia and the First City to be Twice-Temple-Warden," and the Ephesian counter-claim to be "First and Greatest Metropolis of Asia" (Macro, p. 683).

10. Zanker, pp. 76-79.

11. Garnsey and Saller, p. 97.

policy that the recalcitrant people of Britain "were seduced into alluring vices: pillared halls, baths and choice banquets. The simple natives gave the name of 'culture' to this aspect of their slavery" (*Agricola* 21).

Tacitus depicts Civilis, a Batavian military commander well aware of the seductive nature of Roman culture, addressing the people in these words: "Away with those pleasures which give the Romans more power over their subjects than their arms bestow" (*Histories* 4.64.3). In a similar vein is Plutarch's story of Sertorius, the Roman governor of Spain, written about 75 C.E. Sertorius is depicted as seducing the previously hostile local militia in this way:

> He bestowed silver and gold upon them to gild and adorn their helmets, he had their shields worked with various figures and designs, he brought them into the mode of wearing flowered and embroidered cloaks and coats, and by supplying money for these purposes and joining with them in all improvements, he won the hearts of all. (*Sertorius* 13)

The Romans also knew that the local elite could be successfully controlled through "education." The education given by the colonizer sought to erase the memory of local culture and hence resistance to Roman rule:

> He [Sertorius] sent for the sons of noblest parentage out of all their tribes, and placed them in the great city Osca, where he appointed masters to instruct them in Greek and Roman learning, that when they came to be men, they might, as he professed, be fitted to share with him in authority, and in conducting government, although under this pretext he really made them hostages. (*Sertorius* 14)

If those who openly resisted Rome could be seduced by Roman "culture," what chance would a people have who actively sought patronage from Rome? Roman power may have been resisted here and there in the more remote provinces, but in Asia it was embraced wholeheartedly by the elite.

IMPERIAL ECONOMICS

Ancient historians, who were devoted to the recording of political intrigue and the waging of war, did not concern themselves much with economic or social history.[12] They saw the economy as subordinate to political and military events. Furthermore, as a consequence of the social pyramid, the lives of those outside the elite classes were considered vile and repugnant. There is, therefore, very little information concerning the economic life of the provincials. This was especially true of the lower classes who were the vast majority of the Empire's population.

---

12. Grant, pp. 57-60.

It is agreed, however, that agriculture was the economic foundation of the Roman Empire:

> Despite the growth of urban and semi-urban settlements throughout the Empire . . . by far and away the greater population dwelt in the country and engaged in rural activities. The Empire's economy was firmly linked with agriculture. . . . The primacy of land both as a measure of status and a form of investment was never doubted in the ancient world.[13]

Such an economic foundation inevitably produced tension between, as Fernando Belo notes, "the peasant class, which is organized into village communities . . . and the class-state, which directly appropriates the surplus for itself."[14] In arguing that the Roman elite appropriated the agricultural surplus, Belo understates the situation. As Aelius Aristides admits, and frequent food shortages bore witness, the export of grain frequently cut into that required for the mere *subsistence* of rural workers. As a result, the peasant class was mostly very poor.[15]

Diagram 1
The Vertical Roman Hierarchies

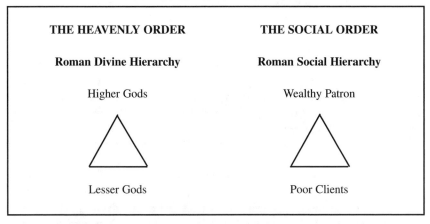

THE HEAVENLY ORDER   THE SOCIAL ORDER

Roman Divine Hierarchy   Roman Social Hierarchy

Higher Gods   Wealthy Patron

Lesser Gods   Poor Clients

Defying gravity, wealth accumulated at the top of the social pyramid. The social pyramid was a mirror of Rome's heavenly order. There a heavenly hierarchy of gods also had a pyramidal structure. Each pyramid lent legitimacy to the other. Understood in this way, the divine Roman hierarchy can be seen as legitimating the system that transferred wealth from the many poor to the elite few.

The patronage system precluded more collective or communal systems of organization. Richard Horsley comments that the "exchange of goods and ser-

---

13. Wacher, p. 8.
14. Belo, p. 60.
15. A. H. M. Jones, p. 38.

vices in patron-client relations stands diametrically opposed to the horizontal associations and reciprocity embodied in kinship and villages."[16] Poor people entered into patronage relationships to gain some measure of security, yet the "success" of the patronage system "lay as much in their [the patrons'] power to refuse as in their readiness to deliver the goods."[17] The patron–client system, then, was an effective means of social control.[18]

The imperial policy of urbanization initiated by Augustus and promoted particularly by Vespasian and Hadrian[19] also contributed to socioeconomic tension. The ancient city consumed much more than it produced. The cities were only viable because of Rome's transfer of food from the countryside to the cities. High Roman taxes increased the burden on rural producers. The Asian cities of Ephesus (with approximately 200,000 people), Pergamum (120,000), Sardis (100,000), and Smyrna (75,000) were the third, sixth, seventh, and fourteenth largest cities in the Roman Empire of the first century.[20] Having such large cities in close proximity made Asia a prime site for socioeconomic tensions between city and country, rich and poor.

At the same time as the process of urbanization was under way, the momentum of *latifundia* ("extensive estates") was increasing. *Latifundia* referred to the practice of removing productive land from the hands of the peasants and consolidating it in the hands of the wealthy city- or estate-based landowners. The ownership of agricultural land was removed from those who engaged in subsistence farming. Those who remained on the land became tenants of the wealthy landowners. Others who lost their land migrated to the cities, adding to social pressures there. Operating under the imperative of the market rather than the imperative of local need, the large estates reduced production of grains and increased production of the more profitable oil and wine. This led to a lack of staple foods like corn and barley, and a surplus of wine and oil, which were of lesser importance to the poor majority. The results of this—inflation and food shortages—are described in Rev. 6:5-6.[21]

This economic system was facilitated for the political elite by those involved in international trade. The exact relationship between the traditional political elite and the emerging commercial elite has been a source of much scholarly contention.[22] There is evidence that the political and aristocratic classes held traders—those on the next lower level of the patronage pyramid—in disdain. From the viewpoint of those in the provincial lower classes, however, the traders' wealth appeared spectacular. The manner in which the traders' wealth was directly dependent on their commercial relationship with Rome might have led some to consider them in the same class as the political and aristocratic elite.

The merchants, traders, and shipowners based in the provincial cities (the

---

16. Horsley (1997), p. 90.
17. Wallace-Hadrill, p. 73.
18. Horsley (1997), pp. 90-91.
19. Macro, p. 672.
20. Stark, pp. 131-32.
21. Wengst, p. 224.
22. See Pleket, pp. 131-33; D'Arms, pp. 11-16.

focus of attention in Rev. 18:11-20) owed their existence to the centripetal pull of all types of agricultural and manufactured goods to Rome and the other major imperial cities. Helen Loane has produced a survey of the range of products that were imported by Rome, and her list is very similar to that found in Rev. 18:12-13. Grain, wine, oil, vegetables and fruits, cheese, meats, honey, fabric, stone, bricks, marble, wood, gold, silver, lead, iron, copper, bronze, pottery, glass, furniture, gems, pearls, animals for games, slaves, and so forth were all imported from different parts of the Empire and beyond to satisfy the consumption of those in Rome.[23] Loane estimates that six thousand ship arrivals at Rome's chief port of Ostia would have been needed annually to feed the population of the capital with grain alone.[24] This grain principally came from Africa, Egypt, and around the Black Sea. Such an immense trade inevitably produced grain shortages in the exporting provinces. Thus, while some saw this as exploitation, others saw it as an example of the glory of Rome.[25]

The trade in foodstuffs aggravated the shortage of food in the provinces, contributing to civil strife in provincial Asia. Klaus Wengst lists a number of examples of grain price hikes in Asia Minor. This occurred, for example, in the town of Antioch in the province of Pisidia (a province neighboring Asia) around 92 C.E. After a severe winter, the price of grain was hugely inflated because the producers held it back to make more profit. A decree from the governor called for the release of whatever grain had been stockpiled and set a maximum price, which was twice that of the previous year.[26]

Philostratus describes a riot in the town of Aspendos in the Roman province of Pamphylia (on the southern coast of Asia Minor) as a result of famine. The scene was one where there was "nothing but vetch on sale in the market, and the people were feeding upon this and anything else they could get, for the rich men had shut up all the corn and were holding it up for export from the country" (*Life of Apollonius of Tyana* 1.15). To calm the riot, Apollonius of Tyana indicted the corn dealers with this charge:

> Apollonius to the corn dealers of Aspendos: The earth is mother of all of us, for she is just; but you, because you are unjust have pretended that she is your mother alone; and if you do not stop, I will not permit you to remain upon her. (Ibid. 15)

The walled construction of Roman cities made expansion of the city area difficult; hence, the populace was crammed into a limited space. Rodney Stark

---

23. Loane, pp. 11-55.

24. Ibid., p. 13.

25. Thus Aristides proclaimed: "Produce is brought from every land and every sea, depending on what the seasons bring forth, and what is produced by all lands, rivers and lakes and the arts of Greeks and barbarians. If anyone wants to see it all he must travel over the whole earth to see it in such a way or come to this city. For what grows and is produced among individual peoples is necessarily always here, and here in abundance" (*Eulogy to Rome* 11).

26. Wengst, p. 223.

argues that the population densities of these cities were comparable to those in the most crowded Third World cities of today.[27] These high population densities produced a host of problems. The primary residential unit in the Roman city was not the spacious villa portrayed by Hollywood but the multistory tenement divided into small cubicles. These overcrowded tenements could come crashing down and were in constant peril of rapidly spreading fire.[28]

High population densities also placed high demands on sewage systems, and despite the famed aqueducts and public baths of ancient Rome, these were not adequate for the task of removing human waste.[29] The buildup of sewage in the streets inevitably produced disease.[30] The high rate of disease led to low life expectancy. In fact, mortality rates were so high that it was only the constant influx of people from the rural areas that allowed the cities to maintain their population levels.[31]

Thus, a sizable proportion of the population consisted of recent newcomers, people who were strangers to the city and to each other. This influx of diverse peoples also led to the formation of ethnic enclaves. Some cities were officially partitioned along ethnic lines. Other cities were unofficially segregated.

In such a situation, with chronic overcrowding, poor sanitation, disease, death, a high proportion of strangers, and endemic poverty, the ancient city was not a pretty place. It is no wonder that efforts were made to beautify the public sectors of cities with temples, public buildings, monuments, and so forth. But such public works were often unable to pacify the populace, and social tensions regularly erupted into riots.[32]

Ramsay MacMullen argues that social connection among neighbors and those engaged in trades were enhanced by the crowded conditions.[33] Residential units had no cooking facilities, which forced everyone to eat in public. Similarly, people had no private indoor plumbing. These needs were provided by public services in the cities, which brought people into contact with one another. The cities included ample public spaces in which people socialized. Cities had festivals organized around a particular street or locality in the city. Every city had groups of tradespeople who gathered for worship, mutual support, and social events. Living in such close proximity made for keen awareness of the lives of neighbors. This served to develop social cohesion in what would be otherwise frightening and lonely places. People such as Christians who refused to participate in the normal activities of Roman life (such as the imperial and local cult or com-

---

27. Stark, pp. 149-50. Ramsay MacMullen (1974), pp. 62-63, stresses the high population density of the ancient city. He describes how the ancient city might have up to one-quarter of its space taken up by public areas, concentrating the population even further.

28. Stark, p. 151.

29. Ibid., pp. 152-53.

30. Ibid., p. 154.

31. Ibid., p. 155.

32. Ibid., p. 159.

33. MacMullen (1974), pp. 64-65.

merce) would have been conspicuous by their absence from public events. It was impossible to keep such resistance secret.

In sum, the economic structure of the first-century Roman Empire produced a number of social tensions. The first was the tension between city and country. Within the city there was tension between the elite, who owned and controlled the food supplies, and the poor majority, who were dependent on food aid. In the rural areas there was tension between the tenanted peasants and the owners of the large estates, and between the peasants and those representatives of the empire who taxed them. There was also tension between the center of the empire—Rome—and the provinces, which benefited the provincial elite and impoverished the majority. Thus, while some praised Rome for its prosperity created by conquest and trade, for others this was a source of deep disaffection.

IMPERIAL CULTURE

It is the cultural realm that provides cognitive coherence to the entire range of practices, structures, and relationships that constitute a given society. That is, we make sense of our society by the way in which our culture presents itself to us.[34] This presentation may be official or unofficial. It makes use of the totality of available media, and it may be packaged with much solemnity or as mere entertainment. The way the cultural code is presented tends to make the prevailing social arrangements seem the natural order of things. The culture says to us: the way things are is the way things should be, in accordance with the "divine" will.

Culture, if it is in the service of empire, will not allow a serious discussion of alternatives. It will not permit any suggestion that the current order may not last forever, or that it is arranged with anything other than the best of intentions by the holders of power. Any breaches of this cultural code will be met with a range of sanctions, up to and including the threat or practice of violence. In a well-run empire, the complex range of cultural phenomena will act in concert to reinforce the imperial view. This will ensure compliance with the social, political, or economic agendas of the powerful. As Ched Myers explains:

> Every national holiday and patriotic event, every ritual of pomp and parade, every liturgy of remembrance or election serves to remind us of this system. Its structures and discourses socialize individuals and groups to conceive of their vocation according to prescribed values and limits set by class, race, and gender.[35]

---

34. In *The Social Construction of Reality* (1966), Peter Berger and Thomas Luckmann argue that everything we understand about ourselves and our culture is "socially constructed." That is, while we may believe our society to be a naturally given reality, it has been socially "constructed" over time. We examine this concept in more depth in chapter 4.

35. Myers (1988), p. 70.

The cultural order of the Roman Empire of the first century was conducive to the aims of the Caesars and their friends. Like societies today, it utilized a range of public rituals, rhetoric, and symbolic imagery to give coherence to the imperial construction of reality. The *imperial cult* and the *local cults* of Asia were key components of the complex web of symbols that constituted the imperial cultural order. In turn this cultural order lent legitimacy to the entire sociohistorical arrangement of the first-century Roman Empire.

The Imperial Cult

The imperial cult was an indispensable element of the imperial order. In his work on the imperial cult in Asia Minor, S. R. F. Price describes the cult as an integral part of a complex "web of power" by which the inhabitants of the empire understood themselves to be connected with Rome and the emperor.[36] It was a large part of the social glue that kept the disparate peoples of the far-flung empire together. That the imperial cult was a social "glue" is reflected in the word "religion." In ancient Rome *re-ligio* meant "the ties that bind people together." In its social function, this is what the imperial cult did. Unfortunately, the modern understanding of "religion," which often refers to a private belief system separate from the political realm, has distorted our understanding of ancient *religio*. In the ancient world no strict demarcation was made between the secular and the religious. John Elliott, for example, argues that in antiquity "there was no independent religious sector with its independent institutions, organizations, and social activities . . . religion was instead embedded within all sectors of the system as a whole."[37] The imperial cult, then, was a social phenomenon that influenced all of life.

For the vast bulk of the provincial population, the imperial cult was the only way in which the emperor was known. No emperor visited Asia in the first century, and only a handful of the local elite ever visited Rome to meet the emperor. By and large, it was through the imperial statues, temples, inscriptions, coins, public festivals, and holidays that the populace came to "know" the emperor.

The cult of the Roman ruler began in earnest with the ascendancy of Augustus. Within a few years of his coming to power, temple construction began in Asia Minor. It is important to note that this was not done at the initiative of Augustus. In Asia, it was the local elite who requested permission to honor the emperor in this way. Once under way, the building of imperial temples became a key part of the age-old civic competition among the cities of Asia.

These cities were leaders in this rush to honor the emperor. The city of Pergamum, for example, was in the process of constructing a temple to Rome and Augustus in 27 B.C.E., a scant four years after the victory of Augustus.[38] Other cities followed Pergamum's example, either building new temples or adapting

---

36. Price.
37. J. Elliott (1986), p. 16; cf. J. Elliott (1995), p. 129.
38. Taylor, p. 273.

current ones to honor the emperor. There were temples dedicated to emperors, altars dedicated to emperors set up in temples to other gods, and priests who attended both these cultic arrangements. In the first century the cult of the emperors was located in each of the seven cities addressed by Revelation, as shown in table 11.[39]

The city of Pergamum was home to the temple of Roma and Augustus. This temple was the meeting place of the provincial assembly of Asia and the repository for decrees of the provincial assembly and letters from Rome.[40] In Pergamum there was also an imperial altar in the temple of Aesclepius. In Ephesus there was a temple of Roma and Julius Caesar, an altar of Augustus within the temple of Artemis, and a huge temple of Domitian. Smyrna dedicated a temple of Tiberius and the Roman Senate in 26 C.E. Sardis maintained a temple of Augustus. Laodicea honored Domitian with an imperial altar. The major cities that maintained temples in the first century—Pergamum, Smyrna, and Ephesus—were granted the title "Temple-Warden [of the Imperial Cult]," a title of civic pride.

The imperial cult is a good example of how the language of power in antiquity knew no real distinction between politics and cult, court and temple, rulers and gods. The same honorific titles were given to kings, emperors, and gods. Throughout antiquity the court of the earthly ruler and the court of the god were described in much the same way. This invested the ancient ruler with divine qualities, and the gods with earthly ones. No doubt this served earthly rulers well. In applying divine language to the emperors, the harsh realities of Roman power were clothed with divine authority. This strengthened the power of the ruler. It also reflected the desire of many subjects and citizens, who in investing their ruler with a divine aura, themselves gained a sense of security and stability.

The imperial cult was a *religio* in that it bound the residents of the cities together in the broader context of empire. All members of the city were expected to participate in the imperial cult. While there were times and places where this participation was an official command, this was not the case in the cities of Asia at the time of Revelation. Rather, there was a social expectation that one would voluntarily participate as a demonstration of one's "faith" in the empire. This is akin to the way Australians and Americans are expected at sporting events to stand while the national anthem is played. There is no law requiring this, but not to do so may cause great social affront.

The temples played a role in the economy of the cities of Asia, operating both as banks and marketplaces. Large-scale financial transactions were impossible without recourse to the banking facilities in the larger temples. In Rome the temple of Saturn was the headquarters of the state treasury.[41] The temple of Artemis in Ephesus was the financial headquarters of the province of Asia. These temples lent money at interest and took mortgages on property. They received income

---

39. L. Thompson (1990), p. 159; see also Price, pp. xviii-xxv.
40. Mellor, p. 978.
41. Stambaugh, p. 586.

Table 11
THE LOCATION OF THE IMPERIAL CULT IN THE SEVEN CITIES

Asian City	*Imperial Temple*	*Imperial Altar*	*Imperial Priest*
Ephesus	✓	✓	✓
Smyrna	✓	✓	✓
Pergamum	✓	✓	✓
Thyatira		✓	✓
Sardis	✓	✓	✓
Philadelphia	✓		✓
Laodicea		✓	

through large-scale bequests and through ownership of land and livestock.[42] Trade guilds and markets also operated in the temple precincts. The tradespeople and sellers made use of the temple as a central public space where all levels of commerce could be transacted. This meant that the temples were key to the economic life of the city and the empire. Anyone who wished to buy or sell, borrow or lend, was compelled to cooperate with the temple. The role of temples in the economic life of the Roman Empire made them more like both the stock exchange and the craft and produce markets of our day, rather than like our churches.

In the book of Revelation (Rev. 2:14, 20; as in Paul's correspondence with the Corinthians, 1 Cor. 8:1-13; 10:23-11:1) the issue of eating meat sacrificed in the temples was a touchstone of participation in the empire as a whole. This meat was the portion of the animal left over after the ritual burning of the inedible body parts.[43] When the amount of meat exceeded that which could be eaten by the priestly caste and their retinue, the remainder was either sold in the marketplace or eaten in ritual meals. Only the wealthy could afford to buy sacrificed meat, and only the elite were invited to the ritual banquets. These banquets, organized by the temple officials, were another manifestation of the patronage system in their rigid recognition of the relative social status of each guest. The banquets served to legitimate the patronage system, the imperial cult, and the privilege of the elite classes.

Participation in the temple cult had numerous benefits. For the elite it served as an opportunity to offer patronage, which enhanced their reputation and status. It also helped qualify them for citizenship, and undoubtedly benefited them in

42. Oster, pp. 1718-19.
43. Aune (1997), p. 192.

their relations with imperial officials and in business. The remainder of the population benefited from participation in the imperial cult by the sense of social inclusion it gave through being part of trade guilds or other organizations that took part in the civic activities. To a great extent the best that the city had to offer was mediated through the imperial temples: worship, commerce, culture, and celebration. These were the *religio* that bound the people of the Asian cities together in the broader circle of empire.

Local Cults in Roman Asia

To the modern eye and ear, the spectacle of cults such as Cybele, Isis, and Mithras might seem bizarre and grotesque. Our religious sensibilities tend to recoil at the idea of rituals that include the dripping of blood from a bull carcass onto the robes of a priest-initiate. Our tame and controlled liturgies pale in comparison to the noisy boisterousness of street processions bursting with wild dancing, sacred statues, and loud tambourines. Yet these practices were already ancient in the Asia to which John wrote the record of his visions. These cults were a major part of what we might call the "dominant culture" of the time. Just as today's churches either incorporate or rail against manifestations of popular culture such as rock or rap music, so the *ekklēsiai* of the first century had to decide: How does God call us to respond to the diverse expressions of popular ritual around us?

Just as we have seen how Revelation's roots extend back to the days of Israel's exile, so Roman Asia's local cults had venerable histories. For example, one of the most popular cults was that of Cybele, the earth mother. Some scholars see traces of her worship in Phrygia (the indigenous name for the inland portion of the Roman province of Asia) that go back over six millennia before Christ.[44] As agriculture began to replace hunting in the river valleys of India, Mesopotamia, and Egypt, there was a correlative increase in the social and economic importance of women. Hence, the need to root women's social roles in a divine model generated the various earth mother cults throughout the region. Powerful and complex myths of origin developed around the earth mother, who became known in Phrygia as Cybele, but who was also assimilated into cults of various Greco-Roman goddesses, such as Artemis, Diana, and Demeter.

By the third century B.C.E., the cult of Cybele was so powerful in Phrygia that the Romans saw her as a source of security amid the war with Carthage in northern Africa. After consulting the Sibylline Oracles, a delegation was sent to Phrygia to bring to Rome a powerful symbol of the goddess, the so-called Mother of Pessinus, a town within the then-kingdom of Pergamum. A great black stone figure was transferred to Rome with tremendous pomp and ceremony and installed on the Palatine Hill in the Temple of Victory, where she stood as a guarantor of Rome's military success.[45] Cybele received her own temple in Rome in 191 B.C.E.

---

44. Turcan, pp. 29-30; Ferguson, p. 14.
45. Turcan, pp. 35-37; Ferguson, pp. 27-28.

Thus, by the time of Revelation, Cybele worship was nearly three hundred years old in Rome itself, and countless years older in Asia.

Because of its popularity in Asia and in Rome, the cult of Cybele also serves as an apt example of the nature of worship and ritual in these traditions. A central event in the lives of Cybele worshipers was the week of powerful rituals introduced to Rome by Claudius during his reign (41-54 C.E.). The ceremonies began on March 22 with the Entry of the Tree, during which a great procession of worshipers and priests carried a pine tree through Rome like a funeral cortege in memory of the tree at whose feet the mythical Attis, friend or lover of Cybele, had castrated himself in despair. The next day included another mourning procession, this time accompanied by blasts from sacred trumpets. On March 24, the Day of Blood marked the peak of the mournful portion of the cycle. The high priest led a wild dance around the sacred pine, while flagellating himself and the other priests, known as *galli*, with a whip hung with knucklebones, accompanied by the sounds of cymbals, timbrels, and other instruments. Meanwhile, the ordinary worshipers beat their bare breasts with pine cones until their blood spurted onto the sacred tree. At the moment of highest frenzy, the *galli* slashed their testicles with broken glass or flint in memory of Attis's emasculation, which completed their initiation into the Cybelic priesthood. The pine, now covered with strips of colorful cloth and flowers, was buried, as had been done by Cybele to Attis's own corpse. The following day, the Festival of Joy, or *Hilaria*, celebrated the resurrection of Attis. By the third century C.E., it had become one of the great festivals on the Roman calendar. It corresponded to what was understood to be the first day after the spring equinox, when the power of day once again overcame night. The emperor himself took part in the triumphal procession along with knights, senators, and other dignitaries, accompanied by the most prestigious works of art and sculpture.[46]

This "holy week" was followed a short time later by the *Megalensia* from April 4 to April 10. This celebration recalled the transfer of the Black Stone from Phrygia to Rome with days of street theater, feasting, public games, and other forms of merriment. The culmination of the *Megalensia* was a procession through Rome's Circus Maximus led by a statue of Cybele in her traditional pose riding on a lion's back (see figure 1). She was led by a toga-bedecked magistrate and great musicians in a celebration of Rome's victory over her enemies.[47]

As one can see, the Roman Empire adapted the formerly local cult of the Phrygian earth mother into a powerful symbol supporting Rome's own mythology. Indeed, in the imperial era, virtually all of the local cults were deeply supportive of the empire. As Ramsay MacMullen has pointed out regarding not only the local cults but all Roman religion,

It was certainly recognized throughout antiquity, at least by people able to look at their world with any detachment, that religion served to strengthen

---

46. Turcan, pp. 44-46; Ferguson, pp. 28-29.
47. Turcan, p. 47; Ferguson, p. 28.

the existing social order. Explicit statements to this effect . . . can be found across a string of well-known writers.[48]

Of course, the original role of these local cults was precisely to strengthen the social order existing within the city-states of the Hellenistic era. However, what had formerly been cults of rival gods and goddesses supporting the rivalry of their correlative cities, became, under the empire's all-embracing arms, often interchangeable expressions supportive of empire itself. As MacMullen puts it, the empire

> had been assembled out of many peoples, each of which had its own system of faith. In the course of time, conflict had brought into being successively fewer but larger states that drew strength from the absorption of divine, as of human, resources. . . . The process was now over. Rome's Empire under our gaze was complete, and completely tolerant, in heaven as on earth.
>
> Perhaps not quite completely: Jews off and on, Christians off and on, Druids for good and all, fell under ban, in the first century of the era.[49]

One can see how this imperial tolerance and peace were threatened by Christians in particular in Luke's account of the silversmiths' riot in Acts 19. In Ephesus, the earth mother was worshiped under the name of Artemis, whose statue-makers felt deeply threatened by Paul's preaching against what he saw as "idolatry." Luke tells how the smiths successfully aroused public anger with their argument:

> "Men, you know that we get our wealth from this business. You also see and hear that not only in Ephesus but in almost the whole of Asia this Paul has persuaded and drawn away a considerable number of people by saying that gods made with hands are not gods. And there is danger not only that this trade of ours may come into disrepute but also that the temple of the great goddess Artemis will be scorned, and she will be deprived of her majesty that brought all Asia and the world to worship her."
>
> When they heard this, they were enraged and shouted, "Great is Artemis of the Ephesians!" The city was filled with the confusion; and people rushed together to the theater, dragging with them Gaius and Aristarchus, Macedonians who were Paul's travel companions. (Acts 19:25-29)

The shouting continued for two hours before the local magistrate could restore calm. As Luke's story indicates, economics, religion, and local identity became deeply intertwined in the worship of Artemis in Asian Ephesus.

What were the attractions of these strange cults for Roman citizens? What would lead people to beat themselves into a bloody pulp as a form of religious

---

48. MacMullen (1981), p. 57.
49. Ibid., p. 2.

Figure 1
TYPICAL IMAGE OF CYBELE ASTRIDE A LION

devotion? For one thing, we need to recall that many residents of the great imperial cities were migrants: soldiers given a pension and freed slaves sent to cities
such as Corinth to settle,[50] as well as former farmers pushed off their land by the
growth of the *latifundia*.[51] Many of these people found themselves adrift in a foreign culture, and adherence to the cults of their places of origin provided some
sense of community in the new cities, much as immigrants to the United States
found solace in continuing the practices of the "old country."[52]

Second, with the advent of the Roman Empire, the role that local politics had
played in generating a sense of community among the Hellenistic city-states was
lost. As Robert Turcan states,

---

50. Witherington, p. 6.

51. E.g., Turcan, p. 16.

52. See, e.g., Auerbach; and Cowan and Cowan for examples of the tension facing Jewish immigrants in turn-of-the-century America.

This void was favourable to the formation of marginal groups. Where the individual no longer plays an active, direct and personal part in the running of the city, he inevitably loses interest and seeks responsibilities elsewhere, in other solidarities, other "fraternities." Religious micro-societies and "mystery" sects assure him of a kind of reintegration and existence, when traditional frameworks and institutional authorities are in decline or failing in their mission.[53]

Thus, cult practices provided a sense of community among people who otherwise might have felt lonely and alienated within the crowded, dangerous, and impersonal cities of the empire. Beyond the spectacular public rituals, participation in the cults included sharing of ritual and honorary meals that created a social circle within which a person could conduct business, find mutual protection against economic insecurity and street violence, and be assured of other social benefits.[54]

Finally, the cults provided a great deal of emotional and spiritual adventure amid the "blasé and weary world" of the empire.[55] The sheer sensory power of both public and "mystery" rituals was overwhelming, both for devotees and bystanders. As MacMullen describes it, people in Asia Minor found that

> their senses were assaulted by messages directing their attention to religion: shouts and singing in public places, generally in the open air, not in any church, and to an accompaniment as loud as ancient instruments could sound; applause . . . enactment of scenes from the gods' stories performed in theaters and amphitheaters . . . the god-possessed swirl of worshipers coming down the street to the noise and rattle of drums; and all of this without the onlooker's offering a pinch of incense or so much as glancing at a temple.[56]

But for devotees, the spiritual dimension often was the ultimate attraction. Many of the rituals offered experiences that invited people out of ordinary consciousness into contact with the world of the gods. Unlike the Olympian gods, who were distant and invulnerable, the gods and goddesses worshiped by the local cults shared in human experiences such as suffering and triumph and "broke down the barriers of a very ancient segregation between heaven and earth."[57] Communion with these beings through ritual offered ordinary people a share in divinity, an "impression of being born into a new life."[58]

This invitation to spiritual "travel" into the realm of the gods should be seen

---

53. Turcan, p. 17.
54. MacMullen (1981), p. 40; cf. Garnsey and Saller, pp. 102-3.
55. Turcan, p. 18.
56. MacMullen (1981), p. 27.
57. Turcan, p. 22.
58. Ibid., p. 20.

in light of Revelation's grounding in a similar claim. For example, cultic initiation into the popular cult of Isis included the purifying of the initiate in a bath, followed by dressing in a new linen robe, after which the initiate was conducted on a journey through both astral and infernal realms as a revelation of the power and reality of the god.[59] Although the Isis cult did not have direct, early imperial support as did Cybele worship, the emperor Domitian was personally a great devotee of Isis, whose statues and monuments could be found all over the empire during his reign.[60] Similar claims of astral and otherworldly travel could be found among the devotees of Mithras, whose rituals were so akin to Christian practices as to be condemned by early church fathers as "demonic" counterparts of Christian liturgies.[61]

Another aspect of the attractiveness of the local cults was their voluntary nature. Unlike the imperial cult, violation of which could result in severe consequences, the local cults in the polytheistic culture of the empire could be practiced or not as one saw fit. As Walter Burkert notes, the "mysteries" were like the ancient practice of "votive" religion, in which one made a vow to a god or goddess in exchange for the god or goddess granting a favor, e.g., restored health or gaining wealth or status. If the favor was "granted," the vow was happily practiced. If not, then the seeker could proceed in search of a more "effective" religious object. In a similar way, participation in the mysteries was experimental: if it provided benefits, one remained a devotee; if not, one moved on.[62] In this way, participation paralleled the practice of many modern-day Christians, who "shop" for the denomination or local congregation that seems most satisfying to one's personal religious "needs."

If participation in the cults was voluntary, why should the author of Revelation be concerned about them? One factor was the ubiquity of the cults throughout the empire, especially in the eastern portion, where John's *ekklēsiai* were located. MacMullen notes:

> Throughout most of the eastern provinces, cities advertised their principal, most characteristic religious beliefs by sending out delegations of heralds or by issuing small change, that is, bronze currency from their own mints and of their own design. . . . People assembling for commerce could not avoid exposure to the challenge of others' religious beliefs.[63]

Another was the intricate way in which empire and cult were mutually reinforcing in casting a "sacred canopy" over the social structures and practices of the empire.[64] As mentioned, the members of the major cults (Cybele/Artemis, Isis, and Mithras) saw themselves as patriotic supporters of the emperor. Fur-

---

59. Ibid., p. 120.
60. Ibid., pp. 89-90; Ferguson, p. 25; B. W. Jones (1992), pp. 200-201.
61. Ferguson, p. 121; Turcan, pp. 216, 221, 226, 233.
62. Burkert, p. 15.
63. MacMullen (1981), p. 25.
64. Berger.

thermore, the structure of the communities that developed around the cults fit well within the patronage system which undergirded the entire imperial system. Practice of the local cults cost substantial sums of money for the elaborate rituals and meals, priesthood and costumes, temples and shrines. This required support from wealthy patrons. Thus, the fusion of the cultic and patronage systems

> evokes both the divine necessity and the social responsibility of the existing social order. The relationship proposed by the sacrificial system between god and man (inferiority; reciprocity between unequals; providential beneficence; changelessness) is implicitly offered as a model of the relationship between the elite and the rest of the community.[65]

As we will see, one of the primary aspects of John's vision is the biblical heritage of diffused, "horizontal" power relations in contrast to imperial hierarchical, "vertical" relations. Thus, the popular practice of the cults could be seen as an important part of the work of "the Beast," which had been conquered by the Lamb in the cosmic war depicted in Revelation.

Specific Cultic Practices in the Background of Revelation

Beyond these general aspects of the cults, which would arouse John's visionary passion, certain specific practices can be seen as particularly provocative. The following brief survey will give some indication of how cult practices lie behind the imagery of Revelation.

The Taurobolium of Cybele. The taurobolium involved the dripping of blood from a bull's body down from a raised platform onto a linen-clad priest. As Turcan describes it, the ritual involved "being immersed in the spilt blood in order to identify oneself ritualistically, though imaginarily, with the victim. It was a substitution sacrifice. . . . the subject of the taurobolium . . . is the one who is to be consecrated as high priest . . . he was hailed and worshipped, and ended with the conviction that he was 'purified.' "[66]

The ritual included the sacrifice of the bull on behalf of the emperor and his family. From the mid-second century on, the "Mecca" of the mother cult and hence the practice of the taurobolium was the Vatican sanctuary which housed a temple of Cybele, built on what is now St. Peter's Basilica.[67]

The first recorded extant evidence of the taurobolium is in Pergamum around 105 C.E., just after John's time. It seems likely, however, that the ritual or something close to it had been practiced earlier. The notion of the priest becoming purified through the receipt of blood on a linen robe certainly resonates with the

---

65. Gordon, p. 135.
66. Turcan, pp. 50-51.
67. Ibid., p. 52.

otherwise mysterious image in Revelation of the martyrs who "have washed their robes and made them white in the blood of the Lamb" (Rev. 7:14). Given the powerful tradition of Cybele worship in Asia and its eventual enthusiastic acceptance in Rome, it would not be surprising to find that John directed some of his apocalyptic energy at "deconstructing" the cult and its support for imperial propaganda.

The Holy Week of Cybele and Autumnal Solemnities of Osiris and Isis. As noted above, Cybele worship in Rome included the "holy week" rituals that were eerily parallel to the eventual Christian commemorations of Palm Sunday, Good Friday, and Easter. A similar ritual pattern was practiced in the cult of Osiris and Isis, the Egyptian god and goddess popular in Domitian's time. The latter rituals included a cycle of mourning, ritual flagellation, and celebration like that of Cybele, but was practiced in the fall. The celebration, also called the *Hilaria*, rejoiced over the revitalization of the dead Osiris. Turcan notes that the rite "enjoyed a success in the West that exasperated Christians."[68] Both the public processional aspects of these rituals and their focus on the suffering, death, and resurrection of a god-human could easily be seen as parodied in the numerous heavenly liturgy scenes in Revelation (see chapter 7 below).

The Commemoration of the Salvific Work of Mithras. The worship of Mithras has its origins in Zoroastrian Persia, where, despite the monotheism of Zoroaster, the already ancient worship of Mithras continued to attract many devotees. But it was in Asia Minor that the Persian roots became intertwined with Hellenistic culture to produce the Mithraic practices that were conducted during the first century C.E.[69] In contrast to Cybele and Osiris/Isis worship, Mithraic worship was not a public event. It took place largely in symbolic caves and grottoes, befitting the mythical underpinning of the tradition. Mithraic practice paralleled early Christian belief and practice in several ways. First, in the words of an inscription in a Mithraic cave, "And us thou [Mithras] hast saved by shedding the eternal blood."[70] That is, Mithras's life was seen as bringing salvation to humanity, just as Christians saw the life, death, and resurrection of Jesus. Second, Mithraic belief saw earthly life as a time of trial for the "soul," which must pass through seven planetary spheres on its way "down" to earthly life. The combination of personal moral effort by the devotee and the knowledge revealed in the mystery rites provided the means to shake off the accumulated weight of the impurities gathered in each sphere.[71] As John Ferguson states, "For this is what Mithraism is about, the battle between light and dark, day and night, life and death, summer and winter, good and evil. The Mithraist was, in the most literal sense, on the side of the angels."[72]

---

68. Ibid., p. 118.
69. Ibid., p. 200.
70. Quoted in Turcan, p. 226.
71. Ferguson, p. 121.
72. Ibid.

Mithraism, like the other cults, was supportive of the Roman Empire. In fact, it became a favorite among the members of the Roman legionary forces.[73] Thus, its apocalyptic theology could easily be seen by John as a diabolic perversion of what was revealed in his own otherworldly journey.

One of the central aspects of Mithraic practice was a communal meal. Although little is known of the details of this sacred feast, the Christian writer Tertullian, whose father had apparently been an initiate, denounced it as a demonic copy of the eucharistic liturgy.[74] We do know that it involved the sharing of bread, water, and wine that were consecrated by the ritual leaders as a way to link those who received with the power of Mithras. These parallels would certainly be enough to raise the hackles on a prophetic figure such as John of Patmos. Perhaps the invitation to the Christians in Laodicea to listen to the voice of the Lamb, so that "I will come in to you and eat with you, and you with me," can be heard in the light of Mithraic ritual meals.

IMPERIAL MYTH

Culture comprises not only the visible structures and relationships that exist between its member parts. Binding these visible aspects of society together is an ideology that lends legitimacy to the culture as a whole. In all cultures, ancient and modern, ideology is conveyed through *myth*. It is easy for us to see the ideologies of ancient or indigenous cultures as "myths." After all, to talk about the world in terms of the Australian Aboriginal "dreaming" or the biblical "miracle" seems absurd to those of us steeped in Enlightenment rationality. Yet on closer examination it becomes clear that ideology, even today, is typically expressed in mythic terms. We are not using the word "myth" in the sense of a fallacious, naïve, or untrue story. Nor are we using it to refer to a tribal or primitive mode of communication. Rather, we use the word to mean symbolic communication within a given cultural and political system.

When myth is understood in this way, it should become obvious that many of the ideological propositions and "truths" that undergird Western capitalist culture, and increasingly undergird the emerging global economic culture, belong to the realm of myth. That fact does not determine whether the myths have validity or not; it is simply a recognition that much of what passes for rational discourse in our culture operates on the symbolic level. David Kertzer argues that the ritual expression of symbol is an indispensable element of contemporary political life. For Kertzer, ritual is a particular manifestation of the broader category of symbol. Symbol-laden rituals are everyday events in contemporary Western culture; they are an important means by which myth is propagated:

> From national party conventions to presidential inauguration, from congressional committee hearing to the roar of the football stadium crowd

---

73. Turcan, p. 195.
74. Ibid., pp. 233-234.

belting out the national anthem, ritual is a ubiquitous part of modern political life. Through ritual aspiring political leaders struggle to assert their right to rule, incumbent power holders seek to bolster their authority, and revolutionaries try to carve out a new basis of political allegiance. All of these political figures, from leaders of insurrections to champions of the status quo, use rites to create political reality for the people around them. Through participation in rites, the citizen of the modern state identifies with larger political forces that can only be seen in symbolic form.[75]

Economics also operates in the mythic realm. The most potent economic ideologies of this century, capitalism and communism, could not have operated without their mythic dimensions. After all, what is the belief that an "invisible hand" and a "free market" can produce a prosperous and free society other than myth? Similarly, the "dictatorship of the proletariat" was a communist myth, operating as it did primarily at the level of symbol. A large portion of the twentieth century was dominated by a war between these two ideologies. This war was played out in mythic language. In "the West" (itself a symbolic reality) the language of myth included the "free world," the "evil empire," the "iron curtain," and "deterrence." This was an ideological war in which symbol was met with symbol, ritual with ritual, ideology with ideology. In chapter 9, we will explore the mythic dimensions of the culture of global capital, and how Revelation might assist in countering the myths of that system.

Like every other culture, the Roman Empire was legitimated by a set of myths that were an intrinsic part of its "construction." Some of these myths varied in time and place across the empire, while others were more regular expressions of Roman ideology. These acted to bind the disparate peoples of the far-flung empire together. The myths functioned to lend legitimacy to rule from distant Rome and to encourage loyalty to both emperor and empire.

The foundational myth of the Roman Empire, which operated throughout the empire and through the first century, was the myth of *Augustus*. This myth accounted for the elevation of Octavian to the position of "Augustus," a title meaning "revered." As we saw in an earlier quotation (see p. 89) the imperial poet and propagandist Virgil created the myth of Augustus by evoking the myth of the "golden age" and linking it to the figure of Augustus.

The myth of the "golden age" is found also in the writings of Hesiod and Ovid. Both these writers saw history as beginning with a golden age, a time of universal happiness. This was followed by a decline through various ages: the silver, the bronze, and then the iron age (cf. Dan. 2:31-46). Ovid described the iron age as characterized by sins against family and kinfolk, as impelled by greed and the absence of justice from the world. The myth of the decline of the ages involved a looking back to a time of peace and prosperity that existed in the imaginary past. The perennial question was: Would this golden age return? If so, when? According to Virgil, the "golden age" had returned under the auspices of

---

75. Kertzer, p. 1.

Augustus. This renewed "golden age" was to be an era of unparalleled peace and prosperity.

The mythic "golden age" in the Augustan era had great power because it coincided with the drawing to a close of a time of disaster for the Roman state. The late Republican period preceding the imperial period was a time of civil war among the Roman elite. A sense of gloom pervaded the circles of the powerful. But while the political atmosphere was one of crisis, the writers and orators offered the hope that a new era would arrive in which peace and prosperity would be restored. With the ascendancy of Augustus, the rhetoricians capitalized on these writings and announced that it was Augustus himself who had inaugurated a new age. This new era was depicted as one of rural idyll: the fulfillment of the promises of an earlier age.

Helmut Koester lists the five planks of this new age:[76]

- The new age is the fulfillment of prophecy, and it corresponds to the promises given in the primordial age.
- The new age includes this earth as well as the world of the heavens: Apollo as *Hēlios* (the "Sun") is the god of the new age.
- The new age is universal; it includes all nations.
- There is an enactment of the new age through the official celebrations of the empire, like the "new age" festivities of the year 17 B.C.E., mirrored by the subsequent introduction of Caesarian games in many places.
- The new age has a savior figure, the greatest benefactor of all times, the "son of god" (Latin *divi filius*), the victorious Augustus.

With this as the new foundational myth of the empire, a web of supporting myths emerged. An examination of the entire set of myths that operated in the Roman Empire would be a massive task. In chapter 8 we examine key myths of the Roman Empire—Empire, Peace, Victory, Faith, and Eternity—and how Revelation exposed these myths as both misleading and seducing the people of the empire.

THE CHRISTIAN *EKKLĒSIAI* AND THE EMPIRE

In the imperial province of Asia, small groups of people tried to live their lives inspired by the memory of Jesus. Jesus had been executed on a Roman cross by order of a Roman official in a rebellious Roman province. The Christian movement from its earliest days had taken the political language of the empire and made it its own. The New Testament language of empire/kingdom,[77] gospel, sav-

---

76. Koester (1992), pp. 12-13.

77. Throughout this book we translate the Greek *basileia*, where it is found in New Testament texts, as "empire." *Basileia* "was the term that Rome used to describe itself. When we encounter it in ancient secular texts or in inscriptions from the period, we translate it as 'empire'" (Patterson [1995], p. 44).

ior, lord, faith, and son of God imbued this movement with a political rhetoric from the beginning. Like most groups, as time goes on and organization becomes more formal and the costs of being different become wearing, some of the Christian communities accommodated themselves to Roman power. The situation is akin to that narrated in 1 Sam. 8, where, despite their history of resistance to centralized forms of social organization, the people of Israel sought a king to rule over them. In their desire to be "like the other nations" the people of Israel forgot their calling to be ruled by YHWH alone. They forgot that the essence of their identity was to be different from the other nations. Similarly, some of the early Christians forgot the implications of the Roman crucifixion of Jesus. The empire, which had crucified their leader, was now seen by some as something that could be lived with. The polar opposition that had at first seemed so clear between the way of Jesus and the way of Rome was becoming blurred. Questions arose: Could one be a faithful follower of Jesus and a faithful follower of Caesar at the same time? How were the followers of Jesus to live surrounded by the great Roman Empire?

This was the situation addressed by the book of Revelation. For John of Patmos, whose visions led him to understand the depth of the crisis facing the *ekklēsiai* of Asia, the situation was critical. For him, Rome was not an order with which one could cooperate. It was, instead, an incarnation of "Satan." It was both a ferocious Beast and a seductive Whore. John did not write his book to manufacture a crisis for a people who had become complacent about the empire. Rather, he tried to reveal that this complacency about Rome *was* the crisis, if only they had "apocalyptic eyes." The primary struggle in which the *ekklēsiai* were urged to participate was resisting assimilation into the dominant Roman imperial ethos. The issue was whether those *ekklēsiai* who had faithfully resisted Rome would continue in that practice, and whether those who had been co-opted by Rome could be renewed in their resistance.

John's confrontation with the empire should not be reduced to a simple critique of the imperial cult, as many academics and church people have argued. In fact, the critique of Rome in Revelation is far broader than that of the imperial cult. While the imperial cult was a clear sign that the Roman Empire had transgressed the prerogatives of God, Revelation casts a critical eye on Rome's economic exploitation, its politics of seduction, its violence, and its imperial hubris or arrogance. To oppose the Roman Empire necessarily involved a rejection of the spirituality that helped the empire run like a well-oiled machine. Yet the rejection of that spirituality, manifest in the imperial cult, was part of a total rejection of the empire. This is a consequence of the inseparability of religion and politics in antiquity.

It was after the destruction of Jerusalem by Roman forces in 70 C.E. and probably during the reign of the emperor Domitian that John was granted on the island of Patmos his vision of the way things really are. John was on the island "on account of the word of God and the witness of Jesus" (1:9). In Revelation this is a technical expression for being a publicly faithful follower of Jesus and implies public consequences for that faithfulness (6:9; 12:11). It is most likely then that John was on Patmos as a "relegated person," that is, as someone who had been exiled by a Roman official. The punishment of exile was imposed on those from the upper classes; crucifixion was reserved for the lower classes.[78] This suggests that John had some social standing that saved him from the penalty of crucifixion. John's relatively high social status has important consequences. It suggests that John did not write Revelation because he was socially powerless and therefore resentful of the wealth and power of Rome's elite. Because John came from the more privileged sectors of Roman society, his critique of Rome would not be a matter of "relative deprivation" but of insight into God's truth about Rome. John, like Third Isaiah, was an active dissenter willing to risk hostility and rejection in order to stay true to the radical tradition of "YHWH alone."

John addressed his book to the followers of Jesus gathered as a community of *ekklēsiai* in Roman Asia. This was done in pointed juxtaposition and competition with the official city assembly.[79] It emphasizes that the followers of Jesus were called to participate in their world as "local communities of an alternative society to the Roman imperial order."[80] This was a renewal of the call made by YHWH to the people of Israel at the beginning of their history: they were not to be like the nations that surrounded them. The call by Revelation to resist empire, then, was not an invitation to engage in a new praxis. Rather it was a reminder to the followers of Jesus of the commitment they had made at their baptism, where they had chosen to enter *ekklēsiai* that were alternative to the social arrangements around them.

Traditionally, Revelation has been seen as having its setting in the context of a great persecution by the Roman Empire against the Christians of Asia. This persecution was thought to have occurred in the reign of the emperor Domitian (81-96 C.E.). The premise was that Domitian had ordered and enforced emperor worship by the people of the empire. When Christians refused to do so, they were subject to brutal persecution. Recent scholarship has refuted this premise. When the historical sources are examined, it emerges that Domitian was no worse than his predecessors in promoting the imperial cult, claiming divine titles, or exploiting the provinces.[81] Nor did Domitian order the systematic or widespread persecution of Christians in Asia or elsewhere.

As a result, some scholars have moved away from the consensus that the text was written in the era of Domitian. They have looked to other times of persecution to account for the book's obvious interest in the matter. The reign of the emperor Nero (54-68 C.E.) and the time of the Judean War (66-70 C.E.) have been the prime candidates. We believe that such an exercise is futile. From a reading of Revelation, it is apparent that social sanctions were exercised only sporadi-

---

78. Hengel, p. 34.
79. Horsley (1997), p. 209.
80. Ibid., p. 209.
81. L. Thompson (1986), pp. 153-62; Aune (1997), p. lxx; B. W. Jones (1992), p. 110.

cally against Revelation's *ekklēsiai*. In Revelation only the experiences of Antipas (2:13, execution) and John himself (1:9, exile) reflect recent instances of the imposition of sanctions against Christians. How then do we explain Revelation's concern for Christians who have been killed for their public witness?

The members of the *ekklēsiai* of Revelation were obviously well aware that agents of the Roman Empire had crucified Jesus. The experiences of the immediate followers of Jesus, too, would have confirmed the existence of a fundamental antagonism between empire and the followers of Jesus. John's vision led him to enjoin the rejection of the Roman Empire—and the wider historical notion of "empire," which Israel had been called to resist throughout its history—upon his colleagues. Their rejection of the empire, if indeed it were practiced, would have involved a wholesale rejection of imperial society. Their knowledge of imperial practice made them aware that such a wholesale resistance to the empire might render them liable to sanctions of various types. Their resistance would bring boiling to the surface the latent antagonism between the Empire of Caesar and the Empire of God.

Sanctions against Christians could take two forms. One was the official persecution of Christians by order of the emperor or provincial governor. Nero sought out followers of Jesus in Rome as scapegoats on which to blame the burning of Rome in 64 C.E. The trial and execution of Christians are reported in the correspondence between the emperor Trajan and governor Pliny (circa 110 C.E.). Persecutions of limited scope also occurred during the rule of Hadrian (117-138 C.E.) and Marcus Aurelius (161-180 C.E.). It was not until the reign of the emperor Decius in 250 C.E. that the first systematic persecution of Christians took place.

The other types of sanction were unofficial in character. If followers of Jesus withdrew from the daily life of the empire, they would place themselves outside the bounds of social acceptability. Depending on the prevailing mood of the city and the time, this could result in social ostracism, exclusion from social events, having one's business boycotted, mob violence and lynching, or being reported to the local authorities.

If the members of the *ekklēsiai* were to reject empire, as Revelation urges, these various types of social sanctions would necessarily follow.[82] To prepare them for such an eventuality, Revelation depicted persecution as a necessary and inevitable consequence of following the Lamb. This accounts, too, for the depiction of empire as Whore and Beast. The myths of the empire were designed to seduce people into the service of Rome. When seduction failed, the threat or use of violence followed. This is the iron law of empire. Against this law stood those faithful followers of the Lamb who were prepared to stand against empire even at the cost of their lives. Revelation asserts that it is only these who would see the end of empire.

---

82. See Slater, pp. 252-56.

REFLECTION QUESTIONS

1. What images or ideas, if any, about the Roman Empire have you grown up with or learned? Take a specific passage from Revelation and try to read it in light of the material presented in this chapter. What sounds different to you, if anything? Try this with a group, with each person selecting a different passage from Revelation and looking for signs of John's understanding of empire.

2. John wrote to tiny Christian *ekklēsiai* within the context of the powerful Roman Empire seeking to guide them in fidelity to God's ways. How does your own church or faith community discern whether its acts are in accordance with God's will? What is its relationship with the dominant culture in which you live?

3. John found it necessary to understand as completely as possible the elements that comprised empire in his day. How do you personally or your faith community collectively endeavor to understand your social world? What sources do you use for coming to this understanding?

4

Revelation's "Bifurcated" Sense of Time and Space

Once we understand the roots of John's apocalyptic tradition and the world of the Roman Empire in which he lived and wrote, our next task is to come to grips with the questions of when and where John expected his visions to be "fulfilled." The prophecy writers, along with many academic commentators, take Revelation's references to "the End" or to "heaven" as being about specific times or places that are "later" or "apart from" the time and place of first-century Roman Asia. The prophecy writers understand the "End" as their own "now" and "heaven" as, if not literally a place in the sky somewhere above the atmosphere, at least in a location accessible only after death or via an act of divine intervention, that is, the Rapture. Scholars usually interpret the "End" as the "Day of the Lord," that is, as the culmination of all history in the distant chronological future. They often demur on the question of where heaven is, finding themselves caught between what they sometimes think is the ancient sense of heaven as literally in the sky and their own scientifically informed knowledge of the physical universe, which precludes such a naïve idea. But have either the prophecy writers or the academic interpreters taken full consideration of how John's audience would have understood his language about "the time is near" or "heaven"? How did people in Roman Asia conceive of time and space? How did the biblical tradition generally, and the apocalyptic tradition specifically, inform John's way of speaking about these basic aspects of reality? It is to these questions that we now turn.

As Peter Berger and Thomas Luckmann argue, from people's earliest perceptions, "reality" is a social construct imposed upon them through the instruments of the dominant culture of their world.[1] When a dominant culture also has the power—whether that of seduction or of military might—to impose its cultural perspective on others, it becomes what we call in this book "empire." Empire typically claims that its own socially constructed reality is the ultimate one, thus displacing the truly ultimate reality—where God lives and reigns—from its rightful

---

1. Berger and Luckmann (1967).

place. The genius of empire is that it is able to establish an aura around itself that says: the way the empire is, is the way things are supposed to be.

In chapter 2 we investigated the roots and development of apocalyptic writing. There we saw that in response to various imperial agendas for Israel, a movement arose that, through visionary experience, *saw* empire as inimical to the ways of YHWH. These visions unveiled the truth of empire and revealed "reality" as existing whenever and wherever God reigned. The apocalyptic tradition that had its roots in the conflict between Third Isaiah and Nehemiah challenged the Persian Empire's and its Jewish elite supporters' attempts to define reality. In chapter 3 we examined the ways in which the Roman Empire constructed people's perceptions of social reality. That construction was seen to involve the creation and adaptation of myth, ritual, and symbol that generated particular ideas about the empire which Revelation challenges head on.

Revelation renewed the ancient call to see with apocalyptic eyes: to look "behind" the screen projected as reality by the dominant culture. There John saw what *appears to be* in the light of what *is*. He saw the truth about the Roman Empire: it was simply the latest manifestation of a false imperial reality that had plagued the people of God since the days of slavery in Egypt.

John's look behind the veil gave him a sense that reality was *bifurcated*. The word "bifurcate" means to divide into two branches. Apocalyptic discourse does this by arguing that there is not only the world constructed by those with social power but also another world hidden by empire's illusions. The world defined by those with power represents one branch. This is the one most people consider "reality" and which attempts to define our very being. The world where God lives and reigns is the other branch. According to the apocalyptic worldview, this latter world is the "real" one, while the other is a parody or counterfeit version of this reality.

Revelation reveals a bifurcated universe in which "ordinary" life and "divine" life *coexist* at all times and places. Traditional interpretations of apocalyptic writings have misunderstood this bifurcated worldview in terms of an absolute separation between present and future. That is, they have viewed Revelation as dividing time into two *consecutive* ages: a present evil age and a future blessed age. Others have understood Revelation as expressing a dualism between heaven and earth: earth below is a place of evil whereas heaven above is a place of good. These understandings are usually combined in varying degrees in standard interpretations of Revelation. They fail, however, to be true both to a close reading of Revelation and to an understanding of how ancient people understood reality.

An example of how reality is bifurcated in Revelation is found in the messages to the *ekklēsiai* at Smyrna and Laodicea. These messages contain God's evaluations of each *ekklēsia*. To the *ekklēsia* at Smyrna, John is told to write: "I know your tribulation and poverty, but you are rich" (2:9). To those in Laodicea, John writes, "You say I am rich and I have become rich and I have need of nothing; you don't know that you are wretched and pitiful and poor and blind and naked" (3:17). John recognizes that in the culture of the cities of Roman Asia, the Smyrneans were materially poor and Laodiceans materially rich. To most observers this would have appeared as a simple "fact." Yet this is not the way things *really* were. From God's "true" perspective as conveyed by John, it is the Smyrneans who are "rich" and the Laodiceans who are "poor" (and "blind and naked" as well).

The Christian communities and the Roman Empire inhabited both of these realities. Revelation calls these realities "heaven" and "earth." On "earth"—that is, the universe as perceived by the empire—the Smyrneans were poor and the Laodiceans wealthy. In "heaven"—the universe where God lives and reigns—the opposite is true: the Smyrneans are wealthy and the Laodiceans poor. On "earth" the Roman Empire was a paragon of power and order. In "heaven" the Roman Empire was a Beast bent on bloodshed and a Whore set on seduction.

These two worlds are competing realities that stand in opposition to each other, but they are not condemned to eternal conflict. Rather, the apocalyptic worldview affirms that the way of God *has already* prevailed *and continues* to prevail over the way of empire. Apocalyptic faith envisions both "practices of liberation *within* and divine intervention from *outside* history."[2] That is, it recognizes that both God and human beings are involved in the struggle against empire. Biblical apocalyptic is adamant that both the various empires of history, and more fundamentally empire itself, will not stand forever. To understand this can save us from the twin outlooks that have paralyzed good people: the "conservative" view that "God will take care of it, so we don't have to," and the "liberal" view that "we are God's hands and feet and without us God is powerless."

The word *apocalypse* (Greek *apokaluptō*) is derived from the word *kaluptō*, meaning "covering" or "veil." It means to unveil, to reveal, to unconceal, to rip the cover from the way things are typically held to be. Because apocalyptic insight comes from God, it has the authority to break through the social consensus. In presenting his apocalyptic insight in the book of Revelation, John calls his audience to choose which world to accept as real: empire or *ekklēsia*.

If the notion of coexisting "universes" or "worlds" seems difficult to grasp, listen to the words of Hans, a twenty-five-year-old sex-worker in São Paulo, Brazil. Hans describes his understanding of the world in this way:

> The two of us belong to the same world. We're all together, but we're not in the *same* world. You, if you enter my world, are a stranger; I, if I enter your world, am a stranger. You wouldn't accept me if you knew that I'd been arrested by the police several times, and I wouldn't accept you knowing that you never stole. You have one world and I have another world. There's a war going on between our two worlds that are, nevertheless, one and the same.[3]

---

2. Myers (1994), p. 404.
3. From an interview in the video program *Ipiranga*, directed by A. Schlaich, 1989, in Arantes, p. 81.

The way Hans grapples with his experience of social worlds is akin to that of apocalyptic bifurcation. While the faithful followers of Jesus "belonged to the same world" as the followers of Caesar (that of the cities of imperial Asia), in a real sense they were "not in the *same* world." If they were faithful to Jesus, they would be "strangers" in the world of the Roman Empire (cf. John 15:19). If they were true to their calling, the subjects of the empire "wouldn't accept them." John's vision revealed to him that there was indeed "a war going on between the two worlds." In that war, neutrality was impossible.

Major obstacles to understanding this bifurcated apocalyptic worldview lie in the future orientation of the United States and some other industrial societies and also in some current conceptions of heaven. We will examine these briefly before investigating how biblical texts expressed a worldview that was conducive to the apocalyptic bifurcation of reality.

TIME

"Lucy, do not look so sad. We shall meet soon again."

"Please, Aslan," said Lucy, "what do you mean *soon?*"

"I call all times soon," said Aslan. . . .[4]

There is a deep human propensity to understand one's own culture as a universal reality and to interpret others' cultures from the perspective of our own. One key category that often differs between cultures, but about which we are largely unconscious, is that of *time*. Using our own time perspectives to interpret cultures or texts with different time perspectives will inevitably produce misinterpretations of those cultures and texts. How does the dominant time perspective in future-oriented society differ from that reflected in the book of Revelation? How might this cultural difference in time perspectives affect our interpretation of Revelation?

Particularly in those "new" societies built outside the domain of traditional Europe, including the United States and Australia, a cherishing of the past or present gave way to a fascination with the future. This future orientation finds classic expression in the notion of "progress." Progress has been the master metaphor that has made it imperative that Western society define the direction of its culture as "growth" and "expansion," metaphors that flow out of the notion of progress. The ideology of Progress asserts that history moves in a ceaseless advance toward a better future. Within societies that adhere to the ideology of progress, it is understood that it is in the future that our present problems will be resolved. An example is how we assume that virtually all of our crises will be fixed by future technological advances.[5] Such a time orientation is alien to members of cultures that look to either the past or present as the primary time of "salvation."

---

4. Lewis, p. 174, emphasis in original.

5. Cf. Grosso, pp. 261-83; he analyzes this dependence under the rubric of "technocalypse now!"

Bruce Malina argues that the future orientation that dominates the "New World" was not a feature of ancient societies generally:

> [F]uture orientation as primary or secondary preference was and is extremely rare on the planet. And it is surely not to be found in any peasant society. . . . Since Mediterranean societies of the first century were examples of classical peasant societies, by and large, the primary preference in temporal orientation at that period and place was the present, with past second and future third.[6]

While it is difficult to distinguish differences in time perceptions among the ancients between city and rural dwellers or the educated and uneducated, what *is* clear is that the overwhelmingly future-oriented concerns of educated Americans and Australians stand in sharp contrast to the present or even past orientations of the ancients generally or even of non-Western people today.[7]

If the future-orientation of educated Australians and Americans has distorted interpretations of the book of Revelation, it is important to understand how differently present-oriented societies apprehend their world. The following table sets out some contrasts between the present- and future-oriented understandings of time.

Table 12
CONTRASTS BETWEEN PRESENT-ORIENTED
AND FUTURE-ORIENTED CONCEPTIONS OF TIME

The Present-oriented Worldview	*The Future-oriented Worldview*
Locates goals and objectives in the present	Locates goals and objectives in the future
Activity occurs in the present, to achieve proximate goals only	Activity occurs in the present, to achieve proximate and remote goals
The "present" has an extended duration	The "present" is a line separating past from future
The present drives what is forthcoming	The future drives what is present

---

6. Malina (1989), p. 5.

7. Damian Thompson shows how the distinction between U.S. future orientation and European past/present orientation is rooted in the pilgrims' and subsequent religious colonists' interpretation of the New World as New Jerusalem, that is, the place where the future is made real in the present (pp. 95-96). Thus, not only did this founding mythology shape American time consciousness for the purposes of our current chapter, but it also allowed for the ongoing expectation of an imminent End that continues to fuel premillennial and other apocalyptic speculations. In Europe, on the other hand, the past-oriented construction of time has not generated similar Endtime speculation.

In his comparison of cultural differences in how time is perceived, James Jones distinguishes between goal setting in present-oriented and future-oriented societies. In a present-oriented culture, it is close, not distant, goals that are the more important. In future-oriented societies, the distant goal is often more important than the immediate one.[8] Jones argues that in a present-oriented culture, the promise of improvement in the distant future lacks relevance and meaning. In this present perspective, the themes of the overthrow of empire and the inauguration of a new reality that characterize biblical apocalyptic cannot be understood as a distant future promise. They must have present significance. Time in present-oriented societies is not bound to hopes for a remote resolution of a current crisis. Salvation begins in the present, not the future.

In present-oriented societies, the realm of the present is invested with tremendous significance. In our future-oriented society, the present typically is flattened into a thin line separating the past from the future. In contrast, the experience of the present in present-oriented societies is as an *enduring* reality. That the enduring present was important in the ancient world can readily be seen in the Christian scriptures. For example, when Jesus declares that "by no means shall this generation pass until all these things happen" (Mark 13:30), he is operating within his primary meaningful time span: the enduring present of a generation of people. Similarly, Jesus speaks in John's Gospel: "Whoever believes in the Son has eternal life" (3:36; cf. 5:24, 39; 6:47). Jesus can speak of his listeners' *having now* the life of God, not of offering them a postmortem opportunity.[9] The life he gives, which is "eternal," remains with them throughout the long "present" of their lifetime, not simply in the specific moment of Jesus.

If the people of antiquity looked primarily to the present and the past as the durations in which crises could be resolved, how did they envision social change taking place? Bruce Malina explains that the "future" in present-oriented society is best understood as what is already in the process of becoming. This notion of "forthcoming" is not identical with how modern people understand the future. Rather, it expresses the idea of what is-to-be as rooted in what is already present. As Malina explains: "something is forthcoming when its later presence is already guaranteed by its present presence. . . . A present that includes the forthcoming is a broad present."[10] In antiquity, change was understood as possible because what *might* happen is *already* in the process of happening. "New Jerusalem," for example, is able to take shape on earth because it *already exists* in heaven (21:2). The followers of Jesus are able to have victory because the "Lamb" has *already* conquered (5:9-10).

This notion of the forthcoming as already present is also expressed in the Gospels. For example, in John, Jesus says: "The hour is coming, and is now here, when the true worshipers will worship the Father in spirit and truth" (4:23; cf. 5:25). This example shows that the sense of forthcoming was not only an apocalyptic convention but an aspect of the biblical concept of time generally.

---

8. J. Jones, p. 25.
9. Howard-Brook, p. 132.
10. Malina (1993), p. 169.

Apocalyptic discourse made sense in cultures that were primarily oriented to the enduring present. If this is so, what, then, are we to make of the *apparent* eschatological timetables and intense interest with the future that feature in so many interpretations of apocalyptic texts? Rudolph Raber argues:

> [D]espite some grammatical look of futurism and a consequent habit of futuristic interpretation, the action of the Apocalypse is to be understood as being *in process.* Any notion that God, living and active, might be sitting about waiting for some predestined moment to commence the eschaton would have been unthinkable to the writer and of no consequence whatever to his first century readers.[11]

Once we put aside our future-oriented lens on time and perceive time from the present orientation of John's world, we can see how Revelation bifurcates time into two simultaneously present realities. Ched Myers argues that in apocalyptic literature

> images of cosmic cataclysm are drawn from the traditional apocalyptic myth of "palingenesis," the surpassing of the "old" order by the "new heavens and new earth." This dualism between world orders is expressed temporally in terms of "two ages." Mythical time, however, is not conceived of chronologically (*chronos*) but archetypically (*kairos*). The two "ages" coexist in human history as "good" and "evil," each with their own respective "pasts" and "futures." . . . [T]he dualism compels listeners to clarify their allegiances in the historical struggle between fundamentally differing social visions.[12]

This insight allows us to interpret Revelation's grammatically future-oriented verb tenses as literal references not to a sequential future but to the always co-present other reality in which God and the Lamb have already conquered empire.

SPACE

What did the fundamental concepts of "heaven and earth" mean to the inhabitants of the first-century Roman Empire? What relationship existed between these "realms"? If the modern concept of time has been a major obstacle to our understanding of apocalyptic discourse, the modern conceptualization of heaven and earth has been no less troublesome.

The major problem with the common notion of "heaven and earth" found in our world is that it posits two distinct places between which there is little inter-

---

11. Raber (1986), p. 297.
12. Myers (1988), p. 338.

change. Theologians split into two distinct realms the integral view of reality that saw a simultaneity between heavenly and earthly aspects of existence. They handed over earthly matters to modern science but preserved a privileged "spiritual" realm immune from scientific confirmation or refutation.[13] A consequence of this was that in modern religion, heaven became a refuge from sociopolitical conflict, not a key player in it. For many modern theologians, theology and politics speak of completely different things.

For biblical discourse, "heaven" has always served primarily as a metaphor for where God "lives." The literal meaning of the Greek term *ouranos,* which is translated "heaven," is "sky," that is, the physical space above the earth. Ancient Israel understood YHWH as a "sky-father" god like Ba'al or other powerful storm-gods of the people around them. We see this in the frequent accompaniment of YHWH's appearances with sky phenomena such as lightning and thunder. Older biblical texts, however, rarely expressly refer to God as dwelling "in heaven."

The specific reference to the "God of heaven" in Hebrew scriptures is a late development, reflecting postexilic Persian influence.[14] It was the name by which the Persian king Cyrus referred to YHWH (Ezra 1:2). As Gerhard von Rad notes, the term refers to "the God who in historical omnipotence controls the destinies of empires and works out his plan for the world."[15] Thus, it is clear that biblical usage of heaven as the place from which divine power comes "down" to earth reflects an understanding common in the ancient world.

After the destruction of the Jerusalem temple and as Israel's exilic and postexilic thinking came to dominate older conceptions of God, YHWH was conceived of as present throughout creation. With this insight, the idea of God as a sky-god was transformed from a literal to a metaphorical notion. This is what we see in the biblical apocalyptic texts discussed in chapter 2 above, where imagery of the divine sky-warrior is used to underscore YHWH's power over all imperial usurpers of divine prerogatives.

That this language had long been understood metaphorically before the time of John of Patmos can be seen, for example, in the following quote from Isaiah:

> For my thoughts are not your thoughts, nor are your ways my ways, says YHWH. For as the heavens are higher than the earth, so are my ways higher than your ways and my thoughts than your thoughts. For as the rain and the snow come down from heaven, and do not return there until they have watered the earth, making it bring forth and sprout, giving seed to the sower and bread to the eater, so shall my word be that goes out from my mouth; it shall not return to me empty, but it shall accomplish that which I purpose, and succeed in the thing for which I sent it. (Isa. 55:8-11)

---

13. Wink (1992), p. 5.

14. Collins (1992), p. 159. Of the twenty-two uses of the term in Hebrew scripture, twelve are in Ezra-Nehemiah, four are in Daniel, and the remaining ones are in other late texts.

15. G. von Rad in *TDNT* 5:508.

Clearly, the prophet is not saying that YHWH's thoughts are literally "above" human thoughts, floating somewhere in the air over their heads! Rather, he is using the tradition of YHWH as sky-father who brings down rain or withholds it as a way of speaking about the *difference* between human and divine ways of thinking.

The writers of Christian scripture inherited this metaphorical tradition. Thus, we see throughout the New Testament the language of "up" referring to God's realm and "down" referring to the realm that humanity seeks vainly to control.[16] Consider these examples from John's Gospel:

> If I have told you about earthly things and you do not believe, how can you believe if I tell you about heavenly things? (3:12)

> The one who comes from above is above all; the one who is of the earth belongs to the earth and speaks about earthly things. The one who comes from heaven is above all. (3:31)

Sadly, interpreters who have not understood the metaphorical nature of this language have sometimes read these comments as suggesting that Jesus is denigrating physical reality. But in fact, Jesus' statements express an opposition between God's ways and the ways of humanity, just as did Isaiah centuries earlier. Thus, we can end up utterly misinterpreting the entire Bible—including Revelation—if we do not recognize how "heaven" and "earth" are used metaphorically.

Revelation, from this perspective, can be seen to draw a fundamental distinction between heaven and earth grounded *both* in the metaphorical tradition just examined *and* in the apocalyptic notion of bifurcation. "Heaven" is holy while "earth" is evil. Earth is the perspective of empire. Heaven, on the other hand, is where John sees that the truth is unveiled. In heaven the followers of Jesus rejoice at the fall of imperial power. Heaven is the source of sustenance for those who would resist this power. Revelation's worldview is not reducible to a world-hating polemic against the natural order or material universe. Rather, wherever the lies and injustices of imperial Rome are given currency—there is earth. Wherever the truth of God is believed and practiced—there is heaven. William Stringfellow stressed this practical notion of heaven:

> Let it be plain that as a biblical term, "heaven" is not a site in the galaxies any more than "hell" is located in the bowels of the earth. Rather it is . . . that vocation, really; that blessedness—to which every human and the whole of creation is called to live *here* in this world.[17]

---

16. Lakoff and Johnson show how powerful the orientational metaphor of "up is good" and "down is bad" has been in shaping Western consciousness (pp. 14-18).

17. Stringfellow (1973), p. 43.

Another aspect of Revelation's use of the apparently spatial language of heaven and earth comes from the way space is marked out as territory controlled by one actor or social group in competition with another. Whether ancient or modern, territory is always the result of a social interpretation of space. It is those who hold power in any social system who most likely shape this interpretation. Yet minority definitions of territory are possible. Such a counterdefinition of territory is in evidence in the book of Revelation. Tina Pippin argues that "the map of the Apocalypse is a political map, for the destruction of the 'world' (the Mediterranean basin) and its reconstruction as the political center of God's power in the New Jerusalem are all central."[18]

Revelation redraws the map of the Roman *oikoumenē* ("inhabited world"), placing the city that comes down from heaven—New Jerusalem—at the center of human territory, and removing the city that dominated the territory—Babylon— from the landscape. New Jerusalem is a territory carved out of empire that embodies an alternative social reality. In Revelation's bifurcated worldview, Babylon and New Jerusalem coexist in time and space as manifestations of empire and of authentic humanity, respectively. This will be examined further in chapter 6.

While modern maps usually confine themselves to terrestrial arrangements, ancient mapping was concerned with the interplay between heaven and earth. The most striking feature of this interplay was its dynamic character. John Gammie points out that the two fundamental rules of space in the ancient world were that "heaven and earth are not operationally distinct or separate, and that there is both contrast and correspondence between heaven and earth; events in the heavens affect the events that transpire on earth, and vice-versa."[19]

In explaining the ancient notion of "correspondence" between heaven and earth, Gammie quotes Hans Bietenhard:

> Everything on earth has its model and prototype in heaven. Every earthly being and event is prefigured in a heavenly being and event. Thus everything which happens and exists in heaven is of primary importance for the earthly. Every country, every river, every city, every temple—indeed the whole earth—has its heavenly model. The things on earth, whether human or sacred, have been patterned after this heavenly model.[20]

Similarly, Mircea Eliade, in his investigation into ancient myth, writes: "The world that surrounds us, then . . . populated and cultivated areas, navigable rivers, cities, sanctuaries—all these have an extraterrestrial archetype, be it conceived as a plan, as a form, or purely and simply as a 'double' existing on a higher level."[21] In this worldview, an appeal to heaven for justice represented not an abandonment of the social world but an engagement with it.

---

18. Pippin (1994), p. 253.
19. Gammie (1974), p. 360.
20. Ibid., pp. 361-62.
21. Eliade, p. 9.

Revelation is filled with just such an understanding of reality. Tangible realities on earth such as the "prayers of the holy ones," when mingled with incense in heaven by angels (Greek *angelos,* literally "messengers"), can then be returned to earth with profound historical consequence (8:3-5). It is possible to realize New Jerusalem on earth, because it comes down from heaven (21:1-3). According to Revelation heaven had a "door," through which one summoned by an angel could enter (Rev. 4:1-2). Thus, heaven was not a remote or inaccessible reality. To summarize: "John sees some things happen in heaven because God has determined that an equivalent event should shortly happen on earth, but other heavenly events take place because earthly events have made them possible."[22]

This correspondence between heaven and earth is typical of the Hebrew scriptures. In an apocalyptic section of Isaiah (chs. 24-27), the causal connections between heavenly and earthly events are clearly expressed:

> For the windows of heaven are opened,
> and the foundations of the earth tremble . . .
> On that day YHWH will punish
> the host of heaven in heaven,
> and on earth the kings of the earth . . .
> Then the moon will be abashed, and the sun ashamed,
> for YHWH of hosts will reign
> on Mount Zion and in Jerusalem. (Isa. 24:18, 21, 23)

Here the host of heaven is obviously in allegiance with the kings on earth, and both will be punished by God. In the victory song of Judges 5 the stars are seen to fight against the king:

> The stars fought from heaven,
> from their courses they fought against Sisera. (Judg. 5:20)

Thus, the "stars," while remaining in their heavenly orbits, fought against the Canaanite military commander on earth!

We saw in chapter 2 how the book of Daniel evokes the image of a battle in heaven led by the heavenly prince Michael as the basis for assuring the audience in imperial-occupied Judea that they had nothing to fear from the apparent success of the reign of terror of Antiochus IV Epiphanes. What Daniel "saw" in heaven in his dream-visions explained what was happening behind the veil of the imperial propaganda of his own time. Heaven was not for Daniel a place that awaited one after death, but an active participant in the fight against evil on earth, as it was for the Persian Zoroastrians, whose influence Daniel reflects.

The simultaneity of heaven and earth in apocalyptic texts makes it obvious that the apocalyptic worldview is completely at odds with modern concepts of heaven and earth. The following excerpt from *1 Enoch* makes this clear:

---

22. Caird (1962), p. 13.

I saw other lightnings and the stars of heaven. And I saw how he called them each by their names, and they obeyed him. . . . And I asked the angel who was going with me and who had shown me the secret things, "What are these things?" And he said to me, "The Lord of Spirits has shown you the parabolic meaning of each one of them: These are the names of the holy ones who dwell upon the earth and believe in the name of the Lord of Spirits forever and ever." (43:1, 3-4)

The "names" of those who believe on earth are seen as lightning and stars in heaven. Such an understanding of spatiality is impossible to reconcile with the modern scientific notion of heaven and earth.

Heavenly Beings

The heavenly beings feature strongly in Revelation, too, and an understanding of their function is crucial to interpreting the text. The heavenly beings in Revelation include what we would see as heavenly bodies such as stars (*astēr*, 1:16, 20; 2:1, 28; etc.), sun (*hēlios*, 1:16; 6:12; etc.), moon (*selēnē*, 6:12; 8:12; etc.) as well as other beings such as the ubiquitous angels, cherubim, and "elders."

Among John's first-century audience, these terms would be identified with the mythic as well as the physical dimensions of heaven. In the Roman east, the cults of Hēlios and Selēnē had a long history. Further, these gods were an established part of the Roman pantheon, along with Mars, Jupiter, Venus, Saturn, and Mercury. When hearing these titles, a first-century audience would think of a Roman deity, who was understood to have its abode in heaven or "the heavens" but who was also active on earth.

By the time of the Roman Empire, the emperors had attached the authority of the celestial powers to their own person. In 43 B.C.E. gold coins were issued that featured the head of Sol (Latin for "sun"), the moon, and five planets. Minted immediately after the death of Julius Caesar, the coins symbolized the approach of the Great Year, a time of cosmic renewal.[23]

Virgil's *Ninth Eclogue* celebrates the rise of Augustus's star:

> Why, Daphnis, upward gazing, do you mark the ancient
> risings of the Signs?
> Behold where Dionean Caesar's star comes forth,
> In heaven, to gladden all the fields with corn,
> And to the grape upon the sunny slopes her colors
> bring! (9.46-49)

For Virgil, the new age, symbolized by the heavenly figures of sun and moon, was fulfilled with the rise to power of Augustus.

---

23. L. R. Taylor, p. 91.

Throughout the first century of the empire, the heavenly powers continued to be identified with the emperors. Tacitus, for example, describes how Nero saw Hēlios as one of the most important gods, and that an "ancient temple" to Hēlios was located in the Circus Maximus in the city of Rome (*Annals* 15.74). Further, Nero had a statue erected that represented himself surrounded by the rays of the sun. Nero wore the radiate crown of Hēlios and is named in inscriptions "the New Hēlios."[24] The emperors Titus and Domitian minted coins depicting the sun and moon, signifying the eternity of the Flavian dynasty.[25]

According to the Roman myth-makers heaven functioned as the authority behind the Roman Empire. Heaven was regularly invoked as a source of legitimacy by emperors and was understood as such by the imperial subjects. Revelation, however, takes issue with the (mis)use of heaven in imperial rhetoric. William Herzog explains the situation in this way: "stars falling from heaven, the sun (associated almost always with the Emperor) refusing to shine, the moon turning to blood, is assaulting the cosmic imagery (and undermining the symbolic universe) invoked to legitimate Roman rule."[26] The downfall of the heavenly powers in Revelation is a way of seeing that behind the veil the Roman Empire really was fallen. While for those with imperial power the falling of *their* stars was a dis-aster, for John and the *ekklēsiai* the falling of the stars was not disaster but a cause for rejoicing.

Battle between Heaven and Earth

Just as heaven was a battleground in which competing claims were played out, the same was true of earth. As we will see in chapter 5, Revelation's visions of earthly destruction are the apocalyptic expression of God's present judgment on empire. Herzog argues that, across a wide range of ancient writings, "plagues, famines, and earthquakes meant that the earth no longer consented to the 'peace of Rome' which had been fortified by appeals to the fruitfulness of the earth and the security of its peoples."[27]

This contrasted strongly with the scenes of rural idyll that poets such as Virgil linked to the leadership of Augustus. Virgil's *Fourth Eclogue* is a prime example of this description of the "golden age" inaugurated by Augustus:

> Earth will shower you with romping ivy, fox-gloves,
> Bouquets of gypsy lilies and sweetly-smiling acanthus.
> Goats shall walk home, their udders taut with milk, and
>   nobody
> Herding them: the ox will have no fear of the lion . . .

---

24. Neverov, p. 189; D. L. Jones, p. 1029.
25. M. P. Charlesworth, p. 127.
26. Herzog (1985), p. 33.
27. Ibid.

> Traders will retire from the sea, from the pine-built
>   vessels
> They used for commerce: every land will be self-
>   supporting.
> The soil will need no harrowing, the vine no pruning-
>   knife;
> And the tough plowman may at last unyoke his oxen.
> We shall stop treating wool with artificial dyes,
> For the ram himself in his pasture will change his fleeces
>   color,
> Now to a charming purple, now to a saffron hue,
> And grazing lambs will dress themselves in coats of
>   scarlet. (4:18-22, 38-45)

In contradiction to these bucolic portrayals of the Augustan age, Revelation depicts a heaven and earth blasted and destroyed by God's judgment against empire (6:12-14; 8:6-12; 16:1-21; 18:1-24). The destruction is systematic and complete, and none of the citizens of empire will avoid it. Images of a peaceful earth that were linked to the myth of the *Pax Romana* were seen in John's visions to be an outrageous lie. The earth was not at peace with Roman rule, but convulsed and tortured by it.

These visions were based on the assumption that the cosmic order reflected the sociopolitical order. The Roman propagandists saw an ordered cosmos because they consented to Roman rule. If one opposed the political order, however, the natural order would also be seen as awry. This is reflected in the following three quotations from Virgil, Philo of Alexandria, and Revelation, respectively:

> First, you must know that the heavens, the earth and the watery plains of the sea, the moon's bright globe, the sun and the stars are all sustained by a spirit within; for immanent mind, flowing though all its parts and leavening its mass, makes the universe work. (Virgil, *Aeneid* 6.724-27)

> The complete whole around us is held together by invisible powers, which the Creator has made to reach from the ends of the earth to heaven's furthest bounds, taking forethought that what was well bound should not be loosened: for the powers of the universe are chains that cannot be broken. (Philo, *Migration of Abraham* 181)

> The seven angels having the seven trumpets prepared themselves so that they might trumpet. The first trumpeted, and happened hail and fire mixed with blood and it was cast to the earth. . . .
>   The second angel trumpeted, and it was as though a great mountain blazing with fire was cast into the sea. . . .

The third angel trumpeted, and a great star fell from heaven, burning as a lamp, and it fell on a third of the rivers and on the springs of water. . . .

The fourth angel trumpeted, and a third of the sun and a third of the moon and a third of the stars was struck. . . .

Then the fifth angel trumpeted, and I saw a star having fallen out of heaven onto the earth. . . . (Rev. 8:6-9:1)

In these selections we see the limits of debate within the ancient social construction of space. Each reflects the understanding that reality is comprised of both visible manifestations and invisible forces that provide coherence. For all of these writers, the physical order is controlled by forces that can operate independently of human beings. These forces, whether of God, the gods, or their agents, also underwrite the sociopolitical order. The two orders work in direct relationship with each other. There is no cosmology without concrete sociopolitical ramifications and no sociopolitical event without cosmological consequences. This much these writers hold in common.

Yet whereas Virgil the Roman claimed that it was the "immanent mind" that "makes the universe work," and Philo the Egyptian Jew asserted that these "powers" were permanent and "unable to be broken," John of Patmos envisioned the crashing of these "powers" from heaven to earth, the diminishing of the sun and stars, and the shaking of the foundations of the earth. The words of Virgil and Philo are reflective of a worldview that sees value in the present sociopolitical arrangements. Revelation represents a worldview in which the end of these dominant arrangements would be seen as liberation. For the writer of Revelation, contrary to both Virgil and Philo, the *universe did not work* as it should, but this maleficent order *was already destroyed*. John saw what Virgil and Philo refused to countenance—the end of the so-called order guaranteed by the Roman Empire.

A reader of Revelation who attempts to construct a literal world from its swirling visions of past and future, heaven and earth, has to either ignore the paradoxes or twist the text into bizarre scenarios. John, though, expects his audience to be familiar with the conventions of apocalyptic writings, which means that "heaven" is not in the sky or after death, but co-present with daily life, hidden only by a veil.

Heaven as the Source of Truth

John's claim that heaven has revealed these things to him is also a claim that authenticates his message. In being invited to "heaven" by a heavenly angel, John of Patmos is given privileged access to the truth of things. As Richard Bauckham explains:

John (and thereby his readers with him) is taken up into heaven in order to see the world from the heavenly perspective. He is given a glimpse behind the scenes of history so that he can see what is really going on in the events of his time and place.[28]

John contends that heaven reveals the "truth" (Greek *alēthinos*, 21:5; 22:6) about the current order. Revelation did not seek to provide an "objective" or "balanced" account of the Roman Empire. Rather it gave a minority report, but one that came with the full authority of God. This gives it a definitive authenticity. Because John of Patmos had personally seen the apocalyptic truth of heaven and had communicated this through his book, the *ekklēsiai* were able to know that it is where God lives and reigns that constitutes the ultimate reality, not the illusory reality of empire.

If heaven is co-present with earth and the definitive manifestation of the real, Revelation's constant appeal to heaven is not abandonment of earth. On the contrary, the heavenly dimensions of apocalyptic discourse "confirm its commitment to concrete history."[29] Revelation, then, sets the heavenly narrative against the imperial narrative that underpinned the Roman order, in order to inspire a circle of *ekklēsiai* in Roman Asia to live in accordance with God's ways.

REFLECTION QUESTIONS

1. Consider your ideas about the relationship between past, present, and future. Which is most real for you? Do you consider that our society and our lives are controlled by too much of an emphasis on the past, present, or future? Why or why not?

2. How do the prospects for the future affect your life today? Consider global concerns such as the environment, poverty, or war/peace as well as personal concerns such as health or job security.

3. What is your sense of the relationship between our life on earth and the forces of the cosmos? For example, do you feel that we're alone amid a lifeless universe or are affected by the stars, sun, planets, and so forth?

4. Where and/or how do you think of "heaven" as existing? How does this affect how you live day to day?

---

28. Bauckham (1993), p. 7.
29. Myers (1988), p. 341.

5

"Vengeance Is Mine!" Says the Lord

Revelation's Language of Violence and the Practice of a Discipleship of Nonviolence

As one approaches the text of Revelation itself, one of the first stumbling blocks for many is the description of terrible violence and destruction. How can the God of love and compassion revealed by Jesus in the Gospels be the same God that John of Patmos encounters in his visions? Is Revelation—and its apocalyptic kin in the New Testament—expressing the same kind of faith as the Gospels?

Numerous writers have found this aspect of Revelation intolerable. For example, novelist D. H. Lawrence opines:

> The Apocalypse of John is, as it stands, the work of a second-rate mind. . . .
> [it] is the revelation of the undying will-to-power in man, and its sanctifi-
> cation, its final triumph. . . . just as inevitably as Jesus had to have a Judas
> Iscariot among his disciples, so did there have to be a Revelation in the
> New Testament. . . .
>
> John of Patmos . . . was a shameless power-worshipping pagan Jew,
> gnashing his teeth over the postponement of his grand destiny.[1]

In a similar vein, modern writer Michael Grosso in his book *The Millennium Myth* offers these phrases to describe John's text:

- a self-righteous indifference to the fate of others . . .
- It is hard to think of a better word than *sadistic* to describe some of the sentiments expressed . . .

---

1. Lawrence, pp. 66-67, 84.

- exults in sheer triumphalism . . .
- the pleasure of salvation lies in becoming privy to the torments of the damned . . .
- tied to images of imprisonment . . . mired in repression . . .
- utterly barbaric . . .[2]

Perhaps ironically, after condemning Revelation, Grosso sings the praises of the *Enuma Elish*, the Babylonian creation myth that is one of the earliest enshrinements of what Walter Wink calls the "myth of redemptive violence"![3]

In this chapter, we will show why these evaluations of Revelation reflect the failure to understand the nature of John's use of the apocalyptic language of violence. There is no doubt that Revelation is replete with images of carnage and bloodshed. And yet, as we saw in chapter 2, the apocalyptic tradition in which John is deeply rooted has generally been an expression of a call to respond to empire not with warfare but with faithful, nonviolent resistance. Revelation is indeed the product of this tradition. But even more, it is the drawing together of the entire biblical story into a story of its own, one that portrays a God whose journey with humanity leads God to change the divine plan in mid-history, so to speak. It is this story that we will tell in this chapter.

"AT ONCE I WAS IN THE SPIRIT": UNDERSTANDING JOHN'S VISIONARY EXPERIENCES

Central to a proper understanding of the message of Revelation is the fact that the entire text claims to be a report of a visionary experience "in the spirit" (1:10; 4:2; 17:3; 21:10). Modern scholars are fairly evenly divided in either attributing to John some sort of actual, ecstatic experience or in seeing the term "in the spirit" as a literary device that allows him to identify himself with the prophetic tradition as a means of achieving authority with his audience. The absence of consensus among scholars seems to us to reflect not so much a problem in deciphering the language of Revelation, but a post-Enlightenment discomfort with visionary experience. The Age of Reason successfully raised up rational thought as the best path to knowledge while reducing mystical experience to the margins. We saw in chapter 1 how this legacy remains with us in the desperate effort of scientists like Dr. Melvin Morse to distance their research into near-death experiences from that of "religion" or "spirituality." Biblical scholars, educated in the same rationalistic paradigm as others trained in universities, have inherited this distrust of the nonrational. We see the extreme result of this in some of the conclusions of members of the so-called Jesus Seminar, whose research into the "historical Jesus" has determined that all stories about healing "miracles," virgin birth, resurrection, and the like are "symbols" not connected to the actual expe-

---

2. Grosso, pp. 24, 25, 36, 37, 39, emphasis in original.
3. Wink (1992), pp. 13ff.

riences the stories purport to describe. It may in fact be the case, of course, that the Gospel stories of roving demons and sudden cures are mythical elaborations of core experiences which were not as dramatic to their original observers as they appear in their canonical texts. The point isn't that the New Testament texts aren't accurate or true in their claims. Rather, it is that the starting point of many rationalistic interpreters is to *assume* that such supernatural events *cannot or did not* take place.

As we also saw in chapter 1, however, shamanistic experiences—whose descriptions closely parallel the Christian language of "in the spirit"—were well known among virtually all ancient cultures, and were among the most highly respected forms of gaining knowledge. Did the early Israelites think that the stories of Moses' experiences at the burning bush or on Mt. Sinai were "literary devices" or reports of actual encounters with YHWH? Or what about the numerous episodes reporting conversations between YHWH and the patriarchs? What would original audiences have understood by the prophets' repeated claims to speak the direct words of YHWH, or by Daniel's or Ezekiel's reports of heavenly visions? It seems clear that those who developed, preserved, and attempted to live in accordance with the biblical tradition deeply believed in a divinity who could and did make contact with humanity. Sometimes YHWH spoke to people who tried to run away from the divine voice. At other times, those contacts were sought and not received, as in the pleas in the Psalms for a response to prayer during hard times. It is not legitimate to write off these stories as expressions of "primitive" thought. We may find that the shoe is on the other foot; we may discover that it is our devotion to "reason" that is the dead end, and that our ancestors understood much more about life than we do.

In studying the reported mystical experiences of the apostle Paul, Alan F. Segal notes: "Mysticism in first-century Judea was apocalyptic, revealing not meditative truths of the universe but the disturbing news that God was about to bring judgment. . . . Paul is a first-century Jewish apocalypticist, and as such, he was also a mystic."[4] Segal goes on to trace Paul's experience to the mystical traditions of Hebrew scripture, pointing out that the "vocabulary of biblical theophanies and the visions of God in the Hebrew Bible imply ecstasy or paranormal consciousness."[5]

If, therefore, we can put aside our rationalistic lenses and try to see with the eyes of first-century people, we can interpret John's claims as no more and no less than what was claimed by Paul and by Jesus himself: an experience of the divine that was received as an unexpected gift of the Spirit. In the end, this is the authoritative premise of all apocalyptic literature: to have revealed to the narrator an aspect of reality not available to rational consciousness that calls the narrator to share what has been revealed to his or her circle of hearers or readers for their enlightenment.

Our premise in this book, then, is that John is telling, in the words available

---

4. Segal, p. 34.
5. Ibid., p. 52.

to him, of what he truly experienced "in the spirit." This does not mean that Revelation has not been crafted in great detail by its author. It is not a transcript. Rather, it is the literary result of John's reflection on his experience in light of his deep knowledge of Hebrew scripture, the Roman imperial world in Asia, and his faith in Jesus. Mystics throughout the ages have always been faced with the difficult task of "translating" ineffable experience into ordinary language. John naturally chose as his vehicle of expression the language of his ancestors, those whom he understood to have had experiences similar to his own. Our modern near-death-experience literature does the same thing in terms of the language available to the experiencer. Christians who have had a near-death experience often report seeing Christ; agnostics describe a "being of light." It is not a matter of determining which is correct, but in recognizing language as an imprecise means for communicating mystical experiences.

John's own language is more like a collection of verbal pictures than like discursive speech; more like an impressionist painting than like a scientific treatise. Failing to understand this is the first reason that many readers of Revelation are repelled by what they read. John's visions convey *truth*, but *not literal truth*. As we showed in chapter 4, a fair reading of Revelation requires that we understand its method of presenting images of a bifurcated reality, grounded but not bounded by John's ecstatic experience. It would be an impossible, and ultimately meaningless, task to attempt to separate "what John saw" from "what John wrote." The various quests for the Jesus "behind" or "before" the Gospels have yielded no clear picture precisely because they fail to take seriously the Gospels as texts witnessing to the Jesus event in the language of the inherited biblical traditions. It would be even more futile to attempt this kind of separating of the "shell" from the "kernel" in the case of Revelation. Therefore, we will focus on the text that John has given us, knowing from the outset that its visual and auditory images point to, rather than describe, the reality on the divine side of the veil.

THE FIRST SCROLL: UNSEALING THE PLAGUES THAT CALL FOR REPENTANCE

After the messages to the angels of the seven *ekklēsiai* (Rev. 2-3), John finds himself in the spirit for the second time (4:2; cf. 1:10). He sees and hears for the first of seven times the heavenly liturgy, which we will look at in detail in chapter 7. For now, our attention will be focused on what follows the worship scene, as John sees a scroll "in the right hand of the one seated on the throne" which is "written on the inside and on the back" (5:1). It is sealed tightly with seven seals. A "strong angel" then proclaims in a loud voice, "Who is worthy to open the scroll and break its seals?" When no one worthy is found, John gives way to bitter weeping. But one of the twenty-four elders who surround the heavenly throne tells John not to weep, because "the Lion of the tribe of Judah, the Root of David, has conquered [Greek *enikēsen*], so that he can open the scroll and its seven seals" (5:5). The first title, Lion of the Tribe of Judah, recalls Gen. 49:9-10. The second title, Root of David, is unique here, but is obviously similar to the messianic expression "root of Jesse" (Jesse = David's father) found in Isa. 11:10. Both titles therefore express warrior strength. The one whose conquest makes him worthy to open the scroll is apparently the mighty Messiah of God. Furthermore, his conquest engages the battle with the Roman myth of *Nikē* described in chapter 8 below. From his first appearance, the Messiah's function in Revelation is to take on the battle against empire.

But then John reports something surprising. The elder had named the worthy one with titles of power, but when John looks, what he sees is "a Lamb standing as if it had been slaughtered, having seven horns and seven eyes, which are the seven spirits of God sent out into all the earth" (5:6). Not a mighty lion but a Lamb! As Richard Bauckham points out, "[t]here is no substantial evidence that the Lamb was already established as a symbol of the messianic conqueror in pre-Christian Judaism."[6] The image is jarring and central to the message of Revelation. The Worthy One is *both* the Messiah of Jewish expectation who would "conquer" Israel's enemies *and* a Lamb slaughtered by those same enemies. Of course, this is also the central message of the wider New Testament tradition: Jesus the Lamb (cf. John 1:29, 36) conquered empire *through* his acceptance of death on a Roman cross. Throughout Revelation, it is made clear that Jesus' power is the "sword of his mouth" (1:16; 2:12, 16; 19:15, 21). The Word of God is truly powerful, but it is a power that, unlike the sword of empire, operates without bloody violence.

The Greek word translated "slaughtered" is one always used in Revelation in relation to the violent acts of empire (e.g., 6:4, 9; 13:3; 18:24; cf. Jer. 52:10; 1 Macc 1:2). In relation to the Lamb, though, we must go back to the first appearance of Jesus in the text's opening vision. After describing the "one like a Human One" in terms borrowed from previous apocalyptic and other biblical traditions, John hears him say, "I was dead, and see [Greek *idou*], I am alive forever and ever!" (1:18). Rudolph Raber explains that the announcement of Jesus' previous death is followed by "the bellowing attention getter, *idou*, a word not rendered strongly enough by the mild English, 'lo' or 'behold'; better, 'NOW HEAR THIS!' or 'ATTENTION!'"[7] The Human One *was* dead at the hands of empire, but God's power of life is stronger than a Roman execution! It is a basic apocalyptic viewpoint, going back to Daniel: what God desires to live *will* live, regardless of human efforts to thwart life.

It is this messianic Lamb, slaughtered but alive forever and ever, who can open the scroll by breaking its seven seals. After a heavenly liturgy affirms the Lamb's worthiness, the seals begin to be opened in Rev. 6. The first four seals are opened in rapid sequence, releasing four riders on horseback, each with a specific mission, as shown in table 13 below.

---

6. Bauckham (1993), p. 183.
7. Raber, p. 299.

Table 13
THE FOUR HORSES AND THEIR RIDERS

Horse's Color	Rider's Equipment and Mission	Interpretation of the Mission
White	Bow and crown: conquering and to conquer	International military conflict
Red	A great sword: Take peace from the earth so that people would slaughter one another	Civil war and other internal, violent conflict
Black	Pair of scales: A quart of wheat for a day's pay, and three quarts of barley for a day's pay, but do not damage the olive oil and the wine!	Economic exploitation of the poor
Pale green	Death, accompanied by Hades: authority over a fourth of the earth, to kill with sword, famine, and pestilence, and by the beasts of the earth	Usurpation of God's power of judgment

The basic imagery combines Zechariah's vision of four chariots and their colored horses, which represent in Zechariah the four winds of heaven who patrol the earth (Zech. 6:1-8), with Jeremiah's and Ezekiel's prophecy of the four kinds of destroyers sent by YHWH to punish God's people for their idolatry and lack of fidelity (Jer. 15:2-3; Ezek. 14:21). John's vision is of powerful forces unleashed to wreak violence and destruction, yet interpreted as the logical consequence of participation in empire. The first three riders express clearly the primary elements not only of the Roman Empire but of all empires, as seen from an apocalyptic perspective. The first represents violence abroad to secure "peace" (i.e., to "conquer").[8] The mounted archer evokes Rome's eastern enemy, the Parthians,[9] who symbolize all foreign enemies of empire. The second horse and rider symbolize domestic (i.e., internal to empire) violence at all levels of society, as indicated by the Greek word *allēlous* ("one another"). The third pair represents

---

8. Many scholars see the white horse and its rider as Jesus himself, based on the parallel white horse and rider in Rev. 19:11-16, who is clearly Jesus. However, apart from the illogic (a dangerous interpretive principle in approaching apocalyptic!) of the Lamb releasing himself with the unsealing, the parallels with Zechariah, Jeremiah, and Ezekiel seem a stronger basis for interpreting the set of four horses and riders as aspects of the human situation under the condition of empire, which is the first "revelation" of the unsealing.

9. Schüssler Fiorenza (1991), p. 63.

systematic exploitation of the poor for the benefit of the wealthy. The term "a day's pay" (literally, Greek *denarius*) refers to the wage of a day laborer, while the price given for wheat is around eight times the normal amount.[10] It is only oil and wine, traditionally associated with grain as part of God's provision of bounty (e.g., Jer. 31:12, Hos. 2:8), which are protected from the ravages of inflation. As we saw in chapter 3, this reflects the growing practice of *latifundia,* where more profitable commodities were produced at the expense of more staple foods. The final rider, Death itself, has usurped YHWH's own authority to punish, as is clear from the use of the phrase "sword, famine and pestilence," found seventeen times in Jeremiah and seven times in Ezekiel, often accompanied by "beasts," and always used to express God's judgment on the unfaithful. Thus, this first wave of violent imagery expresses the apocalyptic insight that the world's suffering is *allowed* by God, but is more fundamentally a result of *sin*.

Immediately after the four horses and riders are released, though, the fifth seal is opened, revealing "under the altar the souls of those who had been slaughtered for the word of God and for the testimony they had given" (6:9). This is the "alternative" consequence of empire: either participate in the war and domestic violence of the empire, or be slaughtered in attempting to resist it! Death in either direction, and yet, those under the altar are obviously alive in that they can cry out to God, whom they call "Master" (Greek *despotēs*). As David Aune notes: "The term *despotēs,* 'master,' is a regular Greek translation of two Latin terms for the Roman emperor, *dominus* and *princeps*."[11] With this title and the description of the double reason for their death, it is clear that they are the counterparts of those faced with the sword of the fourth rider. They are the ones who have been faithful to the One they name *despotēs*.

There is no reason to limit this group to Christians or to specific persons killed during John's lifetime. Rather, they represent all those prophets and holy women and men throughout history who have suffered empire's reaction against them for testifying against its falsity, oppression, and injustice (cf. 1 Kings 19:14/Rom. 11:2-3; Matt. 23:29-35; Acts 7:51-60). John sees them in heaven crying out in a collective loud voice the ancient supplication of those denied justice in this world, "How long will it be before you judge and avenge our blood on the inhabitants of the earth?" (6:10). The anguished cry "How long?" is found more than fifty times in scripture, most frequently in the Psalms (twenty times) and in the exilic prophet Jeremiah (eight times). The question echoes across the ages from the hearts of those seeking not so much revenge as justice, expressing the hope that their willingness to accept the consequences of their faithful endurance will be repaid with a world made right.

Rather than receiving a direct answer to their plea, however, they are given a white robe "and told to rest a little longer, until the number would be complete both of their fellow slaves and of their brothers and sisters, who were soon to be

---

10. Malina (1995), pp. 122-23.
11. Aune (1998), p. 407.

killed as they themselves had been killed" (6:11). The response expresses not divine indifference but divine *mercy*. The plea comes from those whose pain and suffering have limited their ability to maintain their compassion for the "inhabitants of the earth." But apocalyptic literature reveals the big picture of history, in which God's patience and mercy are greater than humanity's. The time will come, indeed, "for destroying those who destroy the earth" (Rev. 11:18), but it is still "not yet." The tension between God's mercy and God's justice, which these passages strain to express, should not be reduced to chronology, however, in which the "little longer" can be measured as ending in some imminent future. Revelation, here as always, is attempting to name a "both/and" situation: there is still a "little longer" in which to repent and turn toward God *and* justice and judgment *are* being meted out!

This exchange is followed by the opening of the sixth seal, releasing a series of cosmic signs that threaten to turn the created order back into primeval chaos (6:12-14) and preparing for the "new heaven and new earth" that will be revealed later (Rev. 21-22). For now, the signs lead "everyone," from "the kings of the earth" to slaves, to call on the mountains and rocks to shelter them from the direct gaze of God, which has been uncovered by the "rolling up" of the sky like a scroll. This image, befitting the scriptural cosmology that imagined the sky as a kind of tent roof between the earth and God's abode,[12] is pure apocalyptic: the veil is lifted, revealing God and the Lamb, in whose presence no one "on earth" can "stand" without fear and trembling (6:17).

Another brief heavenly liturgy celebrates the sheltering presence of God, and then the seventh seal is opened (8:1). It causes a half-hour of silence, which allows the prayers of the saints, carried by the incense within the golden censers held by seven angels, to be received by God and heard (8:3-4). The silence is in striking contrast to the loud singing otherwise taking place day and night around the heavenly throne. In Zech. 2:13ff., the silencing of the people is a prelude to God's rousing himself to rebuke Satan. Here it serves as the interlude between the powers released by the opening of the seals and the series of seven plagues that follow.

There are many fascinating details about the vision of the seven angels and the seven plagues that we cannot discuss here. Our focus is on the role of the trumpet series in relation to the first scroll, which precedes it, and to the second scroll, which follows it (10:2). The first clue is the trumpets themselves. The image is not of a modern-day brass instrument, of course, but of a ram's horn (*shofar*). As Bruce Malina observes, the trumpet was "the loudest controlled sound humans could produce at the time. . . . Trumpets were not musical instruments, but rather instruments to signal power."[13] The image evokes a wide range of biblical passages that associate the trumpet with the encounter with YHWH and with YHWH's function as divine warrior (e.g., Exod. 19:16; Zech. 9:14). They also

---

12. Roloff, p. 92.
13. Malina (1995), p. 106.

serve as a call to battle, a function granted to YHWH alone (e.g., Josh. 6:4ff., seven trumpets). Finally, trumpets were associated with a warning to repent before it was too late (e.g., Ezek. 33:1-20).

All of these memories come together as the seven angels take their turns blowing their trumpets. The consequence of each trumpet blast is a plague reminiscent of those sent by YHWH against Pharaoh, also intended as calls to repentance (cf. Rev. 8:7 with Exod. 9:23ff.).[14] The trumpet plagues affect only a third of their targets, reinforcing that they function as a warning (cf. Ezek. 5:2). There is nowhere to hide from their power, for the first four plagues affect earth, trees, sea, fresh water, sun, moon, and stars. Thus, it would be impossible for the "inhabitants of the earth" (8:13)—that is, those not sealed with God's seal—to be unaware of the power of God breaking into the world and urging repentance.

The four initial plagues are separated from the final three by the loud voice of an eagle in mid-heaven crying out, "Woe, woe, woe!" (8:13). The first two woes mark off the meaning of the first two scrolls, as we shall see (9:12; 11:14), while the third woe is said to be "coming very soon" (11:14), but its arrival is never narrated. This announcement of the woes is followed by the detailed description of some of Revelation's most bizarre creatures, the war locusts from the abyss. Jeremiah had already used the image of locusts as a metaphor for enemy troops or their horses (Jer. 51:14, 27). John's vision combines their Exodus function among the plagues against Egypt with a reversal of Jeremiah's war image, producing a grotesque scene of "locusts like horses" (9:7) which torture people but are forbidden from eating grass. And then we are told that the horrible armored locusts are not serving God, but "have as king over them the angel of the abyss, his name in Hebrew is Abaddon, and in Greek he is called Apollyon" (9:11). The Greek name means "the destroyer," indicating, in case there is doubt, the function of the locusts' ruler. With the onslaught of the locusts, the first woe has passed.

What, then, is the link between the setting in motion of the plagues by heavenly angels and the terrible sting of battle locusts from the ruler of the abyss and the deadly sweep of the battle horses that follow? The response of those who survive these plagues is the key, narrated in 9:20-21:

> The rest of humankind, who were not killed by these plagues, did not repent [Greek *metenoēsan*] of the works of their hands or give up worshiping demons and idols of gold and silver and bronze and stone and

---

14. Exodus states, as many commentators note, that YHWH sent the plagues on Egypt *and* hardened Pharaoh's heart so that the people could see YHWH's power in action, rather than to get Pharaoh to repent. However, what many commentators fail to see is that the "hardening" of Pharaoh's heart was a polite way of "protecting" YHWH's reputation from accusations of impotence. In other words, it "can't" be that the plagues were "ineffective" if YHWH is all-powerful; therefore, it must have been YHWH's plan all along to harden Pharaoh's heart! Given the interpretation of the change in God's plan which we argue is shown in Revelation, this pious cover-up is no longer necessary as an explanation for the inability of the plagues to lead to repentance, despite that being their obvious goal.

wood, which cannot see or hear or walk. And they did not repent of their murders or their sorceries or their fornication or their thefts.

As we will show in chapter 6, the specific list of sins named here is a catalogue of the vices of Rome in particular, and of empire in general. The plagues are clearly directed at getting those who support the imperial program to "repent," to turn away from the imperial and local cults, which support the violence and exploitation released by the four horses and their riders, and to turn toward God. Thus, the plagues are the direct work of "the destroyer," but are intended to fulfill a divine purpose of leading people away from evil and back to God (cf. Wisd. of Sol. 12:8-11). This view is reinforced by Amos 3:6, part of a passage that forms much of the background of the following scene: "Is a trumpet blown in a city, and the people are not afraid? Does disaster befall a city, unless YHWH has done it?"

And, perhaps surprisingly, the plagues are unsuccessful in accomplishing their mission! It is precisely this failure of the plagues to lead people to repentance that provokes another strong angel to bring forth the second scroll, a "little" one (10:2). The description of this tremendous angel with one foot on land and the other on the sea, with a face like the sun and legs like pillars of fire, contrasts radically with the little scroll that he holds. Unlike the first scroll, this one is already open. The angel gives "a loud shout, like a lion roaring," to which "the seven thunders" respond in kind. John is told not to write down the speech of the seven thunders; his attention must remain on the angel and the scroll. After swearing to the Creator that *chronos* (i.e., "earth" time) will no longer prevent *kairos* (i.e., "heavenly" time; cf. Hab. 2:3 LXX), the angel announces, "in the days when the seventh angel is to blow his trumpet, the mystery of God will be fulfilled, as he announced the gospel [Greek *euangelisen*] to his slaves the prophets" (10:7). What is this mystery of God announced to God's slaves the prophets?

THE SECOND SCROLL: FROM PLAGUES TO FAITHFUL WITNESS

As Aune points out, the Greek *mustērion* was sometimes used in ancient Jewish texts to refer to "secrets of state" or the hidden "plans of the king."[15] But in our apocalyptic text, the *mustērion* of the divine king is being revealed before our eyes. To unravel this mystery, we must listen more closely to two biblical texts underlying this proclamation of "good news." First, we hear Amos 3:7-8:

Surely the Lord YHWH does nothing, without revealing [LXX *apocalupse*] his secret [Hebrew *sôdô,* "secret"] to his slaves the prophets. The

---

15. Aune (1998), p. 569.

lion has roared; who will not fear? The Lord YHWH has spoken; who can but prophesy?

Second, we hear Dan. 12:4-10:

"But you, Daniel, keep the words secret [LXX (Old Greek) *kaluptō*] and the book sealed until the time of the end. Many shall be running back and forth, and evil shall increase." Then I, Daniel, looked, and two others appeared, one standing on this bank of the stream and one on the other. One of them said to the man clothed in linen, who was upstream, "How long shall it be until the end of these wonders?" The man clothed in linen, who was upstream, raised his right hand and his left hand toward heaven. And I heard him swear by the one who lives forever that it would be for a time, two times, and half a time, and that when the shattering of the power of the holy people comes to an end, all these things would be accomplished. I heard but could not understand; so I said, "My lord, what shall be the outcome of these things?" He said, "Go your way, Daniel, for the words are to remain secret and sealed until the time of the end. Many shall be purified, cleansed, and refined, but the wicked shall continue to act wickedly. None of the wicked shall understand, but those who are wise shall understand."

The Amos passage is echoed in the angel's reference to the secret/mystery of God announced/revealed to God's "slaves the prophets." Meanwhile, Daniel was told to keep secret (or "unrevealed") and to seal a book until the "time of the end." Daniel heard but did not understand the message of the figure dressed in linen, who, like Revelation's angel, swore by the One who lives forever. The time had not yet come to reveal the secret. As Richard Bauckham points out, the Amos text "makes it clear that to the prophets themselves it remained a secret, while also suggesting its character as the good news of the coming of God's kingdom."[16] This is reinforced by the command to Daniel to "seal" the book until a later time.

In Revelation, however, the scroll which announces the fulfillment of God's mystery is open; the time awaited by Daniel has now come! The difference between the time of Amos and Daniel, on the one hand, and that of John of Patmos, on the other, is the arrival of the Lamb who was slaughtered, the one worthy to open the first, sealed scroll.[17] In a few verses, we will see how this event is revealed as the turning point in history, the public proclamation of a change in God's plan that separates the first scroll from the one now given to John, who is also one of God's slaves the prophets (Rev. 22:9, a verse preceding an echo of Dan. 12:4, 10 in Rev. 22:10-11).

John is told to "take and eat" the open scroll, a phrase with decidedly eucharistic overtones (Matt. 26:26), but also with echoes of Ezek. 3:3. When

---

16. Bauckham (1993), p. 261.
17. Cf. Beale (1999), p. 543.

Ezekiel eats the scroll, which tastes like honey, it empowers him to prophesy to the exiles in Babylon. John, however, finds out, just as the angel predicts, that what tastes sweet in the mouth is bitter in the stomach (10:9-10), and yet it leads John too to prophesy (10:11).

The prophetic authority is given to God's *two witnesses* for "1,260 days," a period identical to that described as "forty-two months" in which the nations will be allowed to "trample over the holy city" and the "time, two times and half a time" heard by Daniel in the passage quoted above (cf. Rev. 12:6, the time of the woman's nourishment in the wilderness; 13:5, the time of the first Beast's authority). The time period, much beloved by prophecy writers as half the time of "the Tribulation," refers here not to a literal period of three and a half years but to the more general "half the time," or, more simply put, "temporarily."[18] There is a beginning and an end to the period of witness, but how long that is to last in human measurement is not revealed (cf. Mark 13:4, 32). The point is not to satisfy human curiosity about the future but to express the more important notion that God's plan *will* come to fulfillment.

We should also resist the temptation to which many mainstream commentators succumb to try to overidentify the two witnesses as specific biblical or historical figures.[19] Rather, we should see them as what the biblical tradition required to legitimate an act of witness, that is, two men (e.g., Deut. 17:6; John 8:17).[20] Nothing can prevent their act of prophetic witness, but once they have completed their testimony, they are defenseless against "the beast that comes up from the abyss [who] will make war on them and conquer them and kill them" (11:7). This deadly opponent, apparently the same figure as the king of the war-locusts (9:11), will be the focus of 13:11-18, where his imperial role as propagandist for the emperor is revealed. In that role, the two prophetic witnesses must be destroyed so that the imperial message cannot be unveiled as the diabolic lie that it is.

Empire is allowed not only to murder God's witnesses but also to dishonor them by leaving their dead bodies in the city's main street and not allow them to be buried, while the inhabitants of the earth celebrate the death of those who "had been a torment" to them (11:8-10). The place of this gruesome scene is "the great city that is called in the spirit Sodom and Egypt, where also their Lord was crucified." Again, we should not attempt to identify this locale only with Jerusalem (where Jesus was crucified) or Rome (where Christians were burned by order of Nero). Rather, we should heed the words of the text, noting that these names are "in the spirit," that is, they are apocalyptic names. The "Great City," as we will show in chapter 6, indicates any imperial power center that attempts to hide itself from God.

---

18. Bauckham (1993), pp. 400-401. Using gematria and ancient numerology, Bauckham develops a complex but fascinating case arguing that in Revelation "rectangular" numbers (such as 42 or 1,260) are ambiguous, "triangular" numbers (such as 666) represent the Beast, while "square" numbers (such as 144) represent God/heaven.

19. Aune (1998), pp. 598-602, surveys the numerous attempts.

20. Giblin (1991), p. 114.

But in the midst of all this demonic gloating, an astonishing event occurs:

After the three and a half days, the breath of life from God entered them, and they stood on their feet, and those who saw them were terrified. Then they heard a loud voice from heaven saying to them, "Come up here!" And they went up to heaven in a cloud while their enemies watched them. At that moment there was a great earthquake, and a tenth of the city fell; seven thousand people were killed in the earthquake, and the rest were terrified and gave glory to the God of heaven. (Rev. 11:11-13)

As with Jesus, who "was dead, but look! is alive forever and ever" (1:18), so too with God's witnesses, whom the imperial forces of death cannot hold. This event, unlike the trumpet plagues, leads first to terror, but then to the giving of "glory to the God of heaven." With this happening, we are told that the "second woe has passed" (11:14). Furthermore, it leads to the long-delayed trumpet blast from the seventh angel, which leads not to a plague like the others but to a heavenly liturgy celebrating the fact that the "empire of the world has become the empire of our Lord and of his Messiah, and he will reign forever and ever" (11:15). How can we now put the two woes and seven trumpets together, and with them, the mystery of the two scrolls?

Scholars have long debated the relationship between the two scrolls. Some have considered them to be the same scroll presented in sealed and open form; others as two different scrolls with no particular relationship to one another; still others as two specific kinds of books known from evidence of royal or temple documents in other ancient cultures. We propose our own interpretation of the scrolls based on the evidence presented in Revelation, the nature of the apocalyptic tradition, and the overarching purpose of the book itself.

We have seen that Revelation frames the story of the scrolls around two specific symbols: the two woes and the issue of repentance. The Lamb opens the seals of the first scroll, and out come both horses/riders and trumpet-angels bringing plagues upon the earth. The scroll itself is never read, at least not for our ears. But the plagues, as we have seen, conclude with failure; they were intended to lead the inhabitants of the earth to repent of their participation in empire and to join in the worship of the One on the throne as the true ruler of all creation.

The second scroll, a little one, contains not plague-causing angels but prophetic witnesses who are killed by empire yet are raised by God to new life. This event, unlike the plagues, is not a failure (despite its initial appearance as such with the murder of the witnesses) but a great success: it leads directly to the giving of glory to God by those who survive and the grand heavenly liturgy acknowledging the sovereignty of God and of God's Messiah.

To put the two scrolls together requires us to consider one of the elements of most apocalyptic texts that scholars usually consider to be absent from Revelation: the *heavenly historical review*. The classic biblical example is Dan. 7-12, in which Daniel's dreams and visions are interpreted by the angel as the story of the rise and fall of recent empires, as seen from a heavenly perspective. The setting of the text's story world in the Babylonian exile—while the text was almost certainly written four hundred years later during the reign of Antiochus IV Epiphanes—leads scholars to refer to this type of historical review as *ex eventu* (or "after the event") prophecy. That is, within the story, Daniel's visions appear to be speaking of the future; however, to even the original audience, they are about the historical past. Only the final narrated event—the actual fall of Antiochus IV Epiphanes—is before-the-fact prophecy, which, as it turned out, incorrectly predicted the means of Antiochus's demise. The point is simply to note the importance to Daniel's purpose of placing the current events of the author's time in the bigger picture of history, that is, to provide a God's-eye perspective on the sweep of time.

Ex eventu prophecy is a common feature of many apocalypses, including ones we have briefly examined such as 4 Ezra and *2 Baruch*. It is an element accompanied by *pseudonymity*, the attributing of authorship to a famous biblical character from the distant past as a means of giving the text authority. Revelation appears not to be pseudonymous; John of Patmos, whoever he was, was certainly not a famous biblical patriarch or sage of the past. Furthermore, the text's ostensible story world—the Asian *ekklēsiai* in the late first century C.E.—appears to be identical to its author's world. Since its narration takes place at the same time as its composition, it does not contain *ex eventu* prophecy and is therefore generally not thought to contain historical review.

At the same time, scholars also recognize that Revelation is unique in many ways within what they define as the genre of apocalypse. For example, the absence of pseudonymity is unusual, if not unprecedented. What if Revelation's uniqueness includes another element, namely, the presence of historical review not as *ex eventu* prophecy but as a summary interpretation of the entire biblical journey leading up to the messianic age of New Jerusalem?

From this perspective, the scrolls suddenly take on a clear and crucial role. The first scroll, filled with plagues, is the story of God's people from the beginning up until the Christ-event.[21] It tells of a God deeply desiring to lead people out of empire's slavery and into freedom, but constantly running into the tendency of the people to be unfaithful, both in terms of practicing idolatry and in terms of failing to live according to the way of YHWH. To empire, God's acts of liberation are plagues. The threat of plagues also hover over God's own people whenever they whore after empire's gods. It is in precisely these terms that the summary conclusion to the story of the first scroll is presented (9:20-21). The evocation of Exodus memories sets the story not specifically in the days of Moses and Egypt, but more broadly along the entire course of Israel's history from Exodus to exile and beyond. God attempted to get the people to repent and

---

21. Of course, the story of Israel's journey also includes the conquest tradition, in which human violence against peoples marked as "enemies of YHWH" is legitimated by claims that YHWH ordered the Israelites to perform it. Revelation does not address this violence directly, although its reservation of "vengeance" to YHWH alone implicitly critiques this tradition. One could well read the conquest tradition as Israel's attempt to justify its own imperialist yearnings with divine authorization for the murder of the people already in the land Israel sought to occupy. Cf. Bailie, pp. 153-66.

return to the Lord through threats of judgment and terrible punishment, as the prophets repeatedly attest. However, in historical Israel as in the story of the first scroll, these threats were largely unsuccessful. Idolatry and accommodation to empire were temptations to which God's people constantly succumbed.

The lesson of the first scroll, then, is that *threats of punishment are not an effective means of leading people to repentance* (cf. Isa. 42:25; 43:19).[22] This is the meaning of the scroll, which was understood only by the Lamb who was slaughtered. Revelation, remarkably, suggests that this was a lesson that God needed to learn! If we are shocked by the idea that God's plan for the course of history could be affected by human behavior, let us pause for a moment to remember the story of Noah and the Flood.

> Now the earth was corrupt [LXX *ephtharē;* note parallel in Rev. 11:18 below] in God's sight, and the earth was filled with violence. And God saw that the earth was corrupt; for all flesh had corrupted its ways upon the earth. And God said to Noah, "I have determined to make an end of all flesh, for the earth is filled with violence because of them; now I am going to destroy them along with the earth." (Gen. 6:11-13)

It is obvious that the destruction that God announces in this passage was not part of the plan according to Gen. 1-3.[23] It is God's experience with humanity that leads to this first change of course: time to wipe the slate clean and start over. John of Patmos, in considering the Christ-event in light of his visionary experience and the pastoral needs of the Asian *ekklēsiai*, studied the scriptures with tremendous attention, as we see in the creative use of earlier biblical texts in nearly every verse of Revelation. In the course of his reflection, we suggest, he came to a startling but powerful understanding: *the death and resurrection of Jesus the Lamb revealed a change in God's plan.* The second scroll, the little one, expresses the new divine strategy. In place of threats of violence, God would lead people to a change of heart by sending prophets—starting with the Hebrew prophets (cf. Rev. 6:9)—so filled with the Word of God that they would be willing to be killed rather than to refrain from witnessing publicly to that Word. And God would vindicate their devotion with the most powerful act of divine sovereignty possible: the returning to life of the dead. This is the conquest that the Lamb made of empire, which subsequent Christians are called to continue in the ongoing-yet-already-won battle between God and empire. And sure enough, the new plan is "successful" where the old one was not. The experience of the murdered witnesses being raised from death leads people to acknowledge God as true sovereign.

---

22. Brueggemann (1998b), pp. 51, 58-59.

23. While scholars might note here that the Gen. 1 story is a "P" (Priestly) text composed at a much later date than the "J" (Yahwist) strand of the Flood story, there is no doubt that even J presents the Flood as YHWH's response to human corruption and violence, not as part of YHWH's original design.

We can now see how John has woven together his biblical sources with his visionary experiences. We noted the clear echoes of the quoted passages from Amos and Daniel that sound in the angelic announcement of the second scroll. Daniel, we recall, was told to seal up for the Endtimes the book telling of God's secret. Daniel could not understand the meaning of the book; it was not yet the time.[24] But Jesus *did* understand what Daniel could not. The mystery that remained a secret to Amos, but which the prophet understood would not always be secret, is now revealed in the death and resurrection of Jesus. That is, while the Hebrew prophets were willing to die for the Word of God, their message continued to express God's threats aimed at repentance. That is, they were "prophets" as John speaks of them, but they did not understand the "secret" of God's changed strategy as Jesus did. While scholars considering Daniel on its own interpret the command to seal up the book as a way to explain why it apparently lay hidden from the time of exile until the time of its proclamation, John of Patmos read it another way. For him, Daniel's book lay hidden not until the time of Antiochus IV Epiphanes but until the time of Jesus. Daniel's sealed book is precisely the second scroll, the one now open in the angel's hand and given to John to eat. It is a bittersweet scroll, for it contains both "good news" and tragedy. God does indeed reign now despite the pretensions of empire, but the earthly power of evil will continue to cause suffering and death for many. The conclusion of the second woe does not announce a future coming of God's reign, but its fulfillment *now*. This is an element of apocalyptic bifurcation that we explored in chapter 4, but it is also a revelation that distinguishes John's text from Daniel's. The victory of the Lamb has already inaugurated the Endtimes. It is this event that leads to the final trumpet blast, the completion of the messages of the scrolls. All that remains is for people to respond by choosing to live in accordance with the ways of the True Sovereign rather than with the ways of empire.

THE BOWL PLAGUES:
DESTROYING THOSE WHO DESTROY THE EARTH

If the events expressed in the context of the two scrolls are in a sense the "whole story," what of the series of seven further plagues poured from the "seven golden bowls full of the wrath of God" (15:7ff.)? If the trumpet plagues were failed attempts to generate repentance, what is the purpose of another series of plagues cast upon the earth? One of the most difficult aspects of divine reality for many inculturated into liberal humanism to accept is that of *judgment*. Most mainline churches have abandoned the old "fire and brimstone" pastoral strategy in favor of a new, Jesus-loves-you approach. This is certainly a healthy develop-

---

24. Although the author of the book of Daniel certainly understood the Endtime as referring to the time of Antiochus IV Epiphanes (i.e., the author's own time; see chapter 2 above), John's use of Hebrew scripture allows him to read Daniel within the wider biblical story and thus interpret his own time as that of Daniel's Endtime.

ment to some extent and, indeed, reflects a pattern similar to the transition from the first scroll to the second. Fire-and-brimstone rhetoric often filled people with fear and guilt, leading them to feel bad both about themselves and about God. However, the dropping of all homiletic references to God's "wrath" or judgment results in an incomplete Christian message, for the voices of the souls under the altar continue to cry out, "How long?" When will there be justice? In other words, will evil ever be banished from our midst, or will we always be faced with the tragic choice of whether to be a part of empire's violence as perpetrators or as victims? These questions have lost none of their urgency in our time, as we pointed out in chapter 1 in examining the reasons for the popularity of premillennialism. The prophecy writers find "the way out" in the doctrine of the Rapture of the holy ones and the destruction of evil in the lake of fire. Is this truly the message of Revelation? Do the bowl plagues simply inaugurate this Endtime chronology?

What premillennialists take seriously that mainline church members should remember is the *necessity of God's judgment against unrepentant evil*. Plagues *were* ineffective as a road to repentance. But the task of the bowl plagues is not repentance but *justice* in response to the cry of those under the altar. They reveal the tragic fact that some people seem unwilling to repent; they are just as committed to the worship of empire's Beasts as the two witnesses and the countless multitude in the heavenly choir are to the worship of the One on the throne and the Lamb. How long will unrepentant evil be allowed to wreak havoc? This is the question that the bowl plagues address.

The pouring out of the first six bowls forms an A-B-A' pattern as follows:

> A: 16:2-4: three angels and bowls
> B: 16:5-7: heavenly acclamation of God's justice
> A': 16:6-12: three angels and bowls

The effect of this structure is to focus the plagues around the proclamation that the purpose of all this violence is the establishment of justice. As the heavenly choir proclaimed upon the blowing of the seventh trumpet,

> The nations raged, but your wrath has come, and the time for judging the dead, for rewarding your slaves, the prophets and holy ones and all who fear your name, both small and great, and for destroying those who destroy [Greek *diaphtheirontas*] the earth. (Rev. 11:18; cf. Jer. 51:25 [LXX 28:25])

The "B" section internally repeats this A-B-A' pattern to underscore the theme:

> A: 16:5: You are just, O Holy One . . . for you have judged
> B: 16:6: because they shed the blood of holy ones and prophets, you
>   have given them blood to drink. It is what they are worthy of!
> A': 16:7: Yes, O Lord God Almighty, your judgments are true and just!

The punishment befits the crime: those who shed blood must now drink blood.

The call for a clearing away of the destroyers is also a clear echo of God's decision to bring on the Flood in the Genesis passage quoted above from the Septuagint, where the verb *phtheirō* ("corrupt" or "ruin") is used four times in relation to the earth. The response of those judged by the plagues is both an acknowledgment that the plagues come from the one who is God and a clear rejection of God's sovereignty over their lives. Twice the people blaspheme, first "the name of God" and second "the God of heaven," and twice they refuse to repent (16:9, 11). As Jacques Ellul writes, this blasphemy and refusal mean "not at all that [humanity] is lost, but that [people] declare [themselves] lost, which is a wholly different thing."[25] The cries of "How long?" clash like cymbals against the softer sounds of God's infinite mercy, leading to the time of judgment against those who, knowing who God is, stubbornly will not submit to God's ways. Like a ticking time bomb in a nursery, or a nuclear weapon in a silo, these "swords" must be *beaten* into "plowshares." For God's people to live in true *shalom*, evil must be demolished, a task that, unfortunately, requires force to carry out.

A brief look at the sequence of bowl plagues (table 14) shows how each one corresponds to a specific "sin" of empire. This should not be understood as a "punishment" initiated by God, as modern fundamentalists have interpreted the link between homosexuality and AIDS or between a "permissive" society and natural disasters, but as the apocalyptic perspective on the *actual* effects of empire's sins. From behind the veil, John sees what is really going on, despite empire's claims that its actions bring "peace and security" (cf. 1 Thess. 5:3). The bowls reveal that justice has already been meted out in accordance with what empire "is worthy of" (Rev. 16:6).[26]

John's deep reading of the biblical tradition and his experience of the tremendous power of the Roman Empire showed how each encounter between God's people and empire results in a wider bifurcation between heaven and earth. As the journey of God's people unfolds, the consequences of abandoning the covenant in favor of empire become worse. The plagues reflect this progression in their images of universal destruction. With Babel, only a tower needed to be demolished and languages diffused in order to dissipate empire's power. With Egypt, what was required to liberate those who chose YHWH was the destruction of Pharaoh's "chariots and charioteers." Israel's own claims to empire were punished with exile, a theretofore unimaginable consequence of disobedience to YHWH. With Babylon, the ante was raised even more: prophetic images of rape and burning polarize the opposing choices more than ever. Now, with Rome, John sees that the choice is all or nothing. Either people choose God, or the whole world is threatened. As we will see in chapter 9, empire today has reached the ultimate opposition to the way of YHWH. Humanity will either reject empire definitively, or the earth's and humanity's future will be literally threatened.

Thus, the bowl plagues reflect John's sense of "both/and" in relation to humanity's refusal to repent. The battle with empire is repeated cyclically

---

25. Ellul (1977), p. 183.
26. E.g., Beale (1999), p. 814.

throughout history, and the increasingly destructive consequences of it will eventually cause humanity to run out of chances. For God's justice to be revealed,
those who cooperate with and promote empire must be allowed to experience the
terrible consequences of their choice. Thus, the judgment described by the bowl
plagues is both the "natural" consequence of imperial sin and the deliberate act
of YHWH in bringing forth justice, albeit justice seen only "behind the veil."

Table 14 THE BOWL PLAGUES		
Bowl Plague	*Reference to Empire's Sin Requiring Judgment*	*Link between Punishment and the Sin*
1. "foul and painful sore came on those who had the mark of the Beast and who worshiped its image." (16:2)	"no one can buy or sell who does not have the mark, that is, the name of the Beast or the number of its name." (13:17)	Participation in empire's economics is revealed as self-destructive
2. "sea . . . became like the blood of a corpse, and every living thing in the sea died." (16:3)	Beast from the sea makes war on the holy ones and sheds their blood (13:1, 7, 10)	The empire's murderous ways pollute its own source: the sea/chaos
3. "rivers and the springs of water . . . became blood." (16:4)	Beast from the sea makes war on the holy ones and sheds their blood (13:1, 7, 10)	Those who collude with imperial murder drink human blood (16:6)
4. "sun . . . was allowed to scorch them with fire" (16:8)	"performs great signs, even making fire come down from heaven to earth" (13:13; cf. 7:16)	This fire "stolen" from heaven (i.e., the claim to divinity) is revealed as self-destructive
5. "throne of the Beast, and its kingdom was plunged into darkness" (16:10)	"dragon gave it his power and his throne and great author-ity." (13:2)	The worship of emperors is revealed as the cause of darkness, not light
6. "great river Euphrates, and its water was dried up in order to prepare the way for the kings from the east." (16:12)	"I rule as a queen; I am no widow, and I will never see grief" (18:7)	An "invasion" by the neigh-boring kingdom of Parthia reveals the *Pax Romana* to be temporary, not eternal
7. "The great city was split into three parts, and the cities of the nations fell." (16:19)	Great city murdered the witnesses and crucified Jesus (11:8)	The attempt by the "great city" to crush Jesus and his followers causes its own collapse

What is absolutely essential to observe, however, is that *this task belongs exclusively to God*. As proclaimed in Deut. 32, a text frequently evident in the background of Revelation,[27] "Vengeance is mine!" says YHWH (Deut. 32:35). This cry is echoed directly in the New Testament in Rom. 12:19 and Heb. 10:30, underscoring the fact that this distinction between divine vengeance and human vengeance was clearly at the heart of the early Christian understanding of justice. Nowhere does Revelation authorize or glorify human violence. To the contrary, its ceding to God of the exclusive authority to act with violence when required by justice marks off this behavior as forbidden to humanity. Human violence is a sign of the "mark of the Beast" (e.g., 16:2). Those who bear God's mark on their foreheads are separated from the followers of the Beast by their refusal to support the legitimation of human violence, which is a central task of the propaganda of empire (13:4, 13-15).[28] They are the ones who receive empire's violence in trust that it is not conclusive (e.g., 20:4).

Thus we see that John's visions have revealed to him and to his audience the "secret" about evil and violence hidden from the prophets but understood by the Lamb who was slaughtered. God continues to call people to repentance, but no longer with threats of violence. God's people—those who dwell in heaven, or as it is called apocalyptically, New Jerusalem, as we'll see in the next chapter—are to bring the cry for repentance into the city streets, knowing that they may be mocked, rejected, or even killed for their efforts. Their resurrection, however, is the new key to God's call for repentance. And for those who refuse to repent, who blaspheme the one they know to be God, there will be judgment and justice. The souls under the altar killed for their witness *do* receive an answer to their question of "How long?" God's justice destroys evil while at the same time God's mercy grants a "little while longer" to those who may yet repent. Revelation does not *resolve* this paradox; it *reveals* it. But it also warns that the time of judgment, like a thief in the night, can arrive just when one is tempted to find rest in the false security of empire.

REFLECTION QUESTIONS

1. Given the entire sweep of biblical narrative, do you think
   - God remains the same throughout the Bible because God cannot change
   - God changed from a violent warrior to a loving parent in response to God's relationship with humanity
   - God didn't change, but people's perception of God changed
   - God changed from warrior to parent in the Gospels, but changes back in Revelation?

---

27. E.g., compare Rev. 9:10/Deut. 32:21-24; Rev. 10:5-7/Deut. 32:40-41; Rev. 17:6/Deut. 32:33; etc.

28. Cf. Beale (1999), pp. 414-15.

2. What is your sense of God's relationship with violence? Does God allow it without response, actively oppose it, or cause it? Consider various types of violence: earthquakes and volcanoes, disease and accidents, wars and other intentional human violence.

3. Do you believe that nonviolence is a reasonable way to live in the world? How would our homes, our churches, and our culture be transformed if we took the call to nonviolence seriously?

4. Do you believe that justice will ultimately be realized? When and how do you conceive of justice taking place? How does this conception affect your idea of God and the way you live?

6

The City of Our God

Babylon or New Jerusalem?

What do the Roman Catholic Church, the United Nations, the United States of America, a New World Order, and a One-World Government have in common? The answer: each has been discerned by various readers of Revelation as comprising "Babylon" in our midst. The images of Babylon and New Jerusalem have galvanized popular religious consciousness and entered our Western cultural idiom. Time and time again people have discerned that Babylon exists in their day. New Jerusalem, too, has been located squarely within history. As we have seen, the colonization of North America was explicitly understood as the embodiment of this "City-on-a-Hill." The impulse that has led so many to read the signs of their own times against Revelation's description of these two cities has a sound foundation. The images of Babylon and New Jerusalem are indeed an apocalyptic discernment of the sociohistorical realities of John's day. Yet before we can apply these apocalyptic metaphors to social realities in our own time and place, we must grapple with how they are presented in the book of Revelation.

We saw in chapter 4 that Revelation presents Babylon and New Jerusalem as coexistent but contrary realities. This pair of apocalyptic cities is the master metaphor of the book. According to Revelation, the truth about these opposing social realities was gained via the medium of John's apocalyptic visions on the island of Patmos. Once the veil of imperial propaganda was lifted, John saw that the Roman Empire was "really" Babylon.[1] This is not to say that there is a literal correspondence between John's vision and the Roman Empire. Nor are these references to literal cities. While John saw Rome as an embodiment of Babylon, the ideological significance of Babylon extends far beyond the historical capital of the Roman Empire. *Rather, Babylon exists wherever sociopolitical power coa-*

---

1. Stringfellow (1973), p. 49.

lesces into an entity that stands against the worship of YHWH alone. Babylon expresses God's judgment on all human attempts to displace God from the center of reality in favor of human power arrangements. John discerned that imperial Rome was such an arrangement. Revelation taps into the biblical memories of Babel and Babylon, but John's visionary experience allows him to see beyond the specifics of historical expressions and into the eternal—and infernal—nature of empire.

New Jerusalem, on the other hand, is not a fairy tale castle in the sky or a dream awaiting our personal death or the "End of the world." Nor should New Jerusalem be equated simply with the seven *ekklēsiai* in Roman Asia, or even with the faithful members of those communities. *Rather, New Jerusalem is found wherever the human community rejects the lies and violence of empire and places God at the center of its shared life.* Revelation exhorts its audience to come out of Babylon and to dwell in New Jerusalem.

Traditional interpretation has seen these cities as existing in chronological succession: New Jerusalem comes down from heaven after Babylon is destroyed. This interpretation, however, is not reconcilable with the text. After depicting the rise and fall of the Beasts and of Babylon, and the elimination of Death and Hades, the coming of New Jerusalem is described. In a linear schema, the arrival of New Jerusalem should follow the end of the evil empire. Yet even with the arrival of the perfect city, evil is still a reality (21:8; 22:15):

> Blessed the ones washing their robes
> that they may have the right to the tree of life
> and that they may enter into the city by the gates.
> Outside are the dogs, and the sorcerers and the fornica-
>   tors
> and the murderers and the idol-worshippers
> and all loving and making illusion. (22:14-15)

That evil still exists outside New Jerusalem has presented a problem for traditional interpreters. Some have ignored the dilemma. Others have argued that the text as we have it was subject to a later re-arrangement by an editor. As Ronald Preston and Anthony Hanson state the problem:

> As they stand, the order of events in ch. 21 and 22 is most confusing; e.g. heaven and earth are passed away in 21:1 and all evil forces have been eliminated by the end of chapter 20, yet in 21:8 and 22:14-15 we have a state of affairs where the wicked are still very much in existence.[2]

Like others before them, Preston and Hanson saw that to resolve this problem it is "almost essential" to posit the existence of an "editor who re-arranged his

---

2. Preston and Hanson, p. 129.

materials."[3] Their solution is to rearrange the text of chapters 20-22. They argue that the original text described two cities—the "Millennial City" on earth and the "Eternal City" in heaven—where the text as we have it describes only one city, New Jerusalem.

But what if the text as we have it is correct? How can we make sense of this apparent problem? In the bifurcated worldview we sketched in chapter 4 the problem disappears. The two cities operate alongside each other in first-century Roman Asia. George Caird named the situation this way: "In the daily life of Smyrna and Pergamum, Babylon and Jerusalem exist side by side. Their citizens rub shoulders in the streets of Sardis and Philadelphia."[4] As Stringfellow expressed it, in Revelation the two cities "become recognizable in the present, common history of the world."[5]

The descriptions of Babylon and New Jerusalem are structured into the climax of the book. They are explored separately in 17:1-19:10 and 21:9-22:9, respectively. These sections were written as parallel units, as is revealed by their almost identical introductory and concluding phrases. This literary construction encourages the audience to draw a dramatic contrast between the two cities. This contrast is fundamental to the apocalyptic bifurcation that stands at the heart of Revelation.

From the outset of the visions, the apocalyptic "Great Whore"[6] is set in stark contrast to the apocalyptic "Bride, the wife of the Lamb." Just as Babylon is both city and "whore," so New Jerusalem is both city and "bride." In fact, virtually every image used to describe the imperial reality represented by Babylon has a counterimage that parodies the reality represented by New Jerusalem. Table 15 lists some of the contrasts that are made between Babylon and New Jerusalem.

The contrast is manifest in the respective descriptions of the two cities. Babylon is depicted as corrupt and corrupting. The city is the dwelling place of evil, a smoking ruin. In contrast, New Jerusalem is depicted as the ideal city. It is filled with the glory of God. In the world of Roman Asia, where civic competition manifested itself in the making of ever grander claims for one's own city versus the city down the road (see chapter 3 above), the assertions contained in these contrasts can be seen as civic competition on a mythic scale. Rather than acrimonious debate about whether Ephesus, Smyrna, or Pergamum was the greatest city, John saw that the real competition is between Babylon and New Jerusalem, between the city of the Beast and the city of the Lamb, between the Dragon's empire and the empire of the faithful followers of Jesus.

---

3. Ibid.

4. Caird, p. 286.

5. Stringfellow (1973), p. 50.

6. Throughout this chapter we translate the Greek word *pornē* as "whore" rather than as "prostitute" to underscore the pejorative connotation of John's description of Babylon. The use is not intended to express any derogation of sex-workers who are driven into their trade because of economic exploitation or other factors related to social oppression.

Table 15
CONTRASTS BETWEEN BABYLON
AND NEW JERUSALEM IN REVELATION

Babylon	New Jerusalem
The great whore (17:1)	The bride (19:7; 21:9)
Seated on many waters (unstable) (17:1)	Built on 12 foundations (stable) (21:14, 19)
Wine of whoring = blood (17:2; 18:3)	Water of life (22:1)
The Beast (17:3)	The Lamb (21:9; etc.)
Gold, jewels, pearls as seductive (17:4)	Gold, jewels, pearls as commonwealth (21:11-21)
Clothed in scarlet and purple (17:4; 18:16)	Clothed in bright, clean linen (19:8)
Practice of abomination and deception (17:4)	No abomination or deception (21:27)
Name of Babylon on forehead (17:5)	Name of God/Lamb on forehead (22:4)
Names not written in scroll (17:8)	Names written in book of life (21:27)
Beast destroys Babylon (17:16)	Lamb marries New Jerusalem (21:2, 9)
Babylon rules the kings of the earth (17:18)	God's servants reign over the city (22:5)
The great city (17:18; 18:16, 18-19)	The holy city (21:2, 10)
Fallen (18:2); thrown down (18:21)	Coming down from heaven (21:10)
Foul and hateful birds and beasts (18:2)	Nothing unclean (21:27)
Dwelling of demons (18:2)	God dwells within (21:3)
Nations intoxicated (18:3)	Nations healed (22:2)
Come out of her (18:4)	Come to see the bride (21:9)
City an eternal smoking ruin (18:9; 19:3)	City an eternal splendid garden (22:2)
Weeping, wailing, mourning (18:11, 15, 19)	No tears or sorrow (21:4)
City appropriates products of nations (18:12-13)	Nations bring glory and honor to city (21:26)
Goods are commodities for trade (18:12-13)	Goods are for the common good (e.g., street of city made of gold, 21:21)
Fruit is gone (18:14)	Fruit each month (22:2)
Sea (18:17, 18:19)	Sea is no more (21:1)
No lamplight, therefore darkness (18:23)	Lamb (21:23) God (21:25; 22:5) is light
No more weddings (18:23)	The wedding of the Lamb (19:7)
Blood, murder (18:24)	Life, healing, no death (21:4)
Nations deceived and corrupted (19:2)	Nations walk in light (21:24)
Wrath of God (19:15)	Glory of God, radiance (21:11)

PRELUDE: MEN TALKING ABOUT WOMEN
AS WHORES AND BRIDES

One of the challenges for us in interpreting the images of Babylon and New Jerusalem is the blatant gender stereotyping of the apocalyptic cities as "evil" or "good" women. After all the light shed in recent decades by feminist scholarship on the violence and injustice wrought over the centuries by such stereotyping, how can two male authors dare to approve of Revelation's imagery?

Feminist biblical scholars have come at the issue from two angles, as mentioned briefly at the end of chapter 1 above. Elisabeth Schüssler Fiorenza articulates three principles necessary to an effective reading of Revelation:

> First, I translate and read the *grammatically masculine language* of Revelation as conventional generic language, unless its interrogation indicates that such language functions as gender-specific language in a particular context and seeks to instill patriarchal meanings. Second, I translate and read the *sexist language and female images* in Revelation first as "conventional" language that must be understood in its traditional and present-meaning contexts. Whoring and fornication as metaphors for idolatry, as well as the symbolic understanding of Israel as bride and wife of Yahweh, are part and parcel of the prophetic apocalyptic tradition. They must be subject to a feminist critique, but their gendered meaning can not be assumed to be primary within the narrative contextualization of Revelation.
>
> Finally, I do not read Revelation just in terms of the sex/gender system but with reference to the Western classical patriarchal system and its interlocking structures of racism, classism, colonialism, and sexism. Such a reading will, for instance, pay attention not only to the sexual characterization of the figure of Babylon but also to its description in terms of high status, ruling power, egregious wealth, and divine aspirations.[7]

Tina Pippin, on the other hand, having started down Schüssler Fiorenza's road, found herself unable to follow Schüssler Fiorenza's lead. She notes that "[r]eading for the 'lives' of the females in the text exposes the deep misogyny of this vision of the end of the world."[8] For example, she points out that the disembodiment of the Whore-Babylon "points to the ultimate misogynist fantasy!"[9] Pippin's work sets out with dark clarity precisely how dangerous these images can be, especially in the hands of men with power over women's bodies. The obvious example of the church's practice of burning women as "witches" underscores how real the consequences of taking such stereotypes as the "word of God" can be.

---

7. Schüssler Fiorenza (1991), p. 14, emphasis added.
8. Pippin (1992), p. 47.
9. Ibid., p. 67.

For Elisabeth Schüssler Fiorenza to choose to treat Revelation's sexual imagery as "conventional language" is one thing; she is, after all, one of the world's leading feminist critics of ecclesial and social patriarchy and sexism. For two First World men of privilege to jump on her bandwagon is another. We hear Tina Pippin's experience of the text as degrading, violent, and hateful of women. We offer no excuses for John's language. It is small solace to suggest that if we were choosing how to express a vision of empire and its alternative, we would find other images than those of women's bodies. It is with acknowledgment of our participation in the privileges of patriarchy and our solidarity with women's cry for justice in the church and in the world that we take on the task of interpreting these difficult images. In case there is doubt, however, let us be clear at the outset. *The images of women used by Revelation were not intended to, nor should they ever, legitimate violence against women of any kind.* They also should not be used to expect women to be submissive to male authority nor to be passive in the face of sexism or other injustice. In the end, Revelation's images of whore and bride are not about human women, but about apocalyptic cities.[10] Any effort to associate them with actual people represents a gross misuse of the text.

BABYLON

The language and imagery used to portray Babylon draws heavily on the prophetic sections of the Hebrew scriptures. These both denounce the political and economic tyranny of the imperial superpowers and powerful city-states of the ancient East and announce their judgment. In drawing connections between these long-gone political entities and the contemporary situation of Roman Asia, Revelation makes the bold assertion that despite the apparent strength of the Roman Empire, its power is not what it seems. Rome is portrayed as an amalgam of all the imperial entities of the past. Yet like all those ancient empires that stood in conflict with God and God's people, Rome too is revealed as fallen.

Before we can investigate how Revelation sought to engage Christians' involvement with the Roman Empire, we should heed the advice of Paul Minear:

> The best procedure is not first to locate Babylon as a particular city, and then to attribute these sins to that city, but first to grasp the character of the sins, and then to infer that where they are found, there is Babylon.[11]

After a look at how Babylon carries forward the biblical attitude toward cities, we shall examine the character of Babylon's sins: whoring, murder, economic exploitation, and arrogance. We shall also examine Babylon through the lens of

---

10. Barbara Rossing argues that Revelation's language of "desolation" (Greek *erēmoō*) and "nakedness" (Greek *gymnos*) as applied to Babylon in Rev. 17:16 describes *urban landscape,* not a woman's body (Rossing, ch. 3).

11. Minear (1966), p. 151.

the vice lists that punctuate the vision of New Jerusalem before turning to the imperative to "come out" of "Babylon, the Great City."

Babylon as City

In the last quarter of the first century, Rome was often referred to as "Babylon" in Jewish and Christian circles.[12] The association of Rome with Babylon was possible because Rome, like the ancient empire of Babylon, had captured and destroyed Jerusalem and its temple. Babylon existed in the popular Jewish and Christian imagination as the imperial power par excellence. The image of Babylon as superempire was cultivated in the prophetic writings, particularly those of Isaiah, Jeremiah, and Ezekiel. Their critique of imperial Babylon was appropriated by Revelation and used against the empire of John's day. By the first century, "Babylon" referred not to a city-state or a long-fallen empire but had become a living archetype of the human propensity to organize "civilization" in opposition to God. By invoking the archetypal Great City, Revelation made an incisive and far-reaching claim: Rome was the current embodiment of Babylon.

The "Babylon myth" did not begin with the capture of Jerusalem by Babylonian forces in 586 B.C.E. Woven among the earliest memories of the people of Israel were traditions that saw the powerful city-states of their neighbors as their primal adversaries. Foremost among these were the centers found in Egypt, Canaan, and Mesopotamia. Their walled city fortresses, soaring towers, and temples typified these centers of power.

Genesis tells the story of how the first city was built by the first murderer. Cain, the first human reported to have rejected the interconnectedness of all life under God's watchful eye, cried out to God:

> Today you have driven me away from the soil,
> and I shall be hidden from your face;
> I shall be a fugitive and a wanderer on the earth. . . . (Gen. 4:14)

As a consequence of this act of fratricide, Cain perceives that his punishment is threefold. His nurturing relationship with the earth (mother) has been ended, his visible relationship with YHWH (father) has also been cut off, and his relationship with the human family has been severed. And yet, three verses later, his wife bears a son named Enoch. Crucially, Cain follows his wife's act of giving birth with one of his own: "he built a city, and named it Enoch after his son Enoch" (Gen. 4:17). In this way, the biblical narrative intimately connects the child born away from God's presence with the dwelling place that acts as a shield

---

12. As we saw in chapter 2, 4 Ezra and the *Fifth Sibylline Oracle,* both written for Jewish communities after the Roman destruction of Jerusalem, identified the Roman Empire with the archetypal empire—Babylon. Of the early Christian texts, 1 Peter also refers to Rome as Babylon. The author of that letter concludes with a greeting from the community in Rome referring to the city as "Babylon." Literally, the greeting was, "the co-chosen in Babylon greet you" (1 Pet. 5:13).

from God's presence. As Jacques Ellul points out, Cain's acts of fathering a child and a city are the root of the human project to "make the world over again," this time, without God's help.[13] In the case of this first city, of course, the protection the city provides is not against foreign aggressors but against God himself. Thus, at its biblical root, the very idea of "city" is tainted with murder, a false sense of independence, and hubris.

One city led to another, and soon the known world was dominated by city-states. Genesis 10 presents a genealogy of empire: the establishment of cities that would become empires and both oppress and seduce God's people through history. The empires of Egypt, Assyria, and Babylon were the inevitable consequence of the building of these first cities.

One of these early city builders was Nimrod. His title "mighty warrior/hunter" (Gen. 10:8) suggests the predatory nature of his work. This is manifested in the cities he built: Babel, Erech, and Accad were all in the land of Babylon (Gen. 10:10). The story of Babel in Genesis 11 is a thinly veiled criticism of the concentration of power represented by the Mesopotamian city-states.[14] The story revolves around the building of a city and a tower. The building of the tower was symptomatic of an archetypal sin: the desire to "make a name for ourselves" (11:4). This phrase expresses the desire to be independent of YHWH, which provokes the intervention of God. Henceforth the city was named Babel—"confusion" (11:9)—and the land around it Babylon.

Babel was a watershed in the larger biblical story. It signaled the end of the transition "from a garden where human beings enjoyed communion with God and the creation to a metropolitan nightmare of hubris and oppression."[15] The Babel story is well known, yet its recurring role in the biblical tradition less so. Isaiah prophesies against the hubris of "every high tower and . . . every fortified wall" (Isa. 2:15) and satirizes the king of Babylon for his ambition to "ascend to heaven" (Isa. 14:13). Jeremiah too spoke of Babylon as Babel: "Though Babylon should mount up to heaven, and though she should fortify her strong height . . ." (Jer. 51:53).

While the city-states of Mesopotamia provided the model for Babel, the experience of slavery in Egypt was another catalyst for an understanding of the nature of the city-state and its oppressive ways. In order to wear down resistance, the Hebrews (*habiru*, "oppressed ones") were forced to build "supply-cities" for Pharaoh (Exod. 1:11). The people of Israel did not willfully build these cities in open defiance of God. Rather, their building was the burden of forced labor under the rule of an oppressive empire. Produce that was exacted as tribute from Egypt's subject peoples was stored in these cities. This practice stood in contradiction to the economic order that would be taught by YHWH in the wilderness.

---

13. Ellul (1970), p. 6.

14. Myers (1994), p. 317. The "tower" of Babel is thought to have been an allusion to the ziggurat structures of ancient Babylon.

15. Myers (1996), p. 5.

There the people were instructed not to store up food beyond the day. YHWH's daily provision of manna for forty years demonstrated the credentials of this alternative economic order (Exod. 16).

In entering the land of Canaan after their time of slavery in Egypt and their wilderness experiment with YHWH's alternative way, the Hebrews encountered the fortress cities of the Canaanites. Walter Brueggemann describes this period:

> The "habiru" mounted a revolution against the tyrannical Canaanite city-kings, rejecting the given social order. Bound to a nonhuman overlord [YHWH] by covenant and the solidarity of the newly formed community, they set about fashioning a deliberate alternative social ordering which became Israel.[16]

This was the first time that the tribal confederacy of Israel had attempted to live out YHWH's agenda in a settled, non-nomadic state. It took place in the midst of an environment where "the cities are large and fortified up to heaven" (Deut. 1:28; 9:1), a description reminiscent of Babel. These cities, built by the inhabitants of Canaan, were problematic for the liberated people of Israel. On the one hand, they bore the curse that fell on any city, built as they were in defiance of YHWH. On the other hand, they would be habitable if the Hebrews practiced everything that YHWH had instructed them in the wilderness and did not live like the former inhabitants of these cities. If the people of a particular city did revert to the practices of the centralized city-states, the whole city was to be razed to the ground and never rebuilt (Deut. 13:12-18).

If Babel typified the Mesopotamian city-state, Jericho typified the Canaanite fortress city. Standing between the Hebrews and land promised them by YHWH, Jericho had closed its gates against the people of Israel (Josh. 6:1). By YHWH's intervention—expressed, as in Revelation, through the image of the trumpet blast—the power of that defiant city was destroyed. Joshua, the leader of the tribal confederacy, made an oath before YHWH: the city was not to be rebuilt under pain of a curse (Josh. 6:26). With the might of the fortress-city broken, the people could enter the land and live not in loyalty to empire, but in loyalty to YHWH alone. That loyalty forswore the oppression, economic accumulation, centralized power, and overweening hubris practiced by the imperial city-states surrounding them.

Opposition to centralized power continued among the biblical traditions despite the centralizing tendency of Israel itself. This tendency manifested itself in its fortress capital, its temple storehouse, and its institution of kingship. These all came together in the reign of King Solomon, who represented a return to the ways of Egypt. Solomon is portrayed in many ways as a new pharaoh. Like Pharaoh, he used forced labor for his building projects (1 Kings 5:13; 9:15; cf. Exod. 1:11) and employed a standing army (2 Chron. 8:5-6; cf. Exod. 14). Worst

---

16. Brueggemann (1993), p. 203.

of all, though, Solomon was a builder of cities. He fortified cities that already existed. He built storage cities (just as Pharaoh had compelled his slaves to do) and fortified them. He centralized his wealth gathered by tribute from the Egyptian border to Mesopotamia and hoarded this in his cities (2 Chron. 8:1-6; cf. 2 Chron. 9:26-27).

The immediate result was civil war and a split in the tribal confederacy (1 Kings 12). The longer-term result was the capture of Jerusalem by Babylon, the destruction of the temple, and the forced migration of the elite. This rocked their faith that YHWH had granted the people land in perpetuity and a temple that would forever provide access to YHWH. The advance of the Babylonian Empire seemed to reveal the powerlessness of YHWH. How could the God who had defeated Pharaoh and the Canaanites surrender the land, the temple, and the people to Babylon? The prophets Second Isaiah, Jeremiah, and Ezekiel accounted for this dilemma in their own way, yet each portrayed Babylon as a corrupt, violent, exploitative, and arrogant power in ultimate conflict with God and God's people. This crisis prompted Israel to see in Babylon all the characteristics of the cities that had been part of the story of Israel. Babylon became the "great city." Jacques Ellul eloquently described the archetypal character of Babylon:

> Babylon, the great city, or Babylon the Great. The biggest in the world. No one can rival her, not even Rome. Not because of her historical greatness, but because of what she represents mythically. All the cities of the world are brought together in her, she is the synthesis of them all. She is the head of, and standard for the other cities.[17]

Babylon as Whore

Revelation envisions Babylon as a "whore" (Greek *pornē*, 17:1, 5, 15, 16; 19:2). The image of "whoring" implies infidelity to one's covenant partner—that is, YHWH. It also suggests the cause of such infidelity: seduction. People usually do not enter rationally and deliberately into a situation of evil; rather, they are seduced into it. Why is empire able to enlist so many into its service? Why do so many good people cheer for empire and give their lives for it? Why do those willing to seek peace, justice, and community always seem so few? The answer resides in the seductive character of Babylon.

As a biblical metaphor, "whoring" has a long history. The Hebrew tradition saw "whoring" as anything that departed from allegiance to YHWH alone, which allegiance involved the construction of YHWH's human order of social and economic egalitarianism. Worshiping idols, making political treaties, and engaging in exploitative commerce were seen as departing from the worship of YHWH alone.

In the book of Exodus, as the people of Moses enter the land of Canaan, YHWH warns their leader:

---

17. Ellul (1970), pp. 20-21.

You will not make a covenant with the inhabitants of the land, for when they whore themselves to their gods and sacrifice to their gods, someone among them will invite you, and you will eat of their sacrifice, and you will take wives from among their daughters for your sons, and their daughters who whore [LXX *porneuō*] themselves to their gods will make your sons also whore themselves to their gods. (Exod. 34:15-16)

It is not that the people of Israel were obsessed with sexual ethics. Rather, the metaphor of "whoring" stood for the selling out of the radical message of YHWH to the practices of the people who lived around them. Here the emphasis is on idolatry as an act of whoring. Idolatry did not involve simply falling down to worship this statue or that tree. Rather, the issue was that by "making a covenant" with their fellow inhabitants of the land, the people of Israel would adopt the cult and the culture that was at odds with their covenant with YHWH.

Whoring also stood for infidelity in the sphere of foreign relations. The prophets declared that when Israel entered into alliances with neighboring regimes, the people of God were whoring themselves. These alliances made good sense according to prevailing notions of *realpolitik*. Israel was small and lacked the resources of its neighbors. By entering into strategic alliances with them, Israel hoped to forestall invasion and to buy security. Yet in Ezek. 16, the prophet depicts Israel's history of imperial alliances as a lifetime of whoring. This chapter is an outrageous parody of Israel's alliances, using a succession of sexually provocative metaphors. For example:

You played the whore with the Egyptians, your lustful neighbors, multiplying your whoring, to provoke me to anger. . . . You played the whore with the Assyrians, because you were insatiable; you played the whore with them, and still you were not satisfied. You multiplied your whoring with Chaldea, the land of merchants; and even with this you were not satisfied. (Ezek. 16:26, 28-29)

The constant temptation for Israel, the people called to allegiance with YHWH alone, was to seek accommodation with the empires that encircled them, even with Rome itself (1 Macc. 8). Revelation takes up this long-standing critique of imperial compromise and applies it to the *ekklēsiai* of Asia in their relationship with Rome.

The Hebrew prophets also condemn the economics of empire as "whoring." Isaiah taunts the city-state of Tyre, which was the "tiger economy" of ancient Palestine, with these words:

It will happen to Tyre as in the song about the whore:
"Take a harp, go about the city,
you forgotten whore . . ."
She will return to her trade, and will whore herself with
all the kingdoms of the world on the face of the
earth. (Isa. 23:15, 16, 17)

168 *THE CITY OF OUR GOD*

Gregory Beale notes that the Hebrew word *zānâ,* translated "whore" in Isa. 23:17 above, was in turn translated in the Septuagint by the Greek *estai emporion,* "to be a market."[18] Thus, by entering into mercantile arrangements across the region, Tyre made itself a whore for "all the kingdoms of the world." The people of Israel, by trading with Tyre, engaged in this "obscene" commerce.

Revelation draws upon the Hebrew tradition that used sexual fidelity/infidelity as a metaphor for faithfulness to the ways of YHWH versus faithfulness to the competing imperial structures of the day. In the biblical world, where sexual imagery was used to speak of power and allegiance, the depiction of Roman imperial power as a "great whore" was both potent and provocative.

In the book of Revelation, Babylon the apocalyptic "whore," is envisioned by John as "sitting on a scarlet beast that was full of blasphemous names" (17:3). We recall that a primary image of the popular goddess Cybele was of her riding astride a lion (see figure 1 in chapter 3). This image was prominently present on the great altar in the city of Pergamum and in the Roman Palatine in the temple of Victory.[19] Thus, John's description of Rome as a whore riding a beast is a parody of the popular cult that Rome had incorporated into its own myth of divine legitimation.[20]

The whore is said to have engaged in "intercourse" with both the "kings of the earth" and the "inhabitants of the earth" (17:2). The "kings of the earth" were the powerful members of society who gave their allegiance to Babylon. In the context of first-century Rome, this term would have applied to

not just client kings who put their kingdoms under the umbrella of the Roman empire, but more generally to the local ruling classes whom, throughout the empire, Rome co-opted to a share in her rule . . . the local aristocracy who sat on the councils of their cities. For such people Roman authority served to prop up their own dominant position in society.[21]

The "inhabitants of the earth," on the other hand, are the mass of the population who either willingly or grudgingly placed their faith in Babylon.[22] In the world of Roman Asia, the "inhabitants of the earth" would have included both free and slaves, rich and poor, city folk and peasants (Rev. 6:15; 13:16; 19:18).

Rome used its seductive power to attract members of the *ekklēsiai* of Asia into accommodation with empire. By trusting in the imperial myths, the disparate peoples of the empire were provided a vision of a unified and secure world. By engaging in imperial commerce, a modicum of prosperity was offered. By participating in the imperial and local cults, a lifestyle of social inclusion and cele-

---

18. Beale (1999), p. 849.

19. Turcan, pp. 35, 37.

20. The image of Rome as whore may have also been a "subversive joke" based on the tradition that the founding infants, Romulus and Remus, were nursed by a she-wolf—in Latin, *lupa,* which had the connotation "whore" (Aune [1998], p. 925).

21. Bauckham (1991), p. 80.

22. Parallel to the "Judeans" in the Fourth Gospel; Howard-Brook, pp. 41-43.

bration was available. By entering into the life of the city, a feeling of pride and achievement was possible. These were some of the seductive entanglements held out to the people of the empire. To those with an "earthly" perspective, these attractions were the height of culture and achievement. Yet to "heaven," they were the mere trinkets and baubles of a wily whore.

Babylon as Murderer

As we saw earlier, in the biblical story the first murderer built the first city. Murder has always been a feature of the human centralization of power, of which Babylon is the most potent biblical metaphor. In Babylon violence has a "sacred" significance.[23] It is clearly seen in the vision of Babylon the whore, drunk with the blood of the saints and witnesses of Jesus (17:6). This vision revolves around the image of the "cup." It unfolds in this way:

1. The "kings of the earth" have "whored" themselves with Babylon (17:2a).
2. The "inhabitants of the earth" were "drunk from the wine of her whoring" (17:2b).
3. The woman was holding a "golden cup" filled with "abominations and the unclean things of her whoring" (17:4).
4. The woman was drunk with "the blood of the saints and with the blood of the witnesses of Jesus" (17:6).

The leaders whore themselves to Babylon, which intoxicates the people. Yet what causes this drunkenness? By implication the people are intoxicated by the contents of the "golden cup" held by Babylon. Bruce Malina explains: "images of gods and goddesses with a cup in one hand, with the other raised, generally depict a posture of blessing."[24] Furthermore, in the Septuagint, the same Greek word for "cup" (*potērion*) was used regularly to symbolize one's acceptance or rejection of God's control over one's destiny.[25] This was the meaning of the eucharistic cup, a very early Christian ritual (see 1 Cor. 10:16). Here, however, the imagery is reversed. Rather than holding a cup of blessing, Babylon holds a cup filled with abominations and unclean things. This cup is shared between the "inhabitants of the earth" (17:2b) and Babylon itself. The latter was seen to be intoxicated with the blood of the executed followers of Jesus. Among the abominations and unclean things contained in the golden cup was the blood of Babylon's victims.[26] This image of Babylon holding the cup of blood is a powerful indictment of empire. It indicates, in a graphic and lurid way, that empire blesses

---

23. Cf. Bailie, p. 155. Gil Bailie, following Rene Girard, has investigated with great clarity how violence has assumed a sacred social role. The sacred character of official violence—that perpetrated by the security apparatus (military, police, etc.)—makes the practice of nonviolent alternatives seem subversive of the sacred order.

24. Malina (1995), p. 215.

25. L. Goppelt in *TDNT* 6:150-55; Sweet (1990), p. 227.

26. In Seneca's *Hercules Oetaeus* (657-658) an identical theme is found: "It is in the cup of gold alone, that blood is mingled with the wine" (Aune [1999], p. 938).

its people with the blood of its victims and that those loyal to empire share in this cup as a sign of their acceptance of empire's control over their lives.

This is also an image of *enthrallment*. The people of empire are typically enthralled by the crucial role that violence plays for empire. Empire routinely engages in killing, yet it claims to be a benign actor in the world. These are not contradictory statements. Rather, it is *because* empire routinely engages in murder that it must claim to be benign. This is the meaning of the myth of the *Pax Romana*, the *Pax Britannica,* and the *Pax Americana*. Just as the Pentagon's high-tech weaponry of the Persian Gulf War enthralled (*thrall*: "one who is in bondage"[27]) so many, Rome's "victory" celebrations captivated the population of the empire.

For our purposes it is helpful to understand violence in two of its dimensions: violence as a *threat* to keep people quiet, and the *actual use* of violence against any perceived threat. The vision of Babylon as Whore suggests that Babylon is usually successful in gaining people's allegiance by co-opting them. But when co-option fails, coercion begins. The Roman Empire employed various forms of execution both as means of eliminating those perceived as threatening the empire and as threats to keep people in line. This is why mass crucifixions occurred along public thoroughfares and on the tops of hills and why people were thrown to the wild animals in the arenas. The mere fact that public executions took place would have been an effective deterrent to many who were dissatisfied with Rome. Where seduction and the threat of force failed, the use of violence inevitably followed.

Revelation clearly portrays Babylon as a place where murder is a method of social control:[28]

> In her was found the blood of prophets and of saints,
> and of all the ones having been slain on the earth. (18:24)

This verse echoes the lament of Jesus for the historical city of Jerusalem, which he saw as responsible for the blood of "prophets, sages, and scribes" (Matt. 23:34-35) or "prophets and apostles" (Luke 11:49-51; cf. 13:34; 19:41-44). But while the Matthean Jesus condemned Jerusalem for shedding the blood of "all the righteous shed on earth" (Matt. 23:35), Revelation broadens the critique to make the city liable for "the blood of *all* the ones slain on the earth" (18:24). Babylon is where people are killed for the sake of the sociopolitical order, not just for being "Christian." John saw that Babylon quenched its thirst with the blood of those who opposed it. This was in accord with the insight that violence—against both external and internal enemies—was the lynchpin of Roman power.

---

27. *American Heritage Dictionary*, p. 1339.

28. The Beasts are seen to operate in the same way. First the "beast from the earth" attempts to seduce the "inhabitants of the earth" to worship the beast from the sea (13:11). Should this prove unsuccessful, the beast had power to kill all who would not worship (13:15).

Babylon as Economic Exploiter

Another characteristic of Babylon is its attachment to wealth. Again and again Babylon is seen as extremely affluent. John sees Babylon as a whore adorned with the accoutrements of opulence:

> The woman was clothed in purple and scarlet,
> and having been gilded with gold
> and precious stones and pearls,
> having in her hand a golden cup. (17:4)

These items were available only to the elite of Roman society. These same goods are listed again as commodities imported by Babylon (18:12), and as the commodities destroyed in the fall of the city of Babylon (18:16).

Revelation 18 contains a concentrated depiction of the affluence of Babylon. This affluence comes to naught in Babylon's fall. Those who had benefited from the city—the kings, the traders, and the seafarers—are envisioned as mourning the loss of the city. Table 16 shows how this chapter is a pastiche of the Hebrew scriptures, particularly those that critique Tyre and Babylon for their economic arrogance and exploitation.

For Isaiah, Tyre was condemned as an economic empire, "the merchant of the nations" (Isa. 23:3), whose "merchants were princes" (Isa. 23:8), and whose commerce spread throughout the eastern Mediterranean. The destruction of Tyre meant a redistribution of the accumulated wealth of the city. That wealth would not be "stored or hoarded" but would be given to "those who live in the presence of YHWH" (Isa. 23:18). Ezekiel 26-28 portrays kings, traders, and sailors lamenting the loss of Tyre's economic might. The economic critique of Tyre, like that of Rome in Revelation, was the prophet's discernment of the social reality of his day. Those who benefited from Tyre's economic activity would have resented Isaiah's and Ezekiel's description of their mercantile arrangements. Yet to the prophets, the economics of Tyre was a crime against the poor and a scandal to YHWH, who would not allow it to stand.

Revelation 18 is structured in the form of a chiasm, which serves to focus the audience's attention on the key elements of the vision. Pablo Richard describes the chiasm in this way:[29]

A: 1-3: Vision of the mighty angel: "Fallen, fallen is Babylon the Great"
   B: 4-8: Voice: "Come out of Babylon"
      C: 9-19: Weeping and mourning for the fall of Babylon—kings, traders, sailors
   B':20: Voice: "Rejoice over Babylon"
A': 21-24: Action of the mighty angel: "Babylon will be thrown down"

---

29. Richard, p. 128; also Giblin (1991), pp. 166-67, 170.

Table 16
ECHOES OF HEBREW SCRIPTURE
IN REVELATION 18

Revelation 18	*Hebrew Scriptures*
"Fallen, fallen is Babylon" (18:2)	Isa. 21:9; Jer. 51:8, 49
It is the place of demons and foul birds (18:2)	Isa. 13:21-22; 34:11-15; Jer. 50:39
All the nations drank her wine (18:3)	Jer. 51:7
"Come out of Babylon" (18:4)	Isa. 48:20; Jer. 50:8; 51:6, 45
Her sins go up to heaven (18:5)	Gen. 11:4; Jer. 51:9
God remembered her injustices (18:5)	Exod. 2:24
Repay her double for her deeds (18:6)	Isa. 40:2; Jer. 17:18
"A queen I sit, and I am not a widow, and sorrow I never see" (18:7)	Ezek. 27:3; Isa. 47:7-8; cf. Zeph. 2:15
In one day will disaster come (18:8)	Isa. 47:9
The kings of the earth (18:9)	Ezek. 27:33; Ps. 2:2; Isa. 24:21
The smoke of the city (18:9, 18)	4 Ezra 15:44
They will stand from afar in fear (18:10)	Ezek. 27:35
The traders of the earth will weep (18:11)	Ezek. 27:36; Isa. 23:8
[Cargo list] (18:12-13)	1 Kings 10:21-29; Ezek. 27:12-24
Everything you own has perished (18:14)	Ezek. 26:12; 27:27, 34
Captains and sailors stood far off (18:17)	Ezek. 27:29
"Who is like the great city" (18:18)	Ezek. 27:32
And they cast dust on their heads (18:19)	Ezek. 27:30; also Josh. 7:6; Job 2:12
A great millstone cast into the sea . . . (18:21)	Jer. 51:63-64
The sound of harpists, musicians, flautists, and trumpeters are heard no more (18:22)	Isa. 24:8; Ezek. 26:13; (the imperial and local cults will be silenced!)
The mill, the lamp, the bridegroom and bride are no more (18:22-23)	Jer. 25:10

Revelation demonstrates a clear awareness of how the economy of Babylon operated and whom it benefited. The center of the chiasm (C) is itself a chiasm:

A: 9-10: kings mourn: smoke of her burning, Babylon the mighty city, one
       hour
  B: 11-13: merchants mourn: gold, jewels, pearls, linen, purple, scarlet
    C: 12-14: all dainties and splendor are lost, never to be found again!
  B': 15-17a: merchants mourn: linen, purple, scarlet, gold, jewels, pearls
A': 17b-19: shippers mourn: smoke of her burning, the great city, one hour

This central section describes the reaction of the global wheelers and dealers to the crash of Babylon. The 1929 Wall Street crash that heralded the Great Depression and the Asian financial crisis of 1997-98 induced grief, fear, and tears among those whose success was dependent on the stability of a global trading system centered in empire. John saw similar reactions accompanying the fall of Babylon among the kings, traders, and sailors (18:9-19). In the paradigm of the imperial economy, sorrow at this unexpected turn of events is entirely understandable. Those who benefit from Babylon have much to lose. However, those who are not part of Babylon have no need to weep and wail. To the contrary, as we will see in chapter 7, those who have "come out" of Babylon celebrate her fall with a heavenly liturgy. The response of each of these three groups is presented in a four-part pattern in table 17.

Included in this vision is a list of the cargoes for which there is no longer a market (18:12-13):

- Gold, silver, precious stones, pearls
- Fine linen, purple, silk, scarlet
- Scented wood, vessels of ivory, vessels of valuable wood
- Bronze, iron, marble
- Cinnamon, spice, incenses, aromatic ointment, frankincense
- Wine, oil, flour, corn
- Cattle, sheep, horses
- Chariots
- Slaves (Greek *sōma,* literally "bodies")
- Human souls (Greek *psuchas anthrōpōn*)

This list is representative of the trade in commodities across the ancient world. It draws upon similar lists of commodities found in 1 Kings (10:21-29) and the prophet Ezekiel (27:12-24). While Richard Bauckham characterizes the list as "very representative of Rome's more expensive imports,"[30] this is not the whole case. It is true that the list included much that was unmistakably in the category of luxury goods. There are other commodities, however, that are more mundane; some are simply the staples of life. Rather than portraying a city that extracted simply *luxury goods* from the entire earth, the list depicts Babylon as appropriating *everything* from the entire earth. In the Hebrew scripture texts from which Revelation's list is drawn, there is an implicit critique of an exploitative imperial economy. Revelation's list similarly critiques Rome's exploitation of the world's wealth, as explained in chapter 3 above.

The insidious nature of imperial trade is underscored by the commodities that conclude the list: "bodies and human souls" (18:13). In ancient Rome slaves were commonly labeled "bodies." This underlined the status of the slave class. They were not considered human beings but commodities that could be bought and sold. People captured in the territories occupied by the Roman legions, those who broke Roman law, and even those who owed a debt could be shipped across

---

30. Bauckham (1991), p. 75.

Table 17
RESPONSE TO THE FALL OF BABYLON (18:9-19)

	Kings of the Earth	*Traders of the Earth*	*Captains/Seafarers*
A description of each group	The kings of the earth, having practiced whoring and lived in luxury with her,	The traders of the earth,	And every captain and everyone who sails to a place and sailors and as many who work on the sea
Their response to the fall of Babylon	will weep and wail over her when they see the smoke of her burning. Standing from afar, in fear of her torment, and saying:	weep and mourn for her, because no one buys their cargo anymore. . . . The traders . . . having become rich from her will stand far off, in fear of her torment, weeping and mourning aloud:	stood far off and cried out seeing the smoke of her burning, saying: "What is like the great city?" And they cast dust on their heads and cried out, weeping and mourning, saying:
Their lament	"Woe, woe, the great city, Babylon the strong city.	"Woe, woe, the great city, having been clothed in fine linen, in purple and scarlet, gilded with gold, precious stones, pearls.	"Woe, woe, the great city, in which those having ships on the sea were rich from her honor.
Their comment on the suddenness of the judgment	In one hour came your judgment."	In one hour all this wealth was made desolate."	In one hour it was made desolate."

the empire to the slave markets of the cities. Within Babylon *everyone* can become a commodity.

Even more than the slave trade, however, the trading in the "human soul" suggests that Babylon buys and sells the very essence of humanity. As Jacques Ellul wrote:

> I believe, without any doubt, that this [the human soul] refers to the interior possession of man. . . . It is his soul that is the object of traffic. He is *alienated* to the great city . . . bound in a completely clear fashion to economic activity, to commerce and enrichment: it is wealth that produces not only exterior slavery but also alienation to the economy and subjection by this interior way.[31]

---

31. Ellul (1977), p. 195, emphasis in original.

Once Babylon has cornered the market in material goods and human beings, it owns the very essence of those who participate in the system. This is precisely what the modern recasting of the philosopher Descartes' famous axiom—"I shop, therefore I am"—means. While someone whose body is owned by empire may be able to resist his or her commodification, those whose soul is owned by Babylon are incapable of realizing that resistance is necessary.

To more fully understand John's vision of imperial economics it is necessary to move from the image of Babylon to that of the "Beast." In Revelation 13, John saw that the earth Beast

> makes all, the small and the great,
> the rich and poor, both free and slaves,
> to be given a mark [Greek *charagma*] on their right hand
> or on their forehead,
> so that no one could buy or sell
> except the one having the name of the Beast or the num-
> ber of its name. (13:16-17)

The crux of the passage is the significance of the *charagma* that is given on the right hand or forehead. The forehead is a site of apocalyptic bifurcation in Revelation. What is present on the forehead is present to the mind of the wearer.[32] Both the citizens of Babylon and the citizens of New Jerusalem have a mark on their forehead. But while the citizens of Babylon have the "mark of the Beast" (13:16; 14:9, 11; 20:4), the citizens of New Jerusalem are "sealed" with the name of God (7:3; 9:4; 14:1; 22:4).[33]

While the citizens of Babylon and New Jerusalem have a sign on their forehead, only the citizens of Babylon have a sign on their "right hand." What is the significance of this? That which is held in the hand and enables buying and selling is the imperial stamp and coin: the medium of imperial commerce. The *charagma* of ancient Rome was not some esoteric symbol but a stamp used to certify deeds of sale,[34] and the impress of the emperor's head on the coinage.[35] The imperial currency bore the image, name, year, and titles of the emperor. This made coinage an important means by which Roman myth was propagated. These coins were an affront to those who resisted empire. As far as Revelation is concerned it was not possible to denounce Rome as satanic and simultaneously to use the empire's medium of exchange—its currency.[36]

---

32. See Deut. 6:6-8, where the people of Israel were commanded to fix the words of YHWH to their foreheads so that they not forget them.

33. In Ezek. 9:4-6, the prophet has a vision where the mark of the Hebrew letter *tau,* resembling a cross, is placed on the foreheads of those who grieve and lament over the abominations practiced in Jerusalem. For Christians this mark could easily have been seen as signifying the crucified Jesus. See Mounce, p. 259, n. 34.

34. Deissmann, p. 341.

35. Caird, p. 173.

36. See ibid.; Collins (1977), pp. 252-53.

John knew that while the right hand was holding the Roman coin, empire would transfix the mind of the bearer. To possess the coin—to bear the "mark of the Beast"—made one a citizen of Babylon. As Beale says, "the mark alludes to the state's political and economic 'stamp of approval.'"[37] Those who grew rich on the back of Babylon —the kings, traders, and shipowners—bore the "mark of the Beast" in great abundance. Yet Rev. 13 is adamant that it is not just the wealthy who must distance themselves from the economy of Babylon: all are marked with the sign of empire if they possess the coin of that realm (cf. Mark 12:14-17). In critiquing the economy of Babylon and the Beast, John was clearing the way for an alternative economy, an issue discussed later in this chapter. Here it is important to understand that in Roman society participants in the "cash economy"—those who had access to free cash and who could therefore take part in the commodity market—were very few in number.[38] In envisioning the *charagma* as a mark of the Beast, John called those members of the *ekklēsiai* who were part of the elite's cash economy into solidarity with the majority of the people of the empire. To reject the "marked" economy of empire would allow alternative modes of economic redistribution, one based on reciprocity and gift, not commodity exploitation.

Babylon and Imperial Arrogance

In his vision of Babylon, John sees that the activities of seduction, coercion, and exploitation in which Babylon specializes are all underpinned by an attitude of imperial arrogance. Isaiah and Jeremiah are John's sources for this insight. Isaiah 14 engages in àn extended satire of the king of Babylon, lampooning him for just this vice. Jeremiah also indicts Babylon for overweening arrogance:

> Repay her according to her deeds;
> for she has arrogantly defied YHWH . . .
> YHWH says:
> "I am against you, O arrogant one . . ."
> The arrogant one shall stumble and fall. (Jer. 50:29-32)

In Revelation, this sin is expressed by the inability of imperial actors to envision the end of empire. Like Babylon in Isa. 47, John sees empire as unaware of the imminence of its judgment:

---

37. Beale (1999), p. 715. Beale adds that Ignatius of Antioch, in his letter to the Magnesians (one of a series of letters to *ekklēsiai* in Roman Asia written within twenty years after Revelation), uses the metaphor of the "two coins" as a description of the choice facing people: "the one of God and the other of the world, and each of them has its own stamp [*charagma*] impressed upon it, so the unbelievers bear the stamp of this world, but the faithful in love bear the stamp of God the Father through Jesus Christ, whose life is not in us unless we voluntarily choose to die into his suffering" (Ignatius, *Magnesians* 5 [Lightfoot and Harmer trans.]).

38. Oakman, p. 205.

> In her heart she says:
> "I am enthroned a queen, and I am not a widow, and sor-
>   row I never see."
> On account of this in one day will come her plagues.
>   (18:7-8; see Isa. 47:7-9)

Empire never admits its fragility or its finitude in time or space. In this respect Rome was no different from its predecessors. The Roman myth of Eternity, which held that Rome would last forever, was a manifestation of that shortsight-edness (see chapter 8 below). Arrogance at the top of sociopolitical structures blinds rulers to the fallout from their actions. Where the citizenry see this arro-gance as a sign of power, the blindness is intensified. Yet the Bible contends that such arrogance is self-destructive: by its very nature it is bound to fall.

Babylon as the Fallen City

Because it is so seductive, because it is prepared to murder any who pose a danger, because it regards everyone and everything as a commodity, and because it is blinded by arrogance—Babylon is "fallen." While the grim state of fallen Babylon is shown in great detail in Rev. 18, an angel has already announced the judgment on Babylon: "Another angel, a second, followed, saying: 'Fallen, fallen, Babylon the Great, all the nations were made to drink of the wine of the anger of her whoring'" (14:8). And another has announced: "Babylon the Great was remembered before God, to give it the cup of wine of the anger of God's wrath" (16:19). What John sees in 17:1-19:10 is not something new. It is some-thing that has already been announced as accomplished.

John is invited to see the "judgment" (Greek *krima*, 17:1) of Babylon. That this word has a legal significance should not be overlooked. In the heavenly courtroom of God (which exists behind the veil) Babylon has *already* been tried and found guilty. Similarly, Babylon is pictured as "fallen" *now*. Stringfellow explained that "the fallenness of this same Babylon is empirically evident and, indeed, enacted everywhere, everyday."[39] For as long as empire exists, it will always be fallen.

Babylon is depicted as fallen in a variety of ways:

- desolate and naked (17:16)
- inhabited by demons, a prison for every unclean spirit and unclean and hated bird (18:2)
- plagued by disease, mourning, famine (18:8)
- burned with fire: the smoke of her burning rises for ever and ever (18:8, 9, 18; 19:3)

---

39. Stringfellow (1973), p. 50.

In these dramatic images of desolation and ruin, the reversal of imagery is total. Whereas every empire prides itself on its grandeur and power—and in this Rome was no different—John sees empire's complete destruction. Everything that was a source of imperial pride—the temples, monuments, culture, order, and achievements—are seen by John as utterly desolate.

In powerful poetic verse, John envisions everything as lost (18:22-23):

- the sound of harpists and minstrels, of flautists and trumpet players—no more
- craftspeople of any craft—no more
- the sound of the millstone—no more
- the light of the lamp—no more
- the voice of the bridegroom and bride—no more
- everything that humanizes civilization—music, art, industry, light, love—no more

In contrast to the friends of Babylon whom we saw earlier weeping and wailing because the "great city" had fallen (18:9-19), the "holy ones and apostles" and a "great crowd in heaven" are invited to "rejoice" at the "judgment" of the city (18:20; 19:1-4). Rejoicing and mourning are contradictory responses to the same vision. These paired responses to the announcement that Babylon is fallen are crucial to Revelation's persuasive power. How would the members of the seven *ekklēsiai* in Roman Asia receive the vision? Would they mourn like the kings and traders or rejoice like the holy ones and apostles?

The members of the *ekklēsiai* with a stake in the Roman economy might empathize with the traders and shipowners. If there were traders among the members of the *ekklēsiai,* this vision of Babylon as fallen would be extremely discomfiting. The wealthy followers of Jesus at Laodicea, for example, would have felt harshly indicted by this vision. The faithful followers of Jesus, such as the poor members of the *ekklēsia* at Smyrna, would have the opposite reaction. For them, the announcement that "Babylon is fallen" would bring great joy and a sense of vindication. It would encourage them to continue their resistance to Rome. Each vision brings both challenge and comfort, an indictment and a justification. Richard Bauckham underscores the point:

> By no means all of his readers were poor and persecuted by an oppressive system: many were affluent and compromising with the oppressive system. The latter are offered not consolation and encouragement, but severe warnings and calls to repent. For these Christians, the judgments which are so vividly described in the rest of the book should appear not as judgments on their enemies so much as judgments on themselves . . . whether the visions bring consolation and encouragement or warning and painful challenge depends on which group of Christians depicted in the seven messages a reader belongs to.[40]

---

40. Bauckham (1993), pp. 15-16.

This was a powerful way of opening the eyes of the followers of Jesus to the truth of the crisis confronting them.

The Vices of Babylon

The criteria that determined whether one was a citizen of Babylon or New Jerusalem were eminently practical: Did one engage in the vices of empire or not? The listing of the vices of Babylon is a stark reminder that God's city conflicts with the ways of empire. Three times in the latter part of Revelation, the vices that characterize Babylon and preclude citizenship in New Jerusalem are listed:

> . . . the *cowards,* and *faithless,* and those having practiced *abomination,* and *murderers,* and those who practice *whoring,* and *sorcerers,* and *idol-worshippers,* and all those who propagate *illusion.* (21:8)

> . . . the one practicing *abomination* and *illusion.* (21:27)

> Blessed the ones washing their robes so that they may have the right to the tree of life and that they may enter into the city by the gates. Outside are the dogs, and the *sorcerers,* and those who practice *whoring,* and the *murderers,* and the *idol-worshippers,* and all loving and practicing *illusion.* (22:14-15)

This last excerpt envisions a contrast between those on the "outside" and those who "enter the city" by "washing their robes." The "washing of robes" is the struggle to either break or remain free of the practices of Babylon so as to be faithful disciples of the Lamb. The use of the present participle—"washing"—stresses the ongoing character of this task. Breaking free of empire is, by its very nature, an ongoing task.

Perusing these three lists, eight types of imperial vices are in view: murder, whoring, illusion, sorcery, worship of idols, abominable practices, cowardice, and faithlessness. These do not correspond one-to-one with any particular social practice in the Roman Empire. Rather, the vices were considered to be sins typical of empire and are hence appropriately attributed to those who collude with empire. While the types of activities signified here are described in biblically pejorative ways, in the world of Roman Asia they were everyday events that were not regarded as obscene or unusual at all. To most, they would have been seen to embody civic virtue.

The vices that characterize Babylon and exclude people from New Jerusalem were not simply the preserve of the imperial elite or the "nonbeliever." In fact, it was the practice of these vices by members of the *ekklēsiai* that constituted the crisis that pervades the pages of Revelation. That those who professed allegiance to Jesus were practicing them constituted the deepest scandal. Thus, among those who found themselves on the "outside" of New Jerusalem were members of the *ekklēsiai* who had not repented of their imperial sins.

Murder. Throughout the scriptures, the word used here for killing refers to the unlawful or unjust taking of life. We saw above that John envisioned Babylon as responsible for shedding the blood of prophets, holy ones, and of all who had been slain on earth (18:24). Those who embrace Babylon are portrayed as drinking the blood of these victims of empire. Thus, those who perform the violence and the multitude who are enthralled by it are guilty of murder. As John saw it, those who shed blood are given blood to drink (16:6). This is the justice of God operating behind the apocalyptic veil. The vice of murder puts the lie to the myth of the *Pax Romana*—the belief that the empire had brought an unsurpassed era of peace to the world. Those who embrace and participate in empire are murderers (cf. John 8:44).

Whoring. As we have seen, "whoring" does not refer to sexual activity. Rather, it conveys a truth about the seductive character of empire. The naming of "whoring" as an imperial vice includes a critique of those who were the agents of imperial seduction and those who let themselves be seduced. Outside the Christian communities, those who might be labeled the whore's "clients" included the provincial rulers, the imperial and local cult priests, and the poets of Roman propaganda. Inside the communities the "whores" were those who argued for an accommodation with the Roman Empire. Twice Revelation links the eating of meat sacrificed in the temples to "whoring." For example, "Jezebel," a figure condemned in the letter to Thyatira, was guilty of advocating the "whoring" of eating meat sacrificed in the imperial cult (2:20; also 2:14). As we saw in chapter 3, this practice legitimated both the imperial cult and the entire patronage system of Roman society. To refuse to participate in this practice was to escape the seductiveness of empire.

Illusion. As far as Revelation is concerned, the Greek words that are usually translated "lie" and "liar" (*pseudos/pseudēs*) are reflective of a more profound departure from the truth than is conveyed in the modern sense of the word "lie." The term is reflective of a systemic untruth that presents itself as reality. Those who propagate the myths of empire by word and deed are those who "love and practice illusion." As Beale puts it, those who engage in this sin express thereby "a desire to benefit from both the spiritual advantages of church membership and the economic security of participation in the ungodly world."[41] Throughout Revelation, Rome is presented as an illusory reality that survived by claiming support from the divine order. Those who propagated illusion about empire, then, were grave enemies of the truth. The propagation of imperial illusion was the task of the imperial rhetoricians, the history writers, and speechmakers, collectively referred to by John as the power of the "second beast," which "spoke like a dragon," "makes the inhabitants of the earth . . . worship the first beast," and "deceives the inhabitants of the earth" (13:11-14). It was found in the temples

41. Beale (1999), p. 1141.

and monuments located throughout Asia. It was found on the coins that circulated through the empire praising the emperor. It was also found in the hearts and minds of ordinary people whose captivation by the empire led them to ask in wonder: "Who is like the Beast and who can fight against it?" (13:4), meaning: which empire is as great as our empire, and who could possibly defeat it?

Sorcery. Like many of the listed vices, "sorcery" (Greek *pharmakoi*) was a long-standing concern of the biblical writers. In the Hebrew scriptures it denoted a range of practices considered hostile to the covenant with YHWH alone. In Exodus, for example, the *pharmakoi* practiced their art of political divination in the court of Pharaoh (Exod. 7:11, 22; 9:11). In Deuteronomy the *pharmakoi* were said to have practiced among the nations that which was not acceptable within the community of Israel (Deut. 18:10). Isaiah attributed sorcery to imperial Babylon. He contrasted the powerlessness of the imperial *pharmakoi* with the power of YHWH (Isa. 47:9, 12; cf. Nah. 3:4). The book of Daniel placed the *pharmakoi* in the court of King Nebuchadnezzar, where they acted as advisers to the imperial court (Dan. 2:2). It is clear from the Hebrew scriptures that "sorcery" is a vice that belonged to the realm of empire. As such it stood at odds with the ways of YHWH.

Worship of Idols. The critique of idol worship has a long tradition in the Hebrew scriptures. Such worship was considered a fundamental challenge to the worship of YHWH alone. Idols were associated with the numerous nations and empires with which Israel came into contact. Idolatry is best characterized as "fetishism": the substitution of something inferior for the true God, typically human-made objects. Revelation takes up the critique of idols in the language of the Hebrew prophets:

> They did not repent of the work of their hands, nor give up worshipping of demons and idols of gold and silver and bronze and stone and wood, which cannot either see or hear or walk. (9:20; cf. Pss. 115:4-8; 135:15-18; Isa. 17:8; 44:9-20; Dan. 5:4)

The worship of human-made objects, of course, took place in the temple cults that stood at the heart of the cities of Asia. But the ancient idol was not a self-referential object. Rather it referred beyond itself to the system that it was produced to legitimate. As we have seen, the idol (or imperial and local cults supporting the idol) was the glue that gave the people of Asia a sense of social cohesion. Sacrificing to an idol not only paid homage to the empire and its gods; it also bolstered the systems of patronage and the commodity economy of which the temple was a key component. Those who participated in the temple cults were the worshipers of idols. In doing this, they demonstrated their loyalty to Babylon and the Beast. They could have no part in New Jerusalem.

Abominable Practices. "Abomination" (Greek *bdelugma*) refers primarily to participation in the cultic practices of empire and nation. In Deuteronomy, the people of Israel were reminded of their experiences among the nations:

> You know how we lived in the land of Egypt, and how we came through the midst of the nations through which you passed. You have seen their detestable things [LXX *bdelugma*], the filthy idols of wood and stone, of silver and gold. (Deut. 29:16-17)

The defining distinction between the people of Israel and the people of the nations—allegiance to the imperial, national, or local idols—was at stake.[42]

The issue of "abomination" was also at stake in the different strategies pursued in the Maccabean and Danielic resistance to the Seleucid program of cultural reformation. As we saw in chapter 2, both 1 Maccabees and Daniel express disgust at the Seleucid placement of statues of Zeus in the Jerusalem temple. Both label this symbolic takeover as an "abomination that desolates" (1 Macc. 1:54; Dan. 9:27; 11:31; 12:11). John saw that the cultic practices, imperial and local, of Roman Asia were of the same character.

Cowardice. In the ancient Mediterranean world, the charge of cowardice was a grave accusation. The use of the word here, however, would turn upside down the concept of courage/cowardice, as it was commonly understood (cf. John 16:33). In all ancient Mediterranean cultures, standing up to a challenge to personal, kinship, or national honor was a manifestation of courage (e.g., 1 Macc. 2). War was the primary forum where courage manifested itself as the defense of perceived slights to the national honor. From heaven's perspective, the existence of the Roman Empire was a serious challenge to the honor of God and Jesus. This placed Rome in conflict with God for honor. The "war" against empire required great courage. To acquiesce to the power of empire, then, was an act of cowardice. Those members of the communities who had succumbed to the might or grandeur of Rome were "cowards" in the struggle against the empire. They did not have the endurance needed to gain victory over empire.

Faithlessness. As we will see in chapter 8, "faith" was considered an imperial virtue. It represented the placing of trust and loyalty in the person of Caesar. One could place one's faith in the empire, as virtually everyone did, or one could place one's faith in the crucified Jesus and his God. The labeling of those who acquiesced with empire as "faithless" was a radical reversal of the prevailing ideology. It matched the official Roman charge against Christians that "justified" capital punishment: *atheism.* As Rome claimed that Christians did not worship the approved divinities and were therefore subject to death, so Revelation claims

---

42. Other key texts that discuss "abomination" include 1 Kings 11:7; 2 Kings 23:13; Jer. 7:30; 13:27; 32:34; Ezek. 5:11; 7:20; 11:21; 20:7-8.

that those who follow Rome's practices cannot enter into the life of God in the New Jerusalem.

The Imperative: "Come Out" of Babylon

Babylon stands in diametric contrast to the ways of God. John's discernment that Babylon was embodied in the Roman Empire of his day had clear ramifications. By claiming to be followers of Jesus but actually being obedient subjects of the Roman Empire, the members of the *ekklēsiai* demonstrated a lack of understanding of both the God of Jesus and the Roman Empire. This is the context of the call to "come out" of Babylon (18:4).

> And I heard another voice out of heaven saying:
> "Come out, my people, out of her,
> so that you do not share in her sins,
> and so that you not receive her plagues;
> because joined together her sins go up to heaven,
> and God remembered her injustices." (18:4-5)

The inspirations for this directive are the words of the prophets to those in exile in Babylon. Second Isaiah announced to those exiled in Babylon: "Go out from Babylon, flee from Chaldea" (Isa. 48:20; 52:11). Jeremiah expressed a similar imperative: "Flee from Babylon, and go out of the land of the Chaldeans" (Jer. 50:8; 51:6, 45). These words of Isaiah also echo the story of liberation from Egypt. Isaiah reminds those whom he calls to leave Babylon that YHWH gave water in the desert to those fleeing Egypt (Isa. 48:21; cf. Exod. 17:1-7). He tells them that YHWH would march at their head and protect their rear (Isa. 52:12; cf. Exod. 13:21; 14:19). In the Bible there is really only one story: that of a people struggling to leave empire behind and set out to follow God. That story was to be relived whether in Egypt, Babylon, Rome, or elsewhere.

This call to "come out" served as both encouragement and warning to the *ekklēsiai*. Those faithfully resisting Rome were encouraged to continue in their resistance. Those colluding with empire were warned that the time to leave was *now*. In the apocalyptic worldview that bifurcates reality between God's realm and empire, the members of the *ekklēsiai* faced a crisis: it is not possible to be a citizen of more than one city. A defection from one to the other necessarily diminishes the one departed and enhances the other. In calling people to leave Babylon and enter New Jerusalem, Revelation called upon the members of the *ekklēsiai* to assist in the diminishment of Babylon. As Paul Minear explains: "Babylon's kingdom depends for its very existence upon the continued allegiance of her subjects; their exodus marks her doom."[43]

In Revelation, the imperative to "come out" of Babylon is not a geographical

---

43. Minear (1968), p. 152.

proposition as it was for the exilic prophets. It does not mean physically to leave Rome, Ephesus, or Philadelphia. It is not a call to flee the city for the country, the First World for the Third World. Rather, it is a call for the *ekklēsiai* to discern the true character of where they were and how to distance themselves from the imperial seduction of their time and place. As Pablo Richard explains, "This departure from Rome is not understood in the physical sense, but is to be economic, social, political, and spiritual; the idea is to resist, to refuse to participate, to create alternatives."[44] What would this creative alternative have looked like in the lives of the *ekklēsiai* of Asia? We shall investigate this after we have looked at how John envisions New Jerusalem.

NEW JERUSALEM

Babylon is fallen (18:2). The two Beasts are thrown into the lake of fire (19:20). The kings of the earth are slain with the sword of truth (19:21). The Satan/Dragon, too, is hurled into the lake of fire (20:10), as are those "whose name could not be found in the book of life" (20:15). God and the Lamb have defeated the coalition that claimed divine status yet practiced incalculable injustice. In seeing these things behind the veil, John was reminded that God is more powerful than empire. The vision of Babylon as fallen prepares the way for the vision of New Jerusalem. As John Sweet puts it, the "slum-clearance" of Babylon has made room for New Jerusalem.[45]

We have seen that Babylon exists wherever human society becomes empire, asserting its power over creation and usurping the privileges of God. Similarly, New Jerusalem is found wherever human community resists the ways of empire and places God at the center of its shared life. Unfortunately, as Stringfellow observes, it is much easier to discern the operation of Babylon than that of New Jerusalem in our world:

> If one speaks of Babylon, there is little hindrance in locating Babylon; it is not so very difficult to discern the Babylonian character of nations or other principalities. But if one bespeaks Jerusalem, as the new or renewed society of mature humanity, where is this Jerusalem?[46]

The most compelling fact about the two cities is that they are presented as polar opposites. Babylon is a consistent image of ruin and doom, while splendor and light abound in New Jerusalem. John sees Babylon as a parody of New Jerusalem. In the vision, New Jerusalem is the ultimate reality, while Babylon is a gross counterfeit of that reality. Presented with such a picture, who would want

44. Richard, p. 135.
45. Sweet (1990), p. 301.
46. Stringfellow (1973), p. 58.

to live in Babylon? The answer: Most of us! For as Daniel Berrigan wrote, "Those who dwell in Babylon do not know they are there."[47] We were raised and educated to see the "great city" as something if not quite perfect at least livable. This is the potency of John's vision. In seeing behind the veil, John saw beyond the propaganda and myths that filled his world. He saw the depths of the problem, and just as important, the glorious alternative.

New Jerusalem, like Babylon, is envisioned in imagery that comes from the Hebrew scriptures, especially from those sources which exemplify the struggle against imperial co-option of the radical message of YHWH (see chapter 2). Table 18 outlines the sources for the visionary imagery of the "holy city."

The Place Where God and People Live Together

Those who faithfully reject empire and embrace the way of God are the residents of New Jerusalem. It is with these people that God lives:

> Behold, the dwelling of God is with people,
> God will dwell with them,
> and they will be God's people,
> and God's self will be with them. (21:3; also 22:3-4)

God's dwelling with the citizens of New Jerusalem is expressed in a number of ways. Perhaps the most significant is the presentation of God and the Lamb as the temple of the city. John's vision of New Jerusalem has much in common with Ezekiel's final vision (Ezek. 40-48), yet it differs in key ways. As we saw in chapter 2, while in exile in Babylon, Ezekiel saw a vision of a restored Jerusalem in which a reconstructed temple dominated the scene. In his vision, ritual purity and adherence to *torah* controlled by the priestly elite regulated admission to the temple (Ezek. 44). Ezekiel's vision maintained the division between the people and the priests. In John's vision, however, there is a crucial difference: in New Jerusalem there is no temple, since God and the Lamb are its temple: "I saw no temple in it, for the Lord God the Almighty and the Lamb is its temple" (21:22; cf. Mark 11:22-25). Furthermore, all those who live with God are "priests" (1:6; 5:10; cf. Exod. 19:5-6).

The biblical tradition itself is divided on the question of temple. With the newly founded institution of kingship in Israel (which itself went against the covenant with YHWH alone; e.g., Judg. 9; 1 Sam. 8) came the building of the Jerusalem temple. A centralized political authority was complemented by a centralized cult. The cult helped maintain the power and wealth of the king; therefore the king maintained the power of the cult. The temple project of David and Solomon was a rejection of the radical egalitarianism of God's plan for the people of Israel (2 Sam. 7; 1 Kings 12). This antitemple tradition was recalled by Third Isaiah in the face of the pro-Persian movement to rebuild the temple after exile.

---

47. Berrigan (1983), p. 107.

Table 18
ECHOES OF HEBREW SCRIPTURE
IN THE IMAGERY OF NEW JERUSALEM

Revelation 21-22	*The Hebrew Scriptures*
New heaven and earth (21:1)	Isa. 65:17; 66:22
Bride prepared for marriage (21:2)	Isa. 61:10
God's home among them, they are God's people (21:3)	Lev. 26:11-12; Jer. 31:33; Ezek. 37:27; Zech 8:8
God-with-them (21:3)	Isa. 7:14
God wipes away tears (21:4)	Isa. 25:8
No more death (21:4)	Isa. 25:7
No mourning, crying, or pain (21:4)	Isa. 35:10; 65:19
The vision is true (21:5)	Dan. 2:45; 8:26
Alpha and Omega (21:6)	Isa. 44:6; 48:12
Water without price (21:6)	Isa. 55:1
"I will be his God and he will be my son" (21:7)	2 Sam. 7:14
Vice does not enter the city (21:8, 27)	Isa. 52:1
Fire and brimstone on those who practice vice (21:8)	Ezek. 38:22
In the spirit he carried me to a very high mountain and showed me a city (21:10)	Ezek. 40:2
The city has the glory of God (21:11)	Isa. 60:1-2
Wall of the city (21:12)	Isa. 60:18
Three gates on the four walls, named after twelve tribes of Israel (21:12-13)	Ezek. 48:31-35
Measure the city (21:15)	Ezek. 40:3
City as a square (21:16)	Ezek. 48:16-17
City as a cube (21:16)	1 Kings 6:20
Wall of jasper (21:18)	Isa. 54:12; Tob. 13:16
Streets of gold (21:18, 21)	Tob. 13:16
Foundations adorned with every jewel (21:19)	Isa. 54:11
Twelve jewels (21:19-20)	Exod. 28:15-21; Ezek. 28:13
Gates of pearl (21:21)	Isa. 54:12
No need for sun or moon; God is light (21:23; 22:5)	Isa. 60:19-20
Nations will come to its light (21:24)	Isa. 60:3
Its gates are never closed (21:25)	Isa. 60:11
Nations bring their honor and wealth to Jerusalem (21:26)	Isa. 60:11; 66:20
Book of life (21:27)	Exod. 32:32; Isa. 4:3; Dan. 12:1
River of life (22:1)	Gen. 2:10; Ezek. 47:1-9; Zech. 14:8
Tree of life (22:2, 14, 19)	Gen. 2:9; Ezek. 47:12
Twelve crops, leaves for healing (22:2)	Ezek. 47:12
Every curse abolished (22:3)	Zech. 14:11

At the same time, there was a biblical tradition in favor of the centralized cult. This voice can be heard especially in the exilic message of Ezekiel and the post-exilic messages of Haggai, Zechariah, and Ezra/Nehemiah discussed in chapter 2 above. This tradition maintained vitality until the Roman destruction of Jerusalem in 70 C.E.

John's radical vision, like that of the Gospel writers, sides with the antitemple tradition. He saw the Jerusalem temple as no different from the temple of Augustus in Pergamum or the temple of Artemis in Ephesus. All were manifestations of a centralized system that stood against God. Rather than having a priestly class standing above the people, John sees the entire people who resist empire as a nation of priests (1:6). This egalitarian vision saw God and the Lamb as living in the city among the people.

The Architecture of New Jerusalem

The architecture of New Jerusalem would have made it a perfect city in antiquity's conception. Ancient (like most modern) cities were typically constructed in a haphazard way. Cities were shaped both by the landscape on which they were constructed and by the contingencies of history. An exception to this was the ancient city of Babylon, at least in its description by the first Greek historian, Herodotus (c. 480-425 B.C.E.). Herodotus described Babylon built as a square (*History* 1.178). To the Greek mind, a square was a symbol of order. John sees New Jerusalem, like Babylon, aligned with the points of the compass in all directions (21:13, 16).

But more than this, New Jerusalem is a *cube*: it is as high as it is long and wide (21:16). The cube was the symbol of perfection par excellence. The cubic structure of New Jerusalem likened it to the "Holy of Holies" of the Jerusalem temple, believed during monarchical Judah to be the exclusive dwelling place of YHWH (1 Kings 6:20). In contrast, John's vision sees God dwelling throughout New Jerusalem.

The measurements of the city's dimensions are also significant. The city is measured at 12,000 *stadia* wide, long, and high (21:16). The number 12, of course, is characteristic of the city itself. The "thousand" represents simply a very large number.[48] Given that there were eight *stadia* to the Roman mile, this would make one side of the city about 2,400 kilometers or 1,500 miles long![49]

To the cubic perfection of New Jerusalem is added the factor of twelve. The city has twelve gates, with an angel standing sentinel at each gate, and the city is

---

48. Herodotus describes each side of Babylon as 120 *stadia* in length. At 12,000 *stadia* each side of New Jerusalem is one hundred times as long as those of Babylon: "such is the size of the city of Babylon; and it was planned like no other city whereof we know" (*History* 1.178).

49. To grasp the size of New Jerusalem these figures might help. The city has a surface area of over five million square kilometers. This amounts to just under two-thirds of the Australian landmass or over one-half of the total area of the United States! This clearly puts the city outside the realm of the literal.

built on twelve foundations. Twelve was a number of great significance throughout the Mediterranean world, especially as linked with zodiacal symbolism.[50]

So who are these people who have removed themselves from empire's
embrace? They are those who live their allegiance to YHWH alone by worshiping God and the Lamb. Inscribed on twelve gates of the city are the names of the
"twelve tribes of the children of Israel" (21:12). The gates signify that this
counter-imperial people live in continuity with the very beginning of God's
covenant project. On the twelve foundations of the city the names of the "twelve
apostles of the Lamb" are written (21:14). The foundations indicate that Jesus
and the *ekklēsiai* have continued the heritage of allegiance with YHWH alone
begun so long ago.

Like the Mesopotamian and Canaanite fortress cities, New Jerusalem too has
a "great and high wall," measuring 144 cubits (21:12, 17; 65 meters). This number (twelve times twelve) signifies social perfection. The wall of the ancient city
was constructed to protect the city from external attack. Yet the wall of New
Jerusalem was not built for defense—after all, its gates are always open (21:25).
This description of the city with its gates always open makes New Jerusalem different from the walled city-states of Egypt, Canaan, Babylon, and Persia. This
vision of open gates builds on Third Isaiah's opposition to the accommodation to
Persia examined in chapter 2. There we saw that the closed gates of Jerusalem
(Neh. 7:3) signified collusion with the Persian Empire. The open gates of Third
Isaiah's Jerusalem (Isa. 60:11) were a rejection of the Persian Empire's plans for
the city, just as New Jerusalem's open gates express dependence on God rather
than empire for security.

Further, the vision of the wall of New Jerusalem maintains that while everything inside the city is in harmony with the ways of God, there *is* an outside that
remains imperial in character. The wall serves to demarcate the imperial and the
divine, earth and heaven. It is not a rigid boundary dividing specific people from
one another. Rather it is a porous boundary the open gates of which allow people who are "washing their robes" to enter. The gates of the city are always open
to receive those who come out of Babylon.

After describing the measurements of the wall and the city in his vision, the
depiction turns to an account of the materials that adorn the city (21:18-21). The
wall, foundations, gates, and street are built with precious gems and metals. Just
as the fine linen worn by the bride was identified with the "just deeds of the holy
ones" (19:8), so we should also understand the precious jewels that decorate the
city as a symbol of the just practices of the followers of Jesus.[51]

Both Babylon and New Jerusalem are described as having great wealth. But
while the wealth of Babylon was a commodity achieved by exploitation, the
wealth of New Jerusalem was part of the commonwealth of the city. The wealth
of New Jerusalem surpasses that of Solomon's temple (2 Chron. 3). Yet the fact
that the wealth of the city is used in communal ways—it lined the streets and

---

50. Malina (1995), p. 85.
51. Fekkes, pp. 286-87.

gates and walls—repudiates the centralization of wealth under the Solomonic regime (2 Chron. 9). The wealth of New Jerusalem was gained by an altogether different economy, as we shall now see.

New Jerusalem as Garden

While it is the amplified features of urban architecture that dominate the first part of the description of New Jerusalem, the city is also envisioned as the primeval garden—Paradise or Eden (cf. 2:7). The image of the garden is conveyed by the presence of both the "river of life" (22:1) and the "tree of life" (22:2), which are found in the Genesis creation myth:

> Out of the ground YHWH God made to grow every tree that is pleasant to the sight and good for food, the tree of life also in the midst of the garden. . . . A river flows out of Eden to water the garden, and from there it divides and becomes four branches. (Gen. 2:9-10)

Ezekiel took these images of river and tree and applied them to the reconstructed temple:

> Then he [YHWH] brought me back to the entrance of the temple; there, water was flowing from below the threshold of the temple toward the east. . . . On the banks, on both sides of the river, there will grow all kinds of trees for food. Their leaves will not wither nor their fruit fail, but they will bear fresh fruit every month, because the water for them flows from the sanctuary. Their fruit will be for food, and their leaves for healing. (Ezek. 47:1, 12; cf. Zech. 14:8)

This image of Eden was a feature of other apocalyptic texts. 4 Ezra, written about the same time as Revelation (see chapter 2), contains a similar vision:

> It is for you that Paradise is opened, the tree of life is planted, the age to come is prepared, plenty is provided, a city is built, rest is appointed, goodness is established and wisdom perfected beforehand. (4 Ezra 8:52)

While using Ezekiel as the chief source of its imagery, Revelation places the origin of the river at the "throne of God and of the Lamb" (22:1), not at the threshold of the temple as in Ezekiel. This is consistent with John's antitemple vision. The sovereignty of God and the Lamb, not empire's spurious claims to sovereignty, is the origin of the "river of life." While the "water of life" flows from the throne of God and the Lamb, the "blood" of murder flows from the throne of empire.[52] In the biblical tradition, the "water of life" signified God's

---

52. For the relationship between blood and empire, see Rev. 1:5; 5:9; 6:10; 7:14; 12:11; 14:20; 17:6; 18:24; 19:2.

gracious provision of the requisites of life. In Revelation, New Jerusalem is the place where this original harmony is restored.

The "water of life" was introduced earlier in the vision: "I will give to the thirsty free from the fountain of the water of life" (21:6; see 22:17). This verse connects the "water of life" image with Isa. 55, which also depicted a renewed Jerusalem:

> Everyone who thirsts, come to the waters;
> and you that have no money,
> come, buy and eat!
> Come, buy wine and milk without money and without
>   price. (Isa. 55:1)

In this context, water freely given contrasts the economy of God with the economy of empire. In New Jerusalem, the water freely given by God prevails over the imperial economy of exploitation and debt.[53]

Similarly, the "tree of life" is also evocative of God's economy. The "tree of life" produces fruit for the citizens of New Jerusalem and leaves for the "healing of the nations." Again John transforms Ezekiel's vision of the restored Jerusalem. Whereas Ezekiel saw trees lining the banks of the river, John saw a *single* tree growing on the street of the city and on either bank of the river. This is, of course, not literally possible. Yet it expresses the unity out of which God's bounty is provided for the diversity of peoples who populate New Jerusalem. Similarly, while Ezekiel saw the leaves of the trees as being "for healing," John sees that they are "for the healing of *the nations*." God's economy, in addition to serving the needs of its own participants, is able to bring healing to the nations previously seduced by the economy of empire.

This vision of the garden restored does not mark a return to a primeval state. This is not a vision of rural idyll or primordial bliss. Rather it is a vision of the "greening" of the city. The city, which had its origins in murder and the desire to be independent of God, is transformed by the presence of God and the praxis of Jesus. Now the garden erupts right through the pavement, so to speak, of the

---

53. God's alternative economy depicted as a garden is complemented by John's vision of the new earth as not containing a "sea." As Barbara Rossing explains: "The disappearance of the 'sea' (*thalassa*) in Rev. 21:1 is the most pointed contrast between the political economies of New Jerusalem and Babylon: New Jerusalem will have no sea, and therefore no shipping economy. Long-distance maritime trade in luxury goods which was so prominent in Babylon's economy will now come to an end. Most scholars interpret the pronouncement about the disappearance of the sea in terms of chaos traditions, with the sea representing terrifying and mythological evil forces. Such a mythological element of primordial terror has not been the principal critique of the sea for Revelation, however. Rather, Revelation portrays the sea quite realistically (as well as mythologically) as a location of evil (Rev. 13:1) and a place where commercial ships sail (Rev. 8:9; 18:11-17). . . . [Revelation] promises an alternate economic vision of an eschatological city where sea trade in luxury goods will be supplanted by an economy that provides the essentials of life 'without payment' (Rev. 21:6; 22:17)" (Rossing, chapter 5).

main street of New Jerusalem. This vision of the "greening" of the city occurs against the background of the general antiurban bias of the biblical tradition, of which Babylon became the archetype. In envisioning New Jerusalem as both God's temple and God's garden, the human project is redeemed. No longer is human organization doomed to repeat the mistakes of history. With the Lamb as exemplar, it is possible to break the cycle of violence, of economic acquisition and scarcity, of the rise and fall of political power.

The Joyous Life in New Jerusalem

Revelation envisioned life in New Jerusalem not as a grim contrariness to Babylon but as a joyous alternative to empire, which constituted "real" living. Authentic community is a place where life can be celebrated, songs can be sung, and human relationships can flourish. In his vision of New Jerusalem, John appropriated much of the joyous and liberating vision of Third Isaiah.

One of the key changes from life in Babylon to life in New Jerusalem is the healing of all pain and suffering (21:4). This is presented not as if it were a fairy-tale dream but as the concrete consequence of a community living in harmony with its Creator and with the Lamb as its shepherd. The apocalyptic insight is that mourning, crying, and pain all result from a life situation compromised by the power of the Beasts disrupting the creative unity of God's design. When people choose to live God's ways fully, normal life processes such as aging will be experienced not as loss but as part of the continuous ebb and flow between Creator and creation. Remarkably, the healing of our alienation from God will conquer death itself. As Paul says, "The last enemy to be destroyed is death" (1 Cor. 15:26). This process begins with the movement away from the competitive distrust of Babylon to the harmonious mutuality of New Jerusalem.

A related aspect of life in New Jerusalem is the absence of darkness or the need for any source of light other than God's own glorious illumination (21:23-25). Throughout the New Testament we hear the echoes of Isaiah's grand announcement, "[t]he people who walked in darkness have seen a great light; those who lived in a land of deep darkness—on them light has shined" (Isa. 9:2; cf. Matt. 4:16). In John's Gospel, of course, Jesus himself is the light of the world (9:5; 11:9). Or in the words of the First Letter of John, "God is light and in God there is no darkness" (1 John 1:5). Revelation shares with the rest of the New Testament the trust that living in God's presence offers an unrivaled clarity and beauty of vision to all who choose it. Life in New Jerusalem is like a summer day at the extreme latitudes, extending its long horizon beyond the constricted vista of empire.

Empire's economic exploitation is reversed in New Jerusalem. Rather than stealing wealth and resources from the world, people and nations will freely bring their glory to the Holy City. The traditional image of nations bringing tribute to Zion is democratized to express people's universal sharing of God's gifts with one another (22:24, 26; cf. Isa. 61:6). The residents of New Jerusalem live in an economy of *gift*, not of wage slavery or measured rewards. Abundance provided by God overflows on all without hoarding or greed.

Finally, people in New Jerusalem live without fear of future judgment: "No curse [Greek *katathēma*] will be found there any more" (22:3; cf. Zech. 14:11). The Greek word refers to the "ban of destruction" ordered against cities living in disobedience to God, used in the verse from Zechariah which John adapts here. Thus, it is not a matter of the removal of specific objects, but of the risk of being "cursed," that is, being sentenced to divine destruction.[54] Those within New Jerusalem are immune from the risk of facing God's wrath. They truly live in *shalom*.

The Alternative Praxis of the Followers of the Lamb

In John's time, the counterimperial praxis of New Jerusalem was meant to exist *alongside* the imperial praxis of Roman society. The call to transfer citizenship from Babylon to New Jerusalem places the stress on the practical imperatives of change. While it is God's sovereignty that assures that the pseudo-sovereignty of empire is exposed, it is the daily and persistent endurance of the followers of God and the Lamb amid the difficulties of resisting empire that constitutes their "victory." The downfall of Babylon is not brought about by a passive waiting on God. Rather, it is won by joining forces with God and the Lamb in active resistance to empire and creative participation in New Jerusalem. Thus, the followers of God and the Lamb were called to say "*no* and *yes* simultaneously . . . [to] expose the reign of death in Babylon while affirming the aspiration for new life."[55] Both this resistance to death and creative embrace of life were to be operative in the political, economic, and cultural spheres of the *ekklēsiai* of Roman Asia.

The Sociopolitical Sphere. We saw in chapter 3 the many ways in which Asian Christians would be tempted and pressured to participate in Rome's seductive attractions. How were they to attempt to live Revelation's radical alternative from within their urban settings? As preposterous as it may sound, fidelity to the apocalyptic good news called for the creation of an entire parallel social universe. It took the form that Greeks called *ekklēsia,* and which we have come to call "church."

Our diluted expectations of the role of churches as comprising alternative worlds have frequently closed off our imaginations to the possibilities that John's vision anticipated. Just as Paul refers to his fellow Christians with the radical titles of "brother" and "sister"—thus declaring them to be family—John's vision expects the *ekklēsia* to be the place in which a new "government" is born. The Greek *ekklēsia* was an assembly, a coming together of people for political purposes. So, too, the Christian *ekklēsia* was expected to be the foundation for com-

---

54. Bauckham (1993), p. 316.
55. Stringfellow (1973), p. 63.

munity life based on the principles expressed in the New Jerusalem vision. This meant that all would participate with equal status and with mutual respect, regardless of gender, race, nationality, or other imperial marks of status.[56] It is one of the tragic ironies of history that this process was reversed with the conversion of the Roman emperor Constantine in the fourth century. With Constantine, the *ekklēsia* took on the shape of imperial Rome, a form that it continues to bear today in its hierarchy and decision-making process. And yet, for those willing to lift the veil, John's vision remains bright and hope-filled as presenting the possibilities for an alternative political structure.

The Socioeconomic Sphere. What might such an economy grounded in the New Jerusalem vision have looked like? As we have seen, a network of patron–client relationships formed the pyramidal structure that constituted Roman society. Nothing happened in terms of economics outside the rigid structure of this pyramid (see diagram 1, p. 97). By envisioning a New Jerusalem where God and the Lamb dwell among the people (21:3), the heavenly hierarchy that legitimated economic exploitation was flattened. God no longer resides above the people but in their midst. The (vertical) pyramid is replaced by a (horizontal) egalitarian communion between God and humanity. Because the heavenly order mirrored the social order, this necessarily repudiated the social pyramid sustained by the patron–client network. As a consequence of God living among the people, social hierarchy disappears.

In New Jerusalem, horizontal associations and reciprocal economic relationships would replace the vertical exchange of goods and services that characterized the patron-client network. In this order, acquisition and scarcity would be replaced by a system in which there would be enough for all. For the Asian *ekklēsiai*, this would have involved mutual support among the members of the communities, and between the communities in the different cities (cf. Rom. 15:25-28; 1 Cor. 16:2-3). This linking of the *ekklēsiai*, if projected on a wide scale, would have destroyed the patron–client network on which Rome relied for its continuance. If community members traded with each other rather than with those who had the mark of the Beast, a new economic order would be born. This accounts for the different characterization of the wealth possessed by Babylon and New Jerusalem. The wealth of Babylon, gained as it was through the patron–client network, was a sign of luxuriousness and corruption. The wealth of New Jerusalem, however, gained through voluntary and reciprocal gift, was a sign of God's bounty.

The Sociocultural Sphere. As we have seen, the cities of Roman Asia contained numerous sites where the empire represented itself to the residents of the Asian cities. These included the temples in which the imperial and associated cults were manifested, the public buildings dedicated to Rome, the games and

---

56. Cf. Giblin (1991), p. 194.

theatrics sponsored by or held in honor of Rome, and the administrative and legal offices of the empire located in the major cities.

John calls on the members of the *ekklēsiai* to have nothing to do with these manifestations of Roman power and patronage. As we have seen, this included a rejection of the meat sacrificed in the temples (2:14, 20) and a refusal to participate in the temple cults themselves (20:4; cf. 1 Cor. 10:14). The refusal to participate in the cultural activities of the city placed the followers of Jesus at odds with the entire social world of the Asian cities. As Klaus Wengst comments: "Anyone who as a Christian withdrew from them was alienated from the world and made himself an outsider."[57] To be on the outside of an all-encompassing order had certain social, economic, and possibly legal consequences. There was little social or economic protection available for those who deliberately and publicly placed themselves outside the system.

To withstand such pressure, strong social bonds between members of the *ekklēsiai* would have been necessary. Those who sought to follow Jesus in the cities of Roman Asia did so in the context of the *ekklēsia* of which they were members. The *ekklēsia* itself was part of an international movement of people committed to the way of Christ Jesus. These *ekklēsiai* were the imperfect vehicles in which the Christians of the Asian cities attempted discipleship. Revelation recognized that despite the faults displayed by members of the *ekklēsia,* this was the communal context that created the possibility for an alternative reality. As the sociologist Peter Berger contends, "it is well nigh impossible in the long run to keep up alone and without social support one's own counter-definitions of the world."[58] People require a social order in which to maintain any social belief and practice. Berger argues that without a social collectivity that provides support for the holding of social counterdefinitions (such as that manifested in Revelation), endurance for the long haul is impossible. A network of viable *ekklēsiai* was crucial to the ability of the followers of God and the Lamb to "come out" of empire. This is where the stories were told and retold, baptism and Eucharist practiced, liturgy celebrated (as discussed in chapter 7 below) and service to the poor and public witness to the world woven as basic practices into the cultural fabric of God's new community.

The Effectiveness of Counterimperial Praxis. Revelation presents John's insight that behind the veil, empire was a fallen reality: it had already been conquered by the Lamb. It was the already-won victory of the Lamb that enabled the followers of the Lamb to share in this victory themselves. While apocalyptic insight revealed that empire is already fallen, it is clear that if enough people withdrew from empire and began to practice God's alternative way, empire would lose its power, even from the earthly perspective. One reason that empire flourishes is because otherwise good people do nothing. Yet what would happen if good people began to resist empire?

57. Wengst, p. 121.
58. Berger, p. 39.

In a letter by Pliny, governor of the province of Bithynia-Pontus, to the emperor Trajan (c. 110 C.E.) we find a hint of the effectiveness of counterimperial praxis. Pliny wrote to the emperor requesting a policy for a procedure to deal with those in his jurisdiction who were accused of being followers of Jesus. In that letter Pliny wrote:

> At any rate it is certain enough that the almost deserted temples begin to be resorted to, that long disused ceremonies of religion are almost restored, and the flesh of sacrificial victims finds a market, whereas buyers until now were very few. (Pliny, *Letter to Trajan* 10.96)

In this excerpt Pliny blames Christian nonparticipation in key imperial practices for a decline in those practices across the province. Although at the time of writing the downward trend has been reversed, Pliny is adamant that the "wretched cult" of Christianity had had an impact on the life of the empire. Because of their alternative practices the temples had been "almost deserted," the ceremonies of religion were "long disused," and buyers in the meat market were "very few." While it is difficult to know the exact nature of the impact of faithful discipleship on the empire—ancient writers were quite prone to exaggeration—it would seem that the governor of this province that neighbored Asia was very concerned for the civic life in his jurisdiction.

The refusal by followers of Jesus to engage in temple worship and to buy meat sacrificed in the temples had concrete consequences. The Christian defection from Rome in the province of Bithynia-Pontus was experienced as a shock to the body politic. For a time, the empire's carefully structured façade was in disarray. It is both the seductive power of empire and its preparedness to threaten social sanctions that holds the people of empire in subjection. Would not the labeling of that seductiveness as "whoring" and the refusal to be thus seduced represent a blow to the power of empire? Would not a group of people who refused to participate in empire because it was "Babylon" represent a real shift in the world's balance of power? Would not the unveiling of empire signal a new social mind that could conceive of alternatives to empire and hence threaten its absolute hold over the populace? Would not a people who were ready to die rather than submit to empire represent a serious challenge to empire's violence? The answer to these questions is, we believe, yes.

REFLECTION QUESTIONS

1. What is your sense of the value of "cities" generally speaking? That is, are cities inherently opposed to God, or are they neutral realities that depend on circumstances? Is the good life easier in the city or the country? Why do you believe what you do about cities?

2. Reflect on your reaction to the use of female imagery in Revelation's presentation of the apocalyptic cities. Consider other traditional uses of

female imagery, such as storms or ships. Might there be other, less sexist ways to describe what one sees "behind the veil"? Brainstorm such possibilities in a group.

3. Take some time to imagine a world that you would like to live in. How does it differ from the world around us? What aspects of Revelation's portrait of New Jerusalem seem attractive to you? Are there aspects that don't seem attractive to you? Why or why not?

7

"The Empire of the World
Has Become the Empire
of Our Lord and of His Messiah"

Liturgy and Worship in Revelation

One of the greatest differences between Revelation and other New Testament texts is Revelation's portrayal of numerous scenes of liturgy and worship. The Gospels never show the followers of Jesus in prayer, although Jesus prays regularly (e.g., Mark 1:35; 6:46; 14:35; John 11:41-42; 17:1-26), teaches his followers how to pray (e.g., Matt. 5:44; 6:5-9; Mark 11:25), and harshly criticizes the hypocritical prayer of the Jerusalem elite (Mark 12:40; Luke 18:11-14). Similarly, Paul refers many times to his own prayer and offers advice to his communities on how to pray and conduct themselves during worship (e.g., 1 Cor. 11, 14; 1 Thess. 5:17), as do the other epistle writers (e.g., James 5:13-16; 1 Pet. 4:7; Jude 1:20).

Revelation, though, like the work of a good novelist, *shows* rather than *tells* its audience how to offer prayer and worship. As we will demonstrate, the powerful images of loud and dramatic liturgy serve several crucial functions:

1. They encourage the audience to remember that *God is listening and will respond* to their prayers for justice and peace.
2. They generate solidarity in the *ekklēsiai* through shared song and other forms of communal prayer.
3. They drown out and parody the liturgy of both the imperial and mystery cults in Roman Asia.
4. They contrast with the silencing of song in fallen Babylon (Rev. 18:22; see also chapter 6 above).
5. They remind listeners which events call for celebration, namely, the enthronement of God and the Lamb with royal power over all creation.

Not surprisingly, there are exactly *seven* scenes of worship in Revelation, all of which take place in "heaven." Each scene is unique, but there are several elements common to most of them, as shown in table 19 below. As is true throughout Revelation, many passages from Hebrew scripture are echoed in these scenes, although most are modified to fit John's theological goals grounded in his visionary experience. The most frequently used source for John's forms and content of worship is the book of Israel's praise, the Psalms. In particular, John has reworked themes from Psalms 95-100, a collection of songs celebrating the victory and enthronement of the divine warrior in heaven over all the gods of the earth. To a Jewish mind, the most shocking innovation in Revelation's portrayal of heavenly worship is the presence with God of *the Lamb who was slaughtered* as also worthy of praise, honor, and thanksgiving. As was shown in chapter 5 above, it is this worthiness of the Lamb, because of his acceptance of death at the hands of empire in witness against empire's evil, that empowers him to open the scroll and explain the meaning of history.

We invite you to follow along as we proceed through Revelation's scenes of worship, explaining how each one calls its listeners to renew their faith in the One who truly reigns and in his Messiah. As we go, you might reflect on how different the heavenly liturgies presented in Revelation are from those most people experience in their weekly church services, asking why it is that we tend to settle for much less than our text calls us to when we gather to offer God praise and thanksgiving.

Table 19
LITURGY AND WORSHIP PASSAGES IN REVELATION WITH HEBREW SCRIPTURE CROSS-REFERENCES

Scene	Who Offers Worship	Titles for Those Who Receive Worship	Forms of Worship	Content of Worship
[After the messages to the ekklēsiai] (prologue: 4:2-7) 4:8-11	Four living creatures with six wings and full of eyes *(Ezek. 1:18)*	Lord God Almighty The One who is and was and is to come	Ceaseless prayer *(Ps. 1:2)* Prostration *(e.g., Ps. 95:6)*	Holy, holy, holy *(Isa. 6:2-3)* Glory, honor, power you created *(e.g., Pss. 95:4-5; 100:3)*
	24 elders	The One seated on the throne *(God on heavenly throne: 9 times in Psalms; see esp. Ps. 99:1; Isa. 6:1; 66:1; Dan. 7:9)*	Casting of crowns	

Scene	Who Offers Worship	Titles for Those Who Receive Worship	Forms of Worship	Content of Worship
		The One who lives forever and ever *(Dan. 4:34; 12:7)* Our Lord and God		
[After the Lamb has been found worthy to open the scroll] 5:8-14	Four living creatures 24 elders Myriads of myriads *(Dan. 7:10)* of angels Every creature in heaven and on earth and under the earth and in the sea, and all that is in them	The Lamb that was slaughtered The One seated on the throne	Incense in golden bowls (the prayers of the holy ones) *(e.g., Num. 7:14; 1 Kings 7:50)* A new song *(Isa. 42:10ff.; Pss. 96; 98)* Singing in a loud voice *(e.g., Pss. 95:1; 98:4; 100:1)* Prostration	You are worthy to take the scroll and to open its seals, for you were slaughtered and by your blood you ransomed for God holy ones from every tribe and language and people and nation; you have made them to be an empire and priests *(Exod. 19:5-6)* serving our God, and they will reign on earth. Worthy is the Lamb that was slaughtered to receive power and wealth and wisdom and might and honor and glory and blessing! Blessing and honor and glory and might forever and ever!
[After the opening of the first six seals] 7:9-12 (with explanation at 7:13-17)	Great multitude that no one could count, from every nation, from all tribes and peoples and languages robed in white with palm	The Lamb Our God who is seated on the throne	Crying out praise in a loud voice Prostration Singing Worship day and night	Salvation belongs to our God who is seated on the throne, and to the Lamb! Amen! Blessing and glory and wisdom and thanksgiving and honor and power and might

Scene	Who Offers Worship	Titles for Those Who Receive Worship	Forms of Worship	Content of Worship
	branches *(Lev. 23:40)* in their hands Angels Four living creatures 24 elders			be to our God forever and ever! Amen.
[After the seventh trumpet] 11:15-18	Loud voices in heaven 24 elders	God Lord God Almighty	Loud voices in proclamation Prostration Singing	The empire of the world has become the empire of our Lord and of his Messiah, and he will reign forever and ever. We give you thanks, Lord God Almighty, who are and who were, for you have taken your great power and begun to reign. The nations raged *(Ps. 2:1),* but your wrath has come, and the time for judging the dead, for rewarding your servants, the prophets and holy ones and all who fear your name, both small and great, and for destroying those who destroy the earth.
[After the beastly liturgy] 14:1-5	144,000 virgins *(Jer. 18:13; Amos 5:2; Lam. 2:13)* with name of Lamb and name of his Father written	The Lamb standing on Mt. Zion The throne	New song *(Pss. 96, 98; Isa. 42:10ff.)*	Not revealed

Scene	Who Offers Worship	Titles for Those Who Receive Worship	Forms of Worship	Content of Worship
	on their fore-heads *(Ezek. 9:4)* who have not defiled themselves with women, the first fruits for God *(Lev. 23:9-14)* and the Lamb; they have no lie in their mouth *(Isa. 53:9; Zeph. 3:13)* and are without blame			
	Voice from heaven like many waters, loud thunder, harpists playing			
	(Four living creatures and 24 elders are present but not partici-pating)			
[After the angels with the seven plagues are first seen] 15:2-4	Those who had conquered the beast and its image and the number of its name	Lord God Almighty Lord King of the nations *(Jer. 10:7)*	Singing the song of Moses *(Deut. 31:30-32:44; Exod. 15:1-18)*, the servant of God, and the song of the Lamb	Great and amazing are your deeds, Just and true are your ways Who will not fear and glorify your name? For you alone are holy. All nations will come and wor-ship before you, for your judgments have been revealed.
[After Bab-ylon is revealed as fallen] 19:1-8	Great multi-tude in heaven 24 elders Four living creatures	Our God Lord our God the Almighty	Loud voice of praise like many waters and mighty thunder-peals	Hallelujah! *("praise YHWH": 35 times in Psalms)* Salvation and glory and power to our God for his judg-ments are true and

Scene	Who Offers Worship	Titles for Those Who Receive Worship	Forms of Worship	Content of Worship
	Four living creatures			just; he has judged the great whore who corrupted the earth with her fornication, and he has
	Voice from the throne			avenged on her the blood of his servants.
				Hallelujah! The smoke goes up from her forever and ever.
				Hallelujah! For the Lord our God the Almighty reigns. Let us rejoice and exult *(Isa. 61:10)* and give him the glory, for the marriage of the Lamb has come, and his bride has made herself ready; to her it has been granted to be clothed with fine linen, bright and pure —for the fine linen is the righteous deeds of the holy ones.

"HOLY, HOLY, HOLY, LORD GOD ALMIGHTY!" (REV. 4:2-11)

The moment John has completed his dictation of the angelic messages to the *ekklēsiai* in Asia, he is swept up into the heavenly throne room, where he sees and hears the flashing lightning and crashing thunder that accompany the ceaseless praise of God. The link between Patmos and heaven is a "door," parallel to that seen in Ezekiel's initial experience (Ezek. 1:1). While the image of a door or gate to God's realm was one familiar from the Hebrew scriptures (Gen. 28:17; Ps. 78:23; also *1 Enoch* 14:14-15), it was also one found in Roman temples. More specifically, the great temple of Artemis (Cybele) at Ephesus featured a door that was apparently used for part of a ritual epiphany of the goddess.[1] But unlike the Roman temple doors, a voice coming from this door calls John directly to heaven. Before he is given a chance to respond, he is "at once in the spirit" and gazing upon the heavenly throne and the One seated upon it.

Rather than "tell" us that the One is God, John "shows" us the glorious scene in and about the throne. The description of the One as like "jasper and carnelian" echoes the description of the breastplate of the Aaronic priest at Exod. 28:17. The priestly vestment was but an image of the real thing which John sees. The throne is surrounded by a green iris, usually translated as "rainbow," but more precisely referring to a circle of light.[2] While a rainbow seen from an earthly perspective is always an arc, this light is a full circle, revealing the completeness of the throne and the inspired vantage point from which John observes.

The throne is also surrounded by an array of twenty-four additional thrones upon which sit twenty-four elders dressed in white robes with golden crowns on their heads. This is not a temple scene but that of a royal hall with the king's advisors forming a circle around the royal presence.[3] Many efforts have been made to pinpoint the meaning of the specific number of elders, but no single interpretation captures the significance of twenty-four, whether the hours of the day, the number of Israelite tribes plus the twelve apostles, the signs of the zodiac plus the apostles, the number of books traditionally counted as part of the Hebrew Bible, astral deities presiding over sectors of the sky, or many others.[4] The elders are a staple of heavenly worship in Revelation, present in six of the seven scenes. White robes are mentioned eight times in the book, with the elders' outfits as a paradigm of the purity required for a place in the divine presence (cf. Rev. 3:4-5, 18; 6:11; 7:9-14). Their golden crowns are a parody of the imperial cult priests in Asia, who also wore gold crowns.[5]

The throne emanates lightning, rumblings, and thunder, traditional phenomena accompanying the coming of the divine warrior in Israel's memory (e.g., Exod. 19:16; Ezek. 1:13-14; Dan. 10:6). In Roman tradition, lightning was said to come from the planets associated with the most powerful gods, Jupiter and Saturn, and the god of war, Mars.[6] Now John's attention shifts to the front of the throne, where seven flaming torches are named as the "seven spirits of God." These seven spirits were first introduced in 1:4 as part of John's initial greeting to the *ekklēsiai*, but now they are directly associated with the seven burning lamps seen by Zechariah in his vision of the restored temple (Zech. 4:1-14). As always in interpreting apocalyptic literature, we run into trouble if we ask overly

---

1. Aune (1997), pp. 280-81.
2. Louw and Nida, 1.38.
3. Schüssler Fiorenza (1991), p. 59.
4. Aune (1997), pp. 289-91; Malina (1995), pp. 93-96; Beale (1999), p. 326, notes that the tradition linking the twenty-four elders with the books of the Hebrew Bible "is an especially attractive view if the 'book' in Rev. 5:1ff. is identified as the Old Testament itself," as we argued above in chapter 5.
5. Aune (1997), p. 293.
6. Malina (1995), pp. 91-92.

literal questions about visionary imagery, such as whether what John sees undermines the unity of the Holy Spirit as understood by later trinitarian theology. Instead, we should read "seven" as a symbol of the completeness of the spirit associated with the throne (cf. Isa. 11:2). The image also parodies Babylonian astral symbolism, which associated seven sky-spirits with the sun, the moon, and the then-known five planets, which were worshiped as deities who controlled time.[7] Furthermore, torchbearers were a common feature of the imperial cult, symbolizing the perpetuity of the emperor's power, which will be seen as nothing compared with the power of the One on the heavenly throne.[8]

Also in front of the throne is "something like a sea of glass, like crystal." Ezekiel saw this crystalline structure as a dome (Ezek. 1:22), but John's image associates it with the huge bronze water basin in Solomon's temple known as "the sea," which was used to recall the Exodus event until it was specifically broken and the pieces removed by the Babylonians during their ransack of the temple (1 Kings 7:23-24; Jer. 52:17). In the heavenly context, it can be imagined as the divider between God's abode and John's vantage point. The throne is visible, but even John must keep some distance from the spectacular panorama upon which he has been allowed to gaze.

At their posts representing the four directions are what the Greek text calls *zōa*, usually translated as "living creatures," but almost certainly referring to what are called in Hebrew *cherubim*. Ezekiel saw them, too, although John's description varies in several ways from that in Ezek. 1:5-14. Like the twenty-four elders, they are fixtures around the heavenly throne, present in five of the seven liturgical scenes in Revelation. Like Ezekiel's cherubim, they are seen as "full of eyes in front and behind," an image that suggests both the starry sky and their all-seeing power.[9] Each looks like a creature that specifically associates it with one of the four zodiacal creatures from Babylonian astrology who control the seasons as follows:

Lion (Leo) = spring = fire
Bull/ox (Taurus) = summer = earth
Human face (Scorpio) = fall = water
Eagle (Pegasus) = winter = air[10]

Later Christian writers associated these images with the four Gospels, emphasizing the sense that John's entire conception is aimed at undermining the various imperial mythologies in favor of trust in the one, true God. One might pause here to take in the dizzying array of cosmic creatures, sounds, and lights that John presents. Before the actual worship is described, we are presented with images making any earthly liturgical scene seem puny in comparison. This was no easy task, for both imperial and local cult celebrations pulled out all the stops in drawing their audiences into their assertions of divine authority.

---

7. Krodel, p. 83.
8. Aune (1997), p. 295.
9. Malina (1995), p. 98.
10. Ibid., p. 99; Giblin (1991), p. 72.

In moving on to the description of the worship itself, John shifts his primary source from Ezekiel to Isaiah 6, where six-winged "seraphs" attending the divine throne call out, "Holy, holy, holy is YHWH of hosts; the whole earth is full of his glory" (Isa. 6:3). In John's vision, the cherubim are said to "sing" a similar refrain "day and night without ceasing," a specific opposition to the total cessation of musical celebration in fallen Babylon (18:22). Their proclamation of the One on the throne as "Lord God Almighty" directly echoes the war-cry shout of Isaiah's seraphs. The central image of God in Revelation is thus seen to be the divine warrior-king, the one who can and *already has* conquered every earthly imperial pretender, including the Roman emperors of John's own day. God's time is *all* time: "who was and is and is to come" in 4:8 and "who lives forever and ever"[11] in 4:9, contrasted with that of the Beast "who was and is not" (17:8, 11).

Beginning with the threefold proclamation of God as holy, a series of epithets forms a central aspect of this first scene of heavenly worship. Each term used by the cherubim and the elders as an attribute of God gives to God something otherwise offered to the emperor himself or to gods in the Greco-Roman pantheon and celebrated in the local cults. Holiness itself implies that God is special and worthy of awe and worship. "Glory and honor"—used twice (4:9, 11)—combine to form a single attribute drawn from the Roman system of patronage described in chapter 3. Because a client cannot repay a patron in kind with the type of material or social benefits that flow from the superior status of the patron down to the inferior status of the client, the only suitable response by the client is public acclamation of the patron's honor. In other words, the client's shout of "honor!" raises the patron's status even higher while simultaneously acknowledging the client's dependence on the patron's ongoing support. A specific practice known from the Roman world of John's time was the morning *salutatio*, in which clients would gather around the door of the patron's house in vocal acclamation, prepared to follow the patron on his morning rounds and to applaud his speeches and other public acts.[12] Here the acts of honor given to God are not simply a morning routine, but a ceaseless celebration of God's power magnanimously poured out on those who acknowledge his reign. Similarly, "thanks" in 4:9 (Greek *eucharistian*), paralleled by "power" in 4:11, affirms the status of God as ultimate patron.

The reason given for God's worthiness as patron is the divine act of creation of all things (4:11). This includes, of course, the empire itself, part of the mystery apocalyptically revealed in Revelation. As we saw in the discussion in chapter 2, God's status as Creator is one of three central powers that affirm God's holiness (e.g., Isa. 44:23-26). The other two, well represented in Revelation's liturgies, are the power of judgment and of deliverance/redemption. Here the affirmation excludes the possibility that other gods or goddesses had any part in the establishment or maintenance of the created order.

---

11. The term is very rare in the Hebrew scriptures, but is found in Dan. 4:34; 12:7; cf. Isa. 57:15.
12. Garnsey and Saller, p. 99.

The sung words of praise are accompanied by a highly charged ritual act: the elders' prostration and casting of their crowns before the throne. As Gregory Stevenson writes,

> In antiquity a common sign of vassalage was the taking off of the diadem (symbol of royalty) by the conquered ruler and the placing of that diadem at the feet of the conqueror. . . . The performance of the elders should be understood as an imitation of such an act of subordination.[13]

All power is now acknowledged to belong to the One on the throne. *Worship is shown to be primarily a political act*: one worships whomever or whatever one affirms as possessing true power to affect people's lives, the central currency of politics in all ages. Just as in John's Gospel the affirmations of Jesus as "savior of the world" (4:42) and as "my Lord and my God" (20:28) are made in terms specific to the praise of the emperor Domitian but now attributed to Jesus,[14] so the casting of crowns and the proclamation of "our Lord and God" in Revelation place the One on the throne in direct opposition to Domitian. It is important to note that while earlier scholarship understood Domitian as calling for worship of himself as *dominus et deus*, more recent investigation has shown this not to be the case. Rather, flatterers seeking Domitian's patronage initiated this practice, which the emperor did not discourage.[15] Similarly, the elders before the throne initiate the acclamation of their patron-ruler. In our modern world of separation of church and state, most churchgoers have not been called upon to consider the inherently political nature of worship. In Revelation's world, though, this connection was obvious and went without saying. What is surprising in Revelation is not that worship was political, but that worship of the One on the throne *excluded* worship of other gods or deified emperors. In Rome's polytheistic culture, worship of emperor and local or national gods could take place simultaneously. For John's Jewish-Christian mentality, though, strict monotheism was a given (e.g., Rev. 15:4). This is at the heart of the subversive nature of Christianity, both then and now: proclaiming God as worthy of honor, glory, and thanks means *not* offering similar laud to any other claimant to divine authority. We will explore some of the implications of this consequence in chapter 9 below.

The act of prostration, which is frequently performed by the elders, is described with the Greek word *piptō*, which means "to fall down." It is the same word that is used to refer to the "fallen" status of Babylon (14:8; 18:2; cf. 2:2; 11:13; 16:9) and the star that falls from heaven to earth (9:1). As part of the liturgical response of those in heaven, it expresses another aspect of God's power: either one falls down voluntarily in worship before the Holy One, or one falls down in destructive ruin in refusing to participate in such worship. It is, of course, not a matter of condemning agnostics or atheists in the modern sense. In

---

13. Stevenson, pp. 268-69.
14. Howard-Brook (1994), pp. 113, 462.
15. B. W. Jones, pp. 108-9.

the world of Roman Asia, the only "atheists" were Christians, a legal charge used against them by the Romans! Revelation does not condemn theological uncertainty. Rather, it condemns empire and those who consciously support empire's evil program. The double use of the term "fallen" simply underscores the fact that there is no escaping from the apocalyptic crisis. Once one knows that there is a God and that God stands against empire, one must choose whether one falls down in joyous worship or in stubborn resistance to that God.

"WORTHY IS THE LAMB THAT WAS SLAUGHTERED!" (REV. 5:8-14)

Between the first and second liturgical scenes stands the drama of the sealed scroll in Rev. 5:1-7. The worship that unfolds is the direct response to the taking of the scroll by the Lamb, who is seen standing, literally "in the middle of the throne and the four cherubim and in the middle of the elders" (5:6). He is described as having seven "horns" and seven eyes, which are said to be "the seven spirits of God sent out into all the earth." Whereas in the first scene the seven spirits were flaming torches in a fixed location before the throne, they are now the eyes of the Lamb himself and are "sent" (Greek *apestalmenoi*). The verb for "sent" is found in Revelation only here outside the beginning and ending frames, where it refers to an angel (1:1; 22:6). It clearly expresses the mission of Jesus to the world, the consequence of which was his being "slaughtered," a term common in Revelation but rare elsewhere in the New Testament, which refers both to animal sacrifice and murder by empire. It is juxtaposed in this passage with the previous description of the one who can open the scroll as "the Lion of the tribe of Judah, the Root of David," messianic images adapted from Israel's tradition (Gen. 49:9-10; cf. Isa. 11:10 [root of Jesse]). Richard Bauckham explains how the juxtaposition of these messianic and sacrificial images generates a new and unexpected symbol:

> [B]y placing the image of the sacrificial victim alongside those of the military conqueror, John forges a new symbol of *conquest* by sacrificial death. Insofar as 5:5 expresses Jewish hopes for messianic conquest by *military violence,* 5:6 replaces those hopes; and insofar as 5:5 evokes narrowly nationalistic expectations of Jewish triumph over the Gentile nations, 5:6 replaces those expectations. But insofar as the Jewish hopes, rooted in Old Testament scriptures, were for the victory of God over evil, 5:6 draws on other Old Testament scriptures to show *how* they have been fulfilled in Jesus.[16]

With this in mind, we can observe the specifics of the narrated liturgical acts. The elders again prostrate themselves, but this time it is before the Lamb, not the

---

16. Bauckham (1993), p. 215, emphasis in original.

One on the throne. Each elder is holding a lyre (Greek *kithara*), an instrument common in the liturgies of the local and imperial cults. In the other hand are golden bowls full of incense which is "the prayers of the holy ones" (cf. Rev. 8:3; 16:1-21).[17] Incense was also a frequent feature of Greco-Roman ritual in both imperial and local cults. The reference to "holy ones" (sometimes translated as "saints") is not to those already dead, but rather to the faithful and enduring members of the *ekklēsiai* (cf. 11:18; 13:7, 10; 16:6; 17:6; 18:20; etc.). Thus, the incense offered by the elders to the Lamb is the prayer of those on earth who acknowledge the Lamb's worthiness to receive worship along with God.

The elders then "sing a new song," a practice long associated in the Bible's liturgical texts with the celebration of a divine act of liberation (Pss. 40:2-4; 96; 98; 144:9-11; 149; Isa. 42:9-10; cf. Jonah 2; Acts 16:25ff.). And it is precisely such a deed that is now named: "by your blood you redeemed [Greek *ēgorasas*] for God holy ones from every tribe and language and people and nation" (5:9). The word for "redeemed" is an economic term, meaning "to cause the release or freedom of someone by a means which proves costly to the individual causing the release."[18] In this case, of course, the cost to the Lamb was of his life itself, which turned out, however, to be only a temporary loss (1:18). Those redeemed come from every social grouping known to humanity, echoing the universality of Third Isaiah (Isa. 56:6). Membership in the new tribe of the slaughtered Lamb is not limited by any human-devised boundary, but is open to all who accept the way of the Lamb as being the way of the one God.

The consequence of the establishment of this new, multicultural community is their composition as "an empire and priests serving our God and they are reigning on earth" (5:10). It is a reinterpretation of God's word through Moses in Exod. 19:5-6: "if you obey my voice and keep my covenant, you shall be my treasured possession out of all the peoples. Indeed, the whole earth is mine, but you shall be for me a priestly kingdom and a holy nation." John's text hears the first part of the divine condition as central to the whole concept of being "God's people": obeying God's voice and keeping God's covenant. The declaration that they "are reigning on earth" should not be taken as a literal offer of a worldly monarchy, but rather of an affirmation that those who are living in accordance with the divine ways are in fact those who "reign," a reality invisible except to the apocalyptically informed.

The proclamation of the redemption and reign of the holy ones is followed by an uncountable choir of angels who sing with voices loud enough to drown out the high-volume imperial and local cult liturgies. Their description as comprising "myriads of myriads" recalls Dan. 7:10, where an identically named assembly serves the One on the throne. In Revelation, their song affirms the worthiness of the Lamb to receive sevenfold honor in words that are inclusive of all possi-

---

17. We should not bother ourselves with logical questions about how these elders can be prostrating themselves while bearing arms full of liturgical objects! It is simply another reminder that Revelation presents visionary images, not rational descriptions, of reality "behind the veil."

18. Louw and Nida, 37.131.

ble forms of giftedness. This speaks to the concern that worship of the Lamb alongside God amounted to bitheism, a charge to which Jews would be extremely sensitive.[19] Revelation makes clear that the Lamb is not Creator nor Judge, but rather has had delegated to him God's power of redemption. As Daniel Berrigan has written, "Revelation does not attempt to answer the haunting question of Jesus; but it poses the question in a hundred voices, tones, signs, gestures."[20]

Their song is joined by "every creature in heaven and on earth and under the earth and in the sea, and all that is in them." Again, we should not seek logical consistency between this all-inclusive choir and the repeated refusal in Revelation of many to worship either God or the Lamb. The phrase is John's way of saying that in "heaven," all creatures joyously affirm their Creator and the Creator's Chosen One. Rather than be jealous that none from among them was found worthy except the Lamb (5:3-4), they sing with all their power of the eternal "blessing and honor and glory and power to rule [Greek *kratos*]" of God and of the Lamb. The liturgy concludes with the cherubim's "Amen!" and the prostration of the elders.

This second scene, then, adds to the first scene the inclusion of the Lamb who was slaughtered as a recipient of heavenly worship. This is key to the entire direction of Revelation. Those throughout the ages who have read Revelation as a violently vindictive text have ignored the central feature that holds the entire narrative together. It is God the Creator, King, Warrior, and Judge *and* the Lamb slaughtered for his nonviolent witness who are due honor in place of emperors and lesser deities.

"WHO ARE THESE, ROBED IN WHITE, AND WHERE HAVE THEY COME FROM?" (REV. 7:9-17)

The third liturgical scene is narrated after the story of the opening of the first six seals on the scroll taken by the Lamb. As we saw in chapter 5 above, the unsealing of the first four seals releases a series of colored horses and political effects with which each is associated. The fifth seal reveals "under the altar the souls of those who had been slaughtered for the word of God and for the testimony they had given" (6:9). This is followed by the sixth seal's cosmic signs, which remove the veil separating heaven from earth and evoke the terrified attempt by those "of the earth" to hide from "the face of the one seated on the throne and from the wrath of the Lamb" (6:16).

The scene is followed by the "sealing" of God's people in protection from a series of impending plagues, just as in the first Exodus (Exod. 12:7-13; cf. Ezek. 9:4-6). John *hears* the number of those sealed ("144,000 out of every tribe of the people of Israel"), and then *sees* something different:

---

19. Aune (1997), p. 92, explores the relationship between a similar passage in Revelation (1:13-14) and the ongoing rabbinic debate over the "two-powers heresy," current at least as early as 110 C.E.

20. Berrigan (1983), p. 29.

> a great multitude that no one could count, from every
>   nation,
> from all tribes and peoples and languages,
> standing before the throne and before the Lamb,
> robed in white, with palm branches in their hands. (7:9)

As John Sweet has noted, what John hears is often described differently from what he sees (e.g., 5:5-6, 11-13; 9:1, 13, 16-17, etc.).[21] In this case, it suggests that there are not two groups present but one seen under two different aspects. The countless multitude from every nation, tribe, peoples, and language *is the new Israel*, the perfectly complete number represented by the twelve thousand from each of the twelve historic tribes. John's vision, as usual, reinterprets the biblical tradition. What had first been the forming of an ethnically pure tribal confederation from out of Egypt and within Israel now is revealed to be a multi-national, multicultural, multilinguistic multitude, defined simply as those "standing before the throne and before the Lamb, robed in white, with palm branches in their hands" (7:9). "Robed in white" signifies, as the angelic interpreter explains, their having been "washed" "in the blood of the Lamb" (7:14). The counterexperiential image of being made white via blood serves two important functions. First, it mocks the priestly initiation of the cult of Cybele, in which white-robed candidates were dripped with bull's blood in order to "purify" them (see p. 111 above). Second, it reverses the logic of Israel's tradition of holy war, in which persons who killed during war were required to wash their robes to remove the blood of their enemies in order to be purified (e.g., Num. 31:19-20). In Revelation, it is not the enemy's blood that must be removed to achieve purity, but a sharing in the Lamb's blood itself which generates purity. The immediate context in which this sharing takes place is the *ekklēsiai*'s eucharistic worship, which itself points to the willingness to share one's blood by offering oneself in sacrifice to the empire.

An interpreting elder uses imagery from the feast of Tabernacles in noting that these are the ones whom the One seated on the throne "will shelter" (Greek *skēnōsei*, literally, "will tent"). Thus, when the tent roof of the sky is rolled up, those on earth attempt to hide from God. Those, however, who are washed in the blood of the Lamb experience that same reality as providing shelter from hunger, thirst, and the scorching heat of the sun.

The Lamb who will be their shepherd will "guide them to springs of the water of life, and God will wipe away every tear from their eyes" (7:15-17). The imagery is taken directly from Isa. 49:10 and 25:8, to which John has added the presence and role of the Lamb. It is a wonderfully joyous image of God's tender, parental role in New Jerusalem which some find "out of place" amid the scenes of plagues, violence, and vengeance. Rather than being out of place, though, it recognizes that people's experience of God depends on how they live in the midst

---

21. Sweet (1990), pp. 125-26, 150-51.

of empire. Those who stubbornly refuse to repent will experience God as angry judge (16:1, 5-11); those who grant all authority to the One who is Holy and True (6:10) will experience God's and the Lamb's community of intimacy and compassion.

Thus, the revealing of the power of heaven that caused those "of the earth" to hide in terror causes the white-robed multitude to celebrate with prayerful joy. The liturgy itself is simple and very similar to those that preceded it. All that is new is the proclamation, "Salvation belongs to our God who is seated on the throne, and to the Lamb!" (7:10). "Salvation" was officially something provided exclusively by the Roman emperor, a result of the *Pax Romana*.[22] In John's vision, those who have been washed clean in the Lamb's blood are precisely those who have refused to abide by this imperial propaganda. They have been willing to exchange the "shelter" provided by empire for the shelter provided by God and the Lamb. All others remain in fear and trembling, hoping desperately to avoid judgment.

"THE EMPIRE OF THE WORLD HAS BECOME THE EMPIRE OF OUR LORD AND OF HIS MESSIAH!" (REV. 11:15-18)

Charles Giblin has shown how the fourth and sixth liturgical scenes form the outer frames of a chiasm extending from 11:15 to 15:8 as follows, with the fifth liturgical scene at the center:

A: 11:15b-19: *liturgy*—song celebrating the messianic empire; opening of heavenly sanctuary

  B: 12:1-18: a great sign in heaven

    C: 13:1-18: beasts from the sea and the earth (empire worship); here is the endurance and fidelity of the holy ones

      D: 14:1-5: *liturgy*—Lamb on Mt. Zion with the redeemed singing a new, secret song

    C': 14:6-20: angels dealing with true worship of God and worship of empire; here is the endurance and fidelity of the holy ones

  B': 15:1: another sign in heaven, great and amazing

A': 15:2-8: *liturgy*—Song of Moses and the Lamb; opening of heavenly sanctuary[23]

The chiastic structure underscores the centrality of worship and liturgy to Revelation's message. Each liturgy features a song celebrating God's power and victory over the would-be usurpers, the God "wannabes." We will look at each one in sequence.

The first scene of this set and the fourth overall comes after the pronounce-

---

22. Schüssler Fiorenza (1991), p. 68.

23. Giblin (1991), pp. 117-19.

ment that the second of three "woes" has passed with the resurrection of the faithful witnesses who were killed by the Beast from the abyss, followed by the earthquake which kills 7,000 and destroys a tenth of the "great city that is called in the spirit Sodom and Egypt, where also their Lord was crucified" (11:8, 13). This combination of new life for the faithful witnesses and terror for the unrepentant is precisely the image with which the previous liturgical scene ended, part of Revelation's strategy of repetition and restatement of its basic themes.

Suddenly in 11:15, the "seventh angel" blows a trumpet, and loud voices in heaven proclaim, "The empire of the world has become the empire of our Lord and of his Messiah, and he will reign forever and ever." The proclamation generates an immediate response from the twenty-four elders, who prostrate themselves as before and sing a song of thanksgiving to the Lord God Almighty. The liturgy echoes the transition in Revelation's story from the first biblical era to the second. The elders' song continues with the pronouncement that the time (Greek *kairos*) has come for judgment, reward, and destruction of the earth's destroyers. This *kairos* is a face-off between the wrath of the nations and the wrath of God, each for refusing to conform to the will of the other. This might be read as a confrontation between royal tyrants as with so many international struggles over the ages, if it were not for the fact that one wrath belongs to the Creator of all! It is crucial to recognize that God is not being reduced here to the image of a worldly emperor bent on increasing his power, but rather, the world's emperors are being *parodied* for their own attempt to compare themselves with God.

While it is tempting to read modern-day environmental concerns into the promise to destroy the earth destroyers, it is not fair to the text to see in it a "prediction" of our latter-day troubles. If the premillennialist readings are to be critiqued for their propensity toward this practice, we cannot allow a similar method to slip in when the imagery echoes more progressive concerns. Instead, staying faithful to the text in its context, we can read this promise as an expression of biblical "karma," the sense that God allows one's evil to come back upon one's own head. For example, in Lev. 26:14-39, God lists a series of terrible consequences that will follow if the people do not practice the sabbath of the earth, the once-in-seven-years resting from planting that was required by the covenant. The punishments listed all befit the "crime" of failing to respect the earth's own need to rest. As God says, if the people practice bad earth stewardship,

> Then the land shall enjoy its sabbath years as long as it lies desolate, while you are in the land of your enemies; then the land shall rest, and enjoy its sabbath years. As long as it lies desolate, it shall have the rest it did not have on your sabbaths when you were living on it. (Lev. 26:34-35)[24]

---

24. The question of relationship between the sabbatical/Jubilee traditions rooted in Lev. 26 and apocalyptic texts such as Daniel and Revelation is a fascinating and complex one that has barely been touched upon by scholars. One connection involves the sabbatical connotations of "rest" (Greek *anapausin*) in texts such as Lev. 25:4-8 and Rev. 6:11; 14:11, 13. Another involves the use and reuse of sabbatical/Jubilee-based schemes of sevens and seventies, rooted in Lev. 26 (sevenfold punishment

While attributed to direct acts of divine intervention by a people who see every event as controlled by the hand of YHWH, the prediction of desolate land is nothing more nor less than keen insight into the consequences of endless exploitation of the soil. In a similar way, the promise in Revelation is no more nor less than a prediction that each empire's endless exploitation *will* come to an end, and *all* empires will become their own victim, as we described in relation to the bowl plagues in chapter 5 above.

"THEY WORSHIPED THE DRAGON . . .
AND THEY WORSHIPED THE BEAST" (REV. 13:1-15)

Between the fourth and fifth scenes of heavenly worship, John has revealed the demonic parody of true worship conducted "on the ground" by the liturgical machinery of empire. Rev. 13 is arranged as a chiasm as follows:

A: 1-3: first beast: visual description
    B: 4-8: the authority of the first beast; its worshipers are not written in the
         book of life
      C: 9-10: narrator's admonition
    B': 11-17: the authority of the second beast; mark of those who worship it
A': 18: first beast: the number

The scene apocalyptically reveals the Roman imperial and local cult rituals to be conducted not by white-robed priests but by grotesque Beasts arising from the depths of the sea and from the earth. Our purpose here is not to wade into the voluminous speculation about the details of the descriptions of the Beasts, but to focus on the aspects of liturgy and empire worship with which they are associated (see table 20).

The first Beast arises out of the sea and receives the power, authority, and throne of "the dragon," a figure introduced in Rev. 12:3ff. and identified there as "that ancient serpent, who is called the Devil and Satan, the deceiver of the whole world" (12:9). Thus, we see five different mythological and political images used to name the source of the sea Beast's power. Rev. 12 presented a retelling of a story familiar from Greek mythology and the rituals of the Isis and other local cults in Roman Asia. The basic tale involves a pregnant goddess being pursued by a dragon who seeks to devour her unborn child. The link between this myth and the Roman Empire is found in the specific association made between the Dragon and the Beast. Thus, John sees Rome's power, authority, and throne as simply the latest chapter in the ancient combat myth, the story of primeval conflict between the Creator and a powerful, rebellious creature.

---

for failing to keep the earth's sabbath) and Jer. 25:12; 29:10's seventy-year periodization of history and leading to intrabiblical interpretations such as Dan. 9 and eventually to Revelation. See Fishbane, pp. 482-91, for a discussion of sabbatical/Jubilee echoes in Dan. 9.

Table 20
THE WORSHIP OF THE BEAST (REVELATION 13)

Scene	Who Offers Worship	Titles for Those Who Receive Worship	Forms of Worship	Content of Worship
The vision of the dragon and the two beasts]	The whole earth	The Dragon	Making an image of the beast	"Who is like the beast, and who can fight against it"
		The Beast		
	The inhabitants of the earth			
			The image is given breath and speaks	
(13:1-15)	Those whose name is not written in the book of life			

John also weaves into his picture a thread from biblical mythology. Isa. 27:1 tells of a great battle between God and a sea-beast:

> On that day YHWH with his cruel and great and strong sword will punish Leviathan [Hebrew *liwyātān;* LXX *drakōn*] the fleeing serpent, Leviathan the twisting serpent, and he will kill the dragon that is in the sea.

Ezekiel borrows this mythical image to make a political critique:

> Thus says the Lord YHWH: I am against you, Pharaoh king of Egypt, the great dragon [Hebrew *hattannîm;* LXX *drakōn*] sprawling in the midst of its channels, saying, "My Nile is my own; I made it for myself." (Ezek. 29:3)

Of course, in Ezekiel's image, the "dragon" is simply a crocodile, the "twisting serpent" of the Nile. But it is precisely this association that makes Ezekiel's political cartoon effective: Pharaoh, far from the self-styled omnipotent creator, is but a scaly lizard in the hand of the true Creator.

John draws together these traditions to portray the power of Rome both as participating in an ancient line of futile resistance to God and as simply another divine pretender who is powerless in the presence of the true king of all. The scene of empire worship thus is set up with the Dragon, frustrated and angry from his failure to destroy the woman's child, transferring his power to the structures of empire.

The immediate response of "the whole earth" is to follow the Beast in "amazement" and to worship both the Dragon and the Beast (13:3-4). Their liturgical refrain is, "Who is like the Beast, and who can fight against it?" It is an explicit mockery of biblical traditions of praise of YHWH (Exod. 15:11; Mic. 7:18; Ps. 89:8) and expresses the enormous ability of the dragon-inspired Beast to gain allegiance among humanity. Indeed, the power of empire, Roman or otherwise, has been tremendously effective at inculcating loyalty and suppressing resistance, even among otherwise "good" people, as has been seen in recent cases such as Nazi Germany. John recognizes both how powerfully attractive *and* demonic is the power of human evil and violence. It seems invincible to most observers. It can choose to ignore or to crush dissent, depending on its mood. Only those committed to worship of the true Power see past the façade to the satanic reality.

The demonic liturgy continues with unrecorded but "great and blasphemous words" from the mouth of the Beast against God, God's name, and God's "dwelling," which is said to be "with those who dwell in heaven" (13:6). As the cherubim, elders, and multitude praise these divine realities, so the Beast curses them. Of course, empires rarely engage in acts of public blasphemy; we are witnessing an apocalyptic interpretation of political speech making. John's vision sees empire's ritual acts of divine self-legitimation as pompous blasphemy.

The liturgical language appears to be interrupted between 13:4-6 and 13:8 by the announcement that the Beast "was allowed to make war on the holy ones and to conquer them. It was given authority over every tribe and people and language and nation" (13:7). However, the framing of this proclamation of war and imperialistic success with the response of "worship" by the "inhabitants of the earth" shows that John sees war against the holy ones itself as a demonically liturgical act. This war took the form of ritual crucifixions, arena contests with lions, and other public spectacles of execution. John's insight is that these are not merely "political" acts but are liturgical acts as well. Canny empires have always carried out public executions with great care to detail designed to generate religious awe in observers. Indeed, the mechanics of well-oiled courtrooms also partake of this liturgical demeanor, with its robed magistrates, choreographed risings and sittings, collective responses, and other ritual acts and paraphernalia. John's vision reveals this entire scenario for what it is: a blasphemous parody of true worship.

The parody continues with the appearance of another Beast, this one rising out of the earth. In addition to speaking "like a dragon"—that is, with the forked but smooth tongue of the serpent, not with a beastly roar (Gen. 3:1)—the Beast from the earth has all the authority of the first Beast. Furthermore, it "performs great signs, even making fire come down from heaven to earth in the sight of all" (13:13). Gregory Beale shows that for the people of Roman Asia, the Sea Beast would have fit their experience of Rome itself, coming "out of the sea" in ships, while the Land Beast symbolized the native elite which collaborated with Rome.[25] S. R. F. Price provides evidence for concluding that the immediate context of this power is the "provincial cult of Domitian at Ephesus, with its colos-

---

25. Beale (1999), p. 682.

sal cult statue."[26] He shows how part of this imperial liturgy included the apparent performance of "miracles" such as that described in our text. This spectacle deceives people into trusting in the Beast's claims on behalf of empire and its leaders. In other words, the power of the second Beast is, as Jacques Ellul names it, "propaganda."[27] Fire from the sky, great signs, talking images: all these are the means by which empire seduces people into submission and worship. It is not at all a matter of gullible folks being taken in by magic tricks. Rather, it is the highly organized, technologically proficient, and psychologically effective process of developing a systematic, false reality that masquerades as "the way things are."

The liturgy ends on an even darker note, however. For the few who are not taken in by the power of the Dragon exercised by the Beasts, a different fate awaits: the "icon of the Beast" itself "cause(s) those who would not worship" it to be killed (13:15). The Beast does not deign to exercise this power of capital punishment itself. John sees that it has delegated this authority to its "icon" (Greek *eikona*). This close association between the Beast and its icon is continued throughout Revelation (14:11; 15:2; 16:2; 19:20; 20:4). At one level, the icon is the collection of imperial cult objects: the shrines, statues, and coins that bear the image of the emperor and the slogans of imperial propaganda such as "Lord and God." At a deeper level, however, the "icon of the Beast" is the public face of empire: the flags and other patriotic paraphernalia that accompany civic rituals in all imperial settings. Consider how deeply felt are people's emotional reactions to those who refuse to salute the flag, whether the Nazi swastika or the U.S. Stars and Stripes. This is what John's apocalyptic insight has revealed, not only about the Rome of his day, but also more broadly about the nature of how empire gains and keeps its subjects loyal to its demonic agenda. It is this power that both insists on being worshiped and eliminates those who refuse to submit to its authority.

In heaven, though, this demonic death sentence is reversed:

> Those who worship the Beast and its icon, and receive a mark on their foreheads or on their hands, they will also drink the wine of God's wrath, poured unmixed into the cup of his anger, and they will be tormented with fire and sulfur in the presence of the holy angels and in the presence of the Lamb. And the smoke of their torment goes up forever and ever. There is no rest day or night for those who worship the Beast and its icon and for anyone who receives the mark of its name. Here is a call for the endurance of the holy ones, those who keep the commandments of God and hold fast to the faith of Jesus. (14:9-12)

As was shown in chapter 5, this should not be taken as an expression of revenge gleefully observed by those in heaven. Rather, it is an apocalyptic

---

26. Price, pp. 197-98.
27. Ellul (1977), p. 92.

expression of the "real" punishment that befalls those who worship the divine pretensions of empire. It reveals not a future torture but the present reality of what worshiping the icon of the Beast means. What appears to be the "joy" of patriotic fervor is, from the perspective of "heaven," a kind of hell on earth. As we will see in the next scene of heavenly liturgy, the death sentence that empire passes on those who resist it is also reversed in heaven. Revelation shows that this is where authentic joy is: in worship of the true God and of God's sacrificed Lamb.

"IN THEIR MOUTH NO ILLUSION WAS FOUND" (REV. 14:1-5)

The fifth liturgical scene lies at the center of the chiasm extending from 11:15b to 15:8. It comes immediately after the conclusion of the scene of demonic worship.

It expresses more explicitly the "karmic" effect described above in relation to the fourth liturgical scene (Rev. 11:18), here adapted from Jer. 15:2 and 43:11. The holy ones are to accept "captivity" (Greek *aikmalōsian,* 13:10, only Eph. 4:8 elsewhere in the New Testament), a term meaning "prisoner of war."[28] The struggle by those who worship God and the Lamb to resist the lure of the Beast is indeed a war, one that many have given up as unwinnable (13:4). The ironic sign of those who have defeated the Beast is to be taken captive like a war prisoner rather than to engage in the Beast's own tactics of sanctioned murder and systemic lying.

It is precisely these prisoners of war who celebrate with liturgical song at 14:1-5. As in Rev. 7:4, they are labeled as the 144,000, but this time the text says that they are those "who had his [the Lamb's] name and his Father's name written on their foreheads" (14:1). These names mark the 144,000 as the opposite of those with the "mark of the Beast" in 13:16-17. The social consequence of resisting the demonic mark is exclusion from the marketplace, the practical result of refusing to use the coin that bore the emperor's likeness and often a slogan such as *dominus et deus* in reference to Domitian.[29] The "reward" for this resistance, however, is access to the words of the "new song," which only the 144,000 can learn (14:3). Here, in Revelation's characteristically sharply drawn imagery, is the choice: participate in imperial commerce (13:17, Greek *agorasai*) among those who worship the Beast or be "bought" (14:4, Greek *ēgorasmenoi*) by the Lamb to participate in the heavenly choir!

The 144,000 are accompanied by the Lamb. They are all standing on Mt. Zion, referring here not to the earthly site of Jerusalem but to the heavenly site of the Messiah's enthronement as king, as expressed in Ps. 2:6-9, a psalm used many times by John.

28. Louw and Nida, 55.23.
29. Mounce, p. 259.

Once again, what John sees (the 144,000 and the Lamb standing on Mt. Zion) is complemented by what he hears:

> a voice from heaven like the sound of many waters and like the sound of loud thunder; the voice I heard was like the sound of lyre-players playing on their lyres, and they sing a new song before the throne and before the four cherubim and before the elders. (Rev. 14:2-3a)

Whose voice is heard? The text is deliciously ambiguous. At Rev. 1:15, a voice like the sound of many waters is that of the Human One, i.e., the Lamb. However, in the final liturgical scene at 19:6, a voice identically described is that of a great multitude. The current text lies midway between these two and thereby expresses the meaning: what the Lamb began is continued by those bearing his name. Just as he was a witness, so also others witness. As he was slaughtered, so will others be slaughtered. As he was raised up to power and glory, so will others be raised up. Now, as his voice thundered like a great waterfall, drowning out the imperial cult, so does the singing of the heavenly choir comprised of the former prisoners of war—accompanied now by the Lamb but finally on their own—drown out the demonic choir.

The closing description of the 144,000 adds an image that, taken literally, can greatly mislead readers: "It is these who have not defiled themselves with women, for they are virgins; these follow the Lamb wherever he goes" (14:4a). To suggest that John is suddenly and out of nowhere raising up sexual virginity as a key virtue totally misunderstands the message of Revelation and, indeed, of the entire Bible. As we saw in chapter 6, sexual infidelity and prostitution are among the favorite prophetic metaphors for the people of God going after other gods in violation of the covenant to worship YHWH alone (e.g., Deut. 6:4-6). This tradition is at the heart of the conception of Babylon as luxurious whore and of New Jerusalem as beautiful bride. Although the literal idea of temporary celibacy is consistent with Israel's holy war ideology,[30] what is depicted in Revelation is not a temporary state of abstinence but a permanent state of nonparticipation in prohibited "sexuality," a clear metaphor for nonparticipation in idol worship. Only "virgins" are suitable "marriage" partners for the Lamb.[31] That is, the 144,000 virgins *are* the residents of the "bride," New Jerusalem. Thus, one should similarly reject any literal reading of this passage that would limit the gender of the 144,000 to male. In fact, logically speaking, they should all be women in order to comprise the bride who marries the Lamb (19:7; 21:2)!

The contrast between "buying" in the imperial system and being "bought" by the Lamb is reinforced in 14:4b, where the purchase of the 144,000 is named as "first fruits for God and the Lamb." The image of first fruits comes from Lev. 23:9-14, where it marks off the beginning of the harvest as a sacred offering to

---

30. E.g., Deut. 23:9-14; Bauckham (1993), pp. 230-31.

31. It may also express a not-so-subtle parody of the initiation rites of the *galli*, the priests of the cult of Cybele, who engaged in ecstatic self-castration as the culmination of their rituals.

God, Israel's covenant replacement of the common Canaanite practice of offering firstborn children to the gods (Lev. 18:21; 20:2-5).[32] Ironically, it is once again a human offering that is named as first fruits, but not, of course, because cultic ritual requires it, but rather because it expresses the total fidelity (virginity) of the 144,000 to their covenant partner.

The final aspect of the 144,000 given as part of this liturgical scene is that "in their mouth no illusion was found; they are blameless" (14:5; cf. Zeph. 3:11-13; Isa. 53:9). Note the odd juxtaposition of the plural "their" and the singular "mouth." Just as they sing with one voice of thunder, so too do they speak with a united voice that is free from imperial propaganda, that voice of sweet deception which tempted all to worship the icon of the Beast (13:5, 12-15). The fact that they are "blameless" (Greek *amōmoi*) expresses a double entendre: they are both without moral fault and without ritual impurity. In other words, they are fruit worthy of being offered to God and to the Lamb.

"JUST AND TRUE ARE YOUR WAYS, KING OF THE NATIONS!" (REV. 15:2-4)

The sixth liturgical scene follows upon the harvest of which the 144,000 were the first fruits. There are two harvests narrated. The first, the grain harvest, is carried out by the Human One and consists of the faithful and enduring ones on earth. The second, the grape harvest, is carried out by an angel with "authority over fire" (a symbol of judgment) and consists of those who have followed the Beast, who are thrown "into the great wine press of the wrath of God" (14:19). The blood flowing from this pressing runs like an enormous flood outside the city, "as high as a horse's bridle," a standard image in apocalyptic texts from the same period as Revelation (e.g., *1 Enoch* 100:3; *4 Ezra* 15:35-36).[33] It is a ghastly image, designed, like many similar ones in the book, both to shock imperial-compromising members of the *ekklēsiai* in Asia into recommitment to the gospel of the Lamb and to provide a sense of ultimate justice.

In the spiral logic of our text, the twin harvest is followed by the sign that the final plagues—those coming from the overturned heavenly bowls (Rev. 16)—are about to take place to "complete" the wrath of God. At this point John sees before him the setting for the sixth liturgical scene: "what appeared to be a sea of glass mixed with fire, and those who had overcome the Beast and its icon and the number of its name, standing beside the sea of glass with lyres of God in their hands" (15:2). The scene is now familiar, with the 144,000 now described in relation to the Beast. And as always, they are singing, this time "the song of Moses, the servant of God, and the song of the Lamb." The original song of Moses is found at Exod. 15:1-18, proclaiming the divine warrior's mighty act of delivering his peo-

---

32. Cf. 1 Kings 11:7 and Jer. 32:35, indicating the ongoing nature of the problem of child sacrifice within Israel.

33. Bauckham (1993), p. 46.

ple from Egypt. Another version of Moses' song is recited in Deut. 31:30-32:44, a passage echoed many times in Revelation. This second song focuses on YHWH as faithful protector and provider, and Israel as unfaithful worshiper of idols. Israel's infidelity at first provokes YHWH's righteous anger against Israel, but divine anger eventually is turned away from God's people and toward the idolatrous nations. The first song was reinterpreted in the course of Israel's history both by Isa. 12:1-6 and by Ps. 105. Now John hears a new version, which has become the combined song of Moses and of the Lamb. The song is an amalgam of numerous passages from Hebrew scripture, making clear that in many ways, there is nothing new about the song's content at all.[34] There are not two songs sung but one, just as there are not two people of God (Jews and Christians) but one (those faithful to YHWH alone). For the song is sung solely to the glory of the Lord God Almighty, called here "King of the Nations."

The song proclaims the joining together of the faithful nations into the one people of God, reinforcing the previously sung celebration of the multitude arising from "every nation, from all tribes and peoples and languages" (7:9). It thus corresponds to the grain harvest, just as the judgment upon the idolatrous members of the nations corresponds to the grape harvest.[35] The song blends the proclamation of God as powerful and benevolent king, but also as just judge, a capacity desired in any good monarch, and, of course, notoriously lacking in emperors.

It concludes by singing that God's judgments "have been revealed," indicating that there is no reason for people to refuse to give loyalty and praise to God other than sheer hard-heartedness. This truth is systematically shown throughout the sequence that follows, in which people respond to the series of terrible bowl plagues not with repentance or requests for mercy but with blasphemous cursing of God (e.g., 16:9-11; 16:21). That is why the treading of the grape harvest takes place "outside the city" (14:20; cf. 22:15), so that those within may live free of the violence and deceit of the Beast's worshipers, who refuse to respond to the truth that has been revealed.

"LET US REJOICE AND EXULT, FOR THE MARRIAGE OF THE LAMB HAS COME!" (REV. 19:1-8)

The final of the seven liturgical scenes bridges the climactic passages that show horror and grief at the sight of the smoking ruin of fallen Babylon, on the one hand, and the impending joyful marriage of the Lamb to his Bride, on the other. While those whose livelihood depended on Babylon stand far off in mourning and lamentation in Rev. 18, the liturgy reveals the "great multitude in heaven"

---

34. Texts include Exod. 34:10; Deut. 32:4; Pss. 98:1; 111:2; 139:14; 145:17; Amos 4:13; Isa. 2:2; Jer. 10:7; 11:20; 16:19.
35. Bauckham (1993), p. 309.

who are overjoyed at the revelation of the destruction of the locus of evil. Their joy is not that of vengeance but of freedom from terror, just as people would rejoice over the destruction of a bomb in their midst or the putting out of a raging fire.

The proclamation of the multitude celebrates the fulfillment of the promise made in 11:18 to "destroy those who destroy the earth," for we hear them say in their usual loud voice, "he has judged the great Whore who destroyed the earth with her whoring" (19:2). The refrain of their prayer is *hallelujah*, a transliterated Hebrew word meaning "praise YHWH," and uttered more than thirty times in the Psalms. They are joined in their refrain by the elders and cherubim, as well as by an unidentified voice from the throne, but one which might be assumed to be that of the Lamb, the only other being who shares that sacred space with God (7:17).

The song is a simple shout of joy, without the many intricacies found in previous heavenly songs. No longer is there need to plead with God for justice, for justice has been done. Now all is celebration, not just of the destruction of Babylon, though, but of a new event about to take place: "the marriage of the Lamb." Rev. 19:7 echoes Third Isaiah's similar celebration of the God who loves justice and clothes his faithful ones "as a bridegroom decks himself with a garland, and as a bride adorns herself with her jewels" (61:10). In the Isaian passage, the imagery of both bride and bridegroom is used to describe the prophet's own joyous exultation. In Revelation, the images of bride and bridegroom are separated to produce a wedding scene, which will be narrated in Rev. 21. The metaphor of Lamb-as-bridegroom is combined with that of New Jerusalem-as-bride, so that the resulting figure is of a blessed place of peace and harmony in which a faithful covenant will be lived out without the distractions of seductive whores and the dangers of lying Beasts. In the song, this link has not yet been revealed, for the lyrics focus only on the readiness of the Bride, bedecked in "fine linen, bright and pure," which is explicitly said to be "the just deeds of the holy ones" (19:8).

Liturgy and worship in Revelation are thus shown to be powerful tools for generating solidarity and commitment within the *ekklēsiai*. For people of our time whose only experience of liturgy consists of packaged performances lacking spirited participation from the congregation, Revelation's liturgies can seem overwhelming if not shocking. However, for those who have been raised in or have been part of Pentecostal, charismatic, or other surging, song-filled services, Revelation's rollicking rituals will seem joyously familiar. In tribute to the power of Revelation's imagery, many hymnals are filled with songs echoing Revelation's words. Sometimes this is obvious, as with tunes such as "When the Saints Go Marching In" or the "Battle Hymn of the Republic." In other cases, the link may be more hidden, as with the classic "We Shall Overcome," whose title is adapted from the Authorized Version of Revelation. In either case, Revelation called the *ekklēsiai* of Roman Asia, just as it does the Christian communities of our own day, to recognize that when we gather for worship, we are making a public statement of political allegiance. We are taking a stand against empire, and in celebration of the reign of our just and true God and of the Lamb.

REFLECTION QUESTIONS

1. How is the liturgy portrayed in Revelation similar to or different from your experience of liturgy? What accounts for the differences?

2. Consider experiences you've had of powerful liturgies. What made it work for you? What lasting impression has that experience had on you?

3. Gather a group for some sort of experience of public prayer or worship (see Kellermann 1994 for ideas). Reflect together afterward on what the experience was like for you.

8

The War of Myths
between Revelation and Rome

We saw in chapter 3 that the Roman Empire was legitimized by a web of myths. These collectively supported the idea that a "golden age" had been inaugurated by Augustus. The emperors succeeding Augustus each claimed to embody the Augustan achievement in their own rule. We shall now examine five particular myths—Empire, Peace, Victory, Faith, and Eternity—and how Revelation "conquers" them. These myths form part of the "sacred canopy"[1] that covered ancient Rome. The purpose of John's visionary narrative is to "uncover" the reality that these myths hid. This engagement between Rome's legitimating stories and God's truth is what is called the "war of myths."

The term "war of myths" was used by Amos Wilder to describe how the early Christian texts were written to challenge the myths that legitimated both Judaism and Roman-Hellenism.[2] Ched Myers explains how "what is usually described as the 'theology' of the new Testament writers Wilder referred to as their challenge to the dominant symbol systems of both imperial Rome and Palestinian Judaism."[3] These myths were primarily intended to subvert the imperial view of reality in favor of the alternative reality of Jesus.

The myths of the Roman Empire served to legitimate the imperial structures and actors. They also functioned to deny the possibilities of alternatives to the empire. The Roman Empire, in broadcasting its myths via a range of media, instructed people collectively in the way they were expected to understand "reality" in accordance with its imperial interests. This is why *metanoeō* was such a crucial issue for the five of the seven *ekklēsiai* who were not faithfully resisting empire. These five were called to the "transformed understanding" signified by the Greek *metanoeō* (*meta* + *noeō* = change + understand, perceive, imagine; see 2:5, 16, 22; 3:3, 19). While traditionally translated "repentance," the Greek word is suggestive of a radically changed perception or imagination.

---

1. Berger (1967).
2. Wilder (1982), pp. 112-19.
3. Myers (1988), p. 16.

The myths utilized by Revelation were largely drawn from the Hebrew prophetic/apocalyptic tradition. In chapter 2 it was shown that many of these traditions were themselves drawn from more ancient traditions. But John shaped this inherited mythic tradition in the light of the history-transforming event of Jesus' death and resurrection. Just as he had uncovered the lies that enshrouded empire for Saul of Tarsus (Acts 9:4-22; Gal. 1:11-16), so too had Jesus, the one worthy to open the first scroll, revealed the falsity of empire to John. It is this event that focused John's use of the biblical heritage as a "weapon" with which to tear away the veil that protected empire's nakedness before God.

MYTH: EMPIRE

An inscription in the temple of Rome and Augustus in Galatia, a neighboring province of Asia, is prefaced with these words:

> The achievements of the god Augustus, by which he subjected the whole earth to the *imperium* of the Roman people. . . .[4]

These words celebrate the *imperium* of foreign rule by the people of Asia Minor. Those responsible for the imperial temple and its inscription welcomed imperial rule and the god Augustus, who inaugurated it. While some people in Judea, Gaul, Britain, and elsewhere resisted Roman *imperium* with their lives, those in the provinces of Asia Minor celebrated it.

The myth of *imperium* was central to the Roman understanding of its role in the world. *Basileia,* the Greek equivalent of the Latin *imperium*, has traditionally been translated "kingdom" or "reign." In the Greek-speaking world of the first century the word had a primary meaning: the Roman Empire.

> This was the term that Rome used to describe itself. When we encounter it in ancient secular texts or in inscriptions from that period, we always translate it "empire." There was only one empire in the Mediterranean basin in the first century, the Roman Empire.[5]

Put simply, *basileia* was how the Roman Empire presented itself in its Greek-speaking eastern half.

COUNTER-MYTH: THE EMPIRE OF OUR GOD

In appropriating this baldly political term from Rome, the early Christian movement acted quite deliberately. As Stephen Patterson argues: "it is no acci-

---

4. From the Ancyra version of the *Acts of the Divine Augustus*, in Brunt and Moore, pp. 18-19.
5. Patterson, p. 44.

dent that earliest Christians took over this vocabulary [that of Roman politics] and made it their own in the years following Jesus' death. This was a hostile takeover. The polemical intent of the parallelism cannot be missed."[6]

A crucial issue for the early Christian movement was: Who was qualified to rule over empire? Was it the god Caesar or the God of Jesus? This had been an aspect of the battle of myths ever since Jesus first announced the "gospel" (another imperial term) that the "Empire of God" was at hand (Mark 1:1, 15). *Basileia* and associated words occur seventeen times in the text of Revelation.

The first occurrence is in 1:6, where Jesus is said to have constituted his followers as an "empire." Three verses later John informs his audience that he shares "tribulation, empire, and endurance" with them (1:9). This usage immediately countered head-on Rome's claims of *imperium*. As the word "sovereignty" implies, and as history has demonstrated, it is virtually impossible for groups competing for sovereignty to share power. *Imperium/basileia* was an either/or proposition. When and where Rome exercised *imperium* no one else could.

The claim by John that empire belongs to the followers of Jesus contains the implicit subclaim: empire does *not* belong to Rome. This claim, by one who was a prophet in a circle of tiny *ekklēsiai*, was, of course, ludicrous if one accepted Rome's mythology. Yet Revelation claims that Rome's *imperium* had ceased in the *ekklēsiai* who resisted it. This claim, if voiced loudly and publicly, was tantamount to treason, yet it is repeated throughout the text:

> You have made them an empire (*basileian*) and priests to our God and they have imperial rule (*basileuousin*) over the earth. (5:10)

> The empire (*basileia*) of the world became the empire of our Lord and of his Christ, and he will have imperial rule (*basileusei*) for ever and ever. (11:15)

> The salvation and the power and the empire (*basileia*) of our God and the authority of his Christ has come. (12:10)

> They [the citizens of New Jerusalem] will have imperial rule (*basileusousin*) for ever and ever. (22:5)

Most interpretations of the "kingdom of God" fail to appreciate the depth of this mythic challenge to imperial power. They either privatize the challenge (e.g., the "kingdom of God" is inside the human heart), or place it outside the realm of human action (e.g., after death, after the end of the world). Both these tracks fail to capture the radical character of John's vision of empire that turns the whole world upside down.

---

6. Ibid., p. 46.

MYTH: THE ROMAN PAX

The central claim made by Augustus was that he had ended civil conflict and thereby brought peace to the world. Augustus claimed to have inaugurated the *Pax Romana*–the "peace of Rome." For some in the Roman Empire, including the province of Asia, the *Pax* was considered to be a sign of the benevolence of the empire and its emperors. It was believed that the empire had bestowed peace and stability across the inhabited world. In the *Acts of the Divine Augustus*, written by Augustus himself and intended as his epitaph,[7] we read:

> On my return from Spain and Gaul . . . the Senate resolved that an altar of the Augustan Peace should be consecrated next to the field of Mars [the god of war] in honor of my return, and ordered that the magistrates and priests and Vestal virgins should perform an annual sacrifice there. (*Acts of the Divine Augustus* 12)

And further:

> It was the will of our ancestors that the gateway of Janus Quirinius should be shut when victories had secured peace [*victoriis pax*] by land and sea throughout the whole empire of the Roman people. From the foundation of the city down to my birth, tradition records that it was shut only twice, but while I was leading citizen the Senate resolved that it should be shut on three occasions. (*Acts of the Divine Augustus* 13)

Augustus hoped that he would be remembered by the Roman people as the herald of an unparalleled age of peace.

Writing in the middle of the first century C.E., Pliny the Elder extolled the benefits of the Roman *Pax*:

> The boundless grandeur of the Roman Peace, which displays in turn not men only with their different lands and tribes but also mountains, and peaks soaring into the clouds, their offspring and also their plants. May this gift of the gods last, I pray, forever! So truly do they seem to have given to the human race the Romans as it were a second sun. (*Natural History* 28.3)

This view was held by many in the provinces. An inscription at Priene, located near Ephesus and dated 9 C.E., describes Augustus as the author of peace. The

---

7. When Augustus died on August 19, 14 C.E., he left behind "a catalogue of his achievements which he wished to be inscribed on bronze tablets and set up in front of his mausoleum" (Suetonius, *The Life of the God Augustus* 101.4). Interestingly, all three extant sources of the text come from the province of Galatia, a neighboring province to Asia. This is indicative of the importance of Augustan ideology in Asia Minor.

inscription claimed that Augustus "brought war to an end and has ordained peace . . . for the world, the birthday of the god [the emperor Augustus] has marked the beginning of his good news of peace."

Again the words of Aelius Aristides in his *Eulogy to Rome* are telling:

> People no longer believe in wars, indeed doubt that they ever happened; stories about them are usually regarded as myths. But if wars should flare up somewhere on the frontiers . . . these wars quickly disappear again, just like myths, as do the stories about them. So great is the peace that you now have, though waging war is a tradition among you. (70)

These various texts are an expression of the myth of the *Pax Romana*, a belief that the Roman Empire was the beneficent provider of peace, security, and order. This myth was propagated for more than a hundred years and was especially powerful in Roman Asia.

The *Pax Romana*, even as its supporters understood it, was a "peace" built upon military conquest:

> The "altar of the peace of Augustus" was placed on the hill of Mars, god of war. Coins struck under Augustus linked the armed and armored First Citizen with Pax, goddess of peace, trampling on the weapons of subdued enemies, and Victoria, goddess of conquest, treading on the globe itself.[8]

Whether one saw Rome as the author of peace was, of course, in the eye of the beholder. The *Pax Romana* was an expression of the order and security that was experienced by those at the center of the empire: the members of the elite and their friends in the provinces. In fact, this "peace" was an order maintained by armed legions on the borders of the empire and the use of deadly force against dissidents within the empire. Many who witnessed the bloodshed on the frontiers and in the rebellious provinces or the execution of dissidents took issue with the universal "peace" heralded by Rome. Tacitus, for example, writes of Calgacus, who described Rome from his perspective as the leader of a people resisting the Roman military in the north of Britain: "To plunder, butcher, steal, these things they misname empire: they make a desolation and they call it peace" (*Agricola* 30). Like Calgacus, the writer of Revelation had a different understanding of Rome from that expressed by emperors, poets, and propagandists.

COUNTER-MYTH:
BABYLON, THE SHEDDER OF BLOOD

Revelation opposes the myth of the *Pax Romana* with a counter-myth: an image of the Beasts and the Whore as *murderers*. The point of these images is

---

8. N. Elliott (1997), p. 169.

clear. Empire is not benign but murderous. It is not ordered but chaotic. It imposes its will not by grace but by force. Supporters of Rome made the claim that the *Pax Romana* was supported by the gods. Revelation contends that the one true God has revealed this claim to be false.

The most obvious way in which the *Pax Romana* is contested is the assertion that the Beasts and Babylon are involved in murder. This is a constant refrain in the book:

> You did not deny your faith in me even in the days of Antipas, my faithful witness who was killed among you, where Satan lives. (2:13)

> I saw underneath the altar the souls of the ones having been slain on account of the word of God. (6:9)

> It [the second Beast] was allowed . . . to have as many who did not worship the icon of the Beast to be killed. (13:15)

> They spilt the blood of the holy ones and prophets, and blood is what you have given them to drink; it is what they deserve. (16:6)

> I saw the woman [Babylon] being drunk from the blood of the holy ones and the blood of the witnesses of Jesus. (17:6)

> In her [Babylon] was found the blood of prophets and holy ones, and all the ones having been slain on earth. (18:24)

John's visions revealed that empire was nothing more than a mass murderer. It routinely murdered any who opposed it. Revelation's audience was thus challenged to see Rome in this counterimperial way.

Furthermore, Revelation responds to the *Pax Romana* myth by offering the *Pax Divina* as the true source of social harmony. In John's opening salutation we hear:

> Grace to you and peace from him who is and who was and who is to come and from the seven spirits who are before his throne, and from Jesus Christ, the faithful witness, the firstborn of the dead, and the ruler of the kings of the earth. (Rev. 1:4-5a)

Although John does not elaborate this form of the counter-myth, by placing it at the beginning of his text, it forms part of the frame that encloses the entire book. True *pax* comes not from imperial rule but from the rule of "Jesus, the faithful witness."

MYTH: *VICTORIA*

The myth of "Victory" (Latin *victoria*) was a keystone of the Roman Empire. *Victoria* was how the empire was founded and the way in which it was maintained. This is true in its crudest material sense: the empire existed by force of arms and bloodshed. No less important, however, *victoria* was embodied in a living, unique, and permanent way in the ongoing person of the emperor.[9] *Victoria* was thus closely related to the *Pax Romana*. The "Victory" of the empire consisted of the subjugation of those in the frontier provinces. It was this "Victory" that enabled the so-called "Peace."

Victoria was inevitably associated with military conquest. This is readily observable in the imagery used to depict her, as Klaus Wengst describes:

> The evidence of the coinage is very eloquent: Mars the god of war is in full armor, on his left shoulder a standard and on his outstretched right arm the goddess of victory, along with the inscription *Mars Victor*. Another coin portrays Victoria on the hand of the goddess Roma, who is herself sitting on the weapons of conquered opponents. Portrayals of Victoria are particularly frequent; she has her right foot on the globe and is inscribing a shield with the victory which has just been won; standing behind the head of Augustus she is putting a laurel wreath on his brow.[10]

Victoria was a myth that lent legitimacy to the emperors. Thus, Julius Caesar (titled *Victoria Caesaris*), Augustus (*Victoria Caesaris Augusti Imperatoris*), and Vespasian (*Victoria Imperatoris Caesaris Vespasiani Augusti)* were each given the title *Victoria.*[11]

The title was attributed to those emperors whose armies had conquered the peoples of the provinces:

> the deeds of these emperors were epiphanies of specific victories . . . Gallia Capta, Aegyptus Capta, and Judea Capta were, in each instance, miracula attesting a specific manifestation of Victoria and her power operating in the sphere of the emperor's warlike activities.[12]

According to the myth, the emperors had achieved military successes in occupying (Latin *capta*) Gaul, Egypt, and Judea because *victoria* had blessed them. *Victoria's* blessing was the guarantor of Rome's success. Yet this is not how John of Patmos saw it.

COUNTER-MYTH: THE VICTORY OF THE LAMB AND HIS FOLLOWERS

If Revelation redefined "peace," it had also to redefine "victory." The Greek equivalent of the Latin *victoria—nikē* (which we have translated "victory" or

---

9. Fears, p. 737.
10. Wengst, p. 11.
11. Fears, p. 745.
12. Ibid.

"conquest," depending on the context) occurs seventeen times in Revelation. Revelation addresses the question of what makes for "victory": Is it the fruit of imperial conquest, or is it the faithful rejection of empire and embrace of the way of God? Revelation's answer is crystal clear: it is only by rejecting empire and by maintaining loyalty to God and the Lamb that victory is won.

More than simply urging its audience to reject the lie of the *Pax Romana*, as we saw in chapter 5, Revelation exhorted its audience to practice nonviolent witness to the reality of God's victory over empire. This call was based on the apocalyptic insight that true "victory" is founded on the "blood of the Lamb" (12:11; cf. 5:6; 7:14; 17:14). It was Jesus' willingness to be executed rather than to kill that constitutes "victory."

Each of the seven *ekklēsiai* of Asia addressed in the text was called to "conquer" (2:7, 11, 17, 26; 3:5, 12, 21). For Smyrna and Philadelphia, this was to be achieved by remaining faithful. For the others, it was necessary that they engage in *metanoeō* if they were to have "victory." For those who proved victorious, God, not empire, would reward them. These rewards are named in each of the seven letters (Rev. 2-3) and find their realization in New Jerusalem (Rev. 21-22), as shown in table 21.

New Jerusalem is where "the victorious shall inherit these things" (21:7). It is where the tree of life grows, where death is no more, and where Jesus has a throne. These rewards may seem less tangible than those offered by Rome, but, for those with "eyes to see," the victory of the Lamb and his followers is more real than the spurious claims of empire:

> And they conquered him on account of the blood of the Lamb and the word of their witness, and they loved not their lives as far as death. (12:11)

> I saw . . . the ones who conquered the Beast, its icon, and the number of its name standing beside the sea of glass. (15:2)

> They will make war on the Lamb and the Lamb will conquer them, for he is Lord of lords and King of kings, and the ones with him are called and chosen and faithful. (17:14)

Revelation's war on the myth of *victoria* involves a radical shift in the cultural understanding of victory. In empire's myth, military success and the quelling of dissent made for victory. Revelation's apocalyptic insight unveiled victory as the preparedness to lay down one's life in resistance to empire, and the willingness to live the way of God for the long haul.

MYTH: FAITH

Fides (Greek *pistis*) was another Roman myth. The word has traditionally been translated "faith," but in the ancient world meant the "value of enduring social relations."[13] These relations were the "social glue that binds one person to another."[14] In the ancient world, "*fides/pistis*" was a synonym for reciprocal loyalty. Caesar embodied *fides* in his faithfulness to treaty obligations, his justice, and his concern for the welfare of the people. Naturally, it was a social expectation that faith was reciprocated by the people in the form of their loyalty to Caesar. In the ancient world this bond of reciprocal loyalty contained a certain exclusivity. It also involved the submission of the weaker party to the stronger in accordance with patron–client relations. Conquered peoples would offer their *fides* to Rome, where it involved a total surrender to the discretion of the emperor.[15] Faith could not be divided. It was either given to Caesar or not. Not to give it to Caesar was an act of gross insolence. It might even amount to a declaration of war.

Table 21
TABLE OF PROMISES TO THE *EKKLĒSIAI*
AND THEIR REALIZATION IN NEW JERUSALEM

City	Promise in Message	Realization in New Jerusalem
Ephesus	To eat of the tree of life, which is in the paradise of God (2:7).	The tree of life produces fruit and leaves for healing (22:2).
Smyrna	To not be harmed by the second death (2:11).	Those who practice the imperial vices receive the second death (21:8).
Pergamum	To be given a white stone . . . with a new name written on it (2:27).	Slaves receive the name of God and Lamb on their foreheads (22:4).
Thyatira	To have authority over the nations (2:26).	Slaves will have empire forever (22:5).
Sardis	To not have their name blotted from the book of life and to be acknowledged before the Father (3:5).	Those who practice vices are not in the book of life (21:27) and the victorious are proclaimed God's son (21:7).
Philadelphia	To be made a pillar in the temple of God; to have the name of God and the name of the city of God, New Jerusalem, written on them (3:12).	New Jerusalem descends from heaven (21:2, 10); God and the Lamb are its temple (21:22).
Laodicea	To "sit on the throne" with Jesus (3:21).	Slaves will have empire with God and the Lamb (22:5).

---

13. Pilch and Malina, p. 67.
14. Ibid., p. 68.
15. Lintott, p. 17.

COUNTER-MYTH:
KEEPING THE FAITH OF JESUS

If the *imperium* of Rome was counterfeit, could "faith" be placed in it? Revelation's answer is an unequivocal no. Revelation, however, understands faith as the enduring social relations that were necessary to create and maintain a circle of counterimperial *ekklēsiai*. If they were to embrace the difficult process of disassociating from empire, the *ekklēsiai* would need to maintain strong social relations within and between one another and with God.

In Revelation it is Jesus who sets the standard as the "faithful one." He manifested his loyalty through his "witness" to the truth of God (1:5; 3:14; cf. 19:11). The "faith" of Jesus extends in two directions. He is loyal to God and demonstrates this by his witness and execution. He is also loyal to his followers in the *ekklēsiai*. This is proven by his concern for the community and by the victory he wins over empire for their sake.

"Faith" is also proposed as a way of life for the members of the *ekklēsiai*. Those at Pergamum (2:13) and Thyatira (2:19) are commended for their "faith." Particularly important is the issue of faith in times of social sanction. The *ekklēsia* at Smyrna, for example, is warned that some of its members will be imprisoned. They are promised victory if they are "faithful unto death" (2:10). For those at Pergamum, Antipas is commended as "my faithful one" (2:13). This is in recognition of his execution for the sake of his witness to God. His remaining community members are praised for "not denying the faith" despite the communal trauma associated with the execution of their community member.

In times such as these, a loyalty that *endures* is essential or everything will fall apart. As Revelation declares:

Here is the endurance and the faith [*pistis*] of the holy ones. (13:10)

Here is the endurance of the holy ones, those keeping the commandments of God and the faith [*pistis*] of Jesus. (14:12)

The first reference occurs after a description of the power of the Beast to make war on and defeat the followers of Jesus. Where the *ekklēsiai* can stand up to that power, there is endurance and faith. The second follows a description of the consequences of following the Beast: the anger of God and a share in the eternal destruction of the Beast. Those with enduring faith can avoid the eternal torment consequent upon the following of the Beast.

In Roman society those who cooperated with the empire were considered loyal, as possessing "faith." Revelation, however, asserts that those who cooperated with empire were in fact "faithless" (21:8) and that those who had rejected empire were "faithful." Revelation penetrates the true meaning of loyalty to Rome and declares it to be disloyalty.

MYTH: ETERNITY

The myth of *aeterna* was another part of Rome's ideological edifice. In the Roman and Greek world *aeterna* (and its Greek equivalent *aiōn*) implied a state of "durability rather than the transcendental eternity in the Christian sense."[16] In the Republican period, Cicero claimed that Rome was the embodiment of the cosmic order on earth. To Cicero, the Roman state would endure if it were free of civil discord.[17]

We have seen that with the ascendancy of Augustus a new era was proclaimed. Civil disorder had been ended by the victory of Augustus. Virgil depicts Jupiter promising to Venus that Rome would not end.[18] Virgil's Latin contains an ambiguity that permits a double meaning: Rome's physical domain would extend indefinitely, and its continuation in time would endure. The mythmakers typically traced Rome's eternity to the stories of its origins. Thus, the phrase "*urbs aeterna*" ("eternal city") was applied to Rome via its foundation by Romulus.[19] It was believed that Rome's eternal status was granted at the very founding of the city.

In the first century, the myth of eternity was applied to the figure of Augustus, the later emperors, the city, the Roman people, and the empire itself. The expressions of that time—*pax aeterna* ("eternal peace"), *Roma aeterna* ("eternal Rome") and *urbs aeterna* ("eternal city")—evoke this myth. It was in the interests of the successors of Augustus to link themselves with the mythic potency of Augustus, and this they did with alacrity.

With Vespasian's quelling of the civil conflict that saw three emperors come and go in the course of a year, coins were minted with the message *Pax Augusti* (Peace of Augustus) and *Aeternitas Populi Romani* (People of Rome Forever). Vespasian thereby claimed, like his great predecessor Augustus, to have brought peace to a warring Rome and to have guaranteed the empire forever. Titus and Domitian also claimed to embody Augustan eternity.[20] On their coins the goddess *Aeternitas* was depicted holding the sun and moon, themselves symbols of eternity.[21] Throughout the first century, then, the emperors presented themselves to their subjects as guarantors of the eternity of the Roman state and Roman people.

COUNTER-MYTH: THEY WILL REIGN FOREVER

The myth that empire lasts forever is indeed an archetypal imperial myth. After all, who wants to admit that the arrangement in which we have invested

---

16. Turcan, p. 52.
17. Mellor (1981), p. 1019.
18. "*Imperium sine fide dedi*" (*Aeneid* 1.279).
19. Tibullus 2.5.23; Ovid *Fasti* 3.72. Livy, who wrote a history of Rome from its origins to his own era, linked the eternity of Rome to its "foundation" (Latin *condita*) in the phrase "*urbs in aeternum condita*" (4.4.4; 28.28.11).
20. M. P. Charlesworth, pp. 124-26.
21. Mellor (1981), pp. 1022-23.

everything will come to an end? In many times and places, to imagine the end of empire has been considered an act of treason. This is exactly what Revelation does.

The Greek *aiōn* occurs twenty-seven times in Revelation. Twenty-six occurrences are as part of the expression *aiōnas aiōnōn*, which is found thirteen times. This expression is usually translated "forever and ever."

The use of the myth of eternity in the book of Revelation points in two directions. The dominant direction is that it is God, the Lamb, and the followers of the Lamb who possess eternity. Thus, God is described as the one who "lives forever and ever" (4:9, 10; 10:6; 15:7). The claim to live forever and ever is also made by the Human One (1:18). In addition to these claims, the assertion is made that God, Jesus, and their followers possess imperial rule forever.[22] These claims are made:

- of God:

  Blessing and glory and wisdom and thanks and honor and power and strength to our God forever and ever. (7:12)

- of Jesus:

  To you be glory and rule forever and ever. (1:6)

  Christ shall have empire forever and ever. (11:15)

- of God and Jesus:

  To the one sitting on the throne and to the Lamb blessing and honor and glory and rule forever and ever. (5:13)

- of the followers of God and Jesus:

  They will have empire forever and ever. (22:5)

As well as positive claims about the eternity of those who resist empire, there are negative claims of eternity made concerning those who collude with empire:

the smoke of their [the beast worshipers] torment goes up forever and ever. (14:11)

the smoke of her [Babylon] burning goes up forever and ever. (19:3)

they [devil, beast, false prophet] will be tormented day and night forever and ever. (20:10)

---

22. Note also Rev. 14:6, where an angel bears "an eternal gospel," which, as Beale notes, serves as a polemic against the gospel of Caesar, which is thereby shown to be temporary (Beale [1999], p. 750).

Rome's myth of the "eternal city" has been nowhere more effectively opposed than with John's revealing vision that saw "the smoke" of Rome's destruction that "goes up forever and ever" (19:3). To depict the "eternal city" as an eternal smoking ruin is clearly subversive of the Roman myth of *aeterna*. The only eternity that the *urbs aeterna* can lay claim to is the smoke that signals the destruction of empire ascending forever. True eternity, John sees, belongs to those who faithfully resist empire, to the Lamb who was slain by empire, and to the God of the Lamb. These possess "glory and rule and empire" forever and ever.

The language and imagery of Revelation sought to use the popular political mythic idiom of first-century Roman Asia to evoke a radical transformation of the way the empire should be viewed. By showing how the ubiquitous myths of the Roman world had been defeated, Revelation delegitimized the empire and encouraged the *ekklēsiai* of Asia to trust in God's victory. The division between the way of God and the way of empire renewed the stark contrast between God-as-king and Caesar-as-king. As we have seen, this struggle between the ways of God and the ways of empire is central to the history of the people of God. The conflict that began between YHWH and Babel and had been waged against Pharaoh, the Canaanite kings, Babylon, the Persians and the Seleucids was now a struggle against Rome. As we will see in the final chapter, it is a struggle that continues in our time, too.

REFLECTION QUESTIONS

1. What myths have been most powerful in shaping your life? Consider myths of family or church origins, national or ethnic myths, or myths of modern culture. How have these myths been conveyed and reinforced for you, that is, through story, advertising, education, and so forth?

2. Reflect on a myth that you've resisted in some way. For example, "men are aggressive and women are soft," "people have wealth because they deserve it in some way," "war is a sometimes necessary tragedy," and so forth. What has helped or hindered your efforts to resist a specific myth?

3. What elements in your life support your ability to hold an alternative myth in the face of the power of empire to support its own myths?

9

Coming Out of Empire Today

It is one thing to consider the difficult challenge to first-century Christians to withdraw from the Roman Empire and to live according to the way of God; it is quite another to ask the question of how this challenge speaks to us today. As we saw in chapter 1, many Christians succumb to the temptation to read Revelation as if it were speaking exclusively to our generation. This approach leads sometimes to absurd scenarios that expect an imminent End of the World. At the same time, premillennialist and other "prophecy readings" of Revelation have the virtue of at least taking seriously the call of the text to live differently in some way from the prevailing culture in which we find ourselves. How do we begin the process of appropriating Revelation's perennial challenge today?

We have tried to show how Revelation is part of the wider phenomenon of apocalyptic literature, which has always called God's people to become aware of the presence of empire in their midst and to refuse to succumb to empire's seductions. During the nearly two thousand years between John of Patmos's time and our own, many accumulations of power have proudly described themselves as "empire." The sequence began immediately with the Roman Empire itself which, with the conversion of Emperor Constantine, made Christianity—at least in name—the imperial faith. In more recent centuries, we have seen the various European empires take their turn at world domination, each believing it would last forever, each collapsing under the weight of its own arrogance and God's judgment. From time to time, Christian movements arose in resistance to this succession of empires, proclaiming and living New Jerusalem in the midst of their own time's Babylon.

Today, though, no entity explicitly calls itself "empire." The United States, having been born in resistance to the British Empire, could never acknowledge this aspect of its history, even though a quick review of U.S. history easily reveals the imperial earmarks that accompanied the growth of the nation: slave labor; demonization, genocide, and displacement of indigenous people; colonization of distant lands (e.g., Hawaii, Alaska, the Philippines, Guam); cultural arrogance; and global military power. However, a deep reading of the signs of our times reveals that the United States is no longer the dominant imperial force in our world.

To begin our deeper look, consider the definition of "imperialism" offered by two historians of the British Empire: "Imperialism can best be viewed as a mechanism for transferring income from the middle to the upper classes."[1] Nation-states are no longer the primary vehicle for this mechanism. Rather, empire today, we contend, can be found in the complex but discernible phenomena that we call here "global capital."

Numerous observers and analysts, from social critics to mavens of global finance, have noted the power shift in recent decades away from national governments. Consider the view of David Korten, former senior advisor to the United States Agency for International Development and member of the faculty of the Harvard Graduate School of Business: "[The] process of economic globalization . . . is shifting power away from governments responsible for the public good and toward a handful of corporations and financial institutions.[2] Or listen to the words of Kenichi Ohmae, managing director of McKinsey & Co., Japan: "[Governments must] yield to the inevitable—accept the reality that government is obsolete, get out of the way, and let goods and money flow freely in response to market forces."[3] Finally, there is the function of billionaire currency speculator and philanthropist George Soros, as described by one of his partners: "George Soros calls the bluff of governments. Their job is to pretend that they're in control and he represents a force that blows away that illusion."[4]

An emblem of this shift from the nation-state to global capital is found in reports from Juneau, Alaska. In the parking lot of the McDonald's restaurant there, bald eagles search the ground for food scraps. The proud symbol of American national power, which soared above the earth with its keen eye and sharp talons, has been reduced to scavenging consumer castoffs from a global fast-food corporation.

How is the empire of global capital manifested in our world? How is it similar to or different from the Roman Empire of John's day? How might Revelation expect Christians to live in the midst of this powerful imperial reality? These are the questions we will address in this chapter.

EXAMINING GLOBAL CAPITAL
THROUGH THE LENS OF REVELATION

When empire was embodied in clearly defined entities like nation-states, it was relatively easy to trace the contours of imperial power. Global capital, how-

---

1. Lance David and Robert Huttenback, *Mammon and the Pursuit of Empire* (New York: Cambridge University Press, 1986), quoted in Korten, p. 20.

2. Korten, p. 12.

3. Cited in Korten, p. 127.

4. Robert Johnson, quoted in Greider, p. 240.

ever, is a more elusive reality. Nonetheless, it may be startling to see how precisely the reality of global capital matches both that of the Roman Empire in particular and Revelation's wider critique of empire generally.

"Then I Saw Another Beast": ### *Government in Service of Global Capital*

In John's time, as we have seen in chapter 3, the Roman imperial cult served as the propaganda mechanism for the empire itself. Everywhere one looked, the message was found inscribed in stone and metal, proclaimed in public ritual, and announced as "good news": the Roman Empire was the most powerful and blessed reality imaginable; refusing to worship it was to engage in heresy and treason at the same time. Thus, the political and economic functions of empire were propagated as "holy" by the practices of religion.

In our world, formal religious institutions are largely irrelevant to empire's self-serving proclamation. In its place, an array of government officials and government-supported economists proclaim the "divine inspiration" of the "free" market. Many commentators have spoken of the religious nature of belief in the free market and the promotion of this religion by government functionaries and journalists at the service of global capital-controlled media.[5] For example, journalist William Greider notes: "Respectable opinion is now enthralled by the secular faith [in the market] . . . . This faith has attained almost religious certitude."[6] David Korten adds: "free-market ideology has been embraced around the world with the fervor of a fundamentalist religious faith. . . . the economics profession serves as its priesthood . . . to question its doctrine has become virtual heresy.[7]

Korten notes the "dogmas" proclaimed by this priesthood:

1. Economic growth is the only path to human progress.
2. Unrestrained free markets are the best mode of trade.
3. Economic globalization is beneficial to almost all.
4. Privatization improves efficiency.
5. The primary role of government is to protect property rights and contracts.[8]

Proponents of this religion have raised up the name of Adam Smith to the level of "high priest" of the free market. It is instructive, though, to observe just how different was Smith's actual economic vision from the deceiving parody of it offered by free-market missionaries. For example, Smith saw that government was "instituted for the defense of the rich against the poor, or of those who have some property against those who have none at all." The "free market" he sup-

---

5. For example, Cox notes: "The lexicon of *The Wall Street Journal* and the business sections of *Time* and *Newsweek* [turn] out to bear a striking resemblance to Genesis, the Epistle to the Romans, and Saint Augustine's *City of God*" (Cox, p. 18).

6. Greider, p. 53.

7. Korten, p. 69.

8. Ibid., p. 70.

ported was one wherein local buyers and sellers could operate at close range. He stood adamantly opposed to international trade, seeing it as the bastion of the very monopolists whom the colonies were rebelling against. The use of his term "invisible hand" to describe the workings of global capital is nothing less than a diabolic effort to invert Smith's belief in the very kind of local economy which is the antidote to empire.[9]

Since the days of Ronald Reagan, government—first in the United States and then throughout the West—has explicitly embraced and proclaimed this religion. It is important to recognize that the characterization of free-market ideology as "religion" is not simply a rhetorical device, but an essential aspect of apocalyptic re-visioning. John's vision showed him how the Roman imperial cult functioned as a second "Beast" on behalf of the first Beast (the Roman political authority) with the power of the Dragon (Satan/evil). This led him to recognize—and to inculcate this recognition in the members of the *ekklēsiai*—that the acceptance of Rome's mythology was an act of giving worship to evil masquerading as divine authority. Similarly, those today who espouse belief in any economic system other than raw, global capitalism are scorned or ignored as "heretics" and their views pushed beyond the margin of "respectable" debate. Apocalyptic vision allows us to penetrate this veil and to see this ideology for what it is: a demonic lie.

It is important also to have a basic sense of how this religion has established itself formally as well as ideologically. As corporations have expanded beyond the borders of their countries of origin in search of markets, cheap labor, and unregulated access to natural resources, they have been transformed first into what were called "multinationals" and then into "transnationals." As we will examine below, the shift from multinationals to transnationals involved the transition from firms who operated locally around the world in accordance with local regulations and customs to those who attempted to change the local legal and cultural environment to assist the formation of a more "efficient" marketing program. That is, multinationals adapted *to* local realities to produce and sell their goods; transnationals adapted the local realities themselves.

The expressed goal in this process was to become "stateless": to transcend the limitations on capital imposed by nation-states in favor of the free market. While politicians enjoy the rhetorical benefits of proclaiming the success of "our" corporations, the firms themselves nod politely while knowing the truth. As Richard Barnet and John Cavanaugh put it,

> Whereas top bureaucrats talk as if global giants with their headquarters in Detroit or their charter in Delaware are national assets of the United States and instruments of national policy, corporate officials are much more candid in saying who they really are.[10]

---

9. Ibid., pp. 74-78.
10. Barnet and Cavanaugh, p. 342.

For example, Charles Exley, CEO of National Cash Register, says candidly: "National Cash Register is not a U.S. corporation. It is a world corporation that happens to be headquartered in the United States."[11]

To support this process of globalization, a world financial system has developed which is similarly stateless. A few global computer systems located in New York, London, and Belgium allow money to flow freely around the world each day, independent of government regulation or control.[12] The size of this flow is nearly beyond human capacity to comprehend: daily foreign currency exchange has more than doubled since 1989, from $640 billion to over $1.2 trillion.[13] National central bankers are almost literally powerless in the face of this massive financial power held in corporate hands.

In addition to this practical power, global capital has formalized its control over governments through a series of alphabet-soup trade agreements that have systematically transferred legal authority from governments to global corporations. The most important of these has been the General Agreement on Tariffs and Trade (GATT) and its institutional expression, the World Trade Organization (WTO). Established in 1994 by the so-called Uruguay Round of negotiations, the GATT and WTO have created a framework for the replacement of national laws protecting the environment, worker safety, and local economic independence with a regime dictated by global capital. When GATT was up for formal passage by Congress, President Clinton breathlessly proclaimed,

> We have a golden opportunity here to add $1,700 in income to the average family's income in this country over the next few years, to create hundreds of thousands of high-wage jobs, to have the biggest global tax cut in history.[14]

Of course, GATT has done nothing of the kind. Real wages have been stagnant or declining and formerly high-wage jobs continue their migration out of the United States and to lands with cheap and ready labor. But the president's promises were simply the window dressing for a deal that had already been done. GATT was approved easily by Congress, despite strong evidence that most members had not read the text of the agreement, let alone understood its arcane wording.[15]

The key to GATT's power is its explicit command to signatory nations to "ensure the conformity of its laws, regulations and administrative procedures" to

---

11. Quoted in Korten, p. 124.

12. Barnet and Cavanaugh, pp. 387-391.

13. Greider, p. 23.

14. Quoted in Greider, p. 196.

15. Ralph Nader and Lori Wallach have described in detail the undemocratic aspects of GATT's passage, including their offer of $10,000 to the charity-of-choice of any congressperson who could claim to have read the text and was able to answer ten simple questions about its content. Only one senator came forward to take the test.

the text of GATT.[16] Included within the prohibited goals of national laws that GATT would supersede are rules protecting local environments, subsidies for energy conservation, or anything else that might be perceived as limiting the free flow of capital. The WTO is the enforcement mechanism for this authority. Corporations can sue nations in the WTO to have laws invalidated. The WTO procedure is strictly secret. Even the names of the members of the panel who hear cases are kept secret, as are the written arguments of the parties and the official decision of the panel. The burden of proof in these hearings is on the nation to defend its laws.

A regime like the GATT/WTO would seem sufficient to give global capital what it needs. But it isn't enough: under on-again/off-again negotiation has been an even more powerful mechanism of transferring power from nations to global capital—the Multilateral Agreement on Investments (MAI). In the words of Dr. Chandra Muzaffar, Director of the Just World Trust, "It challenges the right of a nation to determine its own economic, social and ethical development."[17] A bipartisan letter to President Clinton from twenty-five members of Congress asked,

> . . . the MAI . . . would allow a foreign corporation or investor to directly sue the U.S. government for damages if we take any action that would restrain "enjoyment" of an investment. . . . Why would the U.S. willingly cede sovereign immunity and expose itself to liability for damages under vague language such as that . . . ?[18]

The congressional question points out the main mechanism of MAI feared by the nations of the south: the removal of any impediments whatsoever from what is known as "direct foreign investment" in a nation's local industries. Under this central provision, global corporations will become the controlling forces in local economies and will be empowered to sue governments that attempt to interfere.

The MAI is an effort to extend to the world the provisions of regional trade pacts such as the North American Free Trade Agreement (NAFTA). The NAFTA treaty, like GATT, was touted by most U.S. politicians as a key opportunity for ordinary Americans to gain the benefits of globalization. Instead, it has strengthened the hand of global capital in dictating the terms of trade both to North American governments and to the people they purport to represent. Although much of the chronicling of the destructive legacy of NAFTA has focused on Mexico, it is instructive to see how the United States' more prosperous northern neighbor has also had its sovereignty undermined by the trade agreement. For example, the "national treatment" clause of NAFTA—a key provision as well in the proposed MAI—requires that foreign firms be treated the same as domestic firms. As a result, only 25 percent of educational book publishers in Canada are

---

16. GATT, Article XVI, par. 4.
17. Preamble Center.
18. Ibid.

Canadian. Many Canadian education officials are concerned that the more powerful U.S. firms will swamp Canadian schools with text and history books providing a U.S. perspective on events that will eventually destroy Canada's sense of national identity.[19] Under NAFTA, the Canadian government is powerless to stop this flood of U.S. books into Canadian classrooms.

While grassroots campaigns have sprung up to oppose MAI just as they did in the face of NAFTA and GATT, it is important to Revelation's perspective to acknowledge that ordinary folks are virtually powerless to stop global capital's efforts to solidify its control over national governments. Just as the Christians in the Asian *ekklēsiai* could not impede the Roman Empire's hegemony over the local city-states, neither can the sincere and energetic efforts of Christians and others today stop the forces of empire from doing what they do. This is not, however, cause for despair. It is rather a challenge to recognize the truth of what is happening in our world today and to seek not that empire stop being empire, but that Christians leave Babylon and become citizens of New Jerusalem.

"The Merchants of the Earth Have Grown Rich from the Power of Her Luxury": Global Capital and the Exploitation of the Poor by the Rich

Behind the veil of divine legitimation, the system of global capital has been and continues to work tirelessly to accomplish the primary mission of empire as noted above: the transfer of wealth from the poor and middle class to the wealthy. Consider just a few facts:

- In 1974, total foreign debt owed to external debtors by developing nations was $135 billion. In 1981, this had risen to $751 billion. In the early 1990s, the total external debt for these nations was approximately $1,945 billion.[20]
- In 1981, the share of U.S. national income going to the top 10 percent of the population was 46.6 percent. In 1989, the share was 53.2 percent.[21]
- In 1973, the average nonsupervisory, production worker in the United States made $11.37/hour and worked 1,683 hours per year; in 1991, the same worker made $10.34/hour (in constant dollars, an 11 percent decline) and worked 1,781 hours per year.[22]

These statistics could be multiplied *ad nauseum*. The relevant issue for our purpose here is, *How* is the process of the rich getting richer and the poor getting poorer taking place? Is it simply the eternal struggle of the elite for more, or is there something different about what's happened in recent decades?

We obviously cannot in this space present the full history and development of the current global economic system in which we live. All we can do is to point out some major events and institutions that reveal what is happening. Readers

19. Barlow and Robertson, p. 66.
20. Greider, p. 282.
21. Barnet and Cavanaugh, p. 179.
22. Korten, p. 245.

interested in more are invited to consult the books noted in the bibliography, which tell this story in greater detail.

To understand how global capital has become empire, we need to go back at least to the post–World War II situation. One of the problems facing the victorious Allies was how to help rebuild the German and Japanese economies so that U.S. and British firms could continue to engage in trade while preventing a resurgence of nationalism within the defeated countries. While the war was ongoing, a memo from the Economic and Financial Group of the Council on Foreign Relations to the president and State Department expressed the need to establish a postwar "Grand Area" which the United States would need to dominate in order to assure a steady market for U.S. corporations. The memo also called for creation of worldwide financial institutions for stabilizing currencies and facilitating programs of capital investment in support of this goal. Out of this plan came the historic meeting at Bretton Woods, which resulted in the creation of two key world institutions: the International Monetary Fund (IMF) and the World Bank (WB). At the opening session, President Roosevelt named clearly the key principle under which the institutions would operate. He insisted that all participants "embrace the elementary economic axiom . . . that prosperity has no fixed limits."[23] In the following years, two additional institutions were created to support and coordinate the actions of the IMF and WB: the North Atlantic Treaty Organization (NATO, 1949) and the Organization for Economic Cooperation and Development (OECD, 1961). Eventually, when Japan had recovered and become a powerful economic player, a final, less formal, institution was created to include Japan: the Trilateral Commission, consisting of, in its own words, "the highest level unofficial group possible to look together at the common problems facing our three areas [the United States, Europe, and Japan]."[24]

In the beginning, the IMF and WB were intended to create pathways for U.S. and western European capital into Germany and Japan. However, the success of these nations in restoring their economies left the new institutions all dressed up with no place to go. They looked around and saw what President Truman was the first to call "underdeveloped countries" in need of "help." As German economics professor Wolfgang Sachs has noted, this move meant that there was a specific image that "the United States projected upon the rest of the world: a country's degree of civilization is indicated by the level of its production."[25]

Of course, people in many of these lands—in Latin America, Africa, and Asia—had not considered themselves "underdeveloped." Although often poor, they had frequently established simple and harmonious communities that had thrived for centuries or longer, subject only to interference from previous empires. But Truman's label and the IMF/WB mission led to an enormous and ongoing program to bring "civilization," "modernity," and "development" to people around the globe.

At first, IMF/WB theorists were split into two strategic groups. On the one

---

23. Cited in Korten, p. 21.
24. Quoted in Korten, p. 137.
25. Sachs, p. 240.

side were the "economic nationalists," who urged a program of import substitution by which local economies would become self-sufficient with the help of loans. On the other side were the "transnationalists," who, in line with the institutions' mandate, sought to open markets for world trade by making local economies dependent on exports to the wealthy nations. Not surprisingly, the transnationalists won the battle and have held control of the IMF and WB ever since.[26]

Over the decades, the primary legacy of these policies was to produce an enormous, unpayable debt among the poorer nations. The long-term, external debt of low-income nations went from $21 billion in 1970 to $110 billion in 1980.[27] This debt produced in the 1970s a crisis for the Western financial institutions that stood behind the IMF and WB. The response was to blame the debtors for accepting the loans that had led them into trouble. The solution was as elegant in theory as it was harsh and unjust in practice: the policy of "structural adjustment." The term became a euphemism for the total reshaping of local economies in accord with the desires of the IMF and WB and the transnational corporations they served. What structural adjustment meant was the removal of any preference for local industries in favor of open markets that treated foreign goods the same as local goods. Furthermore, it empowered the IMF/WB to force upon the debtor nations a series of draconian changes that utterly destroyed local cultural and economic stability.

Consider, for example, the case of Costa Rica, a nation that the IMF/WB considers a "success" story. The Central American nation had previously been relatively egalitarian, supporting a wide base of local farmers. After "structural adjustment," however, thousands of farmers were displaced from their land and forced into low-paying wage jobs in cities. Crime and violence multiplied. Costa Rica became, for the first time, dependent on imports to feed its people.[28]

Or, for a more recent example, consider Mexico.[29] For most of the twentieth century, Mexico had been relatively economically independent under the patronage and tariff system supported by its controlling political party, the PRI, which had held office for fifty years. However, after falling into deep debt thanks to the IMF/WB's initial loan packages, the government accepted structural adjustment in 1982 as a way out of debt. The first five years produced a severe recession and high inflation. In 1988, the government signed a "stabilization pact," which controlled inflation largely by restricting wage increases and reducing government funding for social programs. For example, spending on health and education was cut in half during this time. Structural adjustment also called for the sell-off of state-run industries: between 1982 and 1994, the number of state-run companies dropped from 1,155 to fewer than 150. As a result of all of these policies, Mex-

---

26. Korten, p. 161.

27. Ibid., p. 164. Note that this figure is only a small percentage of the *total* foreign debt noted on p. 242 above.

28. Ibid., p. 49.

29. The full story can be found in Heredia and Purcell.

ico, like Costa Rica, became dependent on imported food: by 1990, 40 percent of beans consumed in Mexico were imported, along with 25 percent of corn and 30 percent of sugar.[30] Meanwhile, foreign debt continued to rise: from $86 billion in 1982 to $140 billion in 1994. Drugs, poverty, and disease are the results of structural adjustment for millions of Mexicans; tremendous increases in wealth are the results for the transnational corporations who engineered the deal. In the words of William Greider, "The case of Mexico illustrates, in the most horrendous terms, that developing nations make a kind of deal with the devil when they open themselves to the animal spirits of global capital."[31] The language of this secular critic implicitly recognizes what Revelation makes explicit: the diabolic nature of collaboration with empire.

The policy of structural adjustment has brought wealth to the few and misery to millions all around the globe. And yet, at an annual meeting of the IMF/WB board in the 1980s, Barber Conable, former U.S. congressman and then World Bank president, addressed the crowd, which had been feted with seven hundred social events during the week, estimated to cost $10 million, by saying:

> Our institution . . . will count for nothing if it cannot look at our world through the eyes of the most underprivileged, if we cannot share their hopes and fears. We are here to serve their needs. . . . Collective action against global poverty is the common purpose that brings us together today.[32]

Just as the Roman Empire looked out at its exploitation of the world of its day and called it good, so do the spokespeople for global capital in our time claim to be serving those whom they systematically impoverish year after year. As scholar Edward Goldsmith has stated,

> In other words, formal colonialism came to an end not because the colonial powers had decided to forego the economic advantages it provided but because, in the new conditions, these could now be obtained by more politically acceptable and more effective methods.[33]

Ephesus vs. Smyrna, Tuscaloosa County vs. Vietnam: Competition among Cities and Nations for the Patronage of Global Capital

As was shown in chapter 3, one of the key features of the patronage system under the Roman Empire was the competition among cities for honor and its concomitant supply of imperial building and other funds. In a strikingly similar way,

---

30. Barnet and Cavanaugh, p. 253.
31. Greider, p. 263.
32. Quoted in Korten, p. 104.
33. E. Goldsmith, p. 255.

the institutions of global capital have managed to persuade U.S. cities to compete with one another for the "privilege" of hosting transnational corporate factories or offices. Even more harmfully, this competition has expanded in what some call a "race for the bottom," as poor nations compete with rich ones for such patronage, offering the only "benefits" they can offer: cheap labor, lack of safety or environmental regulation, and plentiful (for now) natural resources.

A few examples from the auto industry should suffice to illustrate the pattern. At the same time that Detroit automakers were struggling to stay afloat, foreign car companies found fertile soil in the United States. In 1982, the state of Ohio gave Honda $16 million in tax breaks and other benefits to persuade the firm to locate a plant in Marysville. In 1988, Kentucky gave a $125 million package to Toyota to build a plant in its state. In 1992, South Carolina paid $79,000 per job to BMW for a factory there. Finally, in 1995, Alabama paid an astounding $300 million to Daimler-Benz to build a Mercedes factory in Tuscaloosa County, promising to rename the Montgomery-to-Birmingham highway the "Mercedes Benz Autobahn."[34] The Tuscaloosa County Board of Trade Web site trumpets this accomplishment proudly, along with the successful luring of Japan's JVC, Canada's StressCrete, and a British Steel subsidiary.[35]

This stunning progression in payoffs to foreign firms to gain the privilege of jobs is a pathetic recognition of the control of global capital over not only the economies of poor nations but also of local economies in the United States. In the rather startling metaphor of David Mulford, Undersecretary of the Treasury under President Bush, attracting foreign investors "is like a girl trying to get a boyfriend. She has to go out, have her hair done up, wear makeup. . . ."[36] A quick comparison of labor costs around the world (table 22) reveals why governments are so willing to "wear makeup" to get jobs for their citizens. After accepting Alabama's offer, Daimler-Benz built its next plant in Vietnam.

The sudden shift in transnational production from formerly home countries to those of the "lowest" bidder is breathtaking. For example, consider the growth of *maquiladoras*, the Mexican border factories run by global corporations. In 1980, there were 620 plants employing 119,000 workers. In 1992, there were over 2,200 plants employing more than 500,000 workers.[37]

Throughout the Two-Thirds World, global capital is finding temporary bases for its manufacturing: apparel, footwear, and toys are produced almost exclusively in Asia, with sites shifting to poorer and poorer countries as local workers develop demands for a modicum of dignity and safety. The Kader Industrial Toy Company fire in 1993 illustrates this "race to the bottom." The worst industrial fire in the history of capitalism took the lives of 188 workers and seriously injured hundreds more, mostly women and frequently children. The *Washington Post* covered this tragedy on page 25; the *Wall Street Journal* followed the day

---

34. Greider, pp. 93-94.
35. See http://www.tcida.com/exist.html for the Tuscaloosa County Board of Trade Web site.
36. Quoted in Barnet and Cavanaugh, pp. 356-57.
37. Korten, p. 129.

after with a page 11 report.[38] When a similar tragedy took place at the infamous Triangle Shirtwaist Factory in New York around the turn of the century, labor and other activists rallied at once in protest, causing the change of conditions across the U.S. workplace. But nearly a century later, such a fire was greeted with a shrug, simply another in the long series of industrial disasters flowing out of the effort to offer the lowest cost to corporate bidders. As an international labor group reported, when the toy industry began in the late 1980s to move from Thailand to China, Thai toy factory accidents tripled.[39] Although one can point the finger for the Kader fire at the billionaire Thai co-owner who got rich while his workers suffered daily under sweatshop conditions, the responsibility lies elsewhere. As William Greider points out, "The Kader fire was ordained and organized by the free market itself."[40]

Table 22 MANUFACTURING LABOR COSTS AROUND THE WORLD, 1993[41]	
Germany	$24.9/hour
Japan	$16.9
United States	$16.4
France	$16.3
United Kingdom	$12.4
South Korea	$4.9
Hungary	$1.8
China	$0.5

In the face of such scavenging, the desperation of U.S. cities and states to locate jobs in their regions can at least be understood. The triumph of global capital in becoming empire over governments in this regard can be underscored by a brief look at the history of corporations in the United States. Recognizing the tremendous power of royal-chartered corporations such as the East India Company and Hudson Bay Company, America's founders set out to keep total control over the corporate form in the hands of the electorate. Corporate charters were granted as privileges to provide specific goods for specific periods. Violation of the stringent conditions of a charter could lead to revocation, that is, the removal of the corporation's right to do business in a given place.[42]

---

38. Greider, p. 343.
39. Ibid., p. 345.
40. Ibid., p. 344.
41. Hines and Lang, p. 487.
42. For a more detailed history of the origins of corporate charters, see Grossman and Adams.

Over time, however, corporations began to influence politicians to loosen these restrictions. Although charters continued to be revoked during the nineteenth century, by the Civil War period corporate power was making itself felt. Shortly before his death, President Lincoln described it thus:

> Corporations have been enthroned . . . an era of corruption in high places will follow and the money power will endeavor to prolong its reign by working on the prejudices of the people . . . until wealth is aggregated in a few hands . . . and the Republic is destroyed.[43]

The situation described by Lincoln was immeasurably worsened by a U.S. Supreme Court decision in 1886 declaring a corporation a "person" for purposes of constitutional law. Now the reversal was complete: corporations had been granted all the privileges and rights of real people, without bearing any of the responsibility. Not long after, President Rutherford Hayes commented, "this is a government of the people, by the people and for the people no longer. It is a government of corporations, by corporations, and for corporations."[44] By century's end, corporate power was at its first peak, leading to the passage in 1890 of the Sherman Antitrust Act, which broke up some of the larger corporate trusts that had swallowed up local businesses across the nation. But the power of corporations over government, once established, proved virtually impossible to break. Thus, the Kader fire tragedy or the Tuscaloosa Mercedes plant can be seen simply as the logical outcomes of a process of imperial consolidation that has been at work for more than a century.

From Country to City: Global Capital's Transformation of Rural Farmers into Urban Beggars

The Roman Empire systematically took over the rural countryside of its day through the development of *latifundia*, the large-scale farms that were controlled by absentee owners in the cities. As a result, tremendous migrations of peasants took place, as people were displaced from their formerly secure but simple lives in the country into the chaos of the city. This in turn made the formerly self-sufficient farmers dependent on grain handouts by the Roman Empire and its patrons for survival.

Similarly, global capital has transformed most of the world's farmers into refugees and immigrants. Some of this new migration has been the direct result of the corporate takeover of indigenous land. Other portions have been the result of wars and ethnic strife exacerbated by global capital's extraction and removal of local wealth. In 1960, the United Nations estimated that there were 1.4 million refugees worldwide. In 1992, this figure had mushroomed to 18.2 million,

---

43. Quoted in Korten, p. 58.
44. Ibid.

with another 24 million estimated to be displaced within national borders. One should add to this measure of economically initiated displacement the 25-30 million people working outside their country of origin as legal migrants, and the 20-24 million undocumented migrants.[45]

Behind these abstract numbers lies a pattern repeated regularly around the globe. Corporations discover resources for development of exports and IMF/WB programs of structural adjustment replace indigenous food production with production for export, thus making traditional farming irrelevant. The United States experienced the first wave of this process earlier in the twentieth century, as family farms were replaced with corporate agribusiness. A 1944 U.S. Department of Agriculture study of two farm towns in California showed how the family farm-based town was more stable, more involved in civic affairs, and more productive of related local business than a comparable corporate farm-based town. The researcher's results, however, were repressed for decades until the corporate lock on farming was secure.[46] Now, 95 percent of food produced and marketed in the United States is controlled by global capital.[47]

While the Roman Empire's exploitation of the countryside and the resulting mass migration of peasant farmers into cities was motivated largely by the prospect of agricultural profits, today's disruption of rural life is rooted in more complex motivations. In addition to the desire to tap into the soil's productive capacity, global capital makes its power felt in remote regions in order to gain access to oil, minerals, and other local resources. They have found, as we will examine below in connection with the seductive aspect of consumerism, that locals can be brought to heel by dangling Western baubles in their faces, creating desires that had never before existed and leading many to leave their homelands in search of the Holy Grail of material wealth.

An example of this process can be seen most tragically in the story of the people of Ladakh, high in the Tibetan plateau of India. In 1962, the Indian government built a road into this remote region in connection with strife in Tibet, providing access to Western tourists in 1975. Swedish scholar and activist Helena Norberg-Hodge spent more than two decades among the Ladakhi people documenting the transformation of their culture under pressure from global capital. She notes how the Ladakhis had managed to forge a stable but fragile relationship with the earth and with one another in this barren, mountainous region, free of a money economy, cultural tension, or other staples of the West. However, Norberg-Hodge notes that "Within the space of little more than a decade, feelings of pride gave way to what can best be described as a cultural inferiority complex."[48] The presence of U.S. and European tourists, replete with fancy clothes, cameras, and other accoutrements, made the Ladakhis feel for the first time that

---

45. Ibid., pp. 19-21.
46. Morris, p. 226.
47. Lehman and Krebs, p. 123.
48. Norberg-Hodge, p. 34.

they were poor. Television was introduced, along with British-style education, deepening the Ladakhis' sense that their own cultural ways were without value. Fireside storytelling, singing, and dancing were replaced by watching television and listening to Western popular music. Ladakhi youth began to resent their isolation and began migrating into Indian cities looking for "real" work, destroying ancient notions of family and village unity. Low-priced food from industrial farms replaced locally grown food, making the Ladakhis dependent on external trade for survival. Eventually, tensions flowing from this pattern of destructive transformation began to express themselves in violence and ethnic strife between Muslims, Hindus, and Buddhists. Norberg-Hodge sums up the entire process as it has affected Ladakh and other similar places:

> The intensely centralizing force of the present global development model is pulling diverse peoples from rural areas into large urban centers and placing power and decision making in the hands of a few. In these centers, job opportunities are scarce, community ties are broken, and competition increases dramatically. . . . In this situation, any religious or ethnic differences quite naturally become exaggerated and distorted. . . .
>
> In the South, there is an awareness that modernization is exacerbating tensions, but people generally conclude that this is a temporary phase on the road to "progress," a phase that will only end once development has erased cultural differences and created a totally secular society. On the other hand, Westerners attribute overt religious and ethnic strife to the liberating influence of democracy. Conflict, they assume, always smoldered beneath the surface, and only government repression kept it from bursting into flames.
>
> . . . after two decades of firsthand experience on the Indian subcontinent, I am convinced that "development" not only exacerbates tensions but actually creates them. . . . it puts pressure on people to conform to a standard Western ideal. . . . Striving for such an ideal means rejecting one's own culture and roots—in effect, denying one's own identity. The inevitable result is alienation, resentment, and anger. I am convinced that much of the violence and fundamentalism in the world today is a product of this process.[49]

Thus, not only in isolated places like Ladakh but also in other locales in which indigenous, land-based culture has been destroyed in favor of corporate agribusiness and urban wage labor, we can interpret violence and ethnic strife as a direct result of global capital's imperial power.

The flip side of this invasion of the countryside is global capital's tendency to operate out of elite enclaves in global urban centers, where corporate and financial players communicate across global computer networks in utter seclusion

---

49. Ibid., p. 45.

from the masses of poor people who often stand not far from their door. For example, journalist Robert Kaplan has vividly portrayed how the city of Tucson, Arizona, has become such a place. Kaplan notes: "I knew that for the prosperous inhabitants of the Catalina foothills, where I was staying, the South Side [populated by poor people] simply did not exist."[50] He quotes a local city planning-program coordinator:

> "Where you are now could be Santa Fe, Palm Beach, or Long Island," he said. "My neighbors are Pakistani doctors, Silicon Valley types, ingenious local entrepreneurs, wealthy Lebanese, Chinese. They have their computers, their links with friends throughout the globe, and a patina of Spanish culture via the street names of this neighborhood and the villa architecture, and they call it a lifestyle. Of course, these people are the only future Tucson has. You lure—you bribe—high-tech firms to relocate here with those high-paying jobs in order to attract more people like my neighbors to Tucson, because experience indicates that most of the poor, even with training, will never be qualified for such jobs."[51]

Similarly, David Korten describes his experience of major cities in Pakistan. He notes how just outside the city centers in which the elite can go to modern shopping malls and five-star hotels, is a "poor and feudalistic countryside governed by local lords who support private armies with profits from a thriving drug and arms trade." He says that the rich of Pakistan, "in contrast to their knowledge of and interest in the rest of the world . . . had little knowledge of or interest in what was happening in their own country beyond the borders of their enclave cities." The result is a global network of enclaves in which there is "a melding of the world's financial elites into a stateless community in the clouds."[52]

Thus, just as the Roman elite lived in sumptuous luxury in cities in which poverty, filth, crime, and violence were endemic, so, too, do the lords of empire today.

THE VICES OF GLOBAL CAPITAL

In the previous section, we looked at how global capital became empire and exerted its control over the governments and peoples of the world in a pattern strikingly parallel to that of the Roman Empire of Revelation's day. John, though, did not settle for naming Rome as empire. He recognized the necessity of naming not only empire's power, but also its "sin." In chapter 6 above, we saw how Babylon's vices were described clearly and specifically. If we are to understand and to respond to empire in our own world, we must also be willing to look at its vices.

---

50. Kaplan (1998a).
51. Ibid.
52. Korten, p. 114.

Illusion: The Power of Marketing and Media
to Create a False Reality

The key component of empire's ability to create in the minds of ordinary folks a false version of reality has always been control of media. In ancient Rome, this took the form of public processions, statuary and temples, coins and other aspects of daily life that impressed upon people the notion of empire as benevolent and secure. In our high-tech world, empire has more powerful tools at its disposal: the various methods known collectively as marketing and advertising.

It has been estimated that in the United States, the average consumer is exposed daily to approximately three thousand advertising messages, up from 1,600 per day in 1980.[53] Television and radio are only the most obvious forms of this spectacle. More traditional forms, such as those found in newspapers and magazines, bus signs and billboards, have been complemented by newer methods, including Internet advertising. Doritos and BMW cars have been promoted in San Francisco through laser-projected images upon the cloudy sky.[54] Firms have placed ads on building rooftops near airports for perusal by passengers overhead, in school locker rooms, and on virtually every other available surface and medium. In 1989, corporations spent over $240 billion on advertising and another $380 billion on packaging, design, and other promotions.[55]

What is important to note for our purposes is not simply the bombardment we face daily urging us to become consumers, but the worldview that is being consciously and ingeniously created through advertising and marketing. More than the youth-and-beauty orientation is at issue. It is the all-encompassing ideology that presents the world as described in advertising as "reality" that is the goal of empire's illusion-making machinery.

This false reality is also supported through seemingly innocuous phenomena such as theme parks and worlds fairs. In 1901, President William McKinley declared that "expositions are the timekeepers of progress." As Richard Barnet and John Cavanaugh interpret the turn-of-the-century events,

> The designers of the early world's fairs had lessons they wished to impart—views of empire, views of science, views of racial superiority, and views of what constitutes progress.[56]

Disneyland is, of course, the mother of all theme parks. Many French people objected to EuroDisneyland in the French countryside, fearing, with both a combination of national snobbery and abhorrence of what the Disney ideology stands for, that its presence would dilute traditional French culture perspectives. But

53. Barnet and Cavanaugh, p. 172.
54. Ibid.
55. Ibid., p. 171.
56. Ibid., pp. 34-35.

Western-oriented theme parks now act as promoters of global capital's version of reality in such remote places as Romania, India, and China.[57]

While theme parks might not seem a serious threat, the control of supposed sources of "news" and "truth" by global capital certainly is. Writers such as Noam Chomsky have shown how corporate mergers and other acquisitions have placed control of the world's media in the hands of a small elite. This means that the line between advertising and content, news and editorials, is being constantly and intentionally blurred in the minds of media consumers. For example, 75 percent of commercial television air time is paid for by the world's one hundred largest corporations. Furthermore, 50 percent of the support of supposedly noncommercial public television in the United States comes from these same corporations.[58] The networks themselves are owned by global corporations such as General Electric and Westinghouse, and perhaps soon by Microsoft. The result of this interlocking control is, as David Korten puts it, television's goal "to create a political culture that equates the corporate interest with the human interest in the public mind."[59]

This creation of a false reality occurs both through the promotion of images and ideas befitting global capital's imperial goals and by suppressing dissent. Consider, for example, the power of media tycoon Rupert Murdoch's ability to disseminate his own views and to repress others. Murdoch purchased the *Times of London* after then Prime Minister Margaret Thatcher arranged to have the rules of media ownership changed on his behalf; Murdoch then turned the *Times* into a vocal supporter of the Thatcher government. In New York, mayor Rudolph Guliani interceded on behalf of Murdoch's efforts to force his TV station on the local cable network after Murdoch's *New York Post* became a booster of Guliani's regime. On the other side of the ledger, Murdoch withdrew publication of former Hong Kong governor Chris Patten's book critical of Chinese influence in Hong Kong after Murdoch's own firm, HarperCollins, had given Patten a contract and begun release of the book. In noting Murdoch's staunch support for both the communist government in China and the conservative ones in London and New York, a National Public Radio commentator noted laconically, "Murdoch supports people in power."[60]

Murdoch's antics are simply among the most public aspect of what is a systemic reality. One could endlessly multiply examples of how corporate-owned media have refused to cover opinions and actions critical of their view of reality while ceaselessly promoting their own.[61] The effect is to leave most ordinary people with false impressions about crime, economic stability, and other essential elements of reality.

The central tenets of this false reality are the basic dogmas of corporate liber-

---

57. Ibid., p. 31.
58. Mander, p. 311.
59. Korten, p. 149.
60. National Public Radio's *All Things Considered*, 2 March 1998.
61. E.g., Barnet and Cavanaugh, p. 108; Mander, p. 7.

tarianism we saw above: economic growth is good, there is no rational alternative to the unfettered free market, and so forth. Ultimately, as with the illusions propagated by the Roman Empire, the primary illusion generated and maintained by the global capital empire today is that the world is largely as it should be and that efforts to change it are misguided at best, and dangerous at worst. So long as global capital's hold on public consciousness remains strong, all that is necessary to maintain the power of this illusion is to keep dissenting voices on the margins, and to label those whose status allows them occasional access to the mainstream media as "dreamers" or "idealists." Numerous former denizens of the controlling institutions have defected from positions of power, only to find their new opinions ignored or treated with condescension. Former U.S. Strategic Air Command General Lee Butler has renounced his previous support for nuclear weapons and has become an articulate spokesperson for abolition, yet he is treated with predictable contempt by Pentagon planners and defense contractors. Former U.S. Attorney General Ramsey Clark has become a tireless advocate on behalf of the victims of imperial violence in Central America, Iraq, and elsewhere, but his views rarely make the newspapers or TV news. Former World Bank chief economist Herman Daly has turned against the policies of "structural adjustment," which he had previously defended, and is treated with scorn by his fellow economists. So long as mass movements of resistance do not form around the insights of such figures, empire can afford to treat them as flies on the back of an elephant.

But when it is necessary to be more harsh, empire now, as always, is willing to be so. Americans attempting to bear witness to the repression in Chiapas, flowing directly from the peasants' attempt to free themselves from the disastrous effects of NAFTA, have been systematically deported. This was a more subtle reaction than was given to Western witnesses murdered in response to similar events in El Salvador a decade earlier. Indeed, two-thirds of U.S. aid to "developing countries" in recent years has been in the form of "security assistance," a euphemism for support of death squads and other means of repressing dissent.[62] We will examine this more closely in the section below on the sin of "murder."

Thus, as Revelation underscores, a key aspect of being true to our Christian vocation today is to name and resist this illusionary power of empire. Our acts of naming may bring us ridicule or worse; our acts of resistance can bring us freedom and joy.

Whoring: The Seductive Immorality of Global Capital's Offerings

The attractiveness of material wealth and comfort is, of course, nothing new. Ever since the Israelites in the desert yearned to return to the fleshpots of Egypt, people of faith have struggled with how to live true to God's ways amid the temp-

---

62. E. Goldsmith, p. 257; see also Nelson-Pallmeyer.

tations of "the flesh." The purpose here is not to present another diatribe against the sins of "Mammon," but to point out the specifically imperial nature of today's struggle with global capital's seductive power.

In response to the question of why Malaysian women and children would endure sweatshop conditions to earn a few dollars a day, a local observer noted, "What these people want is what the West already has. And why shouldn't they? It is a very nice life, isn't it?"[63] Indeed, this "very nice life" filled with quality food, high-tech toys, fancy cars, and big houses represents precisely the best that money can buy. The "American dream" has enthralled people around the world for decades through the missionary power of pop culture. Music Television (MTV) is seen daily by 210 million households in seventy-one countries. Its slogan is the highly religious phrase, "MTV provides reason to live." And its fare offers a constant bombardment of images of "the good life." As Richard Barnet and John Cavanaugh have said,

> A pop video is many things but it is always an ad—for itself, for other songs, rock groups, concerns, the latest fashion in teenage apparel, or Hollywood films from which bits of sound track may be included.[64]

Thus, illusion gives way to seduction: the false reality is generated and people are lured into its embrace. No one forces people to watch MTV or to eat at McDonald's or to buy a sport utility vehicle. But once the false reality is seen as real, the lure to snuggle into its arms is strong indeed. As one pastor put it in a discussion of the difficulty for middle-class American Christians to stop having "intercourse" with Babylon, "but it feels so good!"

As we have seen, Revelation's protest is not against feeling good. John of Patmos was not inviting people to "eternal Lent" but to New Jerusalem, where *real* joy could be experienced. The key to understanding the seductive quality of global capital's siren call in our time is not to fight against the urge toward pleasure, but to come to recognize the whore-like nature of the beckoning smile on the TV screen or the magazine ad.

In themselves, many of the comforts offered by global capital can be considered to be benefits. From indoor plumbing to heating and air conditioning, the basic elements of what most people might think of as "the good life" do take the edges off life's discomforts. Refrigeration and freezers allow a wide variety of foods to be eaten year round; electric lights create the whole concept of "night life"; cars, airplanes, telephones, and computers allow contact among people who would never otherwise meet (including the two authors of this book). And yet, behind these benefits lie enormous costs. As we saw with the Ladakh people, TV and radio destroyed a tradition of fireside cultural expression. When was the last time you got together with your neighbors for a sing-along or community storytelling? Instead, we offer to one another a shared experience of the latest

63. Quoted in Greider, p. 349.
64. Barnet and Cavanaugh, pp. 138, 154.

video or music CD. The point isn't that commercial films and music are immoral per se. Rather, it is that in turning to global capital to provide entertainment, food, shelter, and other basic aspects of life, we have lost control over our ability to create these things for ourselves. Studies show that, despite the sale of cookbooks, fewer people actually know how to cook than in the past. Fewer write songs or poetry, grow their own food, or build their own houses. What global capital's illusion presents as "freedom from drudgery" is, seen apocalyptically, allowing ourselves to become captive to a seductive whore who, when the pretty clothes and makeup are removed, is revealed to be a Beast.

Just as a prostitute pretends to be attracted to her client to maintain the illusion of love, so does global capital pretend to provide an authentic response to our deepest yearnings and desires for security, rest, joy, and community. "Coke adds life." "Without chemicals [from Monsanto], life itself would be impossible." Mutual funds, investments, and insurance provide peace of mind. In these and a thousand other ways, we are invited to find what we are really looking for in what global capital has to offer.

And, as most of us know, the beastly nature of this seduction is carefully hidden from us as part of the illusion-making power of empire. Just as prostitutes do not speak to clients of sexually transmitted diseases or abuse by their pimps, we are not told by global capital of conditions in the sweatshops that produce our toys, clothes, and sneakers. We do not see the destruction of rainforests and other fragile habitats to grow cattle for McDonald's or flowers for sale in the northern winter. We are shielded from the hordes of refugees and other impoverished folks whose lives have been destroyed so that we can live "the good life." Ched Myers has shown clearly how what he calls the "social architecture of insularity" protects us from knowing the truth about our world and how the methods of retailing similarly cover over the means of production.[65] Revelation calls us to look behind this veil, to see first the Whore and then the Beast, and to run from their grasp and back to the truly authentic life offered by the gospel.

Murder: Death as an Instrument of Global Capital's Empire

While convincing people of the imperial sins we have looked at so far requires substantial evidence because of their very nature as illusion and seduction, global capital's practice of systemic violence is much more visible and apparent. At the grinding level of daily life are industrial accidents like the Kader Toy Co. fire noted above, the poisoning of farmworkers exposed to pesticides and unclean water, the deadly effects of poverty, which cause forty thousand children each day to die from preventable diseases and kill others through malnutrition and crime,[66] and numerous other ways in which global capital's everyday existence

---

65. Myers (1994), p. 206ff.

66. A Harvard study has shown the numerous ways in which global trade has caused the resurgence of long-dormant diseases (Harvard Working Group).

breeds death. We have also noted the "war against the poor" waged on behalf of global capital in Latin America and other places when people are murdered for daring to seek dignity and the basics of life. The infamous School of the Americas, called by its opponents the "School of Assassins" for its training of death squad leaders in Latin America, and the Land Warfare Centre near Brisbane, which trains military personnel from the Southeast Asian region, are visible manifestations of this systemic murder.

More sinister perhaps, although no more important from a divine perspective, are the CIA-backed programs to install and protect political leaders who support IMF/WB initiatives and other forms of global capital's imperial reality. In Guatemala in 1954, Brazil in the 1960s, and Chile in the 1970s, popularly elected rulers were violently toppled in favor of dictators who promised to serve empire as the "kings of the earth" did in Revelation. Colonel Oliver North's chilling Senate testimony in the 1980s regarding the Iran-Contra scandal was a rare opportunity to hear from the mouth of one of its perpetrators how willing empire is to abandon law and morality to accomplish its mission.

This depressing parade of empire's death-dealing ways does not require a conspiracy theory to back it up. We are not claiming that there is a Secret Team orchestrating repression, assassination, and disappearances—although the Christic Institute's 1980s allegations of such an entity are not without evidence. Rather, what is evident is that such a program of accidental and intentional killing is simply a logical outcome of global capital's pursuit and defense of empire.

The continued deployment of nuclear weapons and the unceasing research and development of weapons systems in the First World, particularly in the United States, suggest that the stakeholders in the empire of global capital are intent on maintaining their positions of privilege for the long haul.

Worshiping Idols: Global Capital and "Religion"

As we saw earlier in this chapter, the ideology of global capital has been characterized even by secular commentators in religious terms as a kind of fundamentalism which seeks faithful adherents and condemns heretics. There is another way in which global capital usurps the function of true religion, however. *Religio*, in its Latin root and as practiced in the Roman Empire, is a matter of drawing diverse people into unity. The Roman Empire faced the task of taking a wide variety of ethnic and socioeconomic groups and transforming them into people whose primary loyalty was to Rome. In a similar way, global capital today exerts its influence in attempting to erase ethnic divisions and turn all into loyal members of its empire.

A major participant in this exercise is Coca-Cola. The corporation has made enormous efforts both to sell its products across the globe and to inculcate a sense that it is Coke that will provide the means to transcend ancient and modern divisions within the human family. As former Coke chair Roberto C. Goizueta said, "people around the world are today connected to each other by brand name consumer products as much as by anything else." To solidify the truth of this religious assertion, Coke's 1992 Winter Olympics sing-along ad was broadcast in twelve languages to 3.8 billion viewers in 131 countries.[67] This same corporate official speaks in religious terms when looking out across the global landscape:

> When I think of Indonesia—a country on the Equator with 180 million people, a median age of 18, and a Moslem ban on alcohol—I feel I know what heaven looks like.[68]

In the public realm, global capital presents "heaven" as everyone finding common purpose by drinking Coke; in the private realm, it is admitted that "heaven" is simply the profits that come from all those sales of soft drinks.

Another way in which global capital induces people to worship its idols is through identification of pop culture stars as symbols of universal humanity. For example, a television producer and writer described megastar Michael Jackson, whose contract was purchased at tremendous cost by Sony, as "neither young nor old, neither black nor white, neither male nor female . . . the perfect marketing logo."[69] The eerie echo of Gal. 3:28—"There is no longer Jew or Greek, there is no longer slave or free, there is no longer male and female; for all of you are one in Christ Jesus"—underscores the idolatrous nature of the presentation of pop stars. Obviously, no one is actually confusing Michael Jackson—or Michael Jordan or Madonna—with Jesus or his mother. However, the way in which these figures are presented as sources of unity and wholeness to a divided people strongly parallels the Roman Empire's exaltation of its emperors as symbols of unity. And perhaps it is not irrelevant to recall the slogan on the side of each pack of Marlboro's: *"veni, vedi, vici"*—"I came, I saw, I conquered"—the slogan of Julius Caesar.

Speaking of Marlboro, it is the tobacco companies who have ironically been perceived as protectors of the African American community because of their large financial support of African American causes. Although 90 percent of all cigarette and alcohol billboard advertising is found in predominantly black and Latino neighborhoods and although cigarettes disproportionately kill African Americans, Philip Morris and other firms have garnered support from black leaders because of this financial assistance. When antismoking legislation came before Congress, an editorial in the *National Black Monitor*, a monthly insert in eighty African American newspapers across the U.S., called for opposition to this legislation because it served as a "vehicle for intensified discrimination against this industry which has befriended us . . . in our hour of greatest need."[70] In sim-

67. Barnet and Cavanaugh, p. 169.
68. Ibid., p. 181.
69. Ibid., p. 128.
70. Quoted in Barnet and Cavanaugh, p. 197.

ilarly ironic ways, oil companies have garnered the support of some environmental groups, implicitly portraying themselves as saviors of the very earth their products and the production of their products destroy.

In addition to these subtle and not-so-subtle means of encouraging idol worship, global capital has acted similarly to ancient Rome in leading people to respond to its power with the despairing, "Who can fight against it?" (cf. Rev. 13:4). The old adage "If you can't beat 'em, join 'em" has become the concessionary line of many former and would-be activists who feel powerless in the face of global capital's massive resources. This too is a form of idol worship, if only in the negative sense of giving up hope that there is a force greater than empire to which people can turn in trust when empire seems overwhelming. And, of course, that's all the Roman Empire sought from its members: if enthusiastic worship could not be given, grudging acceptance of imperial authority would suffice.

In this regard, the church has at best a spotty record in offering hope. Corporations have been successful at quieting the resistance of church leaders and members through donations to building campaigns, the illusory offer of job security that provides the foundation for stable faith communities, and official tolerance for Christianity so long as it "stays in its place." The moment, of course, that church leaders dare to challenge global capital's system of false worship, the Beast rears its ugly head, demanding that preachers "stay in their pulpits where they belong" and stop pretending to be economists or political or other "nonreligious" experts. One might recall the powerful resistance from the corporate and government worlds expressed in reaction to the U.S. Catholic Bishops' 1980s pastoral letters on war and peace and on the economy. How dare the bishops criticize the military and economic policies of America! And when individual bishops, such as Raymond Hunthausen in Seattle or Thomas Gumbleton in Detroit, dare to take personal stands in resistance to war or to stand in solidarity with workers in their pursuit of justice, the voices of empire are not afraid to get personal in decrying the bishops for their outspoken ways. Courageous pastors such as these bishops and a few other religious leaders rarely find support among their peers, nor does their courage lead to more widespread local preaching against the evils of empire, for fear of losing financial support. It is, of course, just this sort of compromise with empire that John of Patmos lambasted in his messages to the *ekklēsiai* of Asia. But imagine the response if an ordinary pastor were to stand up in the pulpit and urge his or her parishioners to withdraw from participation in global capital's empire! Nonetheless, we believe that this is precisely what Revelation called for in its own time and continues to call for wherever and whenever empire seduces Christians into worship of its idols.

GLOBAL CAPITAL AS ALREADY FALLEN

One of the remarkable aspects of Revelation's message is that, at the apparent peak of Rome's historical power, John's divinely inspired vision enabled him to see the apocalyptic truth: Rome/Babylon was already "fallen." As we have seen, this was the case both in the biblical sense of fallen-as-sinful-and-judged, and in the historical sense of bearing the seeds of its own physical demise. Do we have apocalyptic eyes to see this same truth about global capital's empire?

At one level, no faith in God is required to come to this conclusion. George Soros, no wild-eyed religious fanatic, in speaking of the accelerating pace of global finance's frenzied pursuit of profit, has declared, "I cannot see the global system surviving. . . . we have entered a period of global disintegration only we are not yet aware of it."[71] Similarly, engineering professor and Tokyo University president Hiroyuki Yoshikawa has said,

> It's my feeling that, yes, the companies can survive but the people cannot survive. . . . we can't go on like this. There will be some kind of disaster. We've already had several kinds of tragedy here in Japan. We can't escape.[72]

Numerous economists, disgusted with global capital's false ideology of "growth," have named the obvious: on a finite planet, growth, contrary to FDR's maxim, cannot continue forever. Environmentalists, population experts, and others have pointed out the limits that eventually must either be respected or will bear terrible consequences for the earth and its inhabitants. Despite the optimistic dreams of corporate technologists, there cannot be "fixes" to every problem that flows from the out-of-control power of global capital's imperial ethos. As Robert Kaplan pointed out in his 1994 *Atlantic Monthly* article entitled "The Coming Anarchy," "scarcity, crime, overpopulation, tribalism, and disease are rapidly destroying the social fabric of our planet."

Thus, while politicians proclaim the American economy the best it has been in decades, and empire's preachers brush off world poverty as a temporary effect of "adjustment" to the emerging global economy, we who call ourselves disciples of Jesus must have the courage and faith to see past this illusion to the apocalyptic truth: as with Rome, so with global capital—empire *is* fallen.

The challenge of this proclamation is where the rubber hits the road in our claim to be Christians. If the Babylon of our time is already, from God's perspective, a smoking ruin, how and where do we find New Jerusalem? Is it really possible to "come out" of empire when it surrounds us so completely? These questions are what lead to the conclusion of our book.

NEW JERUSALEM TODAY: SEEDS OF THE NEW
BEING BORN AMID THE SHELL OF THE OLD

There is no doubt that the overwhelming majority of people in our society, including those who call themselves Christians, live most of their lives firmly ensconced in Babylon. Furthermore, very few seem even to be looking for New

---

71. Greider, p. 248.
72. Quoted in Greider, p. 451.

Jerusalem, at least not where Revelation expects it to be found: not "in the sky" or some after-death condition but right in the midst of empire. The Bible, as always, envisions conversion and transformation of individuals and of society right here on earth, right now.

So why is New Jerusalem not even on most Christians' roadmaps? Part of the problem, we think, lies in the deep roots of the historical church. Once a Roman emperor took on Christianity as an imperial religion, there was no room at the inn for New Jerusalem to be born. As we have repeatedly emphasized, John's vision was of a reality *apart from but in the midst of* empire. Once the *ekklēsiai* became empire, the possibility for New Jerusalem disappeared—unless future visionaries were given the imagination, courage, and energy to create it *despite* the sellout of the church to empire.

Ever since Constantine's "conversion," the church has taken on the forms and mind-set of empire. Its ministry and liturgy resemble those of the imperial cult, admittedly with Jesus rather than Caesar as the focus of worship. Crusades, missionary voyages, and the Inquisition all reek of imperial rather than covenantal practice. Centuries of church history find popes and bishops arm in arm with kings, princes, and generals. The very notion of "Christendom" that prevailed throughout much of the church's history as the primary goal of the church has almost nothing to do with biblical faith and everything to do with imperial power.

This is the situation in which we find ourselves today. Although the church has had its temporal empire taken away, it often continues to think in imperial categories. Edicts are issued, royal pomp surrounds its "princes," and dissent is crushed (at least in theory). The book of Revelation itself sits largely on the shelf, coming out only for an occasional bit part in Sunday worship—and even then, only the "nice" parts are heard. Meanwhile, as we have seen, premillennialism and fundamentalism run rampant. Catholics and other mainline Christians in Latin America are running in droves to fundamentalist and conservative evangelical denominations. Europe is fully post-Christian. Both American and Australian Catholics seem divided among those who attend sacramental occasions largely out of habit and nostalgia, those who yearn for a return to pre–Vatican II forms, those who argue endlessly over relatively trivial issues such as the qualifications for ordination and other formal concerns, and a small number who are trying to rediscover the power of authentic biblical faith. Where might New Jerusalem have a chance to make an appearance in the midst of all this?

Throughout the centuries, it seems there have always been a few hardy souls who have dared to embrace the New Testament vision and to attempt to live it out. Some are famous saints: Francis of Assisi, Teresa of Avila, Ignatius of Loyola. Others have been obscured from view but their stories are not wholly lost to us: the thirteenth-century Beguines; the founder of the seventeenth-century "Diggers" movement in England, Gerard Winstanley; the nineteenth-century "New Jerusalem" community founder Jemima Wilkinson.[73] What links some of

---

73. See Ellsberg for a wonderful compendium of holy women and men; also Keller regarding Winstanley and Wilkinson.

these people is that they saw their discipleship not as an individual adventure but as something calling for *community*. In other words, within the context of the church's imperial captivity, some people have dared to invite and cajole a few friends and others to form *ekklēsiai* in the image of the first Christian communities. The Franciscans, Jesuits, and Carmelites who are the legacies of these saints were founded as signs of contradiction within the formal church. They spoke to their first members' deep faith in Jesus and the possibility of Christian community arising both from within the traditional church and outside it. As we know, over time these religious communities have faced their own struggles to remain more a part of New Jerusalem than of Babylon.

What might this mean for us today? Traditional forms of gender-specific, celibate religious life have always appealed to a certain kind of soul. By definition, they do not include "ordinary" people, that is, working people with or seeking families. But all around us, small *ekklēsiai* are being born, right in the midst of Babylon.

One of the most powerful sources of this band of *ekklēsiai* was the Catholic Worker vision of Dorothy Day. A tremendous amount has been written about this woman, who explicitly hoped that she would not be "trivialized" by being called a "saint."[74] Her basic vision, shared with such friends as Peter Maurin and Ammon Hennacy, was for small communities of Catholics who lived with the poor, labored in solidarity with working people, and actively resisted the evils of government and industry, all in a context of prayer, sacrament, and other spiritual practice. Catholic Worker communities have sprung up around the world since Dorothy Day started the first one in the 1930s. Although not formed specifically out of a reading of Revelation, Catholic Worker communities offer some evidence that it is possible to be church while attempting to resist the lures of empire. As Day said in describing the purpose of Catholic Worker communities, "We are building the new within the shell of the old."

Catholic Worker communities are not, of course, the only forms that these latter-day *ekklēsiai* take. Inspired by the base communities in Latin America, which arose from the teachings of liberation theology, other Christian communities in the northern countries have been founded to give expression to the hope for a living alternative to empire. Some, like the Church of the Savior in Washington, D.C., and the various communities of the international L'Arche movement have established themselves over decades. Others have been born, lived, and died. Our purpose here is not to chronicle the history and breadth of these communities, but simply to point out how such communities might serve to incarnate the New Jerusalem vision of Revelation.

"HOLY, HOLY, HOLY": PRAYER AND WORSHIP

An essential difference between an *ekklēsia* seeking New Jerusalem and a secular, progressive community is the context of prayer and worship in which the

---

74. See, e.g., Cornell; Forest.

former is grounded. As James Douglass and others have made clear, resistance to empire is impossible over the long haul if it does not have as its foundation a celebration of the joyous presence of the true Creator of us all.[75] John's vision clearly showed the centrality of this aspect of life for the *ekklēsiai* in Asia. It remains essential today, as always.

Because the church's liturgical forms and prayers have sometimes carried over their imperial history, it is important that *ekklēsiai* today feel the Spirit's freedom to celebrate and pray in new ways that are faithful to the biblical traditions. For example, the heavenly liturgies in Revelation are always *loud*. African American and some other Christian traditions that have remained in contact with their tribal roots have continued this ancient practice of loud music and prayer. Unfortunately, European-based forms have largely gone quiet, except for the formality of organs and choirs. What would it be like for small communities of faith to open their throats and ears and to allow the Spirit free reign over the volume level? Young people gravitate naturally to loud music, constantly facing the parents' cry to "turn it down!" Perhaps, as Jesus frequently taught, it is time for adults to become like youth and to rediscover the prayerful power of loud liturgy. This is not to say that volume levels are linked with holiness, but simply to point out possibilities for the Spirit to break through the imperial façade that holds us bound, even in church. Of course, silence can also be a powerful means of shattering empire's hold on one's consciousness. Revelation's choirs sing loudly, but the key is restoring the political aspect of worship and using the time in which we gather as Jesus' disciples to remind ourselves of the implications of that commitment in relation to empire.

Another aspect of our tendency toward imperial standards for our worship is the sense that we should seek "quality" music and liturgy. In challenging this dogma, we are not arguing for disorganized or inelegant prayer forms. We are, however, urging the abandonment of notions of "professionalism" that remove participation from the people and put it in the hands of "pros." Liturgy, we recall, means "the people's work." The heavenly choir members in Revelation were not auditioned to find out how well they could sing! True liturgy is not a performance event like a symphony concert, but an interactive sing-along more reminiscent of the campfire gatherings of the Ladakh and other tribal peoples. So many people seem to forgo the joys of singing and offering prayer because of a perception that their sounds and words "aren't good enough." Can we imagine Jesus imposing such a restriction?

Finally, prayer and liturgy belong not only in the safe enclosure of home and hearth, but also in the more challenging space of the *imperium* itself. Bill Wylie Kellermann has written eloquently of the call to public liturgy.[76] Martin Luther King Jr. understood this well in leading marchers and other protestors in prayer and song amid the powers who would arrest or beat them. Some of the authors' own most powerful life experiences have been as part of such public worship events, where, like Elijah against the prophets of Baʿal, we can present our trust

---

75. Douglass; Dyckman and Carroll.
76. Kellermann.

in the God of Jesus in the face of the call to worship empire's idols. Can such experiences be embarrassing to our imperial sensibilities? Yes! But the very experience of such embarrassment can be a good catalyst for reflecting on just how deeply embedded in the approval mechanisms of empire we are.

"BLESSED IS THE ONE READING ALOUD AND LISTENING TO THESE WORDS": BIBLE AND CULTURAL STUDY

Anyone who has gotten this far probably does not need to be convinced of the importance of Bible study! And yet the absence of such a regular practice within the church is probably one of the biggest reasons for the church's largely unconscious captivity to empire. We are in the midst of a quiet revolution in biblical studies. Historically, the Bible has been either proclaimed with little comment in Sunday worship or studied academically by "experts." There has been little effort to bridge this gap. Today, though, an enormous amount of scholarly yet praxis-oriented exegesis is being produced. The use of such material is reenergizing individuals and *ekklēsiai* to the radical message not only of the Gospels but of the entire biblical Story. One of our goals in this book has been to show how the message of Revelation is not really different from that of the whole Bible: to come out of slavery and into the freedom of being children of God. Writers like Megan McKenna and Ched Myers have offered eloquent explanations for the power of Story to lead us along the journey.[77] Baltimore's Jonah House, Los Angeles's Catholic Worker, and many other communities have experienced and taught the power of incorporating Bible study into their daily and weekly life. The power of empire to convey its false story is tremendous. Only by following the admonition of Deuteronomy can we keep our ears open to God's version of the Story:

> Keep these words that I am commanding you today in
> your heart.
> Recite them to your children and talk about them when
> you are at home and when you are away, when you
> lie down and when you rise.
> Bind them as a sign on your hand, fix them as an emblem
> on your forehead, and write them on the doorposts
> of your house and on your gates. (Deut. 6:6-9)

At the same time, we must continue to learn about our world. To comprehend the intricacies of global capital is hard work; to fail to attempt the task is to allow ourselves to remain mystified by lies. The challenge is not to become economists, political scientists, or other "specialists," but to become as conscious as

---

77. McKenna; Myers (1988, 1994).

possible of the conditions of our captivity. Leaders such as Gandhi or King were successful because they knew the enemy well. John of Patmos revealed his knowledge of the Roman Empire. Gandhi studied in great depth the history and structure of the British Empire. King knew all about African American history and the legacy of slavery. If we really seek New Jerusalem, we must be as familiar as possible with the boundaries and contours of Babylon today.

OIKONOMIA:
RECOVERING DIVINE "ECONOMICS"

Both in the Roman Empire and in the global capital empire, one of the key tools of captivity is control over the means of production of goods and services. Contrary to the caricatures sometimes offered by the political and religious right, the alternative to global capital is not Marxism or some form of state control. It is, according to the Bible, local community grounded in God's provident care.

As we have seen, throughout the Bible there is a tension between the tendency to organize and centralize trade and commerce, on the one hand, and the urge to keep it within family and village, on the other. Prophets regularly castigate the former, condemning Israel's kings' trade pacts with foreign nations as betrayals of the covenant. This criticism is not a hidebound rejection of "modern" international dealings but an incisive reminder that the ways of YHWH remain the path to *shalom.* For humans to live in harmony with one another and with the earth requires us to rediscover this ancient wisdom of our ancestors in faith and to abandon the imperial alternative, which presents itself as divinely given.

Many secular critics of global capital have acknowledged that, as a purely practical matter, empire will not stop being empire. For change to take place, good people cannot expect the conversion of empire into something else or its "redemption."[78] Rather, a totally different system must be built alongside the imperial one. [79] Is this just a pipe dream, as unlikely as the descent from heaven of a fully formed New Jerusalem, or does it offer a practical plan of survival?

Many writers, both secular and faith-based, have provided sets of principles that would ground such a local economy.[80] Gandhi began his nonviolent revolution with the Hindu principle of *swadeshi,* the home economy that would liber-

---

78. Walter Wink, in his excellent trilogy on the "Powers" in the Bible, argues that the Powers are created good, are fallen, and are redeemable. Revelation, however, presents a biblical case for the notion that empire is *not* redeemable. Perhaps this apparent contradiction is a matter of semantics rather than substance. If the Power at issue here is "government," then "empire" can be seen as government-as-fallen. From this perspective, "empire" is not redeemable, but "government" is.

79. Korten; Mander and Goldsmith. William Greider, in his otherwise helpful analysis of global capital, rather anachronistically sees as the solution a resurgence of federal government authority over corporations. Although he admits that the conditions of debate that might bring about such a resurgence have been captured by global capital, he offers no local alternative.

80. E.g., Berry, pp. 413-14.

ate Indians from British rule.[81] Debates have developed over the proper scope of the term "local": "bioregion" and "social field" are two options.[82] This is not the place to engage these questions, but simply to refer readers to works in which such questions are being thoughtfully considered. Suffice it to say for our purposes that such a local economy would be based on cooperation, not competition; on needs of whole people, not people-as-consumers; and on respect for the earth.

One writer who has engaged these questions with a keen eye toward the practical is the Irish economist Richard Douthwaite. His excellent *Short Circuit: Strengthening Local Economics for Security in an Unstable World* is a compendium of possibilities gleaned from real-world projects. His book contains wisdom and contact information on the following essential elements of local economies:

- Creating local currencies
- Developing alternative financing institutions, such as credit unions
- Building producer co-ops
- Developing local sources of renewable energy
- Creating local food through community supported agriculture (CSAs)
- Changing human attitudes toward economics and toward one another in engaging economic and financial issues

All of these forms have long histories, which Douthwaite recovers in ways fitting for our world. With the advent of the Internet, interested folk can find information and other people engaged in these pursuits at low cost and without delay.

As an example of how energizing and inspiring such experiments can be, we offer the story of Guadalupe Gardens. The Tacoma Catholic Worker is located in what has been the most abandoned portion of Tacoma, Washington, a working-class city thirty-five miles south of Seattle. The Worker offered hospitality to the homeless in an area surrounded by vacant lots filled with broken glass, rusty car hulks, and used syringes and condoms. A few years ago, an idea came to them. What if one of the vacant lots could be cleaned up and turned into a garden? An elderly widow, frequently confined to her house in fear of street gangs and other possibilities of violence, was approached with a deal: Would she offer the water from her hose if volunteers cleaned up her yard and converted it into a vegetable garden? She accepted the invitation. Before long, weeds and garbage were cleared, topsoil acquired, and seeds planted. Soon sunflowers, corn, and other crops sprang up. Visitors were impressed and joyous over the redemption of the small plot of land. One thing led to another, and within a few years, nine lots on the block had been similarly redeemed. Homeless people were hired at livable wages to tend what was now a working, urban, organic farm. Middle-class folks from outlying areas supported the project by purchasing produce through what became a CSA. Local businesses contributed starter plants, topsoil, and other needed supplies. Before long, the mayor and other city officials were holding up

---

81. Kumar, pp. 418-22.
82. Sale (bioregionalism); Douthwaite, pp. 53-55 (social field in debate with bioregionalism).

Guadalupe Gardens as a model of what could be done to redeem inner cities. The project has gained fame and recognition throughout the region.

It is essential to note that this project happened out of the base of prayer, worship, and study with which this section began. The Tacoma Catholic Worker folks simply trusted that if they started the project, God would provide what they would need. This, we believe, is the way New Jerusalem will be found amid empire in our world.

Revelation impresses many people as a fierce and demanding text. It is that. But its fierceness is what Twelve Step folks call "tough love." John's vision of a powerful God who loves humanity and creation leads him to see clearly the power of empire to seduce Christians into its arms. He knew that he had to counter empire both positively and negatively. If empire threatened traitors with execution, "heaven" had to offer the more powerful threat of the lake of fire. If empire offered the wares of global commerce, "heaven" had to be covered with gold and jewels and choice fruit the year round. These are metaphors, not literal descriptions. They are John's visionary means of reminding people that God's ways are both more powerful and more joyous than those of empire. Revelation will not tolerate compromise with evil, nor should we. For humanity to have hope in the new millennium, we must look not to Rapture but to true redemption. We must expect not sudden and easy answers, but must instead be prepared to engage the sometimes exciting, sometimes dreary, day-to-day process of seeking possibilities for New Jerusalem while living in the midst of Babylon. John's narrative calls us to be nothing more or less than what our Creator has always called us to be. Our discipleship is grounded in our trust that God is more powerful than Caesar, New Jerusalem more joyous than Babylon. If we can affirm this much, Revelation's fierceness can be seen as that of a mother God, who yearns for nothing more than to shield her children within her safe and loving arms. This day, once again, let us affirm this trust and do what we can to take a step on the royal road to God's true home amid humanity.

CONCLUSION:
HOW DO WE TAKE A STEP AWAY FROM EMPIRE
AND TOWARD NEW JERUSALEM?

*The following is not meant as a comprehensive statement of our thoughts on how to live in light of Revelation, nor even less as a complete statement of how to be a First World Christian. All we hope to do in the dialogue that follows is to share stories from some of our own experiences as a way to encourage you to gather with others to reflect on how Revelation calls **you** to respond in your own life situation.*

Wes: Well, it's one thing to say "Revelation calls Christians to leave Babylon and become residents of New Jerusalem," and it's another thing to try to figure out how to do that day to day.

Anthony: I found myself personally prodded, provoked, and challenged to really look at my life and to see where I am—how much I'm a resident of Babylon and how much New Jerusalem's values are part of my life.

Wes: Even as we sit here this moment, comfortably conversing before a nice computer, I recognize how the privileges of empire surround us: the peace and quiet on the street, the plentiful food in our refrigerators and at the local grocery a few blocks away, the Internet at our beck and call, the luxury of time to ponder these questions. Each day as I get out of bed, empire is part of the fabric of my daily life in which I am entangled without having made any conscious choices to be a part of it.

Anthony: For me that's how the seductiveness of Babylon really works: Babylon doesn't present me with difficult choices; it says to me, if I go with the flow, I can lead a happy and meaningful life.

Wes: That's exactly the problem. For people in our inner cities, or most folks around the world, empire arrives as a blunt instrument of oppression. For us, though, it's simply the air we breathe. To attempt to live in New Jerusalem is like trying to breathe different air!

Anthony: When I'm in downtown Brisbane, everything I see—the huge office buildings, the fast-food joints, the rush of buying and selling—says that this is the only "reality." We'd be "crazy" not to like it, and even crazier to think that we can live alternatively to it!

Wes: A couple of examples of that from my own life. When I left the practice of law and went to study theology and ministry at the university, a lawyer friend of mine ran into another lawyer who knew me. The second lawyer said to the first, "I heard that Wes flipped out!" My friend responded, "No, he's at the university studying theology." The second lawyer responded, "That's what I mean!"
Another time, I was working in the garden in front of our house when a neighbor walked by. She asked about the living situation next door to us, where three families we knew were living together in community. The neighbor asked me rather suspiciously, "What's going on next door?" I said, "What do you mean?" She said, "Well, who are all the people who live there?" I told her that they were trying to live in community. She asked, "Why would they want to do that? Are they poor?" I said no, two were physicians and the others were well employed. She asked again, confoundedly, "But why would they want to live all in one house if they could afford to live each in their own houses?" Nothing I said could explain to her why people would voluntarily give up the "freedom" to have as big a private living space as they could afford.

Anthony: So to me, Revelation offers the amazing insight that just because everything around us says, "this is the way things should be," there's a "reality" virtually invisible to us most of the time that says everything that claims to be the only reality is a lie. Revelation vindicates my suspicion that there's more to life than TV or politicians or advertisers would have us believe.

Wes: So where do we start in taking our faltering steps away from the lie and toward God's truth? For me it starts with what we're doing in this book: going back to our biblical tradition and remembering what it has meant to be God's people for thousands of years. When I read the struggles of Third Isaiah to fight against Nehemiah's accommodation to the Persian Empire, or Daniel's powerful revelation to his people of the call to stand firm against the Seleucid Empire, I can feel that I'm part of an ancient struggle to remain faithful in difficult circumstances.

Anthony: Yes, to me the whole of the Bible is one Story of people struggling against different empires and wanting to be faithful to God. So whether it's Pharaoh's Egypt or Caesar's Rome or any of the others since, we're all part of the one Story. The Bible's story didn't end with Revelation!

Wes: And I've found that this insight is news to many sincere, faithful Christians. Many have not been taught that the ancient social and political circumstances tell of more than obscure historical battles; they are archetypes, paradigms of the human condition across all cultures and times that call us to trust in the ways of the Creator of all rather than in human-made substitutes.

Anthony: I can't recall much in my Catholic school or church that showed me that Jesus was about anything more than a model for private virtue. The whole possibility that the Gospels might be about how we live in the midst of empire wasn't even an issue.

Wes: So, this is step one: recover the power of our biblical stories—the one Story—to speak to the whole of life, not just to our individual concerns, and to recognize that those who have gone before us, those who lived, wrote down, and collected these stories actually *learned* something along the way that is valuable in our own efforts to be faithful! I'm often amazed at how Western people in general are the least in touch with the stories of their ancestors of any peoples on the planet. Tribal peoples the world over revere their traditions and the tellers of the stories; they know that their ancestors discovered valuable truths that each generation was to make a part of themselves. But our split between "religion" and "science" has relegated the Bible to the distant margins, not only of our general culture but even within the churches.

Anthony: The world of university biblical studies or even our own private reflections are not the best places to recover these stories. It's in coming together in some sort of community that is the best place to start to peel back the cultural encrustations of these stories and to relearn their power. This isn't an exercise in ancient history, of course, but possibly the one way for us to begin the process of living sane lives today.

Wes: This leads me to consider folks I know or have heard of who are modeling this in one way or another. Unknown to most Christians, there's a wide, informal network of people doing this sort of thing around the United States and throughout the world. One particular group that has meant a lot to me is the Los Angeles Catholic Worker community. They've made Bible study of this kind an integral part of their communal life of prayer, service, witness, and celebration. Their basic ministry—to provide meals and hospitality to the desperately poor of L.A.—would quickly become an intolerable burden if they didn't regularly refresh themselves with reflection on how their story fits or doesn't fit into *the* Story. And their life in L.A. is unquestionably taking place in the very heart of Babylon!

Anthony: One of the peculiarities of Australian society is our "cultural cringe." This means that we don't consider ourselves to have any real culture, so we desperately seek some cultural sustenance from over the oceans. This led a handful of people in Brisbane who sensed that the Christian story they'd heard so far wasn't the full picture, to be drawn to the likes of the Berrigans and the Catholic Workers in the United States. Despite the fact they were half a world away, those people put flesh on gut feelings about life amid empire. These people inspired a group of folks in Brisbane to become a Catholic Worker community. When I heard of this community in this other city—I was living in Sydney at the time, a thousand kilometers away—I was excited and wanted to become part of it.

Wes: What also inspires me about folks like the LACW community is that they always link their efforts to recover the power of the Bible's truth with a willingness to look hard at the story that the Babylon around us tells, to sort out in an ongoing way the lies from the aspects of our culture that we can live with, which *aren't* contrary to the ways of God—like the theologians Karl Barth or Jacques Ellul, who would study the Bible at the same time that they analyzed the daily newspapers to see how Babylon was being presented to them as a "given."

Anthony: Over the years I've come to learn that the Bible helps us cast a critical eye over our culture and our church. Our churches have taken on the standards of empire, deflecting attention from the real issues, using capitalist tools for marketing and fundraising, and presenting church as another form of entertainment! We have to turn the whole thing around. Church is where we recover the Bible Story and use that Story to measure the empire!

Wes: Just as we noted how few Christians were taught to take the Bible's politics seriously, we've not been taught that social analysis is part of our responsibility as followers of Jesus. Just as John of Patmos tried to discern what it meant to be Christians within the specific context of the Roman Empire, we cannot know how to follow Jesus today unless we take a clear-eyed look at the world in which we live. People like the Catholic Worker folks have been doing this for years. And of course, they're not the only ones. There are numerous magazines and other alternative media that have long engaged these questions, like *Sojourn-*

ers, The Other Side, The Witness. And there have been many individual Christians whose social analysis has led them to change their sense of what Christians should be doing to extract themselves from Babylon. I think of leaders such as bishops Tom Gumbleton of Detroit, Oscar Romero of El Salvador, or Juan Gerardi of Guatemala, or the Rev. Martin Luther King Jr., none of whom started off as a radical critic of empire. They became so, however, because of their willingness to see the worlds around them as they were. I also think of folks who held no official power but became leaders because of their willingness to name the discomforting truths that they saw: Dorothy Day, William Stringfellow, the Berrigans.

Anthony: An understanding of how empire operates is, of course, just the first step. The Bible Story wasn't written to be a primary source for academic dissertations, but a handbook for how people are to live in the midst of Babylon. Unfortunately, this invites us out of our comfortable existence into the "main street" to name names, to call a spade a spade, to side with the victims of empire.

Wes: But the empire is so big and powerful and we're so small! I'm often tempted to respond like the folks in Revelation 13, "Who can fight against it?" The challenge for me is not to be overwhelmed and to think, in typical American fashion, that I'm facing a "problem" that can be "fixed." Rather, I'm called to recognize each moment as presenting a choice between Babylon and New Jerusalem. Most of the time, unavoidably, I find myself deeply embedded in Babylon. But I can't let that be an excuse not to struggle in the next moment to rediscover the presence of New Jerusalem! This means trying to take little steps, making the daily choices. For example, each purchase that I make or don't make is an opportunity to recognize empire's seductive nature and to find "New Jerusalem" products or services if they are available.

Anthony: Let's face it: we in the First World, ourselves included, are so deeply mired in the ways of Babylon that whatever we do can seem like a futile gesture. But even something as apparently insignificant as buying a justly produced tea like *Trade Winds* is a step. Revelation tells me that "behind the veil," something as simple as drinking tea that didn't enslave those who sweated to produce it has profound power. Babylon tells us that this is a futile gesture, but John of Patmos saw that what we do in our daily lives causes rejoicing "in heaven."

Wes: My experience in engaging in these small daily choices is that they have become patterns, disciplines, habits. There are some purchases or practices I used to engage in unconsciously that now I don't even consider buying or doing. For example, like most Americans, I grew up watching hours of television and the commercials that pay for the shows. I never thought about it much as a kid or even as a young adult. But after a while, as I became more and more aware of how advertising attempts to seduce us into seeing its products as satisfying of our deepest desires, I became first suspicious and then outraged. As time went on, I found I couldn't take TV ads; they made me too angry. So eventually I just stopped watching TV altogether. It's not a matter of making the choice any more.

I simply don't think about watching TV as an option. And I certainly don't miss it at all! That's one little corner of Babylon that I don't frequent any more.

Anthony: Unlike you, I enjoy TV too much to give it up altogether! While I know that to engage in recreation that celebrates humanness rather than the mainstream media's caricature of life is a rejection of Babylon's seduction, it's much easier just to switch it on. On the other hand, I do enjoy the freedom of never having owned a car. I believe cars are a real curse on our society. In a car-oriented culture such as ours, this has practical consequences for me, like waiting for public buses, and sometimes making things generally inconvenient. So, it's clear that what has become habit for me might be a struggle for you, and vice-versa.

Wes: Indeed it is. It is ironic for me how my work as an itinerant Bible teacher requires me to drive to churches all around the area, even though I agree with you about the evil consequences of automobiles on our society and on our planet. Also, being an active parent of a school-age child, it seems almost impossible to get my son to and from his various activities without a car. So many of our choices that can become disciplines depend on where we work, what our family obligations are, and so forth. But the point is, I think, to start with whatever little choices we can make and develop them into ways of life if possible.

Anthony: I don't think we have to strike out immediately into the unknown. There are lots of steps we need to take along the way. For example, I went into the seminary for what were conventional reasons: to serve God and to serve people in a middle-class sort of way. While I was there, I began to read liberation theology, and, by the mystery of God or good fortune, I met up with the people of the St. Francis community, an inner-city community providing hospitality for some homeless people in Sydney. Just by the simplicity and graciousness of the relationships I encountered there, I was challenged to uncover what the gospel might mean in my life. For me this began as small differences between my seminary friends and myself about what inspired us. Over time, this developed for me into deeper differences. We were moving in different directions. My understanding of the "good news" was changing and I felt called to move in a different direction.

Wes: As I mentioned earlier, when we make choices that become visible to others, people often start to look suspiciously at us, or even question our "sanity." It can lead us to feel, in the words of William Stringfellow, like "strangers in a strange land." Or, as the writer Flannery O'Connor put it, "You shall know the truth and the truth shall make you odd." My son said to me the other day, "Dad, how come I'm the only kid I know who doesn't get to watch TV?" It's hard to answer those questions. If I try to come out of Babylon, the place where everyone around me lives, I *do* feel like a stranger at times. Isn't this what the whole biblical story about wanting to have a king because "we want to be like everybody else" is about? It's very uncomfortable not to fit in with the world around me.

Anthony: And this is where we can begin to understand how the members of the *ekklēsiai* would have felt upon hearing John's message. If they acted upon God's Word, they would have felt very different from their neighbors. By not being part of places like the markets, the temples, the festivals, they would indeed have felt like strangers in a strange land.

Wes: But it gets even "worse," doesn't it? I used to be a lawyer, an easy thing to tell people at parties and other social contexts where people asked, "So what do you do for a living?" What do you think mainstream folks in a liberal U.S. city like Seattle say when I, after squirming a bit, tell them that I'm a Bible study teacher? If they don't instantly assume that I'm a fundamentalist simply for taking the Bible seriously, they look askance and usually try to change the subject as quickly as possible. When our choices move beyond our relatively hidden purchasing or entertainment decisions and into how we make a living or even where we live, the sense of alienation can become greater and greater.

For me, this has meant searching for ways to deepen my participation in community beyond Bible study and cultural critique. I am convinced that Revelation, like all of the Bible, expects the term "people of God" to apply to a community or communities of people who have bonded together to live out the ancient covenant first offered by God so many millennia ago. We've been brought up in our consumer culture to think of "church" as something that we can choose as a way of spending an hour or so on Sunday morning. But an *ekklēsia* is supposed to be a completely alternative society. This is what I'm looking for in a small community setting: people who see their commitment to the gospel as inviting, even compelling them to throw their lot in with one another, not just on Sunday morning, but all week long! Some of the big fundamentalist churches seem to understand this well. They've encouraged people to build their whole lives around their faith and the activities the church provides. They come to see their fellow church members as their primary source of support, their true "family" as St. Paul meant when he called his fellow Christians "brothers and sisters."

Anthony: Exactly! That's what challenged me to leave the seminary and to join the St. Francis Christian community and later the Catholic Worker community in Brisbane. The initial loss of the seminary crowd and the security of church office opened up space for new friends. Friends who resonated together, who laughed at the same things, who were ready to come together for the long haul. For me, this has been easier than it has for you: I'm single, I don't have a career in the conventional sense.

Wes: Yes, one of the struggles of being in a primary life relationship and being a parent while trying to leave Babylon at the same time is that we need to make these decisions together. The nuclear family is such a deeply ambiguous institution in the United States. On the one hand, it is the basic building block of all culture and provides opportunities to practice love, compassion, and daily care for others. On the other hand, it can become a self-enclosed site of greed, abuse, and other ills that work against the possibilities of living gospel community. For example, a parish leader once asked for a workshop that would take family people where they were and offer them something, rather than calling a parent to "one more night meeting" away from the family. I suggested a workshop on how to expand the idea of family to include others, for example, offering an extra bedroom for the hospitality of strangers. This proposal met first with dead silence, and then with the cold response, "That's *way* too radical an idea for our people!" I was stunned. If sharing basic hospitality in our homes is "way too radical," how can we ever hope to develop communities that affect our whole lives? We forget so easily that Jesus asked the question, "Who are my sisters and brothers and mother? Whoever hears the Word of God and does it, that's who!"

Anthony: One of the reasons, I think, that people are so resistant to the idea of living in community is that it's imagined as sort of perpetual Lent, always giving up something "fun" in exchange for something "good." That's, of course, the power of Babylon: to seduce us into thinking that life-as-it-is equals life-as-it-should-be, and that any alternative couldn't possibly be as much fun as life is now. But Revelation unveils the reality that this "fun" isn't ultimately as satisfying as life in New Jerusalem. The call isn't, then, to leave the "good life" for the "correct life," but to leave life in the arms of a whore for life in the arms of loving partners.

For example, in the Catholic Worker community, every Monday morning we'd bake about a hundred loaves of bread for ourselves and for sale to friends and local organic food shops. The simple rhythm of preparing the yeast and kneading the dough while chatting about our lives and the world provided a deep sense of joy which Babylon can't begin to match.

Another example was the process of putting out our quarterly "Mutual Aid" newsletter. While we obviously didn't have Rupert Murdoch's global reach, it was very satisfying committing our lives and our thoughts to paper and communicating this with a circle of people throughout Australia and abroad.

Wes: Yes! These are the truly satisfying moments of life. In the Galilee Circle community in which my wife, Maggie, and I were members, we made sandwiches and sorted through fruits and vegetables we'd glean each week from a local grocery to serve to homeless people in downtown Seattle. What had started as a "statement" against the efforts of some downtown merchants to make the homeless invisible so that their customers wouldn't have their consciences disturbed became for us a joyous sharing of time over the kitchen table.

Anthony: At the same time, to adapt an old phrase to life in community: can't live with it, can't live without it! The fact is, that as First World people, we find it extremely hard to share our lives, our possessions, our space with one another. Life in community is a walk through an uncharted wilderness for people socialized into an individualistic, privatized culture. There once were maps to this territory, but now we've lost them.

Wes: Each step in even trying to *form* a community, as I've experienced, requires negotiating one another's feelings, attitudes, childhood experiences, and all the other aspects of ourselves that have separated us from each other. I've often felt that it's easier to confront the evils of the government or corporations than for us to confront one another about how we get along or don't get along! But that doesn't mean that we're not called to try, to engage this process as a necessary aspect of leaving Babylon.

Anthony: And in addition to the challenge to build new forms of community for mutual support along the road out of Babylon, Revelation also calls us to go public with the call to leave the seductions of Babylon for the deeper joys of New Jerusalem. For our community, we have understood this as a call to confront those realities in our city and country that carry out the agenda of empire. For example, we have stood weekly in silent, prayerful vigil in the busy city mall with images of the victims of nuclear war and war preparation. We hope that this simple discipline provides passersby with an insight into the injustice we all take part in as citizens of Babylon. It is not easy to stand in public with a message that is marginal to the consciousness of most people and could provoke hostility or the attention of the police, but these times are not without moments of grace and growth.

Wes: Another example. Our current group experimented one Advent with spending an hour each week in prayer in a different spot amid the downtown shopping scene. It was very powerful for us to feel the frenzied energy of folks desperately filling their arms with stuff they felt compelled to buy while we tried to be present to the downtown homeless people whose needs were largely being ignored by shoppers. By maintaining our prayerful spirit, we were more or less able to feel that a bit of New Jerusalem was brought into the midst of Babylon.

Anthony: But isn't there another aspect of Revelation's call to public witness? How do we participate in Revelation's call to refuse to take part in the "imperial cult" of the Beast?

Wes: Well, as we know, nobody explicitly worships our political leaders, our nation, our military, or other social institutions, as they might have in the Rome of Revelation's day.

Anthony: But as we also know, the claims made by today's global institutions amount to the same thing. Our resignation in the face of violence and exploitation is one way we worship the Beast. So I see it as one of our tasks to reveal the imperial worship taking place all around us. For example, a group of us went to an Australian army base that trains Indonesian soldiers to prepare them for combat on East Timor. We entered an office, found some documents marked "Indonesia," and poured our own blood on them to reveal our complicity in the murder of the East Timorese people. The federal prosecutor charged us with the lesser crime of trespass because a charge of damaging property would have required the production of the documents in the courtroom, something they definitely did not want!

Wes: In our country, people have acted in similar ways at various military bases. But one of the hardest—and most important—actions of this kind I've ever participated in was at the production plant of the B-2 bomber at the Boeing Developmental Center just across the Seattle border. This was hard because our churches and other nonprofit institutions depend on charity from Boeing for their funding. Criticizing Boeing in Seattle is like Jesus criticizing the temple in Jerusalem; it made almost everybody mad! But that, I think, is one of the necessary consequences of exposing what Revelation calls "the Beast." By going to Boeing and performing a public exorcism, we were announcing our belief that Boeing's military production—and our complicity with it—was contrary to the ways of God and needed to be stopped.

Anthony: The point is not that any *particular* action of this kind is required, but that our communal Bible study, our cultural analysis, and our prayer lead us to see how the Beast manifests itself where we live, and to witness publicly against the Beast's presence in our midst. This *is* hard, but it is also essential to Revelation's vision of discipleship. In our societies, at present, the Beast largely ignores these efforts. However, in naming empire as a Beast, John of Patmos knew that while sleeping beasts may appear tame, when disturbed or threatened, they can react with overwhelming violence. The deaths of Christian martyrs from John's time up through our own stands in testimony to this power of the Beast. And yet our hope and trust as Christians is that the power of the Beast to kill is not as great as the power of God to give life.

Wes: And that's why experiments like Guadalupe Gardens [discussed above] are so important. They show that beyond our individual purchasing choices and our acts of public witness, it *is* concretely possible to construct social and economic worlds that are just and whole. Christians seeking New Jerusalem need to embrace the skills and vision of others as well in trying out some of the kinds of things that Richard Douthwaite talks about in *Short Circuit.*

Anthony: It's one of the ironies of this crazy globalized world we live in that I learned via e-mail from the United States from a book written by the Irish economist Richard Douthwaite that the small town of Maleny, about an hour's drive north from where I live, is "using more of the techniques for an integrated local economy than perhaps anywhere in the world." Since the late 1970s people looking toward an alternative economic way of life have developed, among other things, food cooperatives, a credit union, and a local currency. There *are* people aware of the dangers of global capital, who are practicing different ways of producing and consuming, all around us. We've just got to make the effort to see what's possible.

Wes: Again, little steps count. For example, when school's out for summer, a few of us in our neighborhood choose to form a "summer camp" in which each family commits a parent one day a week to spend with six or eight kids, rather than sending them to "professional" programs. It saves money, has been lots of fun, and the kids get to be with their own parents in their own spaces rather than being "farmed out." It's such a simple idea, really, but we've become so socialized into the dominant culture that the rediscovery of basic sharing seems radical.

Anthony: Another example of this might be the production of hand soap that was part of our community work. This helped both to finance our community and to model an alternative to the two transnational corporations—Unilever and Colgate-Palmolive—that dominate soap production. People have been making their own soap for thousands of years: it's good to start reclaiming the skills we have given away to global capital.

Wes: So, each day, we try to keep focused, despite the distractions and deceptions of empire, on who our God is and how God calls us to live. New Jerusalem may never spring forth, like Athena, fully formed from the hand of God, but we can still endeavor to see its healing fruit and shining streets here and there, like our powerful God, waiting to be revealed as living in our midst.

REFLECTION QUESTIONS

1. What have you been taught about the moral value of capitalism? Where did such teachings come from, e.g., family, school, church? What *feelings* arise within you at the idea that capitalism might be more a sign of empire than of God's reign?

2. For one day, try to think about where the consumer items you use come from, who produced them, and how they were produced. Choose one item that you don't know about and try to find out as much as you can about it. Gather a group and have each person try the experiment with a different item and compare the results.

3. Consider your experience of the process of globalization. Does it seem inevitable and beyond your control, one of many options that people can influence, or as not really happening to the extent that this chapter suggests? How does your response affect your sense of discipleship?

Bibliography

COMMENTARIES AND WORKS ON REVELATION

Achtemeier, Paul J. 1986. "Revelation 5:1-14." *Int* 40: 283-87.

Aune, David E. 1986. "The Apocalypse of John and the Problem of Genre." *Semeia* 36:65-96.

———. 1989. "The Prophetic Circle of John of Patmos and the Exegesis of Revelation 22:16." *JSNT* 37:103-16.

———. 1990. "The Form and Function of the Proclamations to the Seven Churches (Revelation 2-3)." *NTS* 36:182-204.

———. 1991. "A Latinism in Revelation 15:2." *JBL* 110:691-92.

———. 1997-99. *Revelation.* 3 vols. Word Biblical Commentaries. Dallas: Word Books.

Barnett, Paul. 1989. "Polemical Parallelism: Some Further Reflections on the Apocalypse." *JSNT* 35:111-20.

Barnwell, F. Aster. 1992. *Meditations on the Apocalypse: A Psycho-Spiritual Perspective on the Book of Revelation.* Rockport, Mass.: Element.

Barr, David L. 1984. "The Apocalypse as a Symbolic Transformation of the World: A Literary Analysis." *Int* 38:39-50.

———. 1986. "The Apocalypse of John as Oral Enactment." *Int* 40:243-56.

———. 1998. *Tales of the End: A Narrative Commentary on the Book of Revelation.* Santa Rosa, Calif.: Polebridge Press.

Bauckham, Richard J. 1991. "The Economic Critique of Rome in Revelation 18." In *Images of Empire,* edited by Loveday Alexander. JSOTSS 122. Sheffield: Sheffield Academic Press.

———. 1992. *The Climax of Prophecy: Studies on the Book of Revelation.* Edinburgh: T & T Clark.

———. 1993. *The Theology of the Book of Revelation.* Cambridge: Cambridge University Press.

Beale, G. K. 1985. "The Origin of the Title 'King of Kings and Lord of Lords' in Revelation 17:14." *NTS* 31:618-20.

———. 1999. *The Book of Revelation.* NIGTC. Grand Rapids: Eerdmans.

Berrigan, Daniel. 1978. *Beside the Sea of Glass: The Song of the Lamb.* New York: Seabury Press.

———. 1983. *The Nightmare of God.* Portland, Ore.: Sunburst Press.

———. 1988. "War in Heaven, Peace on Earth." *Spirituality Today* 40:36-51.

Boesak, Allan A. 1987. *Comfort and Protest: The Apocalypse from South African Perspective.* Philadelphia: Westminster Press.

Borgen, Peder. 1996. "Moses, Jesus and the Roman Emperor: Observations in Philo's Writings and the Revelation of John." *NovT* 38:145-59.

278

Boring, M. Eugene. 1986. "The Theology of Revelation: 'The Lord Our God the Almighty Reigns.'" *Int* 40:257-69.

———. 1989. *Revelation.* Louisville: John Knox Press.

———. 1992. "The Voice of Jesus in the Apocalypse of John." *NovT* 34:334-59.

Brown, Schuyler. 1966. "The Hour of Trial (Rev 3:10)." *JBL* 85:308-14.

Caird, G. B. 1962. "On Deciphering the Book of Revelation: Heaven and Earth." *Expository Times* 74:13-15.

———. 1966. *A Commentary on the Revelation of St. John the Divine.* New York: Harper and Row.

Callahan, Allen Dwight. 1995. "The Language of Apocalypse." *HTR* 88:453-70.

Charles, R. H. 1920. *A Critical and Exegetical Commentary on the Revelation of St. John.* 2 vols. Edinburgh: T & T Clark.

Cook, Cornelia. 1992. "The Language of Likeness in the Apocalypse." *New Blackfriars* 73:472-86.

Corsini, Eugenio. 1983. *The Apocalypse.* Edited and translated by Francis J. Moloney, SDB. Wilmington, Del.: Michael Glazier.

Court, John M. 1997. "Reading the Book: 6. The Book of Revelation." *ExpT* 108:164-67.

Coutsoumpos, Panayotis. 1997. "The Social Implications of Idolatry in Revelation 2:14: Christ or Caesar?" *BTB* 2723-27.

Craddock, Fred. 1986. "Preaching the Book of Revelation." *Int* 40:270-82.

Cullmann, Oscar. 1956. "The State in the Johannine Apocalypse." In *The State in the New Testament.* New York: Charles Scribner's Sons.

Deutsch, Celia. 1987. "Transformation of Symbols: The New Jerusalem in Rv 21:1-22:5." *ZNW* 78:106-26.

Duff, Paul. 1997. "'I Will Give to Each of You as Your Works Deserve': Witchcraft Accusations and the Fiery-Eyed Son of God in Rev. 2:18-23." *NTS* 43:116-33.

Elliott, John H. 1993. "Sorcery and Magic in the Revelation of John." *Listening* 28:261-76.

Ellul, Jacques. 1977. *Apocalypse.* New York: Seabury Press.

Engels, Frederick. 1957. *On the History of Early Christianity,* Vol. 1. 1894-95 Online version, translated by the Institute of Marxism-Leninism, USSR. http://info.ex.ac.uk/meia/Archive/1894-Christ/index.html.

Enroth, Anne-Marit. 1990. "The Hearing Formula in the Book of Revelation." *NTS* 36:598-608.

Esler, Philip F. 1993. "Political Oppression in Jewish Apocalyptic Literature: A Social-Scientific Approach." *Listening* 28:181-199.

Fekkes, Jan, III. 1990. "'His Bride Has Prepared Herself': Revelation 19-21 and Isaian Nuptial Imagery." *JBL* 109:269-87.

Ford, J. Massyngberde. 1975. *Revelation.* Anchor Bible 38. Garden City, N.Y.: Doubleday.

———. 1993. "The Priestly People of God in the Apocalypse." *Listening* 28:245-60.

Friesen, Steven J. 1995a. "Revelation, Realia, and Religion: Archaeology in the Interpretation of the Apocalypse." *HTR* 88:291-314.

———. 1995b. "The Cult of the Roman Emperors in Ephesos: Temple Wardens, City Titles, and the Interpretation of the Revelation of John." In *Ephesos: Metropolis of Asia,* edited by Helmut Koester, 229-50. Valley Forge, Penn.: Trinity Press International.

Georgi, Dieter. 1986. "Who is the True Prophet?" *HTR* 79:100-126.

Geyser, Albert. 1982. "The Twelve Tribes in Revelation: Judean and Judeo Christian Apocalypticism." *NTS* 28:388-99.

Giblin, Charles Homer, S.J. 1984. "Revelation 11.1-13: Its Form, Function, and Contextual Integration." *NTS* 30:433-59.

———. 1991. *The Book of Revelation: The Open Book of Prophecy.* Collegeville, Minn.: Liturgical Press.

———. 1994. "Recapitulation and the Literary Coherence of John's Apocalypse." *CBQ* 56:81-96.

Gonzalez, Catherine Gunsalus, and Justo L. Gonzalez. 1997. *Revelation.* Louisville: John Knox Press.

Gourgues, Michel. 1985. "The Thousand Year Reign (Rev 20:1-6): Terrestrial or Celestial?" *CBQ* 47:676-81.

Hall, Robert G. 1990. "Living Creatures in the Midst of the Throne: Another Look at Revelation 4:6." *NTS* 36:609-13.

Hanson, K. C. 1993. "Blood and Purity in Leviticus and Revelation." *Listening* 28:215-30.

Heil, John Paul. 1993. "The Fifth Seal (Rev 6, 9-11) as a Key to the Book of Revelation." *Biblica* 74:220-43.

Hellholm, David. 1986. "The Problem of Apocalyptic Genre and the Apocalypse of John." *Semeia* 36:13-64.

Hemer, Colin J. 1986. *The Letters to the Seven Churches of Asia in Their Local Setting.* Sheffield: JSOT Press.

Hill, David. 1972. "Prophecy and Prophets in the Revelation of St. John" *NTS* 18:401-18.

Jeske, Richard L. 1985. "Spirit and Community in the Johannine Apocalypse." *NTS* 31:452-66.

Kallas, James. 1967. "The Apocalypse—An Apocalyptic Book?" *JBL* 86:69-80.

Kirby, John T. 1988. "The Rhetorical Situations of Revelation 1-3." *NTS* 34:197-207.

Kraybill, J. Nelson. 1996. *Imperial Cult and Commerce in John's Apocalypse.* Sheffield: JSNT.

Krodel, Gerhard A. 1989. *Revelation.* Augsburg Commentary on the NT. Minneapolis: Augsburg.

Lawrence, D. H. 1980. *Apocalypse.* London: Penguin.

Lee, Michelle E. 1998. "A Call to Martyrdom: Function as Method and Message in Revelation." *NovT* 40:164-94.

Long, Tim. 1996. "A Real Reader Reading Revelation." *Semeia* 73:79-107.

Maier, Harry O. 1997. "Staging the Gaze: Early Christian Apocalypses and Narrative Self-Representation." *HTR* 90:131-54.

Malina, Bruce. 1990. "From Isis to Medjugorje: Why Apparitions." *BTB* 20:76-84.

———. 1993. "'Apocalyptic' and Territoriality." Offprint from *Early Christianity in Context. Monuments and Documents,* edited by F. Manns and E. Alliata. Jerusalem: Franciscan Printing Press.

———. 1994. "The Book of Revelation and Religion: How Did the Book of Revelation Persuade?" *Scriptura* 51:27-50.

———. 1995. *On the Genre and Message of Revelation: Star Visions and Sky Journeys.* Peabody, Mass.: Hendrickson.

McDonald, Patricia M., S.H.C.J. 1996. "Lion as Slain Lamb: On Reading Revelation Recursively." *Horizons* 23:29-47.

Metzger, Bruce M. 1993. *Breaking the Code: Understanding the Book of Revelation.* Nashville: Abingdon Press.

Michaels, J. Ramsey. 1991. "Revelation 1:19 and the Narrative Voices of the Apocalypse." *NTS* 37:604-20.

Miguez, Nestor. 1995. "Apocalyptic and the Economy: A Reading of Revelation 18 from the Experience of Economic Exclusion." In *Reading from This Place,* Volume 2, *Social Location and Biblical Interpretation in Global Perspective,* edited by Fernando F. Segovia and Mary Ann Tolbert, 250-62. Minneapolis: Fortress Press.

Minear, Paul. 1966. "Ontology and Ecclesiology in the Apocalypse." *NTS* 13:89-105.

———. 1968. *I Saw a New Earth: An Introduction to the Visions of the Apocalypse.* Washington D.C.: Corpus Books.

———. 1970. "An Apocalyptic Adjective." *NovT* 12:218-22.

Moore, Stephen D. 1995. "The Beatific Vision as a Posing Exhibition: Revelation's Hypermasculine Deity." *JSNT* 60:27-55.

Mounce, Robert. 1997. *The Book of Revelation.* Revised ed. Grand Rapids: Eerdmans.

Moysie, Steve. 1995. *The Old Testament in the Book of Revelation.* Sheffield: JSNT.

Murphy. Frederick J. 1993. *Fallen Is Babylon: The Revelation to John..* Harrisburg, Penn.: Trinity Press International.

Oakman, Douglas E. 1993. "The Ancient Economy and St. John's Apocalypse." *Listening* 28:200-214.

Pilch, John J. 1992. "Lying and Deceit in the Letters to the Seven Churches: Perspectives from Cultural Anthropology." *BTB* 22:126-35.

———. 1993. "Visions in Revelation and Alternate Consciousness: A Perspective From Cultural Anthropology." *Listening* 28:231-44.

Pippin, Tina. 1992. *Death and Desire: The Rhetoric of Gender in the Apocalypse of John.* Louisville: Westminster/John Knox.

———. 1994. "Peering into the Abyss: A Postmodern Reading of the Biblical Bottomless Pit." In *The New Literary Criticism and the New Testament,* 251-67. JSNTSS 109. Sheffield: Sheffield Academic Press.

———. 1995. "Jezebel Re-Vamped." *Semeia* 69/70:221-33.

Porter, Stanley E. 1989. "The Language of the Apocalypse in Recent Discussion." *NTS* 35:582-603.

Preston, R. H., and A. T. Hanson. 1949. *Revelation: The Book of Glory.* London: SCM Press.

Provain, Iain. 1996. "Foul Spirits, Fornication and Finance: Revelation 18 from an Old Testament Perspective." *JSNT* 64:81-100.

Raber, Rudolph W. 1986. "Revelation 21:1-8." *Int* 40:296-301.

Ramírez Fernández, Dagoberto. 1990. "The Judgment of God on the Multinationals: Revelation 18." In *Subversive Scriptures: Revolutionary Readings of the Christian Bible in Latin America,* edited by Leif Vaage, 75-100. Valley Forge, Penn.: Trinity Press International. Originally published as "El Judicio de Dios a las transnacionales: Apocalipsis 18," in *Revista de Interpretacion Biblica Latinamericana* 5 (1990): 55-74.

Reader, William W. 1981. "The Twelve Jewels of Revelation 21:19-20: Tradition History and Modern Interpretations." *JBL* 100:433-57.

Reddish, Mitchell G. 1988. "Martyr Christology in the Apocalypse." *JSNT* 33:85-95.

Richard, Pablo. 1995. *Apocalypse: A People's Commentary on the Book of Revelation.* Maryknoll, N.Y.: Orbis Books.

Roloff, Jürgen. 1993. *Revelation.* Minneapolis: Fortress.

Rossing, Barbara. Forthcoming. *The Choice between Two Cities: A Wisdom* Topos *in the Apocalypse.* Harrisburg, Penn.: Trinity Press International.

Scherrer, Steven J. 1984. "Signs and Wonders in the Imperial Cult: A New Look at a Roman Religious Institution in the Light of Rev 13:13-15." *JBL* 103:599-610.

Schmidt, Daryl D. 1991. "Semitisms and Septuagintalisms in the Book of Revelation." *NTS* 37:592-603.

Schüssler Fiorenza, Elisabeth. 1985. *The Book of Revelation: Justice and Judgment.* Philadelphia, Fortress Press.

———. 1986. "The Followers of the Lamb: Visionary Rhetoric and Social-Political Situation." *Semeia* 36:123-46.

———. 1991. *Revelation: Vision of a Just World.* Minneapolis: Augsburg Fortress.

Scobie, Charles H. H. 1993. "Local References in the Letters to the Seven Churches." *NTS* 39:606-24.

Slater, Thomas B. 1998. "On the Social Setting of the Revelation to John." *NTS* 44:232-56.

Smith, Christopher R. 1994. "The Structure of the Book of Revelation in Light of Apocalyptic Literary Conventions." *NovT* 36:373-93.

Stevenson, Gregory M. 1995. "Conceptual Background to Golden Crown Imagery in the Apocalypse of John (4:4, 10; 14:14)." *JBL* 114:257-72.

Stringfellow, William. 1977. *Conscience and Obedience: The Politics of Romans 13 and Revelation 13 in Light of the Second Coming.* Waco: Word Books.

Sweet, John. 1981. "Maintaining the Testimony of Jesus: The Suffering Christians in the Revelation of John." In *Suffering and Martyrdom in the New Testament,* edited by W. Horbury and M. Neil. Cambridge: Cambridge University Press.

———. 1990. *Revelation.* London: SCM Press; Philadelphia: Trinity Press International.

Talbert, Charles H. 1994. *The Apocalypse: A Reading of the Revelation of John.* Louisville: Westminster John Knox Press.

Thompson, Leonard. 1986. "A Sociological Analysis of Tribulation in the Apocalypse of John." *Semeia* 36:147-74.

———. 1990. *The Book of Revelation: Apocalypse and Empire.* Oxford: Oxford University Press.

Trevett, Christine. 1989. "The Other Letters to the Churches of Asia: Apocalypse and Ignatius of Antioch." *JSNT* 37:117-35.

Vanni, Ugo. 1991. "Liturgical Dialogue as a Literary Form in the Book of Revelation." *NTS* 37:358-72.

Victorinus. *Commentary on the Apocalypse of the Blessed John.* Ante-Nicene Fathers, vol. 7. CD-ROM edition.

Wilkinson, Richard H. 1988. "The STULOS of Revelation 3:12 and Ancient Coronation Rites." *JBL* 107:498-501.

Wilson, J. Christian. 1993. "The Problem of the Domitianic Date of Revelation." *NTS* 39:587-605.

Yarbro Collins, Adela. 1976. *The Combat Myth in the Book of Revelation.* Missoula, Mont.: Scholars Press.

———. 1977. "The Political Perspective of the Revelation to John." *JBL* 96:241-56.

———. 1984. *Crisis and Catharsis: The Power of the Apocalypse.* Philadelphia: Westminster.

———. 1986. "Reading the Book of Revelation in the Twentieth Century." *Int* 40:229-42.

ROMAN EMPIRE

Aristides, Aelius P. 1981. *The Complete Works,* Vol. 2, *Orations 17-53.* Translated by Charles A. Behr. Leiden: E. J. Brill.

Brunt, P. A., and J. M. Moore. 1967. *Res Gestae Divi Augusti.* London: Oxford University Press.

Burkert, Walter. 1987. *Ancient Mystery Cults.* Cambridge, Mass., and London: Harvard University Press.

Charlesworth, Martin Percival. 1936. "Providentia and Aeternitas." *HTR* 29:107-32.

D'Arms, John H. 1981. *Commerce and Social Standing in Ancient Rome.* Cambridge, Mass.: Harvard University Press.

Fears, J. Rufius. 1981. "The Theology of Victory at Rome: Approaches and Problems." In *ANRW* II 17:2, 736-826. Berlin and New York: Walter de Gruyter.

Ferguson, John. 1970. *The Religions of the Roman Empire.* Ithaca, N.Y.: Cornell University Press.

Fox, Robin Lane. 1986. *Pagans and Christians.* San Francisco: Harper & Row.

Garnsey, Peter, and Richard Saller. 1997. "Patronal Power Relations." In *Paul and Empire: Religion and Power in Roman Imperial Society,* edited by Richard A. Horsley. Harrisburg, Penn.: Trinity Press International.

Gibbon, Edward. 1869. *The History of the Decline and Fall of the Roman Empire.* London: A. Murray.

Gordon, Richard. 1997. "The Veil of Power." In *Paul and Empire: Religion and Power in Roman Imperial Society,* edited by Richard A. Horsley. Harrisburg, Penn.: Trinity Press International.

Grant, Michael. 1995. *Greek and Roman Historians: Information and Misinformation.* London: Routledge.

Hardie, Philip R. 1986. *Virgil's Aeneid: Cosmos and Imperium.* Oxford: Oxford University Press.

Hengel, Martin. 1977. *Crucifixion.* Philadelphia, Penn.: Fortress Press.

Herodotus. 1926. *History.* London: William Heinemann.

Horsley, Richard A. 1997. *Paul and Empire: Religion and Power in Roman Imperial Society.* Harrisburg, Penn.: Trinity Press International.

Jones, A. H. M. 1974. *The Roman Economy: Studies in Ancient Economic and Administrative History.* Totowa: Rowman & Littlefield.

Jones, Brian W. 1992. *The Emperor Domitian.* New York and London: Routledge.

Jones, D. L. 1980. "Christianity and the Roman Cult." In *ANRW* II 23:2, 1023-54. Berlin and New York: Walter de Gruyter.

Lintott, Andrew. 1993. *Imperium Romanum: Politics and Administration.* London: Routledge.

Loane, Helen Jefferson. 1938. *Industry and Commerce of the City of Rome (50 B.C.– 200 A.D.).* Baltimore: Johns Hopkins Press.

MacMullen, Ramsay. 1974. *Roman Social Relations, 50 B.C. to A.D. 284.* New Haven and London: Yale University Press.

———. 1981. *Paganism in the Roman Empire.* New Haven and London: Yale University Press.

———. 1984. *Christianizing the Roman Empire A.D. 100-400.* New Haven and London: Yale University Press.

Macro, Anthony D. 1980. "The Cities of Asia Minor Under the Roman Imperium." In *ANRW* II 7:2, 658-97. Berlin and New York: Walter de Gruyter.

Magie, David. 1950. *Roman Rule in Asia Minor.* Princeton, N.J.: Princeton University Press.

Mazzaloni, Lidia Storoni. 1967. *The Idea of the City in Roman Thought: From Walled City to Spiritual Commonwealth.* London: Hollis & Carter.

Mellor, Ronald. 1981. "The Goddess Roma." In *ANRW* II 17:2, 950-1030. Berlin and New York: Walter de Gruyter.

Millar, Fergus. 1983. "Empire and City, Augustus to Julian: Obligations, Excuses and Status." *JRS* 73:76-96.

Momigliano, Arnaldo. 1966. "Time in Ancient Historiography." In *History and Theory* Beiheft 6, *History and the Concept of Time.* Middletown: Wesleyan University Press.

Neverov, Oleg. 1986. "Nero-Helios." In *Pagan Gods and Shrines of the Roman Empire,* edited by M. Henig and A. King. Monograph Number 8. Oxford: Oxford University Committee for Archaeology.

North, J. A. 1981. "The Development of Roman Imperialism." *JRS* 71:1-9.

Nutton, V. 1978. "The Beneficial Ideology." In *Imperialism in the Ancient World,* edited by P. D. A. Garnsey and C. R. Whittaker, 209-21. Cambridge: Cambridge University Press.

Ogilvie, R. M. 1965. *Commentary on Livy.* Oxford: Clarendon Press.

Oster, Richard E. 1990. "Ephesus as a Religious Center under the Principate, I. Paganism before Constantine." In *ANRW* II 18:3, 1661-28. Berlin and New York: Walter de Gruyter.

Ovid. *The Fasti of Ovid,* vol. 1. London: Macmillan, 1929.

Owens, E. J. 1991. *The City in the Greek and Roman World.* London and New York: Routledge.

Philo. *The Works of Philo.* Translated by C. D. Yonge. Peabody, Mass.: Hendrickson, 1993.

Philostratus. 1912. *The Life of Apollonius of Tyana.* Translated by F. C. Coneybeare. 1811. London: Heinemann.

Pleket, H. W. 1983. "Urban Elites and Business in the Greek Part of the Roman Empire." In *Trade in the Ancient Economy,* edited by P. Garnsey, K. Hopkins, and C. R. Whittaker. Berkeley: University of California Press.

Pliny the Elder. *Natural History.* Translated by H. Reikhman, W. H. S. Jones, and D. E. Eichholz. London: Heinemann, 1940-63.

Pliny the Younger. *Letters and Panegyricus.* Translated by B. Radice. Loeb Classical Library. Cambridge, Mass.: William Heinemann, 1969.

Plutarch. "Life of Sertorius." In *Plutarch's Lives.* Translated by A. H. Clough. Boston: Ginn & Company, 1902.

Price, S. R. F. 1984. *Rituals and Power: The Roman Imperial Cult in Asia Minor.* Cambridge: Cambridge University Press.

Seutonius. *The Twelve Caesars.* Translated by Robert Grant. London: Penguin, 1979.

Smith, R. R. R. 1987. "The Imperial Reliefs from the Sebasteion at Aphrodisias." *JRS* 77:88-138.

Sordi, Marta. 1986. *The Christians and the Roman Empire.* Translated by Annabel Bedini. Norman: University of Oklahoma Press.

Stambaugh, John E. 1978. "The Functions of Roman Temples." In *ANRW* II 16:1, 554-608. Berlin and New York: Walter de Gruyter.

Tacitus. *Annals.* Translated by Donald R. Dudley. New York and Toronto: New American Library, 1966.

Taylor, Lily Ross. 1931. *The Divinity of the Roman Emperor.* Middletown: American Philological Association.

Tibullus. *The Poems of Catullus and Tibullus.* Translated by Walter Kelly. London: G. Bell & Sons, 1910.

Tomlinson, Richard. 1992. *From Mycenae to Constantinople: The Evolution of the Ancient City.* London and New York: Routledge.

Turcan, Robert. 1992. *The Cults of the Roman Empire.* Oxford and Cambridge: Blackwell. Eng. trans., 1996.

Virgil. *The Eclogues, Georgics and Aeneid of Virgil.* Translated by C. Day Lewis. London: Oxford University Press, 1966.

Wacher, J. 1987. *The Roman World.* London: Routledge.

Wallace-Hadrill, Andrew. 1989. "Patronage in Roman Society: From Republic to Empire." In *Patronage in Ancient Society.* London: Routledge.

Zanker, Paul. 1997. "The Power of Images." In *Paul and Empire: Religion and Power in Roman Imperial Society,* edited by Richard A. Horsley. Harrisburg, Penn.: Trinity Press International.

APOCALYPTIC, JEWISH, AND RELATED HEBREW AND CHRISTIAN SCRIPTURE

Achtemeier, Elizabeth. 1986. *Nahum-Malachi.* Louisville: John Knox Press.

Albertz, Rainer. 1994. *A History of Israelite Religion in the Old Testament Period.* 2 vols. Translated by John Bowden. Louisville: Westminster John Knox Press.

Ascough, Richard S. 1997. "Translocal Relationships among Voluntary Associations and Early Christianity." *Journal of Early Christian Studies* 5:223-41.

———. 1998. "Civic Pride at Philippi: The Text-Critical Problem of Acts 16:12." *NTS* 44:93-103.

Bailie, Gil. 1995. *Violence Unveiled: Humanity at the Crossroads.* New York: Crossroad.

Batstone, David B. 1992. "Jesus, Apocalyptic, and World Transformation." *Theology Today* 49:383-97.

Beardslee, William A. 1971. "New Testament Apocalyptic in Recent Interpretation." *Int* 25:419-35.

Belo, Fernando. 1981. *A Materialist Reading of the Gospel of Mark.* Maryknoll, N.Y.: Orbis Books.

Berquist, Jon. 1995. *Judaism in Persia's Shadow: A Social and Historical Approach.* Minneapolis: Fortress.

Birch, Bruce C. 1997. *Hosea, Joel, and Amos.* Louisville: Westminster John Knox Press.

Blenkinsopp, Joseph. 1990. *Ezekiel.* Louisville: John Knox Press.

Braaten, Carl E. 1971. "The Significance of Apocalypticism for Systematic Theology." *Int* 25:480-99.

Brown, Alexandra R. 1995. *The Cross and Human Transformation: Paul's Apocalyptic Word in 1 Corinthians.* Minneapolis: Fortress Press.

Brueggemann, Walter. 1993. "Trajectories in Old Testament Literature and the Sociology of Ancient Israel." In *The Bible and Liberation,* edited by Norman K. Gottwald and Richard A. Horsley. Maryknoll, N.Y.: Orbis Books.

————. 1998a. *A Commentary on Jeremiah: Exile and Homecoming.* Grand Rapids: Eerdmans.

————. 1998b. *Isaiah 1-39.* Louisville: Westminster John Knox Press.

————. 1998c. *Isaiah 40-66.* Louisville: Westminster John Knox Press.

Carmignac, Jean. 1972. "Les Dangers De L'Eschatologie." *NTS* 17:365-90.

Charlesworth, James H., ed. 1983. *The Old Testament Pseudepigrapha: Apocalyptic Literature and Testaments.* 2 vols. Garden City, N.Y.: Doubleday.

Cohn, Norman. 1993. *Cosmos, Chaos and the World to Come: The Ancient Roots of Apocalyptic Faith.* New Haven and London: Yale University Press.

Collins, John J. 1979. "The Jewish Apocalypses." *Semeia* 14:21-49.

————. 1981. *Daniel, First Maccabees, Second Maccabees.* OTM 15. Wilmington, Del.: Michael Glazier.

————. 1984. *The Apocalyptic Imagination.* New York: Crossroad.

————. 1992. *Daniel.* Hermeneia. Minneapolis: Fortress.

————. 1995. "A Throne in the Heavens: Apotheosis in Pre-Christian Judaism." In *Death, Ecstasy, and Other Worldly Journeys,* edited by John J. Collins and Michael Fishbane. Albany: SUNY Press.

Cook, Stephen L. 1995. *Prophecy and Apocalypticism: The Postexilic Social Setting.* Minneapolis: Fortress.

Cross, Frank Moore. 1971. *Canaanite Myth and Hebrew Epic.* Cambridge, Mass., and London: Harvard University Press. Reprint, 1997.

Davies, Philip R. 1991. "Daniel in the Lion's Den." In *Images of Empire,* edited by Loveday Alexander, 160-78. Sheffield: Sheffield Academic Press.

Day, Peggy L. 1995. "The Personification of Cities as Female in the Hebrew Bible: The Thesis of Aloysius Fitzgerald, F.S.C." In *Reading from This Place: Social Location and Biblical Interpretation in Global Perspective,* edited by Fernando F. Segovia and Mary Ann Tolbert, 283-302. Minneapolis: Fortress.

Deissmann, Adolf. 1910. *Light from the Ancient East: The New Testament Illustrated by Recently Discovered Texts of the Graeco-Roman World.* London: Hodder & Stoughton.

Eliade, Mircea. 1954. *The Myth of the Eternal Return: Or, Cosmos and History.* Bollingen Series 46. Princeton, N.J.: Princeton University Press.

Elliott, John H. 1986. "Social-Scientific Criticism of the New Testament: More on Methods and Models." *Semeia* 35:1-33.

————. 1995. *Social-Scientific Criticism of the New Testament.* London: SPCK.

Elliott, Neil. 1994. *Liberating Paul: The Justice of God and the Politics of the Apostle.* Maryknoll, N.Y.: Orbis Books.

————. 1997. "The Anti-Imperial Message of the Cross." In *Paul and Empire,* edited by Richard A. Horsley. Harrisburg, Penn.: Trinity Press International.

Ellsberg, Robert. 1997. *All Saints.* New York: Crossroad.

Ellul, Jacques. 1970. *The Meaning of the City.* Grand Rapids: Eerdmans.

Fishbane, Michael. 1985. *Biblical Interpretation in Ancient Israel.* Oxford: Clarendon Press.

Fitzgerald, Aloysius. 1972. "The Mythological Background for the Presentation of Jerusalem as a Queen and False Worship as Adultery in the OT." *CBQ* 34:403-16.

Franzmann, Majella. 1995. "The City as Woman: The Case of Babylon in Isaiah 47." *Australian Biblical Review* 43:1-19.

Fretheim, Terence E. 1991. "The Plagues as Signs of Historical Disaster." *JBL* 110:385-96.

Friedman, Richard Eliott. 1987. *Who Wrote the Bible?* New York: Harper & Row.

Gammie, John G. 1974. "Spatial and Ethical Dualism in Jewish Wisdom and Apocalyptic Literature." *JBL* 93:356-85.

———. 1987. "A Journey Through Danielic Spaces: The Book of Daniel in the Theology and Piety of the Christian Community." In *Interpreting the Prophets*, edited by J. L. Mays and P. J. Achtemeier. Philadelphia: Fortress.

Girard, René. 1979. *Violence and the Sacred.* Baltimore: Johns Hopkins University Press.

Golb, Norman. 1995. *Who Wrote the Dead Sea Scrolls?* New York: Scribner.

Gottwald, Norman. 1994. *The Hebrew Bible: A Socioliterary Introduction.* Philadelphia: Augsburg Fortress.

Hanson, Paul D. 1979. *The Dawn of Apocalyptic.* Philadelphia: Fortress.

Harrington, Daniel J. 1988. *The Maccabean Revolt: Anatomy of a Biblical Revolution.* OTS 1. Wilmington, Del.: Michael Glazier.

Herzog, William R. 1984. "Apocalypse Then and Now: Apocalyptic and the Historical Jesus Reconsidered." *PTR* 18:17-25.

———. 1985. "The Quest for the Historical Jesus and the Discovery of the Apocalyptic Jesus." *PTR* 19:25-39.

Howard-Brook, Wes. 1994. *Becoming Children of God: John's Gospel and Radical Discipleship.* Maryknoll, N.Y.: Orbis Books.

Kellermann, Bill Wylie, ed. 1994. *A Keeper of the Word: Selected Writings of William Stringfellow.* Grand Rapids: Eerdmans.

Koester, Helmut. 1992. "Jesus the Victim." *JBL* 111:1-13.

———. 1997. "Imperial Ideology and Paul's Eschatology in 1 Thessalonians." In *Paul and Empire: Religion and Power in Roman Imperial Society*, edited by Richard A. Horsley. Harrisburg, Penn.: Trinity Press International.

Malina, Bruce J. 1989. "Christ and Time: Swiss or Mediterranean?" *CBQ* 51:1-31.

Morgan, Donn F. 1990. *Between Text and Community: The "Writings" in Canonical Interpretation.* Minneapolis: Fortress.

Moxnes, Halvor. 1995. "The Quest for Honor and the Unity of the Community in Romans 12 and in the Orations of Dio Chrysostom." In *Paul in His Hellenistic Context*, edited by Troels Engberg-Pedersen. Minneapolis: Fortress.

Myers, Ched. 1981. "Biblical Apocalyptic as Political Theology." Unpublished.

———. 1988. *Binding the Strong Man: A Political Reading of Mark's Story of Jesus.* Maryknoll, N.Y.: Orbis Books.

———. 1994. *Who Will Roll Away the Stone?: Discipleship Queries for First World Christians.* Maryknoll, N.Y.: Orbis Books.

———. 1996. "The Biblical Suspicion of Imperial Architecture." *Catholic Agitator* 7.

Newsom, Carol A. 1987. "A Maker of Metaphors: Ezekiel's Oracles Against Tyre." In *Interpreting the Prophets*, edited by J. L. Mays and P. J. Achtemeier. Philadelphia: Fortress.

———. 1990. "Apocalyptic and the Discourse of the Qumran Community." *Journal of Near Eastern Studies* 49:135-44.

Pagels, Elaine. 1995. *The Origin of Satan.* New York: Random House.

Patterson, Stephen J. 1995. "The End of Apocalypse: Rethinking the Eschatological Jesus." *TT* 52:29-48.

Pilch, John, and Bruce Malina. 1993. *Biblical Social Values and Their Meaning.* Peabody, Mass.: Hendrickson.

Polzin, Robert. 1980. *Moses and the Deuteronomist.* Bloomington and Indianapolis: Indiana University Press.

————. 1989. *Samuel and the Deuteronomist.* San Francisco: Harper & Row.

————. 1993. *David and the Deuteronomist.* Bloomington and Indianapolis: Indiana University Press.

Schaper, Joachim. 1997. "The Temple Treasury Committee in the Times of Nehemiah and Ezra." *Vetus Testamentum* 47:200-206.

Segal, Alan F. 1990. *Paul the Convert: The Apostolate and Apostasy of Saul the Pharisee.* New Haven and London: Yale University Press.

Silberman, Lou H. 1982. "Wellhausen and Judaism." *Semeia* 25:75-78.

Stark, Rodney. 1996. *The Rise of Christianity: A Sociologist Reconsiders History.* Princeton: Princeton University Press.

Stringfellow, William. 1973. *An Ethic for Christians and Other Aliens in a Strange Land.* Waco, Tex.: Word Books.

Vermes, Geza. 1987. *The Dead Sea Scrolls in English.* 3rd edition. Sheffield: JSOT Press.

Wengst, Klaus. 1987. *Pax Romana and the Peace of Jesus Christ.* London: SCM Press.

Westermann, Claus. 1969. *Isaiah 40-66.* Philadelphia: Westminster.

Wilder, Amos. 1958. "Eschatological Imagery and Earthly Circumstance., *NTS* 5:229-45.

————. 1982. *Jesus' Parables and the War of Myths.* Philadelphia: Fortress Press.

Wink, Walter. 1984. *Naming the Powers.* Philadelphia: Fortress.

————. 1987. *Unmasking the Powers.* Philadelphia: Fortress.

————. 1992. *Engaging the Powers: Discernment and Resistance in a World of Domination.* Minneapolis: Fortress Press.

————. 1993. *Cracking the Gnostic Code: The Powers in Gnosticism.* SBLMS 46. Atlanta, Ga.: Scholars Press.

Winter, Bruce W. 1994. *Seek the Welfare of the City: Christians as Benefactors and Citizens.* Grand Rapids: Eerdmans.

Witherington, Ben, III. 1995. *Conflict and Community in Corinth: A Socio-Rhetorical Commentary on 1 and 2 Corinthians.* Grand Rapids: Eerdmans.

APOCALYPTIC AND MILLENNIALISM GENERALLY

Ahlstrom, Syndey E. 1973. *A Religious History of the American People.* New Haven and London: Yale University Press.

Aukerman, Dale. 1993. *Reckoning with Apocalypse: Terminal Politics and Christian Hope.* New York: Crossroad.

Bawer, Bruce. 1997. *Stealing Jesus: How Fundamentalism Betrays Christianity.* New York: Crown Publishers.

Bloom, Harold. 1997. *Omens of Millennium: The Gnosis of Angels, Dreams and Resurrection.* New York: Riverhead Books.

Boyer, Paul. 1992. *When Time Shall Be No More: Prophecy Belief in Modern American Culture.* Cambridge, Mass., and London: Harvard University Press.

Bull, Malcolm, ed. 1995. *Apocalypse Theory and the Ends of the World.* Oxford and Cambridge: Blackwell.

Bushman, Richard L. 1970. *The Great Awakening: Documents on the Revival of Religion, 1740-1745.* New York: Atheneum.

Cohn, Norman. 1970. *In Pursuit of the Millennium.* New York: Oxford.

Collins, John J. 1979b. "Toward the Morphology of a Genre." *Semeia* 14:1-20.

Dellamora, Richard, ed. 1995. *Postmodern Apocalypse: Theory and Cultural Practice at the End.* Philadelphia: University of Pennsylvania Press.

Festinger, Leon, Henry W. Riecken, and Stanley Schachter. 1956. *When Prophecy Fails.* New York: Harper & Row.

Fuller, Robert C. 1995. *Naming the Antichrist: The History of an American Obsession.* New York and Oxford: Oxford University Press.

Grosso, Michael. 1995. *The Millennium Myth: Love and Death at the End of Time.* Wheaton, Ill.: Quest Books.

Keller, Catherine. 1996. *Apocalypse Now and Then: A Feminist Guide to the End of the World.* Boston: Beacon Press.

Körtner, Ulrich H. J. 1995. *The End of the World: A Theological Interpretation.* Louisville: Westminster John Knox.

Martin, William. 1982. "Waiting for the End." *Atlantic Monthly,* June, 1982, 31-37.

Mojtabai, Grace. 1986. *Blessed Assurance: At Home with the Bomb in Amarillo, Texas.* Boston: Houghton Mifflin.

Norris, Kathleen. 1997. *The Cloister Walk.* New York: Riverhead Books.

O'Leary, Stephen D. 1994. *Arguing the Apocalypse: A Theory of Millennial Rhetoric.* New York and Oxford: Oxford University Press.

Robbins, Thomas, and Susan J. Palmer, ed. 1997. *Millennium, Messiahs, and Mayhem.* New York and London: Routledge.

Russell, Jeffrey Burton. 1997. *A History of Heaven: The Singing Silence.* Princeton: Princeton University Press.

Sandeen, Ernest R. 1970. *The Roots of Fundamentalism: British and American Millenarianism, 1800-1930.* Chicago: University of Chicago Press.

Strozier, Charles B. 1994. *Apocalypse: On the Psychology of Fundamentalism in America.* Boston: Beacon.

Thompson, Damian. 1996. *The End of Time: Faith and Fear in the Shadow of the Millennium.* Hanover and London: University Press of New England.

Weber, Timothy P. 1983. *Living in the Shadow of the Second Coming: American Premillennialism 1875-1982.* Enlarged edition. Grand Rapids: Academie Books.

Yarbro Collins, Adela. 1979. "The Early Christian Apocalypses." *Semeia* 14:61-105.

———. 1986. "Early Christian Apocalypticism." *Semeia* 36:1-10.

MODERN APOCALYPTIC PHENOMENA

Allen, John L., Jr. 1998. "Gimme that end-time (Catholic) religion." *NCR* April 3, 1998.

Bailey, Lee W., and Jenny Yates, eds. 1996. *The Near-Death Experience: A Reader.* New York and London: Routledge.

Balch, Robert. 1995. "Waiting for the Ships: Disillusionment and the Revitalization of Faith in Bo and Peep's UFO Cult." In James R. Lewis, *The Gods Have Landed: New Religions from Other Worlds.* Albany, N.Y.: SUNY Press.

Brinkley, Dannion. 1994. *Saved by the Light.* New York: Villard.

Bryan, C. D. B. 1995. *Close Encounters of the Fourth Kind: Alien Abduction, UFOs, and the Conference at M.I.T.* New York: Knopf.

Carroll, Michael P. 1986. *The Cult of the Virgin Mary: Psychological Origins.* Princeton: Princeton University Press.

Casteneda, Carlos. 1968. *The Teachings of Don Juan: A Yaqui Way of Knowledge.* Berkeley and Los Angeles: University of California Press.

Connell, Janice T. 1995. *Meetings with Mary: Visions of the Blessed Mother.* New York: Ballantine.

Culver, Stanley K. 1995. "Waiting for the End of the World: Catastrophe and the Populist Myth of History." *Configurations* 3:391-413.

Dean, Jodi. 1997. "The Familiarity of Strangeness: Aliens, Citizens, and Abduction," *Theory and Event* (online journal). http://www.press.jhu.edu/journals/theory_&_event/v0001/1.2/dean.html.

Greyson, Bruce, and Nancy Evans Bush. 1996. "Distressing Near-Death Experiences." In Lee W. Bailey and Jenny Yates, eds., *The Near-Death Experience: A Reader.* New York and London: Routledge.

Harner, Michael. 1980, 1990. *The Way of the Shaman.* San Francisco: HarperSanFrancisco.

Huxley, Aldous. 1954. *The Doors of Perception.* New York: Harper & Row.

Jung, Carl G. 1978. *Flying Saucers: A Modern Myth of Things Seen in the Sky.* Princeton: Princeton University Press.

Lewis, James R. 1995. *The Gods Have Landed: New Religions from Other Worlds.* Albany, N.Y.: SUNY Press.

Malina, Bruce J. 1990. "From Isis to Medjugorje: Why Apparitions?" *BTB* 20:76-84.

McMurry, Andrew. 1996. "The Slow Apocalypse: A Gradualistic Theory of the World's Demise." *Postmodern Culture* (online journal). http://www.jefferson.village.virginia.edu/pmc/text-only/issue.596/pop-cult.596.

Melton, J. Gordon. 1995. "The Contactees: A Survey." In James R. Lewis, *The Gods Have Landed: New Religions from Other Worlds.* Albany, N.Y.: SUNY Press.

Moody, Raymond, Jr. 1975. *Life After Life.* New York: Bantam/Mockingbird.

Morse, Melvin. 1995. *Parting Visions: Uses and Meanings of Pre-Death, Psychic, and Spiritual Experiences.* New York: Harper Paperbacks.

Rodriguez, Jeanette. 1994. *Our Lady of Guadalupe: Faith and Empowerment among Mexican-American Women.* Austin: University of Texas Press.

Saliba, John A. 1995. "Religious Dimensions of UFO Phenomena." In James R. Lewis, *The Gods Have Landed: New Religions from Other Worlds.* Albany, N.Y.: SUNY Press.

Thompson, Keith. 1991. *Angels and Aliens: UFOs and the Mythic Imagination.* New York: Fawcett Columbine.

Tumminia, Diana, and R. George Kirkpatrick. 1995. "Unarius: Emergent Aspects of an American Flying Saucer Group." In James R. Lewis, *The Gods Have Landed: New Religions from Other Worlds.* Albany, N.Y.: SUNY Press.

Vallee, Jacques. 1988. *Dimensions: A Casebook of Alien Contact.* New York: Ballantine.

———. 1969, 1993. *Passport To Magonia: On UFOs, Folklore, and Parallel Worlds.* Chicago: Contemporary Books.

Von Daniken, Erich. 1970. *Chariots of the Gods?* New York: G. P. Putnam's Sons.

Whitmore, John. 1995. "Religious Dimensions of the UFO Abductee Experience." In James R. Lewis, *The Gods Have Landed: New Religions from Other Worlds.* Albany, N.Y.: SUNY Press.

Zaleski, Carol. 1987. *Otherworld Journeys: Accounts of Near-Death Experience in Medieval and Modern Times.* New York: Oxford University Press.

————. 1996. *The Life of the World to Come: Near-Death Experience and Christian Hope.* New York and Oxford: Oxford University Press.

Zimdars-Swartz, Sandra L. 1991. *Encountering Mary.* New York: Avon.

GLOBALISM, ECONOMICS, AND OTHER CULTURAL STUDIES

Anderson, Sarah, and John Cavanagh. 1996. "Top 200: The Rise of Global Corporate Power." Washington, D.C.: Institute for Policy Studies.

Arantes, Antonio. 1996. "The War of Places: Symbolic Boundaries and Liminalities in Urban Space." *Theory, Culture and Society* 13:81-92.

Auerbach, Jerold S. 1990. *Rabbis and Lawyers: The Journey from Torah to Constitution.* Bloomington and Indianapolis: Indiana University Press.

Barber, Benjamin R. 1992. "Jihad vs. McWorld." *Atlantic Monthly,* 269, No. 3 (May 1992), pp. 53-65.

Barlow, Maude, and Heather-Jane Robertson. 1996. "Homogenization of Education." In *The Case Against the Global Economy,* edited by Jerry Mander and Edward Goldsmith. San Francisco: Sierra Club.

Barnet, Richard J., and John Cavanaugh. 1994. *Global Dreams: Imperial Corporations and the New World Order.* New York: Simon & Schuster.

Berger, Peter. 1967. *The Sacred Canopy: Elements of a Sociological Theory of Religion.* New York: Doubleday.

Berger, Peter, and Thomas Luckmann. 1967. *The Social Construction of Reality: A Treatise in the Sociology of Knowledge.* New York: Doubleday.

Berry, Wendell. 1996. "Conserving Communities." in *The Case Against the Global Economy,* edited by Jerry Mander and Edward Goldsmith. San Francisco: Sierra Club.

Buchanan, Pat. 1998. *The Great Betrayal: How American Sovereignty and Social Justice Are Being Sacrificed to the Gods of the Global Economy.* New York: Little Brown.

Carney, Dan. 1995. "Dwayne's World." *Mother Jones* (July/August 1995).

Cornell, Thomas C., Robert Ellsberg, and Jim Forest. 1995. *A Penny a Copy: Readings from the Catholic Worker.* Maryknoll, N.Y.: Orbis Books.

Cowan, Neil M., and Ruth Schwartz Cowan. 1989. *Our Parents' Lives: Jewish Assimilation and Everyday Life.* New Brunswick, N.J.: Rutgers University Press.

Cox, Harvey. 1999. "The Market as God: Living in the New Dispensation." *Atlantic Monthly* 283, No. 3 (March 1999), pp. 18-23.

Dietrich, Jeff. 1983. *Reluctant Resister.* Greensboro, N.C.: Unicorn Press.

Douglass, James. 1972. *Resistance and Contemplation.* Garden City, N.Y.: Doubleday.

Douthwaite, Richard. 1996. *Short Circuit: Strengthening Local Economics for Security in an Unstable World.* Dublin: Resurgence Books.

Drozdiak, William. 1998. "Germany's Media Empire: Bertelsmann 'Thinks Global' From Its Small Town Base." *Washington Post,* May 13, 1998, p. A19.

Dyckman, Katherine Marie, S.N.J.M., and L. Patrick Carroll, S.J. 1981. *Inviting the Mystic, Supporting the Prophet.* New York: Paulist.

Eggen, Dan, and Nancy A. Youssef. 1998. "U-Va., Other Schools Weigh Cost of Fund-Raising Push Loss of State Dollars Gives Private Donors Increasingly Bigger Role at Public Universities." *Washington Post,* March 1, 1998, p. B5.

Forest, James. 1994. *Love is the Measure: A Biography of Dorothy Day.* Maryknoll, N.Y.: Orbis Books.

Gladstone, Brooke, and Linda Wertheimer. 1998. Interview regarding Chris Patten and Rupert Murdoch, on *All Things Considered.* National Public Radio, March 2, 1998.

Goldsmith, Edward. 1996. "Development as Colonization." In *The Case Against the Global Economy,* edited by Jerry Mander and Edward Goldsmith. San Francisco: Sierra Club.

Greer, Jed, and Kavaljit Singh. "A Brief History of Transnational Corporations." Reprinted at *CorpWatch* website, http://www.corpwatch.org/trac/globalization/corp/history.html.

Grossman, Richard L., and Frank T. Adams. 1996. "Exercising Power Over Corporations Through State Charters." In *The Case Against the Global Economy,* edited by Jerry Mander and Edward Goldsmith. San Francisco: Sierra Club.

Halstead, Ted, and Clifford Cobb. 1996. "The Need for New Measurements of Progress." In *The Case Against the Global Economy,* edited by Jerry Mander and Edward Goldsmith. San Francisco: Sierra Club.

Harvard Working Group on New and Resurgent Diseases. 1996. "Globalization, Development and the Spread of Disease." In *The Case Against the Global Economy,* edited by Jerry Mander and Edward Goldsmith. San Francisco: Sierra Club.

Heredia, Carlos, and Mary Purcell. 1996. "Structural Adjustment and the Polarization of Mexican Society." In *The Case Against the Global Economy,* edited by Jerry Mander and Edward Goldsmith. San Francisco: Sierra Club.

Herman, Edward S., and Noam Chomsky. 1994. *Manufacturing Consent: The Political Economy of the Mass Media.* London:Vintage Press.

Hines, Colin, and Tim Lang. 1996. "In Favor of a New Protectionism." In *The Case Against the Global Economy,* edited by Jerry Mander and Edward Goldsmith. San Francisco: Sierra Club.

Jones, James M. 1988. "Cultural Differences in Temporal Perspective: Instrumental and Expressive Behaviours in Time." In *The Social Psychology of Time: New Perspective,* 21-38. Newbury Park: Sage Publications.

Kaplan, Robert. 1994. "The Coming Anarchy." *Atlantic Monthly* 273, No. 2 (February 1994), pp. 44-76.

———. 1997. "Was Democracy Just a Moment?" *Atlantic Monthly* 280, No. 6 (November 1997), pp. 55-80.

———. 1998a. "Travels into America's Future: Mexico and the Southwest." *Atlantic Monthly* 282, No. 1 (July 1998), pp. 47-68.

———. 1998b. "Travels into America's Future: Southern California and the Pacific Northwest." *Atlantic Monthly* 282, No. 2 (August 1998), pp. 37-61.

Kellermann, Bill Wylie. 1991. *Seasons of Faith and Conscience: Kairos, Confession, Liturgy.* Maryknoll, N.Y.: Orbis Books.

Kertzer, David I. 1989. *Ritual, Politics, and Power.* New Haven and London: Yale University Press.

Korten, David C. 1995. *When Corporations Rule the World.* West Hartford: Kumarian Press.

Kumar, Satish. 1996. "Gandhi's *Swadeshi*: The Economics of Permanence." In *The Case Against the Global Economy,* edited by Jerry Mander and Edward Goldsmith. San Francisco: Sierra Club.

Lakoff, George, and Mark Johnson. 1980. *Metaphors We Live By.* Chicago and London: University of Chicago Press.

Lehman, Karen, and Al Krebs. 1996. "Control of the World's Food Supply." In *The Case Against the Global Economy,* edited by Jerry Mander and Edward Goldsmith. San Francisco: Sierra Club.

Lewis, C. S. 1980. *The Voyage of the Dawn Treader.* New York: HarperTrophy.

Loy, David R. 1997. "The Religion of the Market." *Journal of the American Academy of Religion* 65:275-90.

Mander, Jerry. 1996. "The Rules of Corporate Behavior." In *The Case Against the Global Economy,* edited by Jerry Mander and Edward Goldsmith. San Francisco: Sierra Club.

McKenna, Megan, and Tony Cowan. 1997. *Keepers of the Story.* Maryknoll, N.Y.: Orbis Books.

McKibben, Bill. 1998. "A Special Moment in History: Running Out of Time?" *Atlantic Monthly* (May 1998).

Mokhiber, Russell. 1996. "The Ten Worst Corporations of 1996." *Multinational Monitor* 17, No. 12 (December 1996).

Morris, David. 1996. "Free Trade: The Great Destroyer." In *The Case Against the Global Economy,* edited by Jerry Mander and Edward Goldsmith. San Francisco: Sierra Club.

Nader, Ralph, and Lori Wallach. 1996. "GATT, NAFTA, and the Subversion of the Democratic Process." In *The Case Against the Global Economy,* edited by Jerry Mander and Edward Goldsmith. San Francisco: Sierra Club.

Nelson-Pallmeyer, Jack. 1989. *War Against the Poor: Low-Intensity Conflict and Christian Faith.* Maryknoll, N.Y.: Orbis Books.

Norberg-Hodge, Helena. 1996. "The Pressure to Modernize and Globalize." In *The Case Against the Global Economy,* edited by Jerry Mander and Edward Goldsmith. San Francisco: Sierra Club.

Preamble Center for Public Policy. 1997. "The MAI in the Words of Framers, Supporters and Opponents." Washington, D.C.: Preamble Collaborative.

Press, Eyal. 1998. "The Voice of Economic Nationalism: Buchanan's World" [book review]. *Atlantic Monthly* 282, No. 1 (July 1998), pp. 96-100.

Sachs, Wolfgang. 1996. "Neo-Development: 'Global Ecological Management.'" In *The Case Against the Global Economy,* edited by Jerry Mander and Edward Goldsmith. San Francisco: Sierra Club.

Sale, Kirkpatrick. 1996. "Principles of Bioregionalism." In *The Case Against the Global Economy,* edited by Jerry Mander and Edward Goldsmith. San Francisco: Sierra Club.

Sforza, Michele. 1997. "Globalization, the Multilateral Agreement on Investment, and the Increasing Economic Marginalization of Women." Washington, D.C.: Preamble Collaborative.

Sforza-Roderick, Michelle, Scott Nova , and Mark Weisbrot. 1997. "Writing the Constitution of a Single Global Economy: A Concise Guide to the Multilateral Agreement on Investment—Supporters' and Opponents' Views." Washington, D.C.: Preamble Collaborative.

Shiva, Vandana, and Radha Holla-Bhar. 1996. "Piracy by Patent: The Case of the Neem Tree." In *The Case Against the Global Economy,* edited by Jerry Mander and Edward Goldsmith. San Francisco: Sierra Club.

Taylor, Mark L. 1993. "Transnational Corporations and Institutionalized Violence: A Challenge to Christian Movements in the United States." In *New Visions for the Americas: Religious Engagement and Social Transformation,* edited by David Batstone. Minneapolis: Fortress.

Weisbrot, Mark. 1997. "The Impact of the MAI on Employment, Growth, and Income Distribution." Washington, D.C.: Preamble Collaborative.

METHODOLOGY

Eagleton, Terry. 1983. *Literary Theory: An Introduction.* Minneapolis: University of Minnesota Press.

Fowler, Robert M. 1995. "Taking It Personally: A Personal Response." *Semeia* 72:231-37.

Gottwald, Norman K., and Richard A. Horsley, eds. 1993. *The Bible and Liberation: Political and Social Hermeneutics.* Revised edition. Maryknoll, N.Y.: Orbis Books.

Henking, Susan E. 1995. "Who Better to Indulge?: (Self) Indulgent Theorizing and the Stuff of Ambivalence." *Semeia* 72:239-45.

Jameson, Fredric. 1981. *The Political Unconscious: Narrative as a Socially Symbolic Act.* Ithaca, N.Y.: Cornell University Press.

Jobling, David, Peggy L. Day, and Gerald T. Sheppard, eds. 1991. *The Bible and the Politics of Exegesis.* Cleveland, Ohio: Pilgrim Press.

Moore, Stephen D. 1989. *Literary Criticism and the Gospels: The Theoretical Challenge.* New Haven and London: Yale University Press.

———. 1995. "True Confessions and Weird Obsessions: Autobiographical Interventions in Literary and Biblical Studies." *Semeia* 72:19-46.

Rohrbaugh, Richard L. 1995. "A Social Scientific Response." *Semeia* 72:247-57.

Schüssler Fiorenza, Elisabeth. 1988. "The Ethics of Biblical Interpretation: Decentering Biblical Scholarship." *JBL* 107:3-17.

Segovia, Fernando F., and Mary Ann Tolbert, eds. 1995. *Reading from This Place,* Volumes 1 and 2: *Social Location and Biblical Interpretation in Global Perspective.* Minneapolis: Fortress.

Staley, Jeffrey. 1995. *Reading with a Passion: Rhetoric, Autobiography and the American West in the Gospel of John.* New York: Continuum.

Sternberg, Meir. 1985. *The Poetics of Biblical Narrative: Ideological Literature and the Drama of Reading.* Bloomington: Indiana University Press.

REFERENCE WORKS

Bauer, Walter, William F. Arndt, F. Wilbur Gingrich, and Frederick W. Danker, eds. 1979. *A Greek-English Lexicon of the New Testament and Other Early Christian Literature.* 2nd edition. Chicago and London: University of Chicago Press.

Holmes, Michael W., ed. 1989. *The Apostolic Fathers.* 2nd edition. Translated by J. B. Lightfoot and J. R. Harmer. The Apostolic Fathers. Grand Rapids: Baker.

Kittel, Gerhard, and Geoffrey Bromiley, eds. 1964-1974. *Theological Dictionary of the New Testament.* 10 vols. Grand Rapids: Eerdmans.

Louw, Johannes P., and Eugene A. Nida, eds. 1992-1994. *Greek-English Lexicon of the New Testament based on Semantic Domains.* CD-ROM Edition. Folio Corp.

Abbreviations

ANRW	*Aufstieg und Niedergang der römischen Welt*
BTB	*Biblical Theology Bulletin*
CBQ	*Catholic Biblical Quarterly*
ExpT	*The Expository Times*
HTR	*Harvard Theological Review*
Int	*Interpretation*
JBL	*Journal of Biblical Literature*
JRS	*Journal of Roman Studies*
JSNT	*Journal for the Study of the New Testament*
JSNTSS	Journal for the Study of the New Testament Supplementary Series
JSOT	*Journal for the Study of the Old Testament*
JSOTSS	Journal for the Study of the Old Testament Supplementary Series
LXX	Septuagint
NCR	*National Catholic Reporter*
NIGTC	New International Greek Testament Commentary
NovT	*Novum Testamentum*
NRSV	New Revised Standard Version
NTS	*New Testament Studies*
OTM	Old Testament Message
OTS	*Old Testament Studies*
PTR	*Pacific Theological Review*
TDNT	*Theological Dictionary of the New Testament*
TT	*Theology Today*
ZNW	*Zeitschrift für die Neutestamentliche Wissenschaft*

Index of Biblical
and Other Ancient Texts

CHRISTIAN SCRIPTURES

OTHER ANCIENT TEXTS

General Index

abomination, 179, 182

Abraham, xxvi

abyss, 144. *See also* Hades/hell

Achtemeier, Elizabeth, 62

Adam, xxvi, 1

Adamski, George, 26

Advent, 275

advertising and marketing, 252-254, 268-269, 270, 271-272. *See also* global capital

Aelius Aristides, 88, 89, 91, 97, 99, 227

Aesclepius, 103

Africa, 99, 243

Age of Aquarius, 33, 34

agriculture: global capital and, 249; in Roman Empire, 97-99; U.S. Department of, 249. *See also* community supported agriculture, *latifundia,* specific products

Ahlstrom, Sydney, 7, 8, 9

Ahura Mazda (Persian divinity), 73

Albertz, Rainer, 52, 54, 71, 76

Alexander the Great, 47, 73

alien abductions, xxix, 25-31. *See also* UFOs

Alpha and Omega, 186

altar, heavenly, 142. *See also* heaven, heavenly liturgy

Ammonites, 65

Amorites, 65

angels: as divine assistants, 133-134, 152, 212; as heavenly messengers, xxvi, 27, 37; as interpreters of visions and dreams, 64; as participants in heavenly liturgy, 200, 208; seven, 143-144; strong/mighty, 139, 145, 171; as symbols of power, 21, 76, 80, 84, 177. *See also* Gabriel, Michael, Ramiel, Uriel

Angra Mainyu (Persian divinity), 73, 74, 75

Antichrist: defined, 4; as part of Endtime scenario, 5, 14

Antipas, 118, 228, 232

Antioch, 99

Antiochus IV Epiphanes, 46, 47-50, 51-52, 76, 82, 130, 149, 151. *See also* Seleucid Empire

Antoninus Pius (Roman emperor), 88, 89, 91. *See also* emperor(s), Roman

apocalypse (literary genre), xxviii, 149; defined, 4. *See also* historical review, pseudonymity

apocalypse habit, 18

apocalypse script, 18

apocalyptic: defined, 4, 122

apocalyptic literature: Christian, 81-86; Jewish, 72, 74, 77-81, 149; purpose of, xix. *See also* Zoroastrianism

apocalyptic tradition, xxiv, xxix, 2

apocalyptic world anxiety, 17-18

Apollo, 115

apostles, 170, 178, 188, 203

Apostolic Brethren, 2

Applewhite, Marshall Herff, 30-31

Armageddon: defined, 4

Arnold, Kenneth, 25, 26

Artaxerxes (Persian king), 65-66, 68, 70, 73. *See also* Persian Empire

Artemis, 103, 105, 107, 110, 187, 202. *See also* Cybele

Asia (continent), 243, 246

Asia (Roman province): daily life, xxix; economic dependence on Rome, 99; history of Roman control, 92; political dependence on Rome, 92. *See also* *ekklēsiai,* imperial cult, local cults

Asian financial crisis, 173

Assyria, xxiii, 164

astral prophecy, 41

astrology: ancient, 40-42, 204; psychological symbolism of, 41. *See also* zodiac

Athena, 277

Auerbach, Jerold S., 108

Augustus: emperor, 88-89, 90, 92, 94, 102, 103, 132, 223, 226-227; myth of, 114-115, 131, 224, 229, 233; temple of, 187. *See also* emperor(s), Roman; Octavian

Also by

Wes Howard-Brook

Becoming Children of God
John's Gospel and Radical Discipleship
Foreword by Ched Myers
ISBN 0-88344-983-8

"Wes Howard Brook's commentary on the Fourth Gospel presents an engaged liberation theological interpretation rooted in the political context of the United States of America. I highly recommend it."
—*Elisabeth Schüssler Fiorenza*

"Wes Howard-Brook unites patient scholarship and a way of faithful resistance to the state. His brilliant journey through John will inspire activists and academics alike to a deeper understanding of becoming God's children."
—*James W. Douglass*

John's Gospel & the Renewal of the Church
ISBN 1-57075-114-5

Challenges readers to take a journey into the heart of the Johannine Gospel, showing how the readings for Lent call us to deepen our baptismal commitment to a life of discipleship.

"Howard-Brook reads John's gospel as a call to radical discipleship to the risen Christ. It helps bring the gospel to life, and if taken seriously, could do the same for our church."
—*John Dear*

Please support your local bookstore, or call 1-800-258-5838.
For a free catalog, please write us at
Orbis Books, Box 308
Maryknoll, NY 10545-0308
or visit our website at www.orbisbooks.com

Thank you for reading *Unveiling Empire*
We hope you enjoyed it.